Exploring New Paths in Language Pedagogy

Equinox English Linguistics and ELT

Series Editors: Anthony Baldry and Paul Thibault

Forthcoming:

Public Information Films
Multimodal, Cross-Cultural and Evolutionary Aspects of Social Advertising
Anthony Baldry and Deirdre Kantz

Virtual Worlds for Learning and Teaching
Applications of Distributed Language
Dongping Zheng

Web-based Concordancing and Annotation
Self-access Project Work and Syllabus Construction through Structured Web Explorations
Anthony Baldry and Francesca Coccetta

The Multimodal Analysis of Online Newspapers
Project Work for Students in Economics, Humanities and Social Sciences
Mariavita Cambria and Rosalba Rizzo

Interaction in CLIL Scenarios
Linguistic and Educational Perspectives
Edited by Rita Kupetz

Exploring New Paths in Language Pedagogy

Lexis and Corpus-Based Language Teaching

Edited by

María Moreno Jaén, Fernando Serrano Valverde and María Calzada Pérez

London   Oakville

Published by Equinox Publishing Ltd.

UK: 1 Chelsea Manor Studios, Flood Street, London SW3 5SR

USA: DBBC, 28 Main Street, Oakville, CT 06779

www.equinoxpub.com

First published 2010

British Library Cataloguing-in-Publication Data

A catalogue record for this book is available from the British Library.

ISBN   978 1 84553 695 4   (hardback)
             978 1 84553 696 1   (paperback)

Library of Congress Cataloging-in-Publication Data

Exploring new paths in language pedagogy : lexis and corpus-based language teaching / edited by Maria Moreno Jaen, Fernando Serrano Valverde and Maria Calzada Perez.
        p. cm. -- (Equinox English linguistics and ELT)
  Includes bibliographical references and index.
   ISBN 978-1-84553-695-4 (hb) -- ISBN 978-1-84553-696-1 (pb) 1. Language and languages--Study and teaching. 2. Second language acquisition. 3. English teachers--Training of. I. Jaen, Maria Moreno. II. Serrano, Fernando. III. Calzada Pérez, María.
  P53.E98 2010
  418.0071--dc22
                              2010038545

Cover design by Manuel Calzada Pérez
Typeset by Nieves Mira Torres, University Jaume I, Spain
Printed and bound in Great Britain by Lightning Source UK Ltd, Milton Keynes.

TABLE OF CONTENTS

Preface — vii
Fernando Serrano Valverde

SECTION I: Second Language Vocabulary Teaching

Introduction to Section I — 3
Fernando Serrano Valverde

1. Analysing vocabulary teaching techniques — 9
Paul Nation

2. Fluency and spoken English — 25
Steven Kirk and Ronald Carter

3. Phrase-noticing or phrase-learning: A question of semantics? — 39
June Eyckmans

4. Coming face to face with N_1 P N_1 sequences in Spanish — 51
Christopher S. Butler

5. Missing words: The vocabulary of BBC Spanish courses for adults — 77
Paul M. Meara and Jesús Suárez García

6. Connectors in EFL learners' essays and in course books — 85
Rosa M. Jiménez Catalán and Julieta Ojeda Alba

7. The treatment of lexical collocations in EFL textbooks — 95
Christián Abello-Contesse and M. Dolores López-Jiménez

8. Access routes to lexical collocations in English learner's dictionaries on CD-ROM — 111
Alfonso Rizo-Rodríguez

SECTION II: Applying New Corpus-based Evidence in Language Pedagogy

Introduction to Section II — 127
María Calzada Pérez

9. Learning outcomes from corpus consultation — 129
Alex Boulton

10. Combining text-based and corpus-based approaches in the learning   145
    and teaching of academic writing in French
    Angela Chambers

11. The death of the adverb revisited: Attested uses of adverbs in native   157
    and non-native comparable corpora of spoken English
    Pascual Pérez-Paredes

12. A web-as-multimodal corpus approach to lexical studies based on   173
    intercultural and scalar principles
    Anthony Baldry

13. Learning from Obama and Clinton: Language classroom corpora   191
    relating to individuals
    María Calzada Pérez

SECTION III: ADELEX: From Theory to Practice

Introduction to Section III   213
María Moreno Jaén

14. 'Very' in predicate adjective constructions: A contrastive   215
    (English-Spanish) discourse-functional approach towards its
    pedagogical implementation
    Judith A. Carini Martínez

15. Developing university learners' collocational competence: 229
    An empirical corpus-based investigation
    María Moreno Jaén

16. Exploring conversational grammar through films in the ELT   245
    classroom: A corpus-based approach
    M. Elena Rodríguez Martín

17. The use of DVD films as multimodal texts to raise contextual   259
    awareness in the acquisition of polite words in English:
    The case of 'please'
    N. Ignacio López Sako

18. ADELEX CAT: A computer adaptive test for the lexical   271
    evaluation of university students
    M. Teresa López-Mezquita Molina

References   287

Appendix: ADELEX and EEL Websites   315

Index   317

Preface

Fernando Serrano Valverde, University of Granada, Spain

After more than forty years of devotion to the demanding task of teaching and research, our friend and colleague Carmen Pérez Basanta is ready to say goodbye. For many friends, her decision to retire is unwise and untimely; for others, she is doing the right thing. For my part, I feel sure that she will always be there, ready to give a hand, a good piece of advice and a cup of tea to anyone, friend or otherwise, who approaches her for help or a chat.

Forty years is a long period to compress into a few lines. If this is applicable as a general statement, it is obviously so in the field of EFL teaching, where it is hardly ever possible, or appropriate, to draw a dividing line between practical and theoretical studies. Carmen's career is a good example. Her work in secondary education has to be placed in the context of the great and deep changes in educational perspectives that have taken place in Spain. In the mid-eighties with the Socialists in power, and with the European Union on the horizon, new winds of change began to blow and the teaching of English at secondary level attracted the attention of the new educational authorities. The *Symposium on Foreign Languages: Towards a New Curriculum in the Teaching of Foreign Languages* (Madrid, 1984) is worth mentioning in this respect. There, some of the best known names in the trade, Strevens, Widdowson and many others, talked about the latest trends in the teaching of English before a massive audience of teachers and educationalists.

These initiatives, and the expectations they brought with them, resounded at the local level. In the particular case of Granada, the hopes for change and efforts to bring them about led a group of teachers, among them Carmen, to found a professional association of teachers of English called *GRETA: Granada English Teaching Association* which succeeded in bringing together members of the teaching profession working at primary, secondary and university levels. Within a couple of years, *GRETA* was able to invite its rapidly growing number of members to annual meetings at which the best-known professionals in the field delivered their papers. Teachers of English in the province of Granada, and very soon many from other parts of Spain, were given the opportunity of personally meeting the brightest names in the profession and of discussing their professional doubts and convictions with them.

Carmen not only took a very active part in carrying out her secondary school teaching duties, she also made a great effort to help change the state of affairs in Secondary School education. She always acted in a down-to-earth way making good use of newly-founded channels and institutions. In this period of her life, she invited a selected group of colleagues to take part in seminars and professional meetings and constantly encouraged them to analyse teaching situations with a view to putting forward and disseminating proposals that would help improve the standard of learning and teaching of English in Secondary Schools throughout Spain. This lively approach, and the atmosphere it created in the teaching world, led *GRETA* to bring out a professional publication, *GRETA: Revista para profesores de inglés*, with Carmen as its founding editor. This journal not only recorded the best contributions to the Association's annual meetings but also kept members informed of news about, and developments in, their field and provided them with an outlet through which to voice suggestions, queries and convictions. Here again, Carmen played a key role, putting her knowledge and personal contacts with the main names in academia and the teaching profession, at the Association's disposal. In this way, we were able to maintain ties with many leading scholars in L2 teaching of English in many parts of the world.

The Association also established ties between two areas that have traditionally remained mutually aloof: university and non-university education (as they are officially referred to). The Department of English Philology at the University of Granada was sensitive to the new winds and accepted the need to include English for Specific Purposes among the new academic subjects on offer. This receptive attitude led scholars such as Pauline Robinson and Ian Tudor, specialists in the field, to be invited to lecture at *GRETA* meetings and run courses and seminars for members of the Department of English.

In this scenario, and after many years of teaching at secondary level and long hours of musing, Carmen made up her mind in 1990 to take part in the Ministry of Education's project for fully qualified teachers with proven merit to apply for a position in University Departments. Whatever the secret reasons for this generous offer may have been, it gave Carmen the opportunity to expand her professional interests and apply her knowledge and intensive experience to exploring wider horizons. Her success in preparing students for the teaching profession is easily measurable from the sheer number of graduates who have entered the field thanks to her. As well as the research programme she co-ordinated for a decade, most remarkable is her contribution at postgraduate level in the light of the number of doctoral students she has supervised, all of whom have reached the professional goal they set out to achieve, something uncommon in University Departments in Spain, at least in the Humanities.

Studies centred on the teaching of vocabulary need to be mentioned in the context of Carmen's efforts to promote good teaching practices that meet internationally recognised standards. Carmen has long been interested in the study of lexis, even at a time when the main emphasis was still being placed on the learning of grammatical structures and when the assumption that vocabulary could be acquired incidentally was prevalent. Carmen, on the contrary, contended that this assumption needed to be proven. Her previous research and teaching experience strongly suggested that, without sufficient mastery of a certain amount of vocabulary, communication would be impossible or, at very best, deficient. Backed basically by the theoretical framework being put forward by the British school of applied linguistics, in particular as developed by John Sinclair at the University of Birmingham, she travelled, as it were, from the ends to the means. Once her research group had demonstrated the need to provide students with a sufficient and precise number of words to 'get along', there was the problem of how to help them with the task of acquiring and using that knowledge consistently.

It was to meet this challenge that *ADELEX: Assessing and Developing Lexical Competence* was launched in 2001. The project has been highly valued at the local, national and European level. For once, even the academic authorities became conscious of the merits of such a project. This recognition, and the consequent financial support from the Ministry of Education, have kept Carmen and her research team active until the present time. It has enabled them to get into touch with groups and individuals who share similar interests through the organisation of, and participation in, international congresses. Rather than giving a list of these initiatives that would go on forever, I prefer to direct the interested reader to the website supporting this volume, where details of the publications and activities (conferences, seminars, meetings, etc.) both organised and attended by this research group are given.

The present volume is intended to express our personal appreciation and deep admiration for a career devoted not only to expanding our field of studies, but also dedicated to establishing human values, permanent ties of friendship and professional support.

Acknowledgements

Words are not enough to thank the Series Editors, Anthony Baldry and Paul J. Thibault for their help at all stages in the book's production, from the time when this volume was only a vague idea in our minds to the very last moment when the final proofs were sent to press. We owe Francisco Gutiérrez Martín, the computer engineer who designed the website supporting this volume, a great debt of gratitude. We also thank him for his hard work and generosity in recent years as a member of the *ADELEX* project. We also are deeply grateful to Nieves Mira Torres for the painstaking work of typesetting and checking the entire volume. The book cover was designed by Dr. Manuel Calzada Pérez, who is thanked whole-heartedly. It goes without saying that our final thanks go to the scholars, some of them members of the *ADELEX* research group, who have demonstrated their friendship and admiration for Carmen through their contributions to this volume.

Carmen Pérez Basanta, 2010

Paul M Meara

First column

Christián Abello-Contesse, Svenja Adolphs, Carmen Aguilera Carnerero, Karin Aijmer, Anthony Baldry, Alex Boulton, Sabine Braun, Christopher S. Butler, Coral Calvo Maturana, Manuel Calzada Pérez, María Calzada Pérez, Mariavita Cambria, Judith A. Carini Martínez, Ronald Carter, Angela Chambers, Suzanne Cloke, Francesca Coccetta.

Second column

Germana Cubeta, June Eyckmans, Francisco Gutiérrez Martín, Tony Harris, Julia Hüttner, Emilia Iglesias, Rosa M. Jiménez Catalán, Deirdre Kantz, Gabriele Kasper, Steven Kirk, Rita Kupetz, M. Teresa López-Mezquita Molina, N. Ignacio López Sako, M. Dolores López-Jiménez, Rafael Luque Reina, Fabrizio Maggi.

Third column

Ivana Marenzi, M. Jesús Martínez-Risco Fernández, Paul M. Meara, Nieves Mira Torres, María Moreno Jaén, Paul Nation, Julieta Ojeda Alba, Anne O'Keeffe, Breffni O'Rourke, Pascual Pérez Paredes, Alfonso Rizo-Rodríguez, Rosalba Rizzo, M. Elena Rodríguez Martín, Christopher Rühlemann, Paul Seligson.

Fourth column

Fernando Serrano Valverde, Olcay Sert, M. Grazia Sindoni, Regina Weinert.

Section I:

Second Language Vocabulary Teaching

Introduction to Section I:
Second Language Vocabulary Teaching

Fernando Serrano Valverde, University of Granada, Spain

In keeping with the idea of a carefully-structured volume functioning both as a compendium for researchers and as a coursebook for specialist undergraduate and postgraduate degree courses, *Section I* of this volume provides a general overview of current issues and state-of-the-art strategies for the analysis of vocabulary in the context of L2 vocabulary teaching. As well as vocabulary teaching and learning, many other spheres associated with L2, such as language planning by national, regional and local educational bodies, textbook writing, textbook selection and teacher training are implicitly embraced. Underpinning the eight chapters in this section is the assumption, expressed with differing degrees of intensity, that lexical patterning has primacy in current L2 theory over grammar, grammar rules in particular. This theme illuminates the first four chapters with their theory-oriented focus just as much as it does the last four, with their focus on field experiments.

The storyboard in the first four chapters is thus essentially the issue of how L2 vocabulary learning relates to general L2 issues such as balancing L2 learner needs, understanding fluency, developing strategies that support learners' active perception of L2 structures and comparison of L1 and L2 patterns.

Chapter 1 proposes a four-point plan that promotes a proper balance in vocabulary learning opportunities, proper training in the use of vocabulary strategies, careful definition and monitoring of syllabuses most suited to students' current level of proficiency, and, of course, reflection on vocabulary teaching techniques. Of the three major ways of researching vocabulary, teaching techniques are investigated in relation to the involvement load hypothesis developed by Laufer and Hulstijn (2001), itself underpinned by Craik and Lockhart's (1972) levels of processing theory, which holds that quantity of learning depends on the quality of mental activity at the moment when learning occurs. The deeper and more thoughtful the processing, the better the learning.

Chapter 2 deals with another general issue: fluency viewed as central to the fields of English language teaching, second language acquisition, and linguistics in general, but not well understood and hard to define. Lay definitions of *fluency* hold speech to be ideally smooth and flowing, while careful analysis shows that dysfluencies in speech (pauses, hesitations, restarts, etc.) are essential to the normal functioning of speech and far from being simply evidence of a lack of proficiency on the part of learners. A difficulty in determining whether temporal phenomena are dysfluent or not lies in the fact that they reflect interactive aspects of the conversation and the underlying psycholinguistic processes of speech production. The limitations and psycholinguistic processes that enable fluent language are carefully described. The chapter suggests that for learners, rather than increasing the speed of their speech, the real need is to improve the efficiency of cognitive organisation and language production processes. Fluency is dependent on the speaker, the listener, the context or situation, cultural norms and the speaker's ability to predict how the listener will interpret the speaker's utterances in context. There are thus two interpretations of fluency, the first a psycholinguistic construct, based on the efficient organisation of language in long-term memory, and rapid access to those memories, manifested in longer uninterrupted runs of speech and higher rate of speech, the second the co-construction of speech by all participants in the interactive event. Chapter 2 also holds that studies in corpus linguistics will continue to find ways of identifying recurrent sequences that correspond to formulaic sequences in native speakers' discourse, and which account for predictable chunks of language. Pedagogically, the role of memorisation in the classroom, and whether this leads to more fluent use of the formulaic sequences that comprise the memorised dialogues, needs to be studied. Finally, there is a need for more longitudinal studies of learners to investigate how formulaic language develops in their speech production, and how they develop confidence and higher-level conversational skills.

Chapter 3 sums up recent findings into the role of lexical phrases in the L2 classroom and discusses the likelihood of incidental phrase learning (*phrase noticing*) in an instructed L2 learning context, comparing it with *phrase learning*, the latter inspired by cognitive linguistics that the author champions. Given the overwhelming corpus evidence, applied linguists have come to recognize the basic role of prefabricated patterns in language acquisition. In fact, psycholinguistic research has convincingly shown the extent to which communicative performance relies on example-based knowledge. Although some authors on phraseology have emphasized the arbitrary nature of word combinations, a fair number of linguists have demonstrated that pointing out the semantic and structural motivation of multiword units makes them more meaningful and more memorable. Research suggests that building a native-like phrasal repertoire through incidental uptake is bound to be a very slow process. Moreover, incidental acquisition through reading may be even more problematic when it comes to chunks. Unfamiliar individual words are more likely to be noticed than combinations of familiar words. Chapter 3 argues that a cognitive linguistic approach responds to the need for explicit language-focused instruction with regard to establishing strong memory traces in learners' interlanguage lexicons. Apart from the criteria of frequency and semantic coherence, what has been called *teaching worth* (Ellis et al., 2008) should be taken into account when establishing a corpus of phrases for foreign language instruction. By testing for phrasal competence, a positive backwash effect may be created towards raising learners' awareness of the idiomatic nature of the target language. In order to promote insightful learning and unlock the mnemonic potential of phrases, teacher-led guidance is essential. Integrative language tests such as the cloze test, the c-test and a relatively new format, called the

Deleted Essentials Test, seem promising when it comes to measuring learners' productive knowledge of phrases across different categories (phrasal verbs, collocations, functional phrases, idiomatic expressions, etc.). However, pedagogical proposals that support this approach to language learning are still limited. Collections of useful phrases are gradually becoming available but comprehensive collections of multiword combinations that include conversational fillers, discourse organizers, referential chunks (i.e. compounds and collocations) and idioms have not yet appeared. While activities for the insightful teaching and learning of such phrases are slowly becoming available, standardized tests for learners' syntagmatic competence are also not yet available.

With its focus on comparison, Chapter 4 rounds off the set of chapters that associate vocabulary teaching and learning with general language issues. The chapter tackles the issue of corpus-based approaches to patternings of word classes in specific languages, focusing on the comparative L1/L2 perspective through a detailed comparison of a recurrent, and perhaps partly grammaticalised, lexical class found both in English and Spanish. Specifically, Chapter 4 investigates the N_1 P N_1 pattern in a 22.8 million word corpus of Spanish, comparing the author's findings with observations put forward by Jackendoff (2008) and Lindquist and Levin (2009). Analysis of the nature and incidence of this pattern reveals a predominantly adverbial function of this structure in Spanish though some combinations containing repeated nouns and prepositions are found as noun postmodifiers and, more rarely, as nominals. The analysis also reveals that N_1 P N_1 combinations in Spanish are more frequent in fiction and news than in oral language, and least frequent in academic writing. By focusing on the internal workings of Spanish (and more indirectly English), Chapter 4 demonstrates the potential usefulness of corpus-based studies for linguistics and translation studies as they relate to L2 teaching and learning. Translators, in particular, need an in-depth knowledge of the delicate lexicogrammatical patterns revealed by corpus analysis, while language learners can likewise benefit from what corpora reveal about the patterning of a language, as this potentially improves the naturalness of their productions. Chapter 4 provides just such information, which could be usefully used both to train translators and interpreters, and, likewise, to guide course designers in the construction of courses in Spanish as a foreign language.

Like the subsequent three chapters, Chapter 4 takes an Anglo-Iberian approach to vocabulary learning. Chapters 4 and 5 explore the rigorous analysis of Spanish lexicon and the hoped-for impact that this will have on those writing Spanish L2 courses for English-speaking learners, whereas in Chapters 6 and 7 the reverse stance is taken: the focus switches to English lexicon and its application to English L2 courses for Spanish-speaking learners, all part of this section's intriguing presentation of similar problems from different perspectives. In this respect, Chapter 5 provides a comparative analysis of the criteria relating to selection of vocabulary in six textbooks for teaching Spanish to adults published in the UK over a 30-year period. The special value of Chapter 5 is its diachronic framework that provides a rare insight into the gradual emergence from an essentially pre-scientific age of vocabulary learning in Spanish studies in the UK to one in which, thanks to the development of specialist word-frequency tools and yardsticks like the *Nivel Umbral*, L2 textbook production is scientifically underpinned.

Indeed, Chapter 5 is the first of three chapters that look into much-needed frameworks for quality assessment and quality controls in the field of vocabulary learning. Such frameworks will be capable of guiding and orienting language and education planners, syllabus designers, trainee and in-service teachers, textbook writers, university researchers and many other social categories including students specialising in communication studies or applied linguistics, publishers and, of course, language learners, the main users of L2 textbooks and materials, vis-à-vis the thorny question of deciding how to evaluate and analyse published L2 courses and textbooks. Such critical frameworks need to be based on clearly-stated methods and fine-grained, systematic analyses, whence the inclusion of very useful comparative tables with precise statistics that help readers to critically evaluate essential criteria.

Chapters 6 and 7, respectively concerned with connectors and lexical collocations, again highlight the contribution of corpus linguistics. Chapter 6, a shining example of university and secondary school collaboration in fieldwork, focuses on the use of connectors within authentic texts: letters written by Spanish learners of English. The basic goal of this research is to ascertain the nature and incidence of similarities or differences between the groups compared. Previous studies on the use of connectors by native speakers versus language learners have demonstrated that learners, even advanced learners, show little variety in the use of L2 connectors; indeed, misuse of connectors is a common tendency. Apart from *and*, EFL learners hardly use connectors in their compositions and on the few occasions they do use them, they resort to a very small range. The novelty in Chapter 6 is the careful linkage of the production of connectors by low-intermediate learners in secondary education to how these cohesive elements are presented in the various textbooks selected for use with Spanish EFL learners. If textbooks do not contain equal input, learners' exposure to the target language cannot be the same, a matter compounded by frequent cases where a connector appears only once in a textbook.

Chapter 7 is the last in the trio of chapters on developing critical frameworks for quality assessment and, like the previous chapters, has important messages for second language planners (if only they would listen) that go to the heart of quality control in L2. Whereas Chapter 6 focused on connectors, this chapter specifically develops a framework for the analysis of lexical collocations, their nature and role in EFL/ESL textbooks. This includes definitions of collocations and criteria for selecting collocations for teaching purposes and was the basis for a questionnaire designed to assess views held by Spanish EFL teachers about vocabulary and, in particular, the presentation of collocations in the textbooks they were using.

Chapter 8 rounds off this section by again connecting up with the theme of quality assurance, only this time in relation to the issue of software's impact on second language vocabulary teaching and hence with the prospect of eliminating printed materials from the L2 classroom – not just textbooks but also dictionaries. With its focus on improving teachers' and learners' access to collocations, Chapter 8 compares the presentation of lexical collocations in five learner's dictionaries of English on CD-ROM in the belief that digital dictionaries will increasingly influence new language learning and teaching methodologies. Chapter 8 thus explores the differences and similarities between digital and printed formats with a view to measuring the precise degree of enhancement vis-à-vis access to collocations. In so doing, it provides a much-needed framework for teachers and lexicographers on which to base judgements and assessments about the relationship between printed and digital learner's dictionaries. The chapter shows insight into the need to accelerate digital dictionaries' independence and autonomy vis-à-vis printed dictionaries, and thus paves the way for the discussion in *Section II* of the application of corpus-based evidence in language pedagogy.

Analysing vocabulary teaching techniques

Paul Nation, LALS, Victoria University of Wellington, New Zealand

1. Where does vocabulary teaching fit in a course?

Which vocabulary teaching techniques work the best? What factors determine the effectiveness of vocabulary teaching techniques? Why do some teaching techniques work well and others don't work well? This paper tries to address these questions.

Before focusing on vocabulary teaching techniques we need to look at where vocabulary teaching fits into a course. At first glance it would seem that making use of good vocabulary teaching techniques would be the major job of a vocabulary teacher. However, this is not so. The most important job of the vocabulary teacher is to plan, that is, to make sure that learners are focusing on the most relevant vocabulary for them, and to make sure that they are getting a proper balance of vocabulary learning opportunities. One way of ensuring this balance is to follow the principle of the four strands (Nation, 2007). This principle says that in order to have a good balance of learning opportunities an equal amount of time needs to be spent on each of the four strands of meaning-focused input, meaning-focused output, language-focused learning, and fluency development. *Table 1* shows what this might mean for a course.

Notice that the bolded parts of *Table 1* – 'direct teaching of vocabulary' and 'intensive reading' – are part of the language focused learning strand of a course, and they make up probably less than half of the strand. This means that the use of vocabulary teaching techniques should typically take up less than one eighth of the time in a vocabulary course.

The four strands	Activities and techniques
Meaning-focused input	Reading graded readers, Listening to stories, Communication activities
Language-focused learning	**Direct teaching of vocabulary**, Direct learning, **Intensive reading**, Training in vocabulary strategies
Meaning-focused output	Communication activities with written input, Prepared writing, Linked skills
Fluency development	Reading easy graded readers, Repeated reading, Speed reading, Listening to easy input, 4/3/2, Rehearsed tasks, 10 minute writing, Linked skills

Table 1: The four strands of a well-balanced vocabulary programme

The second most important job of the vocabulary teacher is to train learners in the use of vocabulary strategies, such as learning from word cards, guessing from context, learning using word parts, and dictionary use. The third most important job of the vocabulary teacher is to test so that learners can get a program which is most suited to their current level of proficiency, and so that teachers can monitor their progress. The fourth most important job of the vocabulary teacher is to teach vocabulary using vocabulary teaching techniques. Although using vocabulary teaching techniques is the fourth most important job of the vocabulary teacher, a teacher needs to be able to make use of the most effective techniques. The focus of this paper is to see how we can decide which are the most effective techniques.

2. Researching vocabulary teaching techniques

There are three major ways of researching vocabulary teaching techniques, although in this chapter we will look only at the first one listed below, technique analysis:

- by doing technique analysis such as looking at involvement load (*Need, Search, Evaluation*) (Laufer, Hulstijn, 2001), or by analysing the goals, learning conditions, signs, and design features of techniques (Nation, 2001);
- by observing the learners thinking aloud during or after a vocabulary learning activity (Hosenfeld, 1976);
- by doing experimental comparisons of vocabulary learning activities (Hulstijn, Laufer, 2001).

3. Analysing vocabulary teaching techniques

The best-known and best researched way of analysing vocabulary teaching techniques is Laufer and Hulstijn's *Involvement Load Hypothesis*. Involvement load involves three factors: *Need, Search* and *Evaluation*. Each of these factors may be absent (-), present with moderate strength (+), or present with full-strength (+ +). *Need* is a motivational factor. Is the unknown word needed to complete the task? *Search* – does the learner have to search for or retrieve the meaning or form of a particular word? *Evaluation* – does the task involve having to compare the form or meaning with other possible words or meanings in order to choose the most suitable one for the context? The sum of the strengths of these three factors represents the involvement load of the task. The greater the involvement load, the better the learning.

Let us look at each of the three criteria in more detail. *Need* is a motivational feature, primarily relating to who has set the task, the teacher (extrinsic motivation) or the learner (intrinsic motivation).

When analysing *Need*, we need to ask these questions. Does the learner need to understand or use the word, because the teacher has said so (1 point), or because the learner wants to understand or use the word (2 points)? If the learner does not need to understand or use the word then the score is 0. *Need* is 0 when the word to be learnt is actually not needed in the activity. For example, if learners are reading a text and they meet an unknown word but that word is not necessary for comprehension of the text or for the completion of any activity then *Need* is 0. *Need* is 1 when the learners have been instructed by the teacher to pay attention to the word or to use the word. If a word is bolded in the text, and the learners are told they need to learn such words, then *Need* is 1. If the learners are answering questions set by the teacher based on the text, and those questions require understanding of the word in the text, then *Need* is 1. *Need* is 2 when the learner feels the need to understand a word when reading, or to use a word when writing, and the learner is interested in doing the reading or the writing.

Search involves retrieval or finding new information about the word. When analysing *Search*, we need to ask these questions. Is the meaning or the word form provided in the activity? If the answer is yes, then there are 0 points for *Search*; Does the learner need to retrieve or look for the meaning of the L2 word – receptive retrieval (1 point)? Does the learner need to retrieve or look for the word form – productive retrieval (2 points)? *Search* is 0 when the needed words or the needed meanings are provided. *Search* is 1 when the learner has to look for or retrieve the meaning of a word from their memory.

In their original formulation of the *Involvement Load Hypothesis*, Laufer and Hulstijn (2001) decided that the scoring for *Search* would be 0 or 1. Laufer (personal communication) has subsequently seen value in distinguishing between receptive retrieval (1 point) and productive retrieval (2 points).

Evaluation means making choices between options or providing a suitable context for a word – Does the learner need to decide which word or sense of the word to use? If the answer is no, then *Evaluation* scores 0 points. If the answer is yes, then *Evaluation* scores 1 point. Does the learner have to use the word in the context and provide that context? If the answer is yes, then *Evaluation* scores 2 points.

The basic idea behind the *Involvement Load Hypothesis* is that the design of the task determines the quality of the learning outcomes. The major theoretical construct supporting this is Craik and Lockhart's (1972) *Levels of Processing Theory*. Put simply, the *Levels of Processing Theory* says that the quantity of learning depends on the quality of the mental activity in the brain at the moment that learning occurs. The deeper and more thoughtful the processing, the better the learning. An important factor in deepening processing is elaboration, namely increasing the quantity and quality of the associations made with a particular piece of learning. The *Involvement Load Hypothesis* is an attempt to operationalise depth of processing.

Here are some examples of vocabulary teaching techniques which have been analysed using the *Involvement Load Hypothesis* (see *Appendix 1* for further examples):

- the learner has to (*Need* 1 [imposed by the teacher]) write original sentences (*Evaluation* 2 [supply collocates, etc.]) using words that have just been explained (*Search* 0 [word form and meaning supplied]). This activity has an involvement load of 3 (1 for *Need* and 2 for *Evaluation*);
- the learner repeats a sentence after the teacher says it. This activity has an involvement load of 1 (*Need* 1, *Search* 0, *Evaluation* 0);
- the learner needs to (*Need* 2 [imposed by learner]) look up the meaning of an unknown word (*Search* 1 [receptive]) met in a reading text (*Evaluation* 1 [choose the right sense of the word]). This activity has an involvement load of 4.

The quality of any analytic measure will depend on the reliability of the analysis. Can teachers and researchers be trained to analyse teaching techniques in a consistent way? The strength of the *Involvement Load Hypothesis* is its simplicity. It consists of three criteria each of which may be absent, present in a moderate form, or in a strong form. If these three strengths are allowed for all three criteria, then a total of nine judgements (3x3) need to be made when applying the criteria, resulting in a score, which could range from 0 to 6. With this relatively small number of judgements to be made, it would be wise when applying the *Involvement Load Hypothesis* to have at least two judges determining the involvement load of each activity. This would help reach a good level of reliability in the analysis of the activities.

Is the reliability of the index improved by

- increasing the number of components;
- increasing the number of response categories for each component;
- providing explicit anchoring labels for each category?

Three notions of reliability are relevant for the index (see *Table 2*).

Notion	Explanation
Rater reliability	Error is due to inconsistencies among raters when viewing the same task, or rating across occasions
Composite reliability	The amount of scale score variance that is accounted for by all the underlying components of the index
Construct reliability	The degree to which the scale score reflects one particular component of the index

Table 2: Three kinds of reliability

What is the effect on reliability of increasing the number of components used in calculating the index (say from three to six)?

It is likely that it would:

- increase the discrimination between tasks, hence increase the composite reliability of the index;
- increase the likelihood that the rating of each component would be consistent across occasions/raters, hence increasing the construct reliability;
- depend on the statistical independence of the components of the index – an empirical question.

Why should the number of response categories used to assess a component of involvement load be expected to affect the reliability of the rating?

Weng (2004) has summarized the arguments that have been put forward in the literature to explain the link between reliability and the number of response categories, namely:

- a scale should be no finer than a judge's ability to discriminate. In other words, if a scale requires finer discrimination than a rater can usually accomplish, the rating is more likely to include measurement error. Thus increasing the number of response categories does not necessarily lead to better discrimination on the part of raters;
- a scale with too few scale points may lose information on differences between tasks and hence lower reliability estimates. On the other hand, with too many scale points, raters may fail to distinguish reliably between adjacent categories.

When the relationship between the number of response categories and reliability is studied empirically (e.g. Weng, 2004), the following results are yielded:

- scales with fewer response categories tend to result in lower reliabilities, especially when ratings are compared on different occasions;
- scales with all response categories clearly labelled are more likely to yield higher reliabilities than those with only endpoints labelled.

It thus seems reasonable to claim that the reliability of the involvement load index would be improved by:

- increasing the number of components used in the calculation of the index;
- increasing the number of response categories used to assess each component;
- clearly labelling each response category.

The involvement load index could thus be improved by:

- labelling *Need* 1 as extrinsic, teacher-imposed motivation, and *Need* 2 as intrinsic, learner-centred motivation;
- labelling *Search* 1 as receptive retrieval of meaning, and *Search* 2 as productive retrieval of spoken or written word form;
- labelling *Evaluation* 1 as decontextualised evaluation and *Evaluation* 2 as contextualised evaluation. As we shall see in the *Section 4*, it is also possible to design an *Evaluation* scale with more components.

4. Testing the Involvement Load Hypothesis

The *Involvement Load Hypothesis* has been directly tested in at least four published experiments (Hulstijn, Laufer, 2001; Folse, 2006; Keating, 2008; Kim, 2008), and one less explicitly (Webb, 2008). These studies have provided support for the testability of the hypothesis, though they have shown that other factors like time-on-task and repetition need to be considered.

The research on the *Involvement Load Hypothesis* provides encouragement for the development of other technique analysis systems. Nation (2001: 60-74) has suggested looking at goals, learning conditions, signs, and design features as ways of observing and improving vocabulary teaching techniques. His system however does not readily allow for the quantification that the *Involvement Load Hypothesis* allows. Although the *Involvement Load Hypothesis* works well, it does not include many features that other research has shown to be important when designing vocabulary teaching techniques. For this reason, it does not provide a good guide for designing and adapting techniques. To meet the dual goals of evaluating and designing techniques, a more elaborate set of criteria is needed. The list in *Table 3* represents a first attempt.

Does it involve normal language use?	0	1	
Does each activity set up useful conditions for vocabulary learning?			
Does the activity motivate the learners to pay attention?	0	1	2
Does the activity involve retrieval?	0	1	
Receptive (0) or productive (1)?	0	1	
Recognition (0) or recall (1)?	0	1	
Does the activity involve generative use?	0	1	
Receptive (0) or productive (1)?	0	1	
What degree of generation?		1	2
Does the activity involve instantiation (1) or imaging (2)?	0	1	2
Does the activity involve a useful focus of effort?	0	1	
Does the activity result in new learning?	0	1	2
Does the activity avoid interference?	0	1	
Total possible			**16**

Table 3: A checklist for technique feature analysis

The points values are used when evaluating techniques. The highest possible number of points is 16.

Let us now look at each of the features listed in the checklist and examine the reasons for their inclusion and how they are applied.

Does the activity involve normal language use?
When looking at an activity, it is always useful to consider how much the activity involves typical language use. Typical language use involves using the language to comprehend or express meaning, performing a typical language use activity like listening, reading, speaking or writing, with the target vocabulary involved being set in a wider context. Recalling the form or meaning of words without a phrase or sentence context would not be counted as normal language use. Making multiple-choice selections would not be normal language use; however assessing the truth value of a sentence in a true/false activity would be counted, and completing a sentence would also be counted. The advantage of having an activity that reflects normal use is that it results in vocabulary learning and the practice of a useful skill. The disadvantage of this criterion is that bizarre activities like the keyword technique and decontextualised activities like using word cards, which both work well, get a zero score on this criterion.

Does the activity motivate learners to pay attention?
Without motivation little will be learned. This criterion is very similar to Laufer and Hulstijn's *Need* factor. However, being told by the teacher to do something would get a score of 0. If the activity brought its own motivation with it, as is the case in crossword puzzles, multiple-choice and matching activities, and recall in previously met items as with the word cards, it would get 1 point. If the attention to the word was the result of the learners' strong interest, as when looking at the word while reading, choosing to put a word on the word cards, or using a word in a genuine conversation, it would get 2 points.

Does the activity involve retrieval?
This criterion is similar to Laufer and Hulstijn's *Search* factor. However, in addition to receptive and productive retrieval, a distinction is made between recognition (as in multiple choice or matching activities) and recall retrieval (as in translation or recalling a word's form or meaning). Matching a word with its meaning in a multiple-choice or matching activity involves receptive retrieval (1 point), and recognition (0 points because the choices are provided). A total of one point. Retrieving the translation of a word when looking at word cards (where the word is on one side and its translation on the back) involves retrieval (1 point) and recall (1 point because the translation cannot be seen while looking at the L2 word). A total of two points. Doing productive retrieval with word cards (look at the translation and recall the L2 word) would get 1 point for retrieval, 1 point for productive use, and 1 point for recall. A total of three points.

Does the activity involve generative use?
There is now a considerable body of research that shows that meeting a word used in a new way (receptive generative use) and using a word in a way that the learner has not met before (productive generative use) strengthens memory for the word (Joe, 1998). Productive generative use would get a total of 2 points and possibly 3 points depending on how different the use was. Joe (1998) devised a scale of generativity.

0   no generation – repeating what is in the text;

1   low generation – small grammatical or inflectional changes;

2   reasonable generation – used with some new collocations or substantial grammatical change;

3   high generation – elaborating the meaning, using new collocations which stretch meaning, applying or removing derivational affixes.

Does the activity involve instantiation or imaging?

Instantiation involves seeing an instance of a word such as when the word is used in a meaningful situation where the object or action or quality referred to is visually present. This criterion partly accounts for why words are remembered if they are used in genuine communication. For example, if learners were following instructions to make something, the target vocabulary would occur in genuine communication which related to something that could be visualised. That is, the visual memory of the situation could be easily recalled later.

Imaging involves deliberately seeing or imagining a visual image related to the meaning of the word, as when the keyword technique is used. Imaging is not quite as powerful as instantiation because it involves a contrived image. In its simplest form it would involve making a mental picture based on a sentence containing the target word. For example, visualising an example sentence found in the dictionary. The keyword technique involves a more complicated procedure because two images are combined into one (Ellis, Beaton, 1993).

Does the activity involve a useful focus of effort?

A few activities involve the learners in work that is not contributing to language learning and is thus not a useful focus of effort. For example, the *Find the words* activity (in *Appendix 1*), typically follows a reading text. There is a list of the meanings of several words that are in the text. The learners have to find the words in the text to match the meanings. Typically the words are not marked in the text by bolding or italicisation. The search for the words is largely time-wasting. Providing cued recall by indicating the first few letters of each word would encourage recall and be better for learning. It would also save time which could be spent on a more useful activity. Another activity like this is the hidden words activity where words are hidden in a grid full of letters. The search for words is not a useful focus of learning effort. Fortunately, most vocabulary learning activities involve a more effective use of classroom time.

Does the activity result in new learning?

Vocabulary learning activities should result in the learning of vocabulary or some aspect of it. Some activities however fill more of a testing function in that they involve already well established knowledge. For example, activities which require the learners to match word forms with definitions may be filling more of a testing role than a teaching role. If however the connection between the form and the meaning of the word is not strongly established, then these activities can result in new learning in that the form-meaning connection is strengthened.

Does the activity avoid interference?
There are several pieces of research showing the negative effects of teaching several unknown words at the same time that are members of a lexical set (Higa, 1963; Tinkham, 1993, 1997; Waring, 1997). The lexical sets causing difficulty were near synonyms, opposites, and words like articles of clothing or names of fruit that could be grouped under a headword like *fruit* or *clothing*. Learning several unknown words together in such sets made learning 50% to 100% more difficult (Nation, 2000) compared to learning several unrelated words. That is, many more repetitions were needed to learn the interfering sets and learners tended to cross-associate the words in the sets. However, in his 1997 study, Tinkham looked at a different kind of relationship among words, what he called a *semantic* relationship but which is more usefully viewed as a syntagmatic relationship. Tinkham's set of meanings in his experiment were *frog, green, pond, croak, slimy, hop*. He found that words in this kind of story relationship were easier to learn than unrelated words and were much easier to learn than words in the sets of fruit and articles of clothing. The basic rule underlying interference is as follows (for a fuller explanation see Nation, 2000):

> If two or more previously unknown items which are related in form or meaning or both are presented together, these relationships between them will encourage association between them, and the differences will be cross-associated with each other.

Some activities deliberately bring unknown related words together, and by doing so make learning more difficult.

Let us now look at the analyses of several activities using both the involvement load index and technique feature analysis as listed in *Table 3* of this chapter. *Appendix 1* contains 12 analysed activities, along with a brief description of each one. Three of these activities are those tested by Hulstijn and Laufer (2001). Let us examine two activities in detail and conclude by comparing the two kinds of analysis – involvement load and technique feature analysis.

Word cards
Learning vocabulary using word cards involves writing unknown L2 words or phrases on small cards and writing the L1 translation on the other side. The learner then goes through the cards at increasingly spaced intervals until the meanings (translations) of the words are known. This is receptive learning. By turning the cards over and looking at the translations and trying to recall the L2 word forms, productive learning can occur. In the analysis of this technique however, only receptive learning has been considered. *Table 4* provides a detailed analysis of this activity.

Criteria	Score	Comments
Normal use	0	Learning using cards is not a normal part of language use. Recalling meanings of L2 words using L1 is a normal part of use, but the criterion requires contextualised not decontextualised use.
Motivation	2	The score of 2 is given because it is assumed that the learners choose the words to go onto the cards and want to learn them.
Retrieval	2	Looking at the L2 word and recalling the meaning involves retrieval so it gets 1 point. It is receptive so gets no further points for that but 1 further point for recall. If productive retrieval (productive recall) was also included, the total for retrieval would be 4 points.
Generation	0	Because there is no context for the word there is no generative use.
Imaging	0	If the keyword technique was used with some of the words then there would be points for imaging.
Useful focus	1	This is a very focused efficient activity.
New learning	2	Learning the form and meaning of an unknown word is very useful new learning.
No interference	1	If the learners know not to include paradigmatically related words in the same pack of cards there will be no interference.
Total	8	

Table 4: Analysis of the Word cards *activity*

Involvement load	Need 2	Search 1	Evaluation 0	3

Need is 2 for the same reasons given for motivation in *Table 4*. *Search* is 1 because the learners are doing receptive retrieval. There is no *Evaluation*.

True/false

The activity involves deciding if a sentence is true or false using real world knowledge. Here is an example:

    1. _____ a. Angela felt fear when she got a good grade in the test.
        _____ b. Our team won. We were fortunate.

Because the example above is intended for beginners, there are two sentences and one is true and one is false. This gives more help in making the true/false decision.

Criteria	Score	Comments
Normal use	1	Deciding if a sentence is true or accurate is a normal part of language use.
Motivation	1	The true/false decision is a motivating challenge often used in quiz shows. The motivation is *Can I make the correct choice?*
Retrieval	2	When reading the sentences, the learner has to do receptive recall of the meaning of the target words in their sentence context. 1 point for retrieval, 0 points because it is receptive, and 1 point for recall.
Generation	2	The activity involves receptive generative use, because the learners meet the word in a new context. The minimum score of 1 is given for the degree of generativeness, but a higher score could be given depending on how different the context sentence is from previous meetings with the word.
Imaging	0	No visualisation or imaging are involved.
Useful focus	1	The activity makes good use of learning time. Vocabulary learning is one of several useful things occurring.
New learning	1	There is new learning because the target words were first introduced earlier in the lesson.
No interference	1	The words in the activity are not related to each other, so there is little chance of interference.
Total	9	

Table 5: Analysis of the True/false with two choices *activity*

Involvement load	Need 1	Search 1	Evaluation 1	3

The designer of the book has chosen the words to focus on, so *Need* scores 1. The learner has to make receptive recall of the meaning of the target words in the sentences, so *Search* scores 1. The learner has to evaluate the meaning of the sentence – True or false, so *Evaluation* scores 1.

The goal of these two analyses is to clarify the criteria used in technique feature analysis. Let us now look at a summary of the analyses of the activities in *Appendix 1* (see *Table 6*). The activities in *Table 6* are ranked by their involvement load score and within that by their technique feature analysis score. There is clearly a lot of disagreement between the two measures. The top three according to involvement load include two of those rated lowest by technique feature analysis. Those rated highest by technique feature analysis with a score of 9 all have only a moderate score of 3 on involvement load. In spite of a small amount of overlap of criteria, the two scales are clearly giving different results.

Activity	Involvement load	Technique feature analysis
Fill the blanks	4	6
Find the words in the text	4	4
Word part table	4	3
Write with target words	3	9
True/false	3	9
Reword the sentence	3	9
Multiple-choice on text	3	8
Word cards	3	8
Read and choose definitions	3	5
Keyword	2	7
Reading plus fill in	2	6
Reading with glosses	1	5

Table 6: Comparison of involvement load and technique feature analysis on twelve activities

There are however reasons to suggest that technique feature analysis might work well for some activities, particularly keyword, and the involvement load ranking of the three activities in the Hulstijn and Laufer (2001) study agrees with the rankings by technique feature analysis.

The weaknesses of technique feature analysis may lie partly in the inclusion of the criteria of *normal use* and *new learning*. Normal use might not be a factor strongly affecting learning. Very effective learning activities like using word cards, the keyword mnemonic technique, and writing using target words do not involve normal language use (the keyword technique involves a very strange procedure!). Because there is plenty of opportunity for normal language use in the strands of meaning-focused input, meaning-focused output, and fluency development, there is no need for language-focused learning activities to include it. New learning is not easy to decide. If an item has only been introduced recently, then follow up activities can more clearly contribute to new learning, particularly if they focus on previously unmet aspects of the word. There are also many aspects involved in knowing a word and not all are equally weighted in their contribution to what it means to know a word. The technique feature analysis scale does not allow for this.

The technique feature analysis scale is clearly in the early stages of development. The comparison with the involvement load index shows that an experimental evaluation of the scale is possible. The scale also provides for the possibility of having a more inclusive scale of features for both the evaluation and design of teaching activities.

Acknowledgements

I am grateful to Jim Dickie for preparing the section on reliability.

Appendix 1: Examples for the Involvement Load Hypothesis

Activity: Multiple choice on a text

Criteria	Score	Comments
Normal use	0	
Motivation	1	
Retrieval	2	recept recall
Generation	2	recept gen
Imaging	0	
Useful focus	1	
New learning	1	retrieval
No interference	1	
Total	8	

Involvement load

Need 1	Search 1	Evaluation 1	3

Activity: Word cards

Criteria	Score	Comments
Normal use	0	
Motivation	2	
Retrieval	2	
Generation	0	
Imaging	0	
Useful focus	1	
New learning	2	
No interference	1	
Total	8	

Involvement load

Need 2	Search 1	Evaluation 0	3

Activity: True/false (2 choices)

Criteria	Score	Comments
Normal use	1	
Motivation	1	challenge
Retrieval	2	recept recall
Generation	2	receptive
Imaging	0	
Useful focus	1	
New learning	1	
No interference	1	
Total	9	

Involvement load

Need 1	Search 1	Evaluation 1	3

Activity: Reword the sentence

Criteria	Score	Comments
Normal use	1	
Motivation	0	
Retrieval	3	prod recall
Generation	4	
Imaging	0	
Useful focus	0	
New learning	1	
No interference	0	interfering
Total	9	

Involvement load

Need 1	Search 0	Evaluation 2	3

Activity: Read words choose definition

Criteria	Score	Comments
Normal use	0	
Motivation	1	
Retrieval	1	
Generation	0	
Imaging	0	
Useful focus	1	
New learning	1	
No interference	1	
Total	5	

Involvement load

Need 1	Search 1	Evaluation 1	3

Activity: Word parts table

Criteria	Score	Comments
Normal use	0	
Motivation	0	
Retrieval	1	
Generation	2	
Imaging	0	
Useful focus	0	
New learning	0	
No interference	0	interfering
Total	3	

Involvement load

Need 1	Search 2	Evaluation 1	4

Activity: Fill the blanks

Criteria	Score	Comments
Normal use	0	
Motivation	1	
Retrieval	0	
Generation	2	
Imaging	0	
Useful focus	1	
New learning	1	
No interference	1	
Total	6	

Involvement load

Need 1	Search 2	Evaluation 1	4

Activity: Keyword

Criteria	Score	Comments
Normal use	0	
Motivation	2	
Retrieval	0	
Generation	0	
Imaging	2	
Useful focus	1	
New learning	1	
No interference	1	
Total	7	

Involvement load

Need 2	Search 0	Evaluation 0	2

Activity: Find the words in the text

Criteria	Score	Comments
Normal use	0	
Motivation	1	
Retrieval	2	
Generation	0	
Imaging	0	
Useful focus	0	
New learning	0	
No interference	1	
Total	4	

Involvement load

Need 1	Search 2	Evaluation 1	4

Activity: Write with target words (H&L)

Criteria	Score	Comments
Normal use	0	
Motivation	1	
Retrieval	2	Words given
Generation	3	
Imaging	0	
Useful focus	1	
New learning	1	
No interference	1	
Total	9	

Involvement load

Need 1	Search 0	Evaluation 2	3

Activity: Reading with glosses (H&L)

Criteria	Score	Comments
Normal use	1	
Motivation	1	
Retrieval	0	
Generation	0	first meeting
Imaging	0	
Useful focus	1	
New learning	1	
No interference	1	
Total	5	

Involvement load

Need 1	Search 0	Evaluation 0	1

Activity: Reading plus fill in (H&L)

Criteria	Score	Comments
Normal use	0	
Motivation	1	
Retrieval	0	
Generation	2	
Imaging	0	
Useful focus	1	
New learning	1	
No interference	1	
Total	6	

Involvement load

Need 1	Search 0	Evaluation 1	2

Descriptions of the activities

Multiple choice on a text
1. What is this story about?

       a. A girl who gets a novel about technology in the mail.

       b. A basketball coach who tells jokes.

       c. A man who takes a direct trip to the local store.

       d. A girl who can control other people.

True/False
Check the sentence that is true:

1 __ a. Being tall is a characteristic of many trees.

  __ b. The snow was quite warm.

Read the word, choose the definition
century

a. first   b. hundred   c. school   d. man

pound

a. to hit hard many times   b. the steps you take

c. the first season   d. metal used in money

Word cards
The learners use word cards with the L2 word on one side and the L1 translation on the other.

Reword the sentence (McCarthy, O'Dell, 1994: 138)
Reword the sentences without changing the meaning:

       I strongly dislike jazz. (stand)

       Beer makes me feel sick. (revolt)

       I don't really care for tea. (keen)

Word parts table

Abstract noun	*Person noun*	*Verb*	*Adjective*
Revolution	Revolutionary	Revolutionise	Revolutionary
Representation			
Election			
Dictatorship			
Presidency			

McCarthy and O'Dell (1994: 109)

Fill the blanks
A list of words is provided, followed by 10 sentences with a blank space where a word needs to be inserted. There are more words than blank spaces.

Keyword
To help remember the meaning of a new word, the learner thinks of a keyword from their first language which sounds like the word or sounds like the beginning of the new word. Then the learner creates a mental image combining the meaning of the new word and the meaning of the keyword.

Find the words in the text
After the text, the meanings of some words are provided. The learners have to search in the text to find the words which go with the meanings.

Reading with glosses (Hulstijn, Laufer, 2001)
The learners read a text. The meanings of some of the words in the text are provided in glosses at the side of the text. Those words are needed to deal with the comprehension questions at the end of the text.

Writing using target words (Hulstijn, Laufer, 2001)
10 words are provided with their meanings and example sentences showing their use. The learners have to do a piece of writing and are told to make use of the 10 words in that piece of writing.

Reading plus fill in (Hulstijn, Laufer, 2001)
The learners read the text which has some blanks in it. The words which are needed to fill the blanks are provided on another page with L1 translations and L2 explanations, and a sample sentence containing the word. The learners choose the words to go in the appropriate blanks. Fifteen words are provided to fill the ten blanks. Here is an example of the information about each word.

> WRATH (noun, uncomfortable)
> Strong fierce anger
> Example: The wrath of the opponents to the proposed bill.
> Dutch = gramschap

Fluency and spoken English

Steven Kirk, Toyo University, Japan
Ronald Carter, University of Nottingham, United Kingdom

1. Introduction

Fluency is a concept that is central to the fields of English language teaching, second language acquisition, and linguistics in general; however, it is still not well understood and notoriously hard to define. Its importance in these fields can be seen in its frequent use in second language teaching methodology, where it is often contrasted with *accuracy*, and its frequent appearance in rubrics for the testing of speaking. In fact, it is one of the main goals of language learning, if not *the* main goal.

Although *fluency* is a central concept, it has proven very hard to define due to ambiguity in the use of the term throughout the field. First, there exists a lay term *fluency* with its own uses and connotations. Second, there are differences in researchers' definitions, with there being two broad categories of definitions. One meaning is close to general proficiency in the language, and the other is a more technical sense, related to particular features in the spoken language, such as rate of speech. This is further complicated by the use of the term to refer to native speakers as well as nonnative speakers. For example, are all native speakers by definition fluent, or do native speakers vary in degrees of fluency? Should nonnative speaker fluency be described in terms of resemblance to native speakers or should nonnative language be analysed on its own terms? Guillot (1999: vii) notes that fluency "crosses over boundaries in a way which has made it resistant to analysis", and then adds:

> Yet it is peculiarly available to all, language specialists and non-specialists, as a measure of oral performance, and is used with a confidence which hardly seems justified in view of the scarcity of accounts governed by anything other than intuition.

Clearly, *fluency* is a term that needs to be unpacked. In this chapter, we will look more closely at previous definitions of fluency in order to clarify this issue and arrive at a clearer and more useful concept for second language acquisition and language teaching pedagogy.

1. 1. Common sense notions of fluency

Definitions of fluency in English language teaching and applied linguistics all share at least one thing in common; they are essentially based on the common sense, non-technical meaning of the word. This sense is exemplified in dictionary definitions such as the

Merriam-Webster Online Dictionary ('fluent', 2008), which gives two relevant definitions. The first is "capable of using a language easily and accurately" and includes the example *fluent in Spanish*, which implies second language users. The second is "effortlessly smooth and flowing", and includes the examples *a fluent performance* and *spoke in fluent English*, which is relevant to first language users, and activities other than speech. There is also a more literal use of the word, defined as "capable of flowing" and "capable of moving with ease and grace". These definitions suggest that there is a conceptual metaphor of fluent speech as smooth motion and flowing as a liquid.

Although the lay definitions of *fluency* describe fluent speech as smooth and flowing, the picture that emerges from looking at natural spoken language is quite different. Goldman-Eisler (1968: 15; cited in Wingate, 1987) observed that

> [s]omehow the phenomenon of speech has become associated with images which suggest continuity of speech production. We speak of even flow [...] and many words relating to speech derive from descriptions of water in motion. [...] The facts however show these images to be illusory. If we measure vocal continuity by the number of words uttered between two pauses and call *phrase* the sequence uttered without a break we obtain a picture of fragmentation rather than continuity.

Koponen and Riggenbach (2000: 13) also note that

> oral proficiency and its perception are so complex in linguistic description that considering them unidimensionally as flows or currents constitutes an overly simplified view of language and speech.

The problem for linguists is how to capture the idea of *ease* of language use, and *smoothness* of speech, while taking into account the realities of spoken language.

2. Fluency as a temporal phenomenon

Fluency research in the 1980s and 1990s particularly focused on identifying quantifiable temporal variables which could distinguish fluent and nonfluent speech. The type of factors considered include length and duration of unfilled (silent) and filled (*erm* and *er*) pauses or hesitations, length of uninterrupted runs, rate of speech, amount of speech, and presence of other dysfluencies such as uncompleted utterances, lengthened sounds (drawls), and restarts. Quantitative studies of fluency have generally found that more fluent L2 speakers have comparatively fewer pauses than less fluent speakers, a higher rate of speech, and longer uninterrupted runs of speech (Lennon, 1990; Riggenbach, 1991; Freed, 1995; Ejzenberg, 2000; Hasselgreen, 2005). The difficulty is that the *fluent* speech of native speakers is full of these apparent dysfluencies, which native speakers are usually themselves unaware of (Wingate, 1987). Also, for learners, there is no linear development in temporal features from, for example, extremely long pauses to no pauses (Fulcher, 1996). That is, there are many reasons for the presence of dysfluencies in speech, with some being evidence of lack of proficiency in learners' speech, but others being normal or unavoidable.

Chafe (1980a) notes that there are many reasons for hesitations in speech, with some of them being dysfluencies but others being a normal part of fluent speech. Pauses are first of all necessary, because speakers must sometimes stop in order to breathe. Furthermore, pauses between clauses or *intonation units* (Chafe, 1994) are necessary for planning the next utterance (Goldman-Eisler, 1968; Dechert, 1980, 1983; Pawley, Syder, 2000). These can be further divided into planning *what* to say and planning *how* to say it.

It is also claimed that the location of the pauses is critical as well, with pauses that are within clauses being more dysfluent. Deese (1980) found that pauses that were within clauses are actually perceived as being longer than pauses between clauses. Chafe (1980a) claims that pauses within clauses are for grammatical or lexical choice rather than planning content, which would explain why they are more frequent with L2 users. Furthermore, less fluent L2 speakers tend to have more clusters of dysfluencies occurring together, which can result in the impression of *choppy* sounding speech (Riggenbach, 1991).

Searching for words is one of the major reasons for hesitations (Chafe, 1980a), and Fillmore (Fillmore, 1979, 2000) suggests that vocabulary size can be one measure of fluency, but that it is situation-dependent in that it depends on whether the other speaker can understand the vocabulary used. Since adult L2 speakers usually have a large mismatch between what they can say in the L1 and what they can say in the L2, they are likely to find themselves in situations where they simply lack knowledge of the needed lexical item, and have to resort to circumlocution, avoidance, reliance on help from the interlocutor, or awkward silences.

There is also evidence that dysfluencies such as hesitation phenomena may not just be necessary from the point of view of the speaker's ability to process language, but may also be helpful in fluent communication. Corley et al. (2007) show that hesitations (*er*, in the case of their study) which preceded words that had low predictability as completions of the sentences in question, were more easily integrated into context, and resulted in greater retention of the following word. Their study implies that hesitations before unpredictable words reduce the cognitive processing required for comprehension by the listener.

Although fluency judgments of learners generally correlate with higher speech rate, Munro and Derwing (2001), based on research by Anderson-Hsieh and Koehler (1988), found that speech rate had a curvilinear relationship with fluency judgments, i.e. there is a best range for speech that is easy to comprehend, with speech that is too fast or too slow being perceived as less fluent. Furthermore, native speakers' preferred speech rate for nonnative speakers was found to be lower than for other native speakers. This could be due to native speakers having more difficulty processing nonnative pronunciation or nonnative-like phraseology.

Restarts or false starts are generally considered to be dysfluencies, although they are often found in native speaker speech as well. However, Carroll (2004), studying conversations of groups of three nonnative speakers, observed that some apparent dysfluencies could be argued to contribute to the overall fluency of the conversation rather than detract from it. By viewing video of the conversations, he found that some restarts were the result of the speaker holding their turn while waiting for full eye contact from the person the utterance was directed to. Once eye contact was made, signaling to the speaker that the recipient was paying attention, the utterance was completed. Carroll claims that this behavior is not dysfluent, but rather shows interactional competence.

The difficulty in determining whether temporal phenomena are dysfluent or not lies in the fact that they are the symptoms of interactive aspects of the conversation and the underlying psycholinguistic processes of speech production. The dysfluencies of spoken language are a window into the limitations of human language production for all speakers, and into the problems of second language production for learners. In *Section 2.1.* we will look at both the limitations and the psycholinguistic processes that enable fluent language.

2. 1. Psycholinguistic basis of fluency

Lennon defines *fluency* as "the rapid, smooth, accurate, lucid, and efficient translation of thought or communicative intention into language under the temporal constraints of on-line processing" (2000: 26). Some researchers associate *fluency* with procedural knowledge as opposed to declarative knowledge (Faerch, Kasper, 1984; Schmidt, 1992). Lennon (1990: 391) asserts:

> Whereas such elements as idiomaticness, appropriateness, lexical range, and syntactic complexity can all be assigned to linguistic knowledge, fluency is purely a performance phenomenon; there is (presumably) no fluency store.

Linguistic knowledge is what is stored in memory, but fluency is the speaker's ability to access those memories and process them into speech within the constraints of real time conversation. For learners, the problem is not simply to increase the speed of their speech, but rather to improve the efficiency of the organisation and production processes of language in the mind, which then result in more fluent speech.

Many dysfluencies, whether considered normal or not, are the result of planning speech, which requires time away from articulation (Goldman-Eisler, 1968). Chafe (1980b) and Pawley and Syder (2000), both looking at the uninterrupted runs of speech, argue that there is an upper limit on what speakers are able to plan for a single utterance. Chafe (1992) proposes that this limit is based on the capacity of working memory (Miller, 1956; Schweickert, Boruff, 1986; Baddeley, 1992) and that speakers can at most plan the lexical content of one new idea, or one focus of consciousness, at a time, which often coincides with a single clause.

Within the limits of working memory, fluency is achieved through automaticity of language production (Schmidt, 1992), although exactly what this means varies in the literature (Dörnyei, 2009). Automatic processing frees working memory capacity for other aspects of speaking, such as planning content. Much of automatic processing also depends on the access of memory. Studying the neurobiological correlates of fluency, Dewaele (2002) states that fluency in both L1 and L2 depends on the existence, accessibility, and retrieval of procedural knowledge from long-term memory. Fluent speech results when the appropriate or required language is present and accessible in long-term memory, when it can be combined efficiently, and when there is sufficient storage in working memory. Problems in any of these areas, such as lack of language knowledge, an individual's lower capacity of working memory, or anxiety in the communicative situation, could lead to problems in fluency. Although it may be possible for fast operation of declarative knowledge to improve fluency to some extent, in general L2 speakers' reliance on declarative knowledge to speak results in reduced fluency due to overloading working memory (Paradis, 1994; Dewaele, 2002).

2. 1. 1. Formulaic sequences

The link between fluency and the use of formulaic language has been recognised for quite some time. In a study of learners' fluency development after a period abroad, Towell et al. (1996) conclude that the observed temporal aspects of fluent speech, i.e. higher rate of speech and longer uninterrupted runs, are a result of more efficient proceduralised knowledge. This could be due to automatisation of the processes of speech production or the use of ready-made chunks of language, i.e. formulaic sequences. Larsen-Freeman and Cameron (2008) note that, although native speakers can theoretically produce infinitely many utterances that conform to the syntactic rules of the language, they rarely do, and rather tend to mix and match frequently used chunks. This is also one of the most important findings of corpus linguistics – that a large part of native speaker speech consists of recurrent chunks (Nattinger, DeCarrico, 1992; O'Keeffe et al., 2007; Schmitt, Carter, 2004).

Wray (2002: 9) defines a *formulaic sequence* as

> a sequence, continuous or discontinuous, of words or other elements, which is, or appears to be, prefabricated: that is, stored or retrieved whole from memory at the time of use, rather than being subject to generation or analysis by the language grammar.

By directly accessing the formulaic sequence, the speaker is able to circumvent application of syntactic rules in the construction of utterances in real time. Connectionist neural network theories propose that as particular sequences of language are repeatedly accessed in memory, their neural connections are strengthened, which leads to faster access later (MacKay, 1982; Gasser, 1990; Strayer, Kramer, 1990). In this way, formulaic sequences in L2 speech can act as *islands of reliability* (Dechert, 1983) between periods of more difficult language production.

It is also possible for an L2 speaker to have idiosyncratic formulaic sequences which are stored and accessed whole in memory, but which are not *nativelike*, and would not be a recurrent chunk found in a corpus of native speaker language. Their use would promote *nativelike fluency* but would not be *nativelike selection* (Pawley, Syder, 1983). However, the use of idiosyncratic rather than nativelike formulaic sequences results in greater processing required by native speaker listeners (Millar, submitted for review), which can result in the perception of weaker fluency from the listener's point of view.

2. 2. Fluency as an interactive phenomenon

Temporal variables are often ambiguous, and psycholinguistic aspects of fluency are generally inaccessible or difficult to measure. For these reasons, measurement of fluency of L2 speakers is usually measured holistically by native speaker raters. Fulcher (1996), creating bands of descriptors derived from studying the language of learners grouped into 5 categories of fluency, found that speakers put into different categories of fluency varied in more ways than just temporal variables. Differences in the 5 bands included listening comprehension, length of utterances, presence of backchanneling, expansion or lack of expansion of utterances, and the ability to repair problems in communication. This suggests that fully capturing what constitutes fluent performance in conversation involves more than just temporal factors on the speaker's side.

Ejzenberg (2000) notes that fluency should be seen from both a speaker-based, psycholinguistic perspective, as well as a listener-based, sociolinguistic perspective. She claims that fluency is a display or manifestation, defined as "the perception of the ease with which a speaker delivers the message, making it appear to be smooth and naturally paced to the listener" (2000: 287), which is variable and dependent on the context or situation. Fluency is ultimately the speaker's ability to project an "image of fluency" (2000: 288) to the listener. Ejzenberg notes the relationship of fluency to overall proficiency, stating that it is one component of oral proficiency, dependent on language knowledge, i.e. grammatical competence and discourse competence, but accomplished mainly by strategic competence, which is the ability to deal with breakdowns in communication (Canale, 1983). Similarly, Hasselgreen (2005: 134) sees fluency as listener-oriented and interactive, defining it as

> the ability to contribute to what a listener, proficient in the language, would normally perceive as coherent speech, which can be understood without undue strain, and is carried out at a comfortable pace, not being disjointed or disrupted by excessive hesitation.

The ease of the speaker's production is one factor contributing to the ease of the listener's comprehension.

Sajavaara (1987: 62) takes a broader view of fluency including both the linguistic acceptability and smooth continuity of speech, stating that fluency "equals the communicative acceptability of the speech act, or 'communicative fit', and expectations concerning this fit vary according to the situation". He also notes that just as native speaker speech contains pauses, hesitations, false starts, and rephrases, it is expected that nonnative speaker speech should also contain these *dysfluencies* (Lehtonen et al., 1977), and therefore, fluency must be evaluated in context (Lehtonen, 1978). In Sajavaara's (1987: 62) words,

> [l]earning to speak fluently does not always imply an uninterrupted flow of speech that is sequentially and grammatically irreproachable. The 'good' speaker 'knows' how to hesitate, how to be silent, how to self-correct, how to interrupt, and how to complete expressions or leave them unfinished. Speech must meet the expectations of the speech community and represent normal, acceptable and relaxed behavior.

Fluency is not only dependent on the speaker, but also on (1) the listener, (2) the context or situation, (3) the norms of the culture, and (4) the speaker's ability to predict how the listener will interpret the speaker's utterances in context. Sajavaara describes participants in conversation as problem solvers, where the problem is to communicate using previous experience and whatever practical means are available, including facial expressions and gestures. Listeners and speakers both construct interpretations by taking the other person and their own discourse history into account.

2. 2. 1. *The role of the listener*

Bavelas et al. (2000) found that listeners' verbal and nonverbal backchannels function to show the speaker that communication has been successful, and more specific lexical backchannels can even contribute to the construction of the speaker's narrative. In their study, when listeners were given a concurrent task which prevented them from backchanneling, the speakers' narratives became much less fluent and often fell apart. Furthermore, speakers tend to use more words when there is no feedback (Krauss, Weinheimer, 1966), and listeners are able to understand more when they can provide feedback (Kraut et al., 1982).

This suggests that fluency in conversation may be co-constructed by both (or all) participants. McCarthy (2005) calls this aspect of fluency *confluence*, and notes that speakers scaffold each other's performance, for example, by finishing each other's sentences or suggesting words that the other speaker might be searching for, which results in a fluent conversation in spite of the apparent dysfluencies of the individual participants.

Fiksdal (2000), studying conversations between native speakers and L2 speakers, found that the periods when the participants felt that the conversation was most fluent were when they were able to match tempo and had good rapport. In fluent conversations, the tempo was maintained in spite of false starts and hesitations. Furthermore, the context, i.e. the relationship to the interlocutor, the level of formality, the topic, and other more social factors, may contribute to fluency, through the ability or lack of ability to build rapport.

Relevance Theory (Sperber, Wilson, 1995) can help to explain how the interaction between participants in a conversation can lead to successful communication and fluency. *Relevance Theory* assumes that utterances are underspecified for meaning, and successful communication is when the listener is able to make the correct inferences intended by the speaker. To do this, participants must be able to identify the communicative intention of the speaker, the context for interpretation of the utterance, the effect of previous utterances, the degree of vagueness or commitment to the utterance, and the state of success of communication so far. Hasselgreen (2005: 135) claims that *smallwords*, which are "small words and phrases, occurring with high frequency in the spoken language, that help to keep our speech flowing, yet do not contribute essentially to the message itself", accomplish many of these functions. These overlap with some of what others refer to as *backchannels*, *discourse markers*, and *vague language*. Smallwords, such as *well*, *right*, *you know*, *like*, and *kind of*, help the speaker by guiding the listener to the appropriate interpretation of the utterance. Hasselgreen (2005) found that in addition to temporal variables such as rate of speech, nativelike use of smallwords is a mark of higher L2 fluency.

2. 2. 2. Turn boundaries

McCarthy (2008a) notes that fluent conversation is a joint enterprise where both participants attend to one another. By attending to one another, every turn is a response to the previous turn. Schegloff (1996) states that turn boundaries are important points in conversation. Turn beginnings help the recipient anticipate the turn shape and turn type of the ensuing turn (Schegloff, 1987), which then helps the listener predict the ending of the turn. Tao's (2003) corpus-based study of turn initial items found that turn beginnings were usually syntactically independent smallwords such as *yeah*, *mm hm*, *oh*, *and*, *well*, and *right*, that served to link that turn with the preceding turn, or comment on the preceding turn.

Smooth turn boundaries are crucial to creating the impression of flow in co-constructed fluency, and are dependent on each participant's ability to predict the endings of the other's turns. Prosody, as well as grammatical and lexical cues, can help the listener to predict these. Wennerstrom (2000) found that the lack of pitch accents to distinguish new and old information, and lack of appropriate boundary tones at the end of turns led to interruptions by native speaker interlocutors. Appropriate use of boundary tones allowed even relatively long pauses to be tolerated without interruption by native speakers. She (2000: 125) concludes by noting:

> Thus it is not longer utterances or shorter pauses per se that lead to a perception of fluent speech; instead, it is the ability to speak phrasally rather than word-by-word, focusing the main idea of each utterance in a coherent manner and collaborating in the turn-taking process.

In summary, it seems that there are two main senses of fluency. One is a psycholinguistic construct, based on the efficient organisation of the language in long-term memory, and rapid access of those memories, which is manifested in longer uninterrupted runs of speech and higher rate of speech. The other sense of fluency is dependent on the psycholinguistic construct, but also co-constructed by all participants in the conversation. The fluency of observed spoken conversation will always be a result of the interaction of both of these.

3. Analysis of a learner conversation

Most fluency research has studied high level learners, or compared the fluency of higher level learners with the nonfluency of lower level learners. There often is a tacit assumption that learners are either *fluent* or *nonfluent*, and that lower level learners are nonfluent. The learner in this conversation is a Japanese university student, whose English proficiency is approximately B1 in the Common European Framework. This conversation in particular is interesting because both the learner and the native speaker felt that the conversation was quite fluent. The native speaker commented that the learner's fluency seemed relatively high, and that she was quite easy to talk with. In addition, the learner commented that she perceived herself as being quite fluent in this conversation. In this section, we will look at what, among the various factors that create fluency in conversation, are present or absent in this conversation.

Before looking at the details of the conversation, the more general circumstances should be noted. The speakers met for the first time just a few minutes before the conversation was recorded. The NNS commented that she was initially nervous, but relaxed about a minute into the conversation when she found she was able to participate effectively. The NNS commented that topics brought up in the conversation (mostly by the NS) were familiar and easy for her to talk about.

3. 1. Strategic competence

First, the conversation is generally led by the NS, who chooses most of the topics and asks most of the questions. However, there are times, increasingly so as the conversation progresses, where the NNS initiates topics and asks questions which move the conversation forward. The NS commented that this is one of the aspects of her conversational ability that impressed him the most, and made the conversation feel more balanced. To attempt to quantify this, the NS asks 23 direct questions during the roughly 6 minutes of conversation, and the NNS asks 8. The numbers may not be equal, but the NS is both a native speaker of the language used and a teacher, which gives him responsibility for leading the conversation.

The NNS also shows good listening comprehension throughout the conversation, and is able to initiate repair when she does not know words. In one case, she does not understand the word *debt*, and immediately repeats it to ask for clarification. There are also two cases where she is able to clarify her meaning when the NS signals lack of understanding. In *Extract 1,* she (A in the transcription) uses an idiosyncratic phrase *dress style*, which is followed by a hesitation and repetition by the NS (B in the transcription). She recognises the problem and rephrases the expression as *one piece* (this is a Japanese loan word from English that means *dress*), which the NS shows he understands.

```
Extract 1
1 B   so er what kind of fashion do you like.
2 A   (0.3) yeah dress style.
3 B   (0.5) dress style like [er:: ]
4 A                          [one p]iece.
5 B   (0.3) oh o[kay. ]
6 A             [yeah.] yeah.
```

Later, in *Extract 2*, when asked where she is from, she uses the Japanese word *shitamachi* in her answer, and then asks the NS if he understands to pre-empt repair.

```
Extract 2
1 B   how is what is er monzennakacho like.
2 A   (0.5) [er::         ]
3 B         [is it a nice] place?
4 A   (.) yes. (.) shitamachi.
5 B   (.) ah [ok.     ]
6 A          [can you] understand?=
7 A   =yeah.=
8 B   =mm hm.
```

Another time, when she gets embarrassed at her lack of knowledge on the topic, she immediately initiates a topic change. Only once is there a problem that is not immediately resolved. At the end of the conversation, she misunderstands part of the question asked of her, and the conversation continues for a few turns until the misunderstanding is brought to her attention by the NS. Her strategic competence shown by her ability to repair and control the topic is quite good compared to her peers and contributes strongly to the impression of high fluency.

3. 2. Turn boundaries

Turn boundaries are important places to find signs of fluent conversation. Out of a total of 164 turn boundaries, 22% were latched, 13% were early (overlapped), and 64% had silent pauses. The silent pauses between turns were a mean length of 0.42 seconds (standard deviation = 0.26), with the longest pause at 1.36 seconds. The total pauses between turns accounted for 11% of the total time of the conversation. Of the five pauses that were longer than 1.0 second, two are cases of the NNS being asked a question that involves a topic change, which could be more taxing on the NNS's comprehension, or require more time to think of a response. One is prior to the NNS giving an answer that was embarrassing. One is where the NNS falters while searching for how to say what she wants to say, until the NS completes her sentence for her. The longest pause (see *Extract 3*) comes when the NS is thinking of something to say on a topic started by the NNS.

```
Extract 3
1 A   so: where do you (0.6) often
2     (0.8) go (.) to buy sh- (0.4) clothes?
3 B   (1.0) nn: i almost never go to buy clothes.=
4 A   =wow. ((both speakers laughter)) wow.=
5 B   =but nn:: (1.4) [yeah sometimes]
6 A                   [you:r         ] wife?
7 B   (0.3) sometimes my wife will buy me a shirt.=
8 A   =oh good.
```

This 1.4 second pause in line 5 is perceived as long by both speakers, as they both begin speaking simultaneously afterwards, until the NS drops out and the NNS finishes her question. The data shows that the NNS is aware of when silences become uncomfortable, and understands that she is also responsible for attempting to keep the conversation going.

Generally, she is able to use appropriate boundary tones to signal the end of turns, or to hold turns (with a low-rise or flat boundary tone). In one case, shown in *Extract 4*, overlap occurs when the NS mistakenly interprets the turn to have ended. In lines 1 to 4, she effectively holds her turn even through long pauses with low-rise and plateau boundary tones, and the phrase *oh yeah*; but in line 5 she uses a falling tone after *worked*. This tone, as well as the fact that grammatically the NS would not expect a following direct object, results in overlap when the NNS tries to complete the sentence.

Extract 4
```
1 A   o:h yea:h
2     (0.9) er:: yest- (0.4) yesterday,
3     (0.3) oh yeah.
4     (0.2) my seven days is almost all days
5     (0.4) i worked. (1.0) [a part time j-      ]
6 B                        a:h  [you have a part time] job?
7 A   yes.
```

Looking at turn initiators used by the NNS, out of a total of 119 turns (backchannels and overlapping speech were also counted as turns here), *yeah,* used 41 times, is by far the most frequent turn initiator. *Yeah* is also the most frequent turn initiator for native speakers, but only accounts for 19% of turns (Tao, 2003), while in this NNS's speech it accounts for 35%. Other frequent turn initiators were *yes* (18), laughter (7), *oh* (6), *er* (5), and *so* (4). Although she lacks the variety of NS speech, she does generally use appropriate turn initiators, which is a characteristic of more fluent non-native speakers (Hasselgreen, 2005). This learner also uses backchannels appropriately, either with *yeah, mm,* or a comment like *oh good.* She also used 2 of the smallwords in Hasselgreen's list of 19 (2005: 163). She used *oh* 10 times to indicate a cognitive change of state, and *I know* once to indicate agreement. She also used *ah* as a smallword, but in the way it is commonly used in Japanese, to express a negative surprise, rather than in the nativelike use of a positive surprise.

In terms of the balance between the speakers in the conversation, the NNS has 119 turns, and the NS has 117 turns. The NNS's speech accounts for approximately 56% of the conversation, and the NS's speech accounts for approximately 48%. The total is greater than 100% due to overlapping speech. The non-native speaker takes up more time with turns, but of course speaks more slowly and pauses more frequently during them, which is to be expected. The number of turns is almost equivalent. Although this is difficult to interpret by the raw numbers alone, looking at the conversation itself, the NNS generally responds to the NS's turns without any problem. Furthermore, as the conversation progresses, the NNS sometimes elaborates her responses without prompting or further questioning from the NS.

3. 3. Temporal factors

In order to evaluate fluency as a temporal and psycholinguistic phenomenon of the speaker, it is necessary to look in more detail at the NNS's turns. To arrive at numbers that are more representative of the NNS's speech during turns, we performed the calculation using all turns that were 4 words or longer and did not contain laughter. The mean length of uninterrupted runs was 2.21 words (SD=1.4), with the longest run at 7 words. This calculation followed Riggenbach (1991) by including filled pauses as words. The subject's mean rate of speech per turn ranged from 90 words/minute to 111 words/minute.

Her pauses within turns averaged 0.39 seconds (SD=0.24), with the longest pause at 1.16 seconds, which actually occurs during overlapping speech, and therefore could be accounted for as her pausing to listen to the other speaker. Many of the pauses that occur during turns are appropriate and normal and should not be considered dysfluencies. After removing pauses that occur between clauses, after discourse markers, and after hesitations like *erm*, there are 34 unfilled pauses that could be heard as dysfluent, spread among the 71 turns consisting of 2 or more words.

Looking more closely at her longer turns, many of them are constructed one or two words at a time, and show a lack of grammatical structure. This single conversation, with 493 tokens and 150 word types, is too small to be subject to corpus linguistic techniques; however, looking at the sequences of words the learner is able to utter as uninterrupted runs suggests that some sequences may be formulaic for the learner. *I want to go* is spoken twice and both times as a fluent sequence. *So where are you from?* is one of her longest spoken runs. One of the longest runs is *Yes do you know Decks Tokyo Beach*. After the turn initiator, the next three words are uttered one other time in the conversation, also as a continuous phrase, and are not infrequent in learner input. The last three words make up the name of a shopping centre, which would almost certainly be stored whole. So, this could very well be three sequences combined together. Sentences that involve more complex grammar result in dysfluent pauses. For example, *So where do you (0.6) often (0.8) go (.) to buy sh- (0.4) clothes* (see also *Extract 1*) involves an infinitival complement after the main verb.

To summarise, the learner in this study was able to create an impression of fluency mainly through showing confidence, being able to take control of the conversation, even if only to a small extent, the ability to repair breakdowns in communication, and the ability to use some nativelike turn initiators. She was also able to keep her turn while encountering language production difficulties by employing low-rise boundary tones, filled pauses, and repetition, and by avoiding long silent pauses. At the level of the conversation as a whole, she shows the ability to recognise when a silence has reached an uncomfortable length, and acts to fill it, which is part of 'keeping up her end of the conversation.' On the other hand, her fluency is lacking in the temporal factors, particularly speech rate and mean length of run. Her fluency is weaker at the psycholinguistic level which is probably due to a lack of vocabulary in general, and a lack of formulaic sequences, which could be used with minimal strain on cognitive processing and working memory. The pedagogical implications of this, in terms of what learners need to learn to be able to contribute to creating fluent conversation will be discussed in the following section.

4. Pedagogical implications and conclusions

One of the most important aspects of developing fluency is the acquisition of formulaic sequences, stored and accessed holistically, which would result in faster processing and ease of listener comprehension. However, not every utterance needs to be or even should be uttered without hesitation, if less predictable or more creative parts of utterances become easier to comprehend when preceded by hesitations. Therefore, the formulaic language that learners need to acquire is what native speakers would perceive as more predictable, which equates to higher frequency and a higher mutual information (MI) score (Ellis et al., 2008). Within usage-based theories of first language acquisition, high frequency can account for holistic storage as formulaic sequences; however, in naturalistic language learning, the words are also situated within a context of use. If the memory of context of use is stored along with the memory of the chunk, then high frequency, low MI score chunks like *and at the* will likely not have recurrent contexts associated with them.

The next and ultimate question is how to teach these to learners. First, it is necessary to understand how learners acquire formulaic sequences. In recent usage-based first language acquisition theory (Tomasello, 2003), language is acquired as sequences first and only analysed into component parts as needed (Wray, 2008), or with greater exposure according to the type and token ratios of the sequences and their components (Bybee, 2008). However, this may be different with adult second language learners, who tend to analyse more and to store smaller chunks of language (Wray, 2008).

Second, another problem that classroom learners face is the overall lower amount of input. If materials are designed to contain recurrent chunks with high frequency and high MI score, then the next step is for the learners to *notice* them (Schmidt, 2001), which can make them more salient and help them enter memory (Skehan, 1998).

Memorisation of larger stretches of language may also prove useful for classroom learners. Although memorising dialogues is certainly not new, the weakness of this technique traditionally has been in the dialogues themselves, which are artificially constructed by textbook writers and not very realistic examples of spoken language. Some more recent textbooks have dialogues based on spoken corpora that are rich in aspects of language crucial to fluency. Dialogues should include hesitations written into the text, as well as turn initiators, discourse markers, and other smallwords. By memorising these more realistic dialogues, learners are memorising phrases that make up whole turns in conversation, along with smallwords and hesitations. Grammatical constructions are also contained in the phrases memorised. Furthermore, they are situated within the context of the conversation, giving the phrases pragmatic meaning as well. Although it may seem that memorising a single conversation is very limited, it is much easier to break the memorised language into constituent parts than to put it together from smaller segments and rules (Lewis, 1993, 1997), and would come closer to solving the *nativelike selection* problem (Pawley, Syder, 1983). Furthermore, if learners can refer to a recording of the dialogue, then learners can imitate the prosody of the original. This could help them to acquire more nativelike use of boundary tones and pitch accents on stressed words, which are also important to fluency.

Many questions still remain to truly understand spoken fluency and its development in learners. As much as possible, corpora of native speaker spoken language and non-native speaker language in conversations should be multimodal, that is, including video, so that non-verbal aspects of fluency can be taken account of. Also, more research needs to be done into how the second language is organised in learners' minds, and particularly how formulaic sequences are acquired by learners. Furthermore, studies in corpus linguistics can continue to find ways of identifying recurrent sequences that correspond to formulaic sequences in native speakers, and that account for the predictable chunks of language. On the pedagogical side, the role of memorisation in the classroom, and whether this leads to more fluent use of the formulaic sequences that comprise the memorised dialogues, needs to be studied. Finally, there is a need for more longitudinal studies of learners to investigate how formulaic language develops in their speech production, and how they develop confidence and higher-level conversational skills.

Acknowledgements

We are grateful to Mike McCarthy for helpful discussions and advice on the material in this chapter.

Phrase-noticing or phrase-learning:
A question of semantics?

June Eyckmans, Erasmushogeschool Brussel and Vrije Universiteit Brussel, Belgium

1. Introduction: second language pedagogy and lexis

Although applied linguists nowadays agree that learning vocabulary should occupy a central place within language teaching pedagogy, the key role vocabulary plays in language learning has not always been reflected in the amount of attention that has been given to it by language teachers and researchers (Eyckmans, 2004). According to Boers and Lindstromberg (2008) the lack of attention for vocabulary learning can be attributed to the persistent popularity of old-school grammar study, on the one hand, and the neglect of the importance of vocabulary in later approaches to language teaching pedagogy such as *audiolingualism* and *communicative language teaching,* on the other. Indeed, in the – not so distant – past, mastery of grammatical structures was seen as central to learning a second language. The main focus in classroom activities and second language acquisition research was on the acquisition of grammatical competence and – at best – the development of functional communication skills (Eyckmans, 2004). Although it can be argued that early *communicative language teaching* made room for a greater emphasis on vocabulary because it emphasized the importance of so-called functional phrases (phrases of evident high frequency in spoken English such as *would you like to…*, etc.), it provided no structured approach to the learning and long-term remembering of new words. The general assumption that foreign language learners pick up vocabulary in the same vein as first language learners do, i.e. incidentally, appears to be a very tenacious one in the history of second language acquisition. The development of the learner's interlanguage lexicon has long been treated as an auxiliary activity and, more often than not, it involved memorizing word lists. Apart from encouraging teachers to help their learners with inferring word meaning from context or from the morphemes words are made up of, little effort was invested in deliberately associating lexical forms with particular meanings.

It took until the early 90s for premeditated vocabulary instruction to move up to its current prominent position in second language acquisition and for language teaching approaches to start emphasizing the importance of a lexical approach to language learning. Cases in point are Lewis' teacher training manuals that revolve around the adage that language consists of *grammaticalised lexis*, not *lexicalised grammar* (Lewis, 1993, 1997) and scholars' assertions that vocabulary needs to be systematically integrated into any language course curriculum (Nation, 1990, 2001; Meara, 1995, 2002; Schmitt, 2000).

The revaluation of the lexical dimension in language learning coincides with the shift in perspective from defining second language learning as primarily involving top-down processing (learning grammar rules and applying them to concrete examples) to perceiving it as being driven by *bottom-up processing* skills (recognizing frequent word combinations from which more general patterns can be extracted). According to Ellis (2002a, 2002b, 2005) language learners continually analyse the distributional characteristics of the language input they receive throughout their life, which makes input frequency the key determinant of language acquisition. This ties in with usage-based theories which define the grammar of any particular language as *a posteriori* conceptualisation of the dynamic process of language development (Barlow, Kemmer, 2000; Bybee, Hopper, 2001; Bybee, 2006). Together with psycholinguists' assertions that natural language is largely built up out of prefabricated multiword combinations that make up the discourse structure of language (Sinclair, 1991; Wray, 2002), these modern views of language acquisition have replaced the generative linguistics' perspective of the lexicon as being separate from the grammar with an integrative conceptualisation of language in which patterns are inherent in language segments.

In this chapter I will sum up some important and recent research findings into the role of lexical phrases in the second-language learning classroom. Starting with the ubiquity of syntagmatic constructions in authentic discourse and text as uncovered by corpus linguistics, I will shed light on the quintessential role assigned to prefabricated patterns in language acquisition (*Section 2*). In *Section 3*, I will discuss the likelihood of incidental phrase-learning (also called *phrase-noticing*) in an instructed second-language learning context. This will be followed by a strong petition for cognitive linguistics inspired phrase-learning and a run-down of available measures to assess phrase knowledge (*Section 4*).

2. The importance of the syntagmatic dimension in language

2. 1. Corpus linguistics and the ubiquity of phrases

The foregrounding of multiword lexis is largely due to the rise of corpus linguistics. Studies of L1 discourse have revealed overwhelming evidence of collocational tendencies that often defied generative grammatical explanation (Pawley, Syder, 1983; Nattinger, DeCarrico, 1992; Howarth, 1998; Foster, 2001; Wray, 2002; Schmidt, 2004). Adult native speakers' phrase lexicon is estimated to consist of many thousands of chunks and estimates on the bases of written corpora have unveiled that half of all written English is made up of lexical phrases (Erman, Warren, 2000; Butler, 2005). Although most of this research involves the English language, studies in Spanish (Corpas Pastor, 1996; Ruiz Gurillo, 2001; Montoro del Arco, 2006), in French (Gross, 1996; Mejri, 1997), and in German (Fleischer, 1997; Burger, 1998) are also surfacing.

In view of the overwhelming corpus evidence that knowledge of one's mother tongue consists very substantially of active and passive knowledge of chunks of language of a wide variety of sorts, applied linguists have come to recognize the quintessential role of prefabricated patterns in language acquisition (Ellis, 1996; Wray, 2002; Schmitt, 2004). In fact, psycholinguistic research has shown convincingly that communicative performance – which is characterized by real-time language processing – relies on this exemplar-based knowledge to a large extent (Ellis, 2002). Strings of words that are stored as single ready-made units are easily accessible and contribute to fluency in real-time situations because learners do not have to construct these language units word by word, as they can be summoned from memory as prefabricated wholes. Because we use these chunks of language, we are capable of freeing up the necessary short-memory capacity for planning and delivering a new stretch of speech.

The fact that a string of words is stored and retrieved as a single ready-made unit is the defining characteristic of a multiword combination in Wray's well-known and much-cited definition of what she calls "formulaic sequences" (2002: 9). Sinclair used the term *semi-preconstructed phrases* and postulated that a substantial amount of language obeys the *idiom principle* (Sinclair, 1991: 110), which restricts the co-occurrence of words for reasons beyond any grammar rules (in contrast to the *open-choice principle* where individual words occupy slots in particular syntactic structures). The number of terms used to refer to multiword units in the literature – Wray (2002) lists over 50 terms – may be indicative of the diversity and scope of the phenomenon, which has also become known as *phraseology*.

2. 2. The consequences for Second Language Acquisition?

If the fluent use of lexical phrases is an essential marker of native-like proficiency then it stands to reason that learners will need receptive and productive knowledge of a vast array of these phrases if they wish to aspire to becoming fluent language users. Unfortunately, many advanced learners of English with significant vocabulary sizes and profound knowledge of the rules of English grammar still sound unidiomatic and awkward (De Cock, 2004; Siyanova, Schmitt, 2007). In fact, it seems that it is language learners' inability to combine words in idiomatic ways that distinguishes the less proficient language learner from the highly proficient one (or from the native speaker). Learners' neglect of the idiom principle often results in excessive reliance on L1 to L2 transfer. Consequently, many sentences generated by language learners sound unnatural or foreign even though they are perfectly 'grammatical' (Pawley, Syder, 1983; Sinclair, 1991). The incremental acquisition of phrases which comes so naturally to the L1 user poses a serious challenge for the L2 learner who simply does not receive sufficient L2 input for associations between words to become strong enough to guarantee their storage as unitary combinations in the lexicon (Deconinck et al., 2009).

Although many studies have shown the problematic nature of learners' command of phrase knowledge (even at an advanced level of language proficiency) in terms of overuse, underuse or misuse (Nesselhauf, 2005), and despite learners' dire need for help in coping with this learning burden, the number of pedagogical proposals furthering a syntagmatic approach to language learning have been limited. Willis (1990) and Nattinger and DeCarrico (1992) took pedagogical initiatives directed at the acquisition of an L2 multiword lexicon within immersion situations. In the field of instructed second-language acquisition – in which the language learners' exposure to the target language is largely confined to the classroom – a phrase-oriented pedagogy has been proposed by Michael Lewis (1993, 1997, 2000a). In his *Lexical Approach*, Lewis promotes noticing activities that raise learners' awareness of the syntagmatic dimension of natural language. He recommends large amounts of language exposure in the classroom and chunking activities that help the learners notice the prevalence of lexical phrases in authentic language material. The assumption is that learners will also engage in this strategy outside the classroom. Regretfully, the autonomous identification of authentic word sequences seems to pose an insurmountable challenge (Eyckmans et al., 2007).

The meagre harvest of phrase-oriented methods when skimming the second-language teaching literature may be due to the multiple taxonomies that have been formulated in order to capture the phraseological dimension of language and the fact that it is notoriously difficult to establish a common core of useful phrases.

2. 3. A common core of multiword units?

In keeping with Schmitt's (2000) proposal that vocabulary should best be taught according to a cost-benefit perspective, it seems evident that teachers and materials writers should target a common core of phrases that is of the most use to their language learners. Surely, this *must* mean that this common core should consist of phrases that are idiomatic and frequently used by most native speakers (so that the learners would succeed in sounding like native speakers of the language they are trying to master). However, the establishment of a core selection of chunks for teaching on the basis of corpora is fraught with difficulties (Moreno Jaén, 2007; Stengers, 2007; Eyckmans, 2009). In the electronic megacorpora that are available nowadays, the concept of collocation is defined quantitatively: statistical significance computation scores indicate the probability of co-occurrence of words within a certain span. However, these 'lexicometrics' need to be interpreted with caution as they are purely mathematical analyses of all items occurring in a set span. Given the prevalence of homonymy and polysemy, it is very hard to obtain unambiguous data and manual checking of the extracted collocations is indispensable. Nevertheless, collections of useful phrases are gradually becoming available. Shin and Nation (2008) compiled a list of the highest frequency collocations of spoken English on the basis of the ten million word BNC spoken corpus and Moreno Jaén (2009) identified 2,688 highly frequent adjective-noun, verb-noun,

noun-verb and noun-noun collocations on the basis of the BNC and the Bank of English. Collections of lexical phrases have also been published in the form of dictionaries (e.g. *The Oxford Collocations Dictionary for Students of English*, *The Collins Cobuild English Language Dictionary*, *The Oxford Idioms Dictionary for Learners of English*). But, as remarked by Boers and Lindstromberg (2009), these dictionaries have been assembled on the basis of formal features, which means that highly fixed combinations such as idioms and collocations have been prioritized. A comprehensive collection of multiword combinations across language classes that includes conversational fillers, discourse organizers, referential chunks (i.e. compounds and collocations) and idioms is not on hand.

3. Phrase-noticing and the incidental learning of phrases

The huge numbers of multiword sequences in native speakers' discourse make phrase-learning a daunting task in the eyes of second-language learners. One could argue that second-language methodologists can only hope for incidental language learning pedagogies such as the *Lexical Approach* (Lewis, 1993, 1997, 2000a) to be successful. However, results from an experiment set up to help estimate the likelihood of learner-autonomous, incidental uptake of lexical phrases contradict this assumption (Eyckmans et al., 2007). In this experiment, upper-intermediate English majors (estimated to be at the B2 level of the European Council's CEFR) who had received classroom training in chunk-noticing along the lines of the *Lexical Approach* were asked to indicate all the word sequences they considered to be chunks in a previously unseen text. Their performance was compared with that of (a) same-level peers who had not received any chunk-noticing tuition, (b) highly advanced learners, and (c) native speakers. The results clearly showed a big variation and a lack of convergence between the participants' selection of chunks. The language learners who had been trained in chunking underlined more chunks than their peers but many of these perceived chunks could not be considered idiomatic by any standard. Thus, a greater sensitivity to the syntagmatic aspects of language does not necessarily lead to more successful identification of idiomatic phrases. Despite the ubiquity and naturalness of phraseology, sharing a sense of what constitutes an idiomatic phrase in English does not come naturally or easily.

Stengers (2009) put the chunk-noticing approach to the test in a longitudinal research design in which she set out to estimate the applicability of a lexical approach beyond the EFL community. She carried out two quantitative investigations. In a first corpus-linguistics inspired study she compared the prevalence of lexical phrases in English and Spanish. In a second empirical study she examined the pedagogical efficiency of a lexical approach in the learning of English and Spanish as foreign languages. Stengers found no evidence for a higher degree of idiomaticity in either English or Spanish and had to conclude on the basis of her comparative analysis that Sinclair's (1991) idiom principle is as pervasive in Spanish as it is in English native discourse. With regard to the benefits of a chunk-noticing pedagogy as advocated by the *Lexical Approach* (Lewis, 1993, 1997, 2000a), i.e. relying on learner-autonomous (semi-) incidental uptake of lexical phrases, she found no differential uptake of chunks between students from the experimental group (who received language instruction along the lines of the *Lexical Approach*) and the students from the control group (who were given the same class materials but whose awareness about the phrasal nature of language had not been raised). In short, the teacher strategy of encouraging learners to notice chunks was insufficient to significantly accelerate learners' uptake of chunks (receptively and productively). The results of both these research projects suggest that building a native-like phrasal repertoire through incidental uptake is bound to be a very slow process, even for learners with enhanced phraseological awareness.

Evidence for the beneficial effect of phrase competence for learners' communicative competence was furnished by Boers et al. (2006). In a (semi)controlled experiment with upper-intermediate learners of English, significant correlations were found between the number of multiword combinations used by these learners and their level of oral proficiency as gauged by blind judges. However, experimental data obtained in the context of interpreter-training research (Eyckmans, 2007) suggest that the positive impact of learners' phrasal knowledge is commensurate with both width and depth of that knowledge, i.e. the repertoire of chunks at the learner's disposal needs to be pretty large and made up of chunks that are mastered sufficiently well for the learner to retrieve them *whole* from memory without much hesitation. Again, it seems that expectations about autonomous, incidental uptake of chunks with a view to accurate productive use of these chunks need to be qualified.

From research on incidental vocabulary acquisition (Laufer, 2005a) we know that rates of vocabulary uptake through reading are generally quite disappointing. One of the many explanations for this is limited processing capacity: as one reads a text, one will typically be interested first in its content (i.e. focus will be on meaning) rather than on the precise choice of words or linguistic features (i.e. focus on form). Moreover, there are reasons to believe that incidental acquisition through reading may be even more problematic when it comes to chunks. Laufer and Girsai (2008) point out that unfamiliar individual words (especially ones that cause text comprehension problems) are more likely to be noticed during meaning-focus than combinations of familiar words (e.g. tell + a lie; make + a presentation).

The sad but inevitable conclusion is that the incidental uptake of lexical phrases through noticing is compromised for several reasons. First of all, noticing chunks is no guarantee for the long-term memory storage of these chunks. Secondly, the successful identification of lexical phrases without teacher-led guidance is doubtful. Thirdly, the precise lexical composition of chunks is often not noticed because language learners process discourse with a focus on meaning rather than on form and because the form of phrases that consist of familiar words does not get noticed at all. It follows that non-immersion second language acquisition contexts require a phrase-learning pedagogy rather than a phrase-noticing one if we want learners' phrase competence to improve.

4. A cognitive linguistic approach to phrase-learning

Although some authors on phraseology have emphasized the arbitrary nature of word combinations (Lewis, 1993; Woolard, 2000), a fair number of linguists, have demonstrated that pointing out the semantic and structural motivation of multiword units makes them more meaningful and therefore more memorable (Boers et al., 2004; Walker, 2008). This is in line with cognitive linguistic views on language and language learning. Within cognitive linguistic theory, language is seen as an integral part of general cognition and linguistic phenomena are taken to reflect general cognitive processes. Linguistic motivation is a key issue in cognitive linguistics and several studies have demonstrated the relevance and pedagogical effectiveness of presenting language as motivated by showing that a greater depth of processing of information leads to better retention rates and language learning results in general (Baker, 1998; Boers, 2000; Charteris-Black, 2000). Because teacher-stimulated phrase-noticing incentives are not enough for learners to turn intake into uptake, we need explicit language-focused instruction with regard to establishing strong memory traces in the learners' interlanguage lexicons. With this goal in mind, a cognitive linguistic approach seems to fit the bill.

4. 1. Broaching the concept of elaboration

According to the *Levels-of-Processing Theory* (Cermak, Craik, 1979; Cohen et al., 1986) more elaborate mental processing leads to better long-term retention. Applied to lexis these *deeper* mental processes are called *elaboration* (Barcroft, 2002). The linguistic motivation of phrases can be encoded and can function as an adequate retrieval cue. Semantic elaboration concerns the meaning of words or phrases (e.g. associating a lexical item with others that are already known). Structural elaboration applies to the formal characteristics of words or phrases (e.g. paying attention to the spelling of words or phrases). Within a cognitive linguistic approach to phrase-learning both types of elaboration can be tapped into so as to form stable memory traces.

The number of chunks with non-arbitrary semantic and formal features that can be exploited to make these word strings memorable seems to be quite large. This means that sizeable proportions of newly encountered word combinations can be committed to memory through elaboration of the semantic or formal aspects of these word strings.

Semantic elaboration is the appropriate line to take when aiming for in-depth comprehension and for retention of meaning. Imagery has been shown to be an effective mnemonic strategy for the semantic elaboration of figurative expressions (Boers et al., 2004; Boers, Lindstromberg, 2009). Through the explanation of the literal usage of an idiom (e.g. *to throw in the towel*), an association can be established between the figurative meaning of an idiom and a mental image of a concrete scene. This dual coding of information (Paivio, 1986) provides an extra pathway for recall (Boers et al., 2004).

Of course, not all multiword combinations lend themselves to semantic elaboration (e.g. verb-noun and adjective-noun collocations). Structural elaboration is not only a welcome complement if we want to cover a substantial part of multiword lexis, it is also much needed when aiming for the productive use of chunks. A beautiful example of structural motivation in language are sound patterns. It seems that the form of many lexical phrases is motivated through patterns of sound repetition such as alliteration or assonance. Classroom experiments have shown that lexical phrases with alliteration are more easily recalled than non-alliterative ones. Drawing learners' attention to this sound repetition as a form of structural elaboration can enhance this mnemonic effect (Boers, Lindstromberg, 2005). Deconinck et al. (2009) have unearthed the external as well as the internal salience of phonemic repetition as pathways for insightful learning. In experiments directed at estimating the internal salience of alliteration and assonance in English, eighty standardized collocations of varying frequency from a format called *Discriminating Collocations Test* (Eyckmans, 2009) were used as filler items in a test that pairs alliterative and non-alliterative pseudo-collocations. Language learners were asked to identify the most common collocation. The results of the experiment confirm that learners are strongly attracted to alliterative stimuli if this sound pattern has been pointed out to them in previous classroom instruction. This means that minor awareness-raising can affect the way in which learners process unknown input and points to the effect of structural elaboration.

These studies illustrate how opportunities for elaboration are often impervious to language learners and need to be unlocked by teachers or through well-developed materials. Also, structural elaboration and semantic elaboration should be carefully balanced in a language course. Structural elaboration consists of *language-focused* instruction since the activity is not directed at conveying meaning and deliberate attention is paid to language features during classroom practice. According to Nation, this kind of teacher-led guidance is highly beneficial for language learners but should not exceed 25% of classroom time so as to not lose sight of the overall focus on communication (Nation, 2007).

4. 2. How to select phrases for teaching?

Given the enormous size of the chunk repertoire in any target language and given that classroom time is limited, the issue of which multiword units to single out for instruction should take priority when talking about a vocabulary acquisition approach that includes targeting multiword expressions. Corpus linguists who have worked in this area seem to agree that it is word strings with a high frequency of occurrence and a high mutual information (MI) score that are bound to be recognized by native speakers as standardized phrases (Ellis et al., 2008). High MI scores indicate that the words in the phrase occur more often than would be expected by chance. These scores can therefore be interpreted as indicators of semantic coherence (allowing us to distinguish the frequently-occurring word string *and at the* from the word string *in other words*). Being able to account for semantic coherence in corpus extraction and selection is an invaluable advantage of corpus linguistics.

However, frequency of occurrence seems to be a more elusive concept than previously thought. The point of selecting words as targets for teaching on the basis of frequency is that these words will be most useful to learners because they are likely to encounter or need them in language-use situations. This is true in the case of beginners but research by Hazenberg and Hulstijn (1996) has shown that the relationship between word frequency and word knowledge depends on vocabulary size. The further you move on from the high-frequency vocabulary, the less significant frequency becomes in an absolute sense. The same may be true for chunks. Also, recent studies have shown that there are relatively few highly-frequent chunks (Shin, Nation, 2008) and that frequency distribution rapidly levels off below the small group of highly-frequent chunks (Boers, Lindstromberg, 2009). Given the fact that the core selection of high-frequency word combinations is small, and the fact that they stand the best chance of being picked up incidentally through repeated encounters anyway, a plea for more classroom attention to word strings of medium-frequency seems well-founded.

Apart from the criteria of frequency and semantic coherence, Boers and Lindstromberg (2009) argue that *learnability* (West, 1953) – also called *teaching worth* (Ellis et al., 2008) – should be taken into account when establishing a corpus of phrases for foreign language instruction. They propose to award the predicate *teachable* to those phrases that have intrinsic mnemonic potential, i.e. phrases that can be made memorable in an efficient way. They are unlikely to be picked up incidentally but give good returns for teacher-assisted learning. Fortunately, activities for the insightful teaching and learning of such phrases are slowly becoming available (e.g. Lindstromberg, Boers, 2008).

4. 3. How to assess phrase knowledge?

Since multiword knowledge is a long-overlooked domain in foreign language acquisition, it stands to reason that the assessment of this particular knowledge and skill has lagged behind as well. Furthermore, phrases are very diverse in lexical composition, as well as function; they comprise the whole stock of collocational patterns of a language, which makes it especially hard to measure the 'phraseomaticity' of learners' interlanguage.

Standardized tests tapping into learners' syntagmatic competence are not available yet. Nevertheless, reasons abound for developing measures of phrasal knowledge. Firstly, it has been suggested in the literature that learners' knowledge of word meanings does not change radically over time whereas knowledge of syntagmatic relationships does (Schmitt, 1998). It follows that tests of phrasal knowledge could be much more suited for measuring learners' progress (especially at an advanced level) than the vocabulary measures we tend to employ today (Eyckmans, 2009). Secondly, empirical studies into foreign language acquisition have shown collocations to be notoriously challenging for L2 learners (Nesselhauf, 2005). Because collocations are often comprehensible in the input, they may not be recognized as problematic by language learners. The errors mostly appear in language production. By administering tests of phrasal competence a positive backwash effect may be created towards raising learners' awareness of the idiomatic nature of the target language. Thirdly, it seems that the use of conventionalized language also relates to other kinds of linguistic development in learners. Yorio reports positive correlations between grammatical proficiency and the successful use of conventionalized language and claims that "although fluency is possible without grammatical accuracy, idiomaticity is not" (Yorio, 1989: 68).

Where receptive knowledge of phrases is concerned, most initiatives reported in the literature have been directed at the recognition of adjective-noun or verb-noun collocations (Barfield, 2006; Gyllstad, 2007; Moreno Jaén, 2007; Eyckmans, 2009). Obviously, adjective-noun and verb-noun collocations only make up one section of a language's much larger spectrum of multiword units. This particular section, however, lends itself reasonably well to categorization and represents a well-recognized and substantial number of chunks in the phrase lexicon so that researchers assume these tests to be reliable and user-friendly indicators of learners' phrase knowledge at large.

The assessment of productive knowledge of phrases is usually measured through contrastive translations or gap-fill tests in which part of the phrase is deleted (Moreno Jaén, 2007). Another avenue for the assessment of phrase knowledge would be the use of integrative test formats such as the (rational) cloze or the c-test (Klein-Braley, Raatz, 1984). Given the fact that half of all English texts are made up of word strings and that the test formats mentioned above rely on the principle of the deletion of every n^{th} word in a text (or in the case of the c-test, the deletion of the second half of every second word in a text), the likelihood that these deleted words are part of a chunk is in n^{th} proportion to the total number of words in the text. An example of an integrative format that has been exploited vis-à-vis the measurement of phraseological competence is the *Deleted Essentials Test* (Eyckmans et al., 2004). In this test format – based on a reading comprehension test (Weir, 1990) – an authentic text is spread out over a number of lines. In each line, one word is deleted. This word is essential for the semantic or structural coherence of the text. It is the test taker's task to supply the word (or an acceptable alternative) and identify the place where the word is missing. Phraseological competence plays a substantial role in this test format since it centres around the probabilistic nature of natural language. Thus it might well prove to be a good candidate for measuring productive multiword lexis.

Clearly, more test development is required if we want to obtain effective tools that track the phraseological dimension of learners' interlanguage. With the advent of parallel corpora in terms of functionalities and corpus composition for different languages, the prospect of developing standardized tests for multiword lexis opens up.

5. Conclusion

In this chapter, a plea has been made for vocabulary instruction that includes a strong emphasis on phraseology. I have illustrated that successful language learning hinges upon the understanding and producing of large numbers of memorised phrases and that spontaneous language interaction is filled with them. Language learners need help with identifying and learning chunks, hence the call for a specific syntagmatic approach to vocabulary in instructed second-language learning.

Since the incidental acquisition of a sufficiently large phrase lexicon is doubtful, phrase-learning will be dependent on the efficiency of classroom-based instruction in which phrases will need to be explicitly taught. In this respect, I have argued for a pedagogy that is centred on the notion of cognitive linguistic motivation. Language that is motivated lends itself well to classroom instruction because it stimulates insightful learning, which is beneficial for long-term retention. Recent literature shows that a lot of word combinations are in fact motivated. The established evidence for the motivation of phrases ranges from studies that examine the use of imagery to comprehend and remember idioms to the phonological motivation behind the lexical selection of compounds and binomials and the memorability of phrases with particular sound patterns such as alliteration and assonance. If we add up the different categories of phrases to which this applies, it is clear that a fair proportion of multiword units are already covered.

In order to promote insightful learning and unlock the mnemonic potential of phrases, teacher-led guidance is essential. The motivated properties of chunks of language need to be pointed out to learners and activities need to be developed in which learners engage in rich and elaborative mental processes so that long-term vocabulary retention is enhanced. Within such a phrase-oriented pedagogy, time and effort will have to be invested in consolidating knowledge of phrases in long-term memory through rehearsal. This will also involve sufficient emphasis on the productive use of phrases so that stronger knowledge can be established than when focusing solely on receptive learning.

Finally, some avenues for assessing multiword knowledge have been laid out. To this day, the tests developed are mainly discrete point formats that focus on the receptive recognition of adjective-noun or verb-noun collocations. However, integrative language tests such as the cloze test, the c-test and a relatively new format, called the *Deleted Essentials Test*, seem promising when it comes to measuring learners' productive knowledge of phrases across different categories (phrasal verbs, collocations, functional phrases, idiomatic expressions, etc.).

In future research, applied linguists might want to focus on the kind of form-focused exercises that are best suited for target languages other than English, since the typological characteristics of a particular language will, to a considerable extent, determine the kind of structural elaboration that is required. Also, learners' transfer of their L1 phraseological patterns to their L2 language use and learners' individual difference variables (i.e. cognitive style) merit closer investigation if we want to secure phrase-oriented pedagogies for different languages that focus predominantly on meaning transference but do not neglect a well thought-out focus on form.

Coming face to face with N_1 P N_1 sequences in Spanish

Christopher S. Butler, Swansea University, University of Huddersfield, and
Centre for Translation Studies, University of Leeds, United Kingdom

1. Introduction

In recent years, corpus-based studies have provided large quantities of information which
is potentially useful in applications of linguistics. Two of the most important of these
are translation and the teaching and learning of languages. Translators need an in-depth
knowledge of the delicate lexicogrammatical patterns revealed by corpus analysis, which
can make the difference between a fluent, natural translation and a stilted one. Language
learners, particularly at the more advanced stages of study, can likewise benefit from what
corpora reveal about the patterning of language, in order to improve the naturalness of
their productions. The present article[1] is intended to provide just such information, which
not only increases our knowledge of the internal workings of Spanish, but could also be
used in training translators and interpreters, and by course designers in the construction of
courses in Spanish as a foreign language.

The inspiration for the work reported in this paper came from two recent articles,
Jackendoff (2008) and Lindquist and Levin (2009), both of which discuss NPN sequences,
illustrated in English by expressions such as 'hand to mouth' or 'cause for concern'. As
both of these accounts observe, a particularly frequent version of this general pattern
shows identity of the two nouns (N_1 P N_1), as in 'day by day' or 'face to face'.

Jackendoff's paper reviews the properties of NPN sequences and concludes that
they are good examples of the kind of "entrenched non-canonical structure" (Jackendoff,
2008: 8) which Culicover (1999) refers to as a 'syntactic nut'. He presents the basic facts
about the behaviour of NPN structures, discusses productive subconstructions with the
prepositions 'by', 'for', 'to', 'after' and '(up)on', and then suggests that because of "the
construction's complex interweaving of regularity and irregularity" (2008: 14-15), it is hard,
if not impossible, to account for using standard syntactic procedures, and is better handled
within the framework of Construction Grammar (Fillmore et al., 1988; Goldberg, 1995,
2006; Goldberg, Jackendoff, 2004). In this family of approaches non-standard pieces of
structure can easily be accommodated, since the concept of construction as a pairing of a
form with a meaning can deal with any systematically observed meaningful unit, from single
words to abstract patterns such as ditransitive clauses, so breaking down the traditional
water-tight distinction between grammar and lexicon. Jackendoff also discusses a number
of syntactic problems posed by the NPN construction, including the syntactic category
to which it belongs, the question of what is the head of the construction, the restricted

possibilities for adjectival modification of one or both nouns, the existence of triples such as 'day after day after day', and the possibility for complementation and modification of the nouns. He finally sketches a lexical entry for NPN. The data for Jackendoff's discussion are largely taken from his own idiolect, though he does cite Google searches at one point.

Lindquist and Levin (2009) concentrate on the N_1 P N_1 pattern, and in particular those structures which involve nouns referring to body parts, linked by 'to'. Their investigation is corpus-based, using the British National Corpus (100 million words) as a main base, and supplementing this with corpora from *The New York Times* and the British newspaper *The Independent* to give a total of around 500 million words. They present a table showing the 16 most frequent N_1 'to' N_1 combinations, and note that half of these involve nouns which denote (or originally denoted) body parts: 'face', 'side', 'back', 'hand', 'head', 'eye' and 'ear'. They postulate two paths of change in the institutionalisation of these structures (Lindquist, Levin, 2009: 176-177): firstly, a change of syntactic role, in which a structure initially used as an adverbial starts to be used as a prenominal modifier in a NP, very often with hyphenation ('a head-to-head contest'), and then eventually as the head of a NP ('a head-to-head'); secondly, there is a change of categorial constituent status, such that two conjoined PPs [('from head') ('to head')] become a noun plus a PP [('head') ('to head')] and eventually a lexicalised noun ('head-to-head'). They also observe that as we move further to the right on these paths, the meaning often becomes narrower and more specialised: for instance, all occurrences of hyphenated 'hand-to-hand' refer to fighting. Lindquist and Levin discuss the frequency of combinations with particular nouns, their collocational behaviour, the rare occurrence of adjectival modification of the second noun, and the layering of literal and less literal meanings (e.g. 'back to back' is used almost exclusively in a metaphorical sense, 'nose to nose' expresses pragmatic meanings but retains the literal component, while 'cheek to cheek' is almost exclusively literal).

NPN constructions have also been studied in languages other than English (see e.g. Postma, 1995 and Poss, 2007 on Dutch; Matsuyama, 2004 on Japanese; Haïk, 2008 on French). Jackendoff (2008: 8) also lists a number of other languages in which NPN constructions are known to occur, and comments that the properties of these constructions are "detailed and idiosyncratic enough to suggest that none of these other languages are likely to be exactly parallel". It therefore seemed interesting to investigate the occurrence and behaviour of structures of this kind in Spanish, in relation to the findings on English reviewed above. Like Lindquist and Levin, I shall concentrate on structures in which the same noun is repeated; I shall not, however, confine myself to a particular preposition or to body part nouns.

2. Materials and methods

For this initial study a much smaller corpus was used than those investigated by Lindquist and Levin, namely the 1900s component of the Corpus del Español assembled by Mark Davies (2002-), consisting of 22.8 million words, equally divided into four subcategories:

oral, fiction, newspapers, academic writing. Apart from allowing users to investigate patterning in different registers of Spanish, this corpus has the advantage of being tagged with parts of speech for each word. However, its small size means that results from the investigation reported here should be regarded as purely preliminary, and need to be amplified by work on a larger corpus. Furthermore, the corpus contains material from both Peninsular and Latin American Spanish, so the results reported here are from a mixture of geographical varieties.

The first step was to search for all types corresponding to the word tag pattern 'noun + particular preposition + noun' occurring with a frequency of 3 or more in the corpus[2], where the full list of individually investigated prepositions was *a, ante, bajo, cerca de, con, contra, de, delante de, desde, detrás de, durante, en, encima de, entre, hacia, hasta, junto a, mediante, para, por, según, sin, sobre, tras*. It was found that *cerca de, delante de, detrás de, durante, encima de, hacia, junto a* and *mediante* formed no patterns of the type 'noun + preposition + noun', whereas *ante, bajo, de, desde, entre, hasta, para, según* and *sin*, although they did have this pattern with different nouns, did not show any occurrences with a repeated noun. Thus only *a, con, contra, en, por, sobre* and *tras* were relevant to the present study. Those combinations which involved the repeated use of a single noun were then selected for further study, and concordances for each combination of noun and preposition were produced. *Table 1* shows the type frequencies of the patterns N P N and N₁ P N₁ for the 7 prepositions occurring in the latter pattern. It can be seen that for *tras*, 8/9 (88.9%) of the N P N types have identical nouns, and that the proportion for *a* (38/316, 11.9%) is also appreciable[3].

Preposition	Most frequent English translation(s)	N₁ + prep + N₁	N + prep + N	% N₁ + prep + N₁
a	to, at	38	316	11.9
en	in, on	14	588	2.4
por	for, by, through	12	226	5.3
tras	after, behind	8	9	88.9
con	with	4	149	2.7
sobre	on, over, about	1	21	4.8
contra	against	1	5	20.0

Table 1: Type frequencies of total N P N and N₁ P N₁

In theory, this procedure should have been sufficient for the isolation of all and only the strings of interest in this study. However, when a check was made by requesting output for specific strings such as *cara a cara* ('face to face') or *día tras día* ('day after day'), discrepancies were found in a few cases. This was due to the fact that despite the use of the best automatic tagger of Spanish available, the parts of speech allocated to words are sometimes incorrect, especially where a word form can represent more than one part of speech. The most striking example of this was *paso a paso* (equivalent to English 'step by step'), where a search for N P N gave just 43 examples, whereas a direct search for the string revealed 72 occurrences, 29 of which had the second *paso* incorrectly classified as the first person singular present tense indicative form of the verb *pasar* rather than as a noun. For this reason, specific combinations with word forms which could represent more than one part of speech were retrieved directly, and adjustments made to the frequencies and concordances. This acts as a salutary reminder that even when the most sophisticated automatic analysis tools are used, the tagging of corpora inevitably carries with it a certain degree of error, in the absence of manual checking, which would be impracticable for a large corpus.

3. The most frequent types

It should be noted that *Table 2* simply indicates the frequency for each 'sequence of items' listed, and is not meant to imply either that this sequence necessarily forms a constituent or that it does not occur in any larger sequence: indeed, we shall see later that some sequences are always (or almost always) preceded by the preposition *de*, as in *de oreja a oreja*, with the constituency [(*de oreja*) (*a oreja*)], while others always, or usually, occur without *de*, and still others show a mixed pattern. The significance of occurrence with and without *de* will be discussed in *Section 6.2*.

Combination	Frequency
día a día	137
paso a paso	72
par en par	67
año tras año	61
cara a cara	56
día tras día	41
mano a mano	29
cuerpo a cuerpo	28
punta a punta	27
boca en boca	24
lado a lado	22
mano en mano	22
casa por casa	21
oreja a oreja	20
casa en casa	18
hombre a hombre	18
tiempo en tiempo	16
trecho en trecho	16
palabra por palabra	15
punto por punto	15

Table 2: The 20 most frequent N_1 P N_1 combinations in the corpus[4]

4. Semantic classification

The various combinations, as used in the corpus (sometimes preceded by *de*), can all be seen as expressions of location, either temporal or spatial. *Figure 1* proposes a set of semantic distinctions for the basic adverbial uses of these sequences, and *Table 3* classifies the 20 most frequent combinations in terms of the semantic categories. Note that 3 of the combinations (*par en par, lado a lado, hombre a hombre*), occur in two of the categories [+movement (source/destination) and state-descriptive].

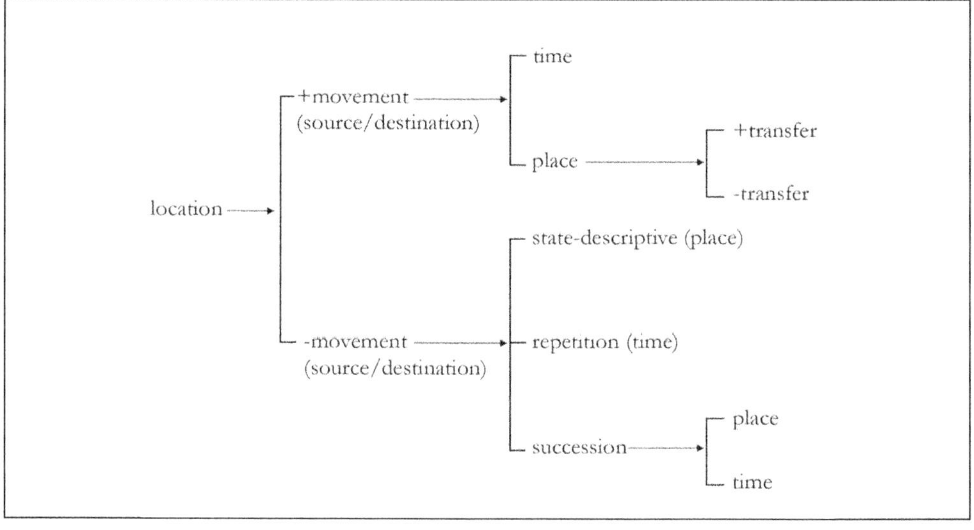

Figure 1: Semantic classification of the 20 most frequent combinations

Semantic category			Combination
+movement (source/destination)	time		tiempo en tiempo
			trecho en trecho
	place	+transfer	boca en boca
			mano en mano
		-transfer	punta a punta
			oreja a oreja
			casa en casa
			par en par
			lado a lado
			hombre a hombre
-movement (source/destination)	state-descriptive		cara a cara
			mano a mano
			cuerpo a cuerpo
			par en par
			lado a lado
			hombre a hombre
	repetition		año tras año
			día tras día
	succession	time	día a día
		place	paso a paso
			casa por casa
			palabra por palabra
			punto por punto

Table 3: Semantic classification(s) of each of the 20 most frequent combinations

One example of each semantic type will be given here; each expression will be analysed in more detail in *Section 5*, where the presence or absence of initial *de* will also be taken into account.

We begin with expressions used to indicate movement from one time or place to another. Idiomatically, temporal expressions of this kind encode the meaning of something happening sporadically, as in *1*[5].

1. | De | tiempo | en tiempo | México | es | parte | del |
    |---|---|---|---|---|---|---|
    | from | time | in time | Mexico | be.PRS.3SG | part | of.DEF.M.SG |

debate	polític-o	de	lo-s	Estado-s	Unid-o-s.
debate	political-M.SG	of	DEF.M-PL	State-PL	United-M-PL [NAME]

    'From time to time Mexico is part of the United States political debate.' (oral, Encuesta: Zedillo)

Spatial expressions indicating movement from a source to a destination can involve transfer, as in *2*, or no transfer, as in *3*:

2. | Iba-n | de | mano | en | mano, | y | no |
    |---|---|---|---|---|---|---|
    | go-IMPPRET-3PL | from | hand | to | hand | and | NEG |

ten-ía-n	nada	extrañ-o	en	el	interior.
have-IMPPRET-3PL	nothing	strange-M.SG	in	DEF.M.SG	inside

    'They went from hand to hand, and they had nothing strange inside.' (news, Perú: Caretas_1467)

3. | Escuch-ab-a | es-a-s | cosa-s | y | mov-ía |
    |---|---|---|---|---|
    | listen-IMPPRET-3SG | DIST-F-PL | thing-PL | and | move-IMPPRET.3SG |

de	lado	a	lado	su	larg-a	cola	de	caballo
from	side	to	side	POSS.3SG	long-F.SG	tail	of	horse

negr-a	como	un	giroscopio.
black-F.SG	like	INDF.M.SG	gyroscope

    'She would listen to these things and move her long black ponytail from side to side like a gyroscope.' (fiction, El profesor)

It should be noted that there are some examples which, although basically static in meaning, can be interpreted in terms of a type of 'subjective motion' in which the conceptualiser sequentially activates points along a path from one point to another (see Langacker, 1987: Chap. 7). A case in point is *4*, where the rainbow is static, but the viewpoint selected by the writer presents this static situation in terms of stretching from one point to another:

4. | Un | arco iris | se | tend-ía |
   | INDF.M.SG | rainbow | PRONOMCLITIC.3SG | stretch-IMPPRET.3SG |

   | de | lado | a | lado | del | arroyo. |
   | from | side | to | side | of.DEF.M.SG | gully |

'A rainbow stretched from side to side of the gully.' (fiction, Angola y otros cuentos)

We now turn to expressions which do not involve movement from a source to a destination. Those which I have termed 'state-descriptive' encode the state in which some entity finds itself. Contrast *Example 3* above with *5*:

5. | Él | ve-ía | lo-s | dos | cuerpo-s, | sent-ad-o-s |
   | 3SG.M | see-IMPPRET.3SG | DEF.M-PL | two | body-PL | sit-PTCP-M-PL |

   | lado | a | lado, ... |
   | side | to | side |

'He saw the two bodies, seated side by side, …' (fiction, La Muerte de Artemio Cruz)

Here, the bodies are being presented as lying side by side: note the difference in the English translation ('side by side' rather than 'side to side' as in *3*), and also the fact that *lado a lado* is preceded by *de* in *3* but not in *5* (see also *Section 6.2.* for further discussion).

Temporal repetition, with the meaning 'one X after another', and an implication of multiple repetition, is illustrated in *6*:

6. | Hora | tras | hora, | día | tras | día | y | año | tras | año |
   | hour | after | hour | day | after | day | and | year | after | year |

   | era | cada | vez | más | joven. |
   | be.IMPPRET.3SG | each | time | more | young |

'Hour after hour, day after day and year after year he got younger and younger.'
(fiction, Nostálgico del Ayer)

This contrasts with *7*, in which we have temporal succession (one X and then another):

7. | Karajan | era | un | fenómeno | que | cambi-ab-a |
   | Karajan | be.IMPPRET.3SG | INDF.M.SG | phenomenon | REL | change IMPPRET-3SG |

   | día | a | día, | imposible | de | conoc-er | con | certeza. |
   | day | to | day | impossible | of | know-INF | with | certainty |

'Karajan was a phenomenon which changed from day to day, impossible to know with certainty.' (Oral, ABC Interview)

Finally, spatial succession is exemplified in *8*, where one element in the procedure is to be checked, followed by the next element in the series, and so on:

8.   … la   única   manera   de   ten-er   la   certeza
     DEF.F.SG   only   way   of   have-INF   DEF.F.SG   certainty

     es   verific-ar   paso   a   paso   el   procedimiento.
     be.PRS.3SG   check-INF   step   to   step   DEF.M.SG   procedure

'The only way to be certain is to check the procedure step by step.' (oral, Encuesta: PAN)

5. Detailed study of the most common combinations

In this section, each of the 20 most common combinations will be examined, grouping the material by semantic class.

5. 1. Expressions involving movement from a source to a destination

5. 1. 1. Temporal: occasional occurrence

The two combinations illustrating the meaning 'from one time to another', interpreted idiomatically as indicating occasional occurrence, are *tiempo en tiempo* and *trecho en trecho*. In all cases, these combinations were preceded by *de*, and the meanings are virtually synonymous ('from time to time', 'every now and then', 'occasionally'). All tokens of both expressions were adverbial in function. An example of *de trecho en trecho* is given in *9*:

9.   Ve-ía-se   de   trecho   en   trecho   un
     see-IMPPRET.3SG-PASS.3SG   from   stretch   in   stretch   INDF.M.SG

     avestruz   que   corr-ía   velozmente, …
     ostrich   REL   run-IMPPRET.3SG   swiftly

'From time to time, an ostrich could be seen running swiftly, …' (fiction, Las vértebras de pan)

Of the 16 occurrences of *de tiempo en tiempo*, 9 were in fiction, 5 in news and 2 in the oral component of the corpus; of the 16 occurrences of *de trecho en trecho*, all but one were in fiction, the remaining example being from the oral part of the corpus. No clear collocational patterning was observed.

5. 1. 2. Spatial, with transfer

We now turn to expressions involving *boca en boca* and *mano en mano*, which are always preceded by *de* and are used in situations where transfer is indicated. All occurrences were adverbial, except one case of *de boca en boca* which was ambiguous as between adverbial and postmodifying usage. An example of *de boca en boca* (24 tokens) is given in *10*:

10.   …en   un   tiempo   record   su   fama   corr-e
         in   INDF.M.SG   time   record   POSS.3SG   fame   run-PRS.3SG

      de   boca   en   boca…
      from   mouth   in   mouth

'… in record time his fame spreads by word of mouth…' (fiction, La reindivicación del conde Don Julián)

The expression collocates primarily with verbs of transfer: *correr* 'run' (6), *pasar* 'pass' (3). It is found primarily in fiction (17, 70.8%), but also in news writing (7, 29.2%).

The expression *de mano en mano* (22 tokens) is illustrated in *11*:

11.   Se   la   fueron   pas-ando   de   mano
      REFL.3PL.DAT   ACC.F.SG   go.INDEFPRET.3PL   pass-GER   from   hand

      en   mano, …
      in   hand

'They passed it among themselves from hand to hand, …' (fiction, Rayuela)

Like *de boca en boca*, this expression occurs mainly in fiction (15, 68.2%), but also in news writing (7, 31.8%). The most frequent verbal collocates are forms of *pasar* 'pass' (12) and *circular* 'circulate' (3), though other verbs of movement also occur.

5. 1. 3. Spatial, without transfer

Expressions with *punta a punta* (27 tokens), *oreja a oreja* (20 tokens) and *casa en casa* (18 tokens) express purely dynamic location involving movement from a source point to a destination point, or at least scanning of a trajectory from one point to another, without transfer of any entity. Consistently with this, all occurrences of *oreja a oreja* and *casa en casa*, and all adverbial uses of *punta a punta* are preceded by *de* ('from'). An example of adverbial *de punta a punta* is given in *12*. In this case, 24 out of 27 occurrences (88.9%) are adverbial, 3 (11.1%) nominal (see *Example 13*):

12.   …deb-ía-n…   recorr-er   la   casa   de
      must-IMPPRET-3PL   go.through-INF   DEF.F.SG   house   from

      punta   a   punta   sin   toc-ar   el   piso…
      end   to   end   without   touch-INF   DEF.M.SG   floor

'… they had to… go through the house from one end to the other without touching the floor…' (oral, Habla Culta: Caracas: M26)

13.   El   ganador   Caña Dulce   realiz-ó
      DEF.M.SG   winner   Caña Dulce [NAME]   do-INDEFPRET.3SG

      un   punta   a   punta…
      INDF.M.SG   end   to   end

'The winner Caña Dulce led from start to finish…' (news, DR: Listín: 98Jun24)

Note that in nominal usage, the gender is masculine, even though the repeated noun is feminine. 15 tokens appeared in fiction, 7 in news, 5 in oral language. The most frequent collocate was *recorrer* 'go all through/over' (5).

The expression *de oreja a oreja* is used adverbially 10 times (see *14*), as a postmodifier 8 times (as in *15*), with one occurrence analysed as having implied predicative adverbial function in a verbless clause (*Example 16*), and one case which is ambiguous as between adverbial and postmodifier function.

14.　… Celina　　　　a　　su　　　　lado　　sonre-ía　　　　　de
　　　　Celina [NAME]　at　　POSS.3SG　side　smile-IMPPRET.3SG　from

　　oreja　a　　oreja…
　　ear　　to　　ear

'… Celina, at his side, was smiling from ear to ear…' (fiction, Los hombres de Celina)

15.　Trejo　　　　　　asint-ió　　　　　　　con　　un-a　　　sonrisa
　　　Trejo [NAME]　　agree-INDEFPRET.3SG　with　INDF-F.SG　smile

　　de　　oreja　a　　oreja.
　　from　ear　　to　　ear

'Trejo agreed, smiling from ear to ear.' (fiction, México-Zambia con tiros penales)

16.　… hac-iendo　　un　　　　　gran　esfuerzo　por
　　　　make-GER　　INDF.M.SG　big　　effort　　for

　　manten-er-se　　　　　en　pie　　y　　la　　　　sonrisa
　　maintain-INF-REFL.3SG　on　foot　and　DEF.F.SG　smile

　　siempre　de　　oreja　a　　oreja.
　　always　　from　ear　　to　　ear

'… making a big effort to stay on his feet and with his smile always from ear to ear.' (fiction, Disfraz)

Of the 20 tokens, 16 (80.0%) occur in fiction, 3 in news, 1 in oral language. As suggested by the examples, *de oreja a oreja* collocates preferentially with *sonreir* 'smile' and its nominal form *sonrisa*.

The expression *de casa en casa* is somewhat hybrid in that, although it indicates movement from one house to another, it implies a series of locations, and so shares characteristics of the 'succession' category discussed in *Section 5.2.3.ii*. All occurrences in the corpus are adverbial. A typical example is given in *17*:

17.　… and-ab-a　　　　　busc-ando　　al　　　　　　　dueñ-o　　　　de
　　　　go-IMPPRET-3SG　look.for-GER　ACC.DEF.M.SG　owner-M.SG　from

　　casa　en　casa.
　　house　in　house

'… he went from house to house looking for the owner.' (fiction: Cien años de soledad)

The expression occurred 11 times in fiction, 4 in news and 3 in oral language. The main verbal collocates were *ir* 'go' (6), *andar* 'go, walk' (3) and *visitar* 'visit' (3).

Combinations which can indicate movement without transfer or state-descriptive meaning are dealt with separately, in *Section 5.3*.

5. 2. Expressions not involving movement from source to destination

5. 2. 1. State-descriptive

Let us begin with the most frequent of the state-descriptive combinations, *cara a cara*, occurring 56 times in the data, with a meaning equivalent to English 'face to face'. A typical example is given in *18*:

18. ... un   día   se   encontr-ó   cara   a
        INDF.M.SG   day   REFL.3SG   find-INDEFPRET.3SG   face   to

     cara   con   El Camisero,   ladrón   español, ...
     face   with   El Camisero [NAME]   thief   Spanish

'... one day he found himself face to face with El Camisero, a Spanish thief, ...'
(fiction, Hijo de ladrón)

Only one occurrence is preceded by *de* as part of the expression itself, as shown in *19*:

19. Seles   y   Sánchez   de   cara   a   cara   siete
     Seles [NAME]   and   Sánchez [NAME]   from   face   to   face   seven

     año-s   después
     year-PL   after

'Seles and Sánchez face to face seven years later' (news headline, CR: PrLibre: 98Jun5)

Of the 56 tokens, 49 (87.5%) function as adverbials, 7 as postmodifiers of nouns: an example of postmodification is given in *20*:

20. En   la-s   carrera-s   cara   a   cara   se
     in   DEF.F-PL   race.PL   face   to   face   REFL.3PL

     suel-e-n   enfrent-ar   en   un   duelo   lo-s
     be.usual-PRS-3PL   confront-INF   in   INDF.M.SG   duel   DEF.M-PL

     caballo-s   de   más   éxito   de   la   temporada.
     horse-PL   of   most   success   of   DEF.F.SG   season

'In face to face races, the most successful horses of the season usually confront one another in a duel.' (academic, Enc: Carreras de caballos)

Of the 56 tokens of *cara a cara* 31 were found in fiction, 18 in news, 4 in the oral component and 3 in academic writing. There was a strong collocational preference for the verb *encontrarse* 'find oneself' and the corresponding noun *encuentro* 'meeting, encounter'; the verb *mirar* 'look' also occurred 5 times as a collocate.

We turn now to *mano a mano*, with a frequency of 29, an example of which is presented in *21* where the preposition *de* is part of the expression *así de* rather than of the following *mano a mano*:

21.   … dos   contertulio-s   no   se   habl-a-n
        two   participant.in chat.show-PL   NEG   REFL.3PL   speak-PRS-3PL

        así de   mano   a   mano.
        so much   hand   to   hand

'Two participants in a chat show don't talk to one another like that, just the two of them.' (fiction, Maladrón: epopeya de los Andes Verdes)

In the corpus, *mano a mano* is strongly associated with bullfighting, where it refers to a situation where two bullfighters, rather than three, are involved. Only 15 out of 29 tokens (51.7%) are adverbial, 13 (44.8%) nominal, and 1 ambiguous as between adverbial and postmodifier. The nominal uses are associated with bullfighting, with other sports such as football, and also political confrontations, as in *22*, where the most natural English translation of *un mano a mano* is 'a head to head' (as with *un punta a punta*, the gender is masculine although *mano* itself is feminine):

22.   ¿Qué   se   pued-e   esper-ar   de   un
        what   IMPERS   be.able.to-PRES.3SG   expect-INF   from   INDF.M.SG

        mano   a   mano   Serpa-Pastrana?
        hand   to   hand   Serpa [NAME]-Pastrana [NAME]

'What can be expected from a Serpa-Pastrana head to head?' (news, Col: Semana: 835)

Not surprisingly, in view of the sporting association, 15 out of 29 tokens (51.7%), including 10 of the 13 nominal occurrences, occurred in news writing, with 7 in fiction, 4 in academic writing and 3 in the oral component. No clear collocational patterns were found.

Finally, let us look at *cuerpo a cuerpo* (28 tokens), for which there were no tokens preceded by *de* as part of the expression itself. The adverbial function is illustrated in *23*, in which *cuerpo a cuerpo* is most idiomatically translated as 'hand to hand':

23.   Cuerpo   a   cuerpo   luch-amos   hasta   que   al
        body   to   body   fight-INDEFPRET.1PL   until   that   at.DEF.M.SG

        fin   su   boca   vomit-ó   un   quejido…
        end   POSS.3SG   mouth   vomit-INDEFPRET.3SG   INDF.M.SG   groan

'We fought hand to hand until his mouth finally emitted a groan…' (fiction, Bazar de cuentos)

However, only 11 out of the 28 tokens (39.3%) are adverbial, 11 (39.3%) being nominal (see *24*) and 6 (21.4%) postmodifying (as in *25*):

24. Ciego-s,   enloquec-id-o-s,   feroces,   luch-a-n   en
     blind-M-PL   go.crazy-PTCP-M-PL   fierce.PL   fight-PRS-3PL   in

     un   cuerpo   a   cuerpo, …
     INDF.M.SG   body   to   body

     'Wild, crazy and fierce, they engage in a hand-to-hand fight, …' (fiction, Maladrón: epopeya de los Andes Verdes)

25. … se   practic-ab-a   el   combate   cuerpo
     PASS.3SG   practise-IMPPRET-3SG   DEF.M.SG   combat   body

     a   cuerpo   con   maza-s,   hacha-s   y   espada-s, …
     to   body   with   mace-PL   axe-PL   and   sword-PL

     '… they engaged in hand-to-hand fighting with maces, axes and swords, …'
     (academic, Enc: Indígenas americanos)

As will be clear from the examples, *cuerpo a cuerpo* tends to collocate with words indicating fighting: *luchar/lucha* 'fight (v/n)', *combatir/combate* 'combat/fight (v/n)'.

5. 2. 2. Temporal repetition

An example of *día tras día* was given in *6*, and also serves to illustrate the other type which occurs in the top 20 list, *año tras año*, as well as the less frequent *hora tras hora*. No token of *día tras día* was preceded by *de*, and in the only case of *año tras año* preceded by *de* this preposition introduced the expression as a postmodifier, rather than being part of the expression itself. All 41 tokens of *día tras día* were adverbial in function, as were all but one of the 61 occurrences of *año tras año*, the exception being the example shown in *26*:

26. Contra su-s   párpado-s   deb-e-n   corr-er   la-s
     against POSS.3SG-PL   eyelid-PL   must-PRS-3PL   run-INF   DEF.F-PL

     imágen-es   de   año   tras   año   y   quizás   también   voces.
     image-PL   of   year   after   year   and   perhaps   also   voice.PL

     'Against his eyelids must flow the images of year after year and perhaps also voices.'
     (fiction, Sobre héroes y tumbas)

Here, *de* introduces a postmodifier of *imágenes*, consisting of the preposition plus *año tras año*, the latter acting as a nominal. Verbal collocates of *día tras día* occurring 3 times or more were *repetir(se)* 'repeat' (4) and *quedarse* 'remain' (3); the first of these also occurred 4 times with *año tras año*, and *ser* 'be', 3 times. *Día tras día* occurred 27 times in fiction, 7 in oral language, 5 in news and 2 in academic language, while *año tras año* occurred 26 times in fiction, 16 in news, 16 in academic language and 3 in the oral component.

5. 2. 3. Succession

i. Temporal succession

The only temporal succession combination in the top 20 list is *día a día*, an example of which was given in *7*. This was the most frequent combination of all, with 137 tokens. Of these, 3 were preceded by *de*, but in one case the preposition introduced a postmodifier containing *día a día* in nominal function (cf. *Example 26* above). The two examples where *de* did seem to form a constituent with *día a día* are shown in *27* and *28*:

27. Est-o-s,   de   día   a   día,   se
    PROX-M-PL   from   day   to   day   3.PL.PRONOMCLITIC

    qued-a-n   atrás.
    remain-PRS-3PL   behind

    'These, from day to day, remain behind.' (oral, Habla Culta: Sevilla: M14)

28. Su   peso   parec-e   vari-ar   de   día   a   día…
    POSS.3SG   weight   seem-PRS.3SG   vary-INF   from   day   to   day

    'His weight seems to vary from day to day…' (fiction, Lo que no sirve, que no estorbe)

The great majority of the tokens (121/137, 88.3%) had adverbial function, but 8 were nominal, 1 acted as a postmodifier and 7 were ambiguous as between adverbial and modifier function. An example of nominal *día a día* is given in *29*:

29. ¿Es-o   se –   se   not-a   en   el
    DIST-N.SG   IMPERS   IMPERS   notice-PRS.3SG   in   DEF.M.SG

    día   a   día   de   lo-s   mercado-s?
    day   to   day   of   DEF.M-PL   market-PL

    'Is this obvious in the day to day fluctuations of the (financial) markets?' (oral, España Oral: CNOT035A)

Occurrence as a postmodifier is shown in *30*:

30. La-s   variacion-es   día   a   día   en   un   área
    DEF.F-PL   variation-PL   day   to   day   in   INDF.M.SG   area

    da-d-a   defin-e-n   su   climatología, …
    give-PTCP-F.SG   define-PRS-3PL   POSS.3SG   climatology

    'The day-to-day variations in a given area define its climatology, …' (academic, Enc: Clima)

Example 31 shows an example where *día a día* is functionally ambiguous: it could be taken as an adverbial modification of the verb *sirvan*, or as a postmodifier of *menesteres*:

31. | Parec-ía | | un | | ensañamiento | el | | de |
| --- | --- | --- | --- | --- | --- | --- | --- |
| seem-IMPPRET.3SG | | INDF.M.SG | | cruelty | 3SG.M | | of |

Solano,	del		que	se		aliment-ab-a
Solano[NAME]	of.DEF.M.SG		REL	REFL.3SG		feed-IMPPRET-3SG

con	placer,	es-o	de	que	lo		sirv-a-n
with	pleasure	DIST-N.SG	of	REL	3.SG.M.ACC		serve-PRS.SBJV-3PL

hasta	en	lo-s	más	baj-o-s	menester-es	día	a	día.
up.to	in	DEF.M-PL	most	low-M-PL	activity-PL	day	to	day

'It seemed a kind of cruelty on Solano's part, which he fed on with pleasure, that they should serve him day by day even in the most menial of activities' OR 'that they should serve him even in the most menial day-to-day activities.' (fiction: Demasiada historia)

Día a día occurs 50 times in fiction, 45 in news, 34 in the oral component and 8 in the academic section. Verbal collocates with a frequency of 3 or more were: *crecer* 'grow' (6) (plus *acrecentarse* 'grow', with just one occurrence), *ser* 'be' (4), *ver* 'see' (3), *aumentar* 'increase' (3), *construir(se)* 'build/be built' (3), *ganar* 'gain, win' (3), *vivir(se)* 'live' (3): the importance of verbs of increase is clear.

ii. Spatial succession

There are 4 combinations which are involved in the expression of succession in place: *paso a paso* (72 tokens), *casa por casa* (21), *punto por punto* (15), *palabra por palabra* (15). No occurrence of any of these is preceded by *de*.

Paso a paso, for which a suitable English translation is often 'step by step' or 'little by little/gradually', was given earlier in *8*. The overwhelming majority (69, 95.8%) of its occurrences are adverbial in function, with just one as postmodifier and one ambiguous as between adverbial and postmodifier. It is most frequent in fiction (39 tokens, 54.2%), with 20 (27.8%) in news, 8 (11.1%) in oral language and 5 (6.9%) in academic writing. The most frequent verbal collocates are *seguir(se)* 'follow' and *bajar* 'decrease'.

The expression *casa por casa* occurs with adverbial function 13 times (see *Example 32*), as a postmodifier 7 times (see *Example 33*), and there is one example which is ambiguous between adverbial and postmodifier. Six of the postmodifiers are in news writing.

32. | ... si | porfi-ára-mos | | en | hall-ar-la | | tendr-ía-mos |
| --- | --- | --- | --- | --- | --- | --- |
| if | insist-PST.SBJV-1PL | | in | find-INF-ACC.3SG.F | | have.to-COND-1PL |

que	seguir	registr-ando	la		ciudad	casa	por	casa.
that	follow.INF	search-GER	DEF.F.SG		city	house	by	house

'... if we insisted on finding her we would have to keep on searching the city house by house.' (fiction, Hijo de ladrón)

33. Oposición   panameñ-a   anunci-a   lucha   "casa
    opposition   Panamanian-F.SG   announce-PRS.3SG   fight   house

    por   casa"   para   imped-ir   reelección   de   Balladares
    by   house   for   prevent-INF   re-election   of   Balladares[NAME]

'Panamanian opposition announces 'house by house' fight to prevent re-election of Balladares' (news headline, Hon: Prensa: 98May20)

There are 11 occurrences (52.4%) in fiction, 8 (38.1%) in news, with 1 in oral language and 1 in academic writing. The most frequent collocate is *lucha* 'fight/struggle (n)', but this is an artefact arising from the multiple occurrence of this collocation in one particular Honduran news article.

All occurrences of *punto por punto* and *palabra por palabra* were adverbial in function, and neither had any collocates of frequency 3 or higher. Examples are given in *34* and *35*:

34. ... un-a   mujer   que   prepar-a   su-s
    INDF-F.SG   woman   REL   prepare-PRS.3SG   POSS.3SG-PL

    clase-s   punto   por   punto...
    class-PL.   point   by   point

'... a woman who prepares her classes point by point...' (oral, Habla Culta: Buenos Aires: M21 B)

35. ... transcrib-o   la-s   respuesta-s   palabra   por   palabra.
    transcribe-PRS.1SG   DEF.F-PL.   reply-PL.   word   by   word

'... I transcribe the replies word by word.' (oral, Habla Culta: Buenos Aires: M14 A)

For *punto a punto*, 6 (40.0%) occurrences were in oral language, 4 (26.7%) in news, 4 (26.7%) in fiction and 1 (6.7%) in academic writing. For *palabra por palabra*, 9 (60.0%) occurred in fiction, 5 (33.3%) in oral language and 1 (6.7%) in news writing.

5. 3. Expressions which can be used for source/destination movement or state-descriptively

Expressions involving *par en par*, *lado a lado* and *hombre a hombre* can be used either to indicate movement from a source to a destination or a static state, which may, but need not, result from such movement. *Par en par* (67 tokens) is always preceded by *de*, and can be translated into English as 'wide', as used in 'wide open'. It occurs 39 times (58.2%) as an adverbial, 24 (35.8%) as a postmodifier and 4 (6.0%) with predicative adverbial function. *Example 36* illustrates the adverbial usage, in a dynamic context:

36. Antuco   abr-ió   de   par   en   par
    Antuco [NAME]   open-INDEFPRET.3SG   from   rafter   in   rafter

    la   ventana   del   patio.
    DEF.F.SG   window   of.DEF.M.SG   patio

'Antuco opened wide the window of the patio.' (fiction, Gran señor y rajadiablos)

In its postmodifying use, *de par en par* indicates a static situation resulting from an earlier movement, and normally follows *abierto/abierta* 'open', as in *37*; however, in two cases it follows a noun, as in *38*:

37. ... la   ventana   est-ab-a   abiert-a   de   par   en   par...
    DEF.F.SG   window   be-IMPPRET-3SG   open.PTCP-F.SG   from   rafter   in   rafter

'... the window was wide open...' (fiction, Barrio palestina: novela)

38. El   cura   joven   me   dedic-a   un-a
    DEF.M.SG   priest   young   1SG.DAT   dedicate-PRS.3SG   INDF-F.SG

    sonrisa   de   par   en   par.
    smile   from   rafter   in   rafter

'The young priest gives me a broad smile.' (fiction, Novios de antaño, 1930-1940)

Example 39 illustrates the predicative adverbial use of *de par en par* in a verbless clause, again in a static situation:

39. ... empuñ-a   el   cuchillo,   lo-s   dedo-s
    take.hold.of-PRS.3SG   DEF.M.SG   knife   DEF.M-PL   finger-PL

    todavía   caliente-s   del   arrancón   del
    still   hot-PL   from.DEF.M.SG   pulling.out   of.DEF.M.SG

    herraje,   de   par   en   par   un   ojo...
    ironwork   from   rafter   in   rafter   INDF.M.SG   eye

'... he takes hold of the knife, his fingers still hot from pulling out the ironwork, one eye wide open...' (fiction, Maladrón: epopeya de los Andes Verdes)

There are 52 tokens of *de par en par* (77.6%) in fiction, 11 (16.4%) in news, 3 in oral language and 1 in academic writing. As indicated above, the overwhelmingly most frequent collocates were the verb *abrir(se)* 'open' and its past participle *abierto/abierta*, used adjectivally.

Examples of *lado a lado* (22 tokens), both in static contexts without *de* and in contexts of movement, including 'subjective motion', were given earlier (*5*, *3* and *4*). This combination occurs 19 times with *de* and 3 without, and all tokens are adverbial in function. There are 15 occurrences in fiction, 5 in academic writing and 2 in news. The expression collocates with verbs of movement [*atravesar* 'cross' (3), also *mover* 'move', *cruzar* 'cross' and others].

Hombre a hombre (18 tokens) occurred 11 times with *de* and 7 without. A clear example of movement from one place to another is shown in *40*:

40. ... se   cern-ió   un-a   enorme   ansiedad   en
    3SG.PRONOMCLITIC   hang-INDEFPRET.3SG   INDF-F.SG   enormous   anxiety   in

    tod-o   el   sector,   comunic-ad-a   de   hombre   a
    all-M.SG   DEF.M.SG   sector   communicate-PTCP-F.SG   from   man   to

    hombre   a través   del   frenesí   de   preparativo-s.
    man   across   of.DEF.M.SG   frenzy   of   preparation-PL

'... an enormous anxiety hung over the whole sector, communicated from one person to another through the frenzied preparations.' (fiction, La casa y su sombra)

The expression occurs in association with football contexts, often in collocation with the verb *marcar* 'mark'[6] or its nominal form *marca*. *Example 41* illustrates its postmodifying function:

41. Muy   a menudo,   la-s   formaciones   defensiv-a-s   comprend-e-n
    Very   often   DEF.F-PL   formation-PL   defensive-F-PL   include-PRS-3PL

    la   defensa   "hombre   a   hombre"   o   individual, ...
    DEF.F.SG   defence   man   to   man   or   individual

'Very often, these defensive formations include 'man to man' or individual defence, ...' (academic, Enc: Fútbol)

There are 7 tokens of *hombre a hombre* in news, 6 in fiction, 4 in oral language and 1 in academic writing. *Marcar/marca* (4) was the only collocate with a frequency of at least 3.

6. Discussion: N_1 P N_1 patterns in Spanish and English

6. 1. Similarities and differences in lexical material used

In some cases there are clear parallels between Spanish and English, in the sense that expressions used with similar meanings contain words which are translations of one another: for instance, *cara a cara* is a literal translation of 'face to face'. There are also cases in which the lexical item is a direct translation equivalent, but the preposition is not: for example, Spanish *de tiempo en tiempo* is translated by English 'from time to time', whereas the preposition *en* would rarely be translated by 'to' in a variety of other contexts in which it occurs; a similar example is *paso a paso*, where English equivalents use 'by' ('step by step', 'little by little'). In other cases, there is no direct equivalence: for example, in the context of close fighting, Spanish prefers to invoke contact of the body (*cuerpo a cuerpo*), while English still uses a body part expression but prefers to refer to hands ('hand to hand'), 'body to body' being somewhat unidiomatic. In yet other situations, Spanish uses a term whose literal translation is totally unidiomatic: *de par en par* translates literally as 'from rafter to rafter'.

6. 2. Presence/absence of initial preposition *de*/'from'

As observed briefly in *Section 1*, Lindquist and Levin (2009), in their work on the English N_1 'to' N_1 pattern, postulate a development from earlier '[from (the) N_1] [to (the) N_1]' structures, with two prepositional phrases, to structures containing just a noun and a prepositional phrase, and eventually to a fully lexicalised noun. They state (2009: 175) that "for most phrases, versions without 'from' and without articles are the norm". Though true, this statement conceals some important facts. In *Table 4* are shown the 16 most frequent N_1 'to' N_1 combinations in the BNC, according to Lindquist and Levin's analysis, together with the frequency with which they are preceded by 'from', the table being sorted on the proportion preceded by 'from'[7]. The frequencies with initial 'from' are in fact slightly conservative for some combinations, since they do not take into account the (rare) occurrence of ellipsis, as in 'from end to end and side to side'.

From this table it can be seen that there is great variability in the extent to which the various combinations are preceded by 'from'. Some ('back to back', 'head to head', 'shoulder to shoulder', 'face to face', 'eye to eye', 'day to day') are never, or rarely (< 10%), preceded by 'from'. At the opposite end of the spectrum, 'place to place', 'strength to strength', 'ear to ear' and 'side to side' are preceded by 'from' in the overwhelming majority (> 90%) of cases. In between, we have a set of combinations ('wall to wall', 'door to door', 'hand to hand', 'house to house', 'person to person') with proportions of initial 'from' ranging from 17.5% to 59.6%.

Combination	Total frequency	With initial 'from'	% with initial 'from'
back to back	160	0	0.0
head to head	79	0	0.0
shoulder to shoulder	62	1	1.6
face to face	797	18	2.3
eye to eye	68	3	4.4
day to day	1308	113	8.6
wall to wall	63	11	17.5
door to door	133	24	18.0
hand to hand	135	37	21.4
house to house	130	37	27.8
person to person	94	56	59.6
year to year	212	171	80.7
side to side	374	351	93.9
ear to ear	57	54	94.7
strength to strength	114	111	97.4
place to place	138	136	98.6

Table 4: Proportion of 16 most frequent N_1 to N_1 combinations preceded by 'from' in BNC

Table 5 shows that a very similar situation occurs with the Spanish data, although these differ in that more than one preposition is involved. Indeed, the distinctions are rather more clear cut, but this may be due partly to the small sample size. While 10 combinations (*año tras año, día tras día, mano a mano, cuerpo a cuerpo, paso a paso, casa por casa, palabra por palabra, punto por punto, día a día, cara a cara*) occur without *de* in all cases or at least in the vast majority, 7 (*tiempo en tiempo, trecho en trecho, oreja a oreja, casa en casa, par en par, boca en boca, mano en mano*) always take *de*, and 3 (*hombre a hombre, punta a punta, lado a lado*) occur with *de* in the majority of cases, but also without this preposition. Where initial *de* occurs, we have the constituency pattern [(*de* N$_1$) (prep N$_1$)], parallel to the situation in English.

Combination	Total frequency	Preceded by *de*	% preceded by *de*
año tras año	61	0	0.0
día tras día	41	0	0.0
mano a mano	29	0	0.0
cuerpo a cuerpo	28	0	0.0
paso a paso	72	0	0.0
casa por casa	21	0	0.0
palabra por palabra	15	0	0.0
punto por punto	15	0	0.0
día a día	137	2	1.5
cara a cara	56	1	1.8
hombre a hombre	18	11	61.1
punta a punta	27	22	81.5
lado a lado	22	19	86.4
tiempo en tiempo	16	16	100.0
trecho en trecho	16	16	100.0
oreja a oreja	20	20	100.0
casa en casa	18	18	100.0
par en par	67	67	100.0
boca en boca	24	24	100.0
mano en mano	22	22	100.0

Table 5: 20 most frequent combinations, sorted by % preceded by de

Two factors are responsible for the data in *Tables 4* and *5*, only one of which is discussed by Lindquist and Levin. The first, not noted by these authors, is the semantic classification of the expression. All the Spanish combinations which always take *de* are concerned with movement between a source and a destination, temporal or spatial[8], while those which never (or hardly ever) take *de* are of the non-movement kind (state-descriptive, repetition, succession). Two of those which sometimes take *de*, but sometimes do not (*hombre a hombre, lado a lado*), are ones which can indicate either source/destination movement or state-description. The third (*punta a punta*) is of the movement kind, and will be examined further in *Section 6.3*.

   A detailed description of the English data along these lines is beyond the scope of this paper, but it is not unreasonable to suggest that a parallel semantic explanation may be available. For instance, 'place to place' is used to indicate movement from one place to another, and so is naturally preceded by 'from'. 'From strength to strength' is more strongly idiomatic, but can be interpreted in terms of a change, or 'movement', from one degree of strength to an even higher degree. 'Ear to ear' is similar to Spanish *oreja a oreja* in that the viewer of the situation mentally scans the trajectory from one ear to another. On the other hand, 'back to back', 'head to head', 'shoulder to shoulder' and 'face to face' are used exclusively or predominantly as state-descriptions, and so do not take 'from'. And it is a reasonable hypothesis, needing further investigation, that those combinations which sometimes take 'from' and sometimes do not are used both to indicate movement and state-descriptively.

   However, there is, as Lindquist and Levin point out, a further factor in play here, which is concerned with the progression from adverbial usage to modifying, and finally nominal, usage. This is the area to which we now turn.

6. 3. Syntactic function and its relationship with form

Table 6 shows the distribution of functions for each of the 20 most frequent combinations in the Spanish data. There is a clear pattern in the data, in that most of the combinations which have the highest proportions of modifying and nominal use are of the non-movement type: state-descriptive (*cara a cara, mano a mano, cuerpo a cuerpo*) or succession (*casa por casa, día a día*). This is natural, in that one would expect expressions which are already state-descriptive in their adverbial use to lend themselves most easily to conversion for use as descriptive modifiers. Furthermore, since these adverbial expressions occur without initial *de*, there is no question of their having to lose this preposition for use as modifiers. However, some combinations with high modifier and/or nominal use are of the movement (source/destination) type (*punta a punta, oreja a oreja*), or the mixed movement/state-description type (*hombre a hombre*).

   Table 5 shows that two of these (*punta a punta, hombre a hombre*) are of the type which sometimes takes *de*, but sometimes does not, whereas the third (*oreja a oreja*) always takes *de*. Clearly, in the last case *de* is retained even in modifying use (there are no nominal uses of *oreja a oreja*), but it is of interest to investigate whether, for the other two combinations, the loss of *de* is associated with the move from adverbial to modifying and/or nominal use, as Lindquist and Levin propose for 'from' in English. Analysis of the data for *punta a punta* reveals that all the non-adverbial uses are nominal, and *de* is always dropped[9]. For *hombre a hombre*, on the other hand, all 5 non-adverbial occurrences are modifying, and *de* is retained in 4 of these cases. We can therefore provisionally conclude that where an expression which normally occurs adverbially with *de* is used as a modifier, *de* is normally retained, but where it is used nominally, *de* is dropped. The conclusions we have drawn about function and its correlation with the form of the expression suggest that Spanish may be somewhat more conservative than English in this area. However, the database from which these conclusions have been drawn is small, and the results clearly need to be checked against a larger corpus.

One further observation which should be made about modifying uses is that they often occur with nouns which are formed by nominalisation from verbs, as with *sonrisa* in *Examples 15* and *38*, *combate* in *25*, *variaciones* in *30*, *lucha* in *33* and *defensa* in *41*. In such cases there is a clear parallel with the 'verb + adverbial' usage.

Combination	Total	Adv	Pred attribute	Mod	Nom	Ambig	% (mod + nom)
día tras día	41	41	-	-	-	-	0.0
boca en boca	24	23	-	-	-	1	0.0
lado a lado	22	22					0.0
mano en mano	22	22	-	-	-	-	0.0
casa en casa	18	18	-	-	-	-	0.0
tiempo en tiempo	16	16	-	-	-	-	0.0
trecho en trecho	16	16	-	-	-	-	0.0
palabra por palabra	15	15	-	-	-	-	0.0
punto por punto	15	15	-	-	-	-	0.0
año tras año	61	60	-	-	1	-	1.6
paso a paso	72	69	-	2	-	1	2.8
par en par	67	39	4	24	-	-	3.0
día a día	137	121	-	1	8	7	6.6
punta a punta	27	24	-	3	-	-	11.1
cara a cara	56	49	-	7	-	-	11.5
hombre a hombre	18	13	-	5	-	-	27.8
casa por casa	21	13	-	7	-	1	33.3
oreja a oreja	20	10	1	8	-	1	40.0
mano a mano	29	15	-	-	13	1	44.8
cuerpo a cuerpo	28	11	-	6	11	-	60.7

Table 6: Proportion of (modifier + nominal) function for 20 most frequent combinations

6. 4. Internal modification

Jackendoff (2008: 9) notes that the N P N pattern is highly constrained in its structure: for instance, with certain exceptions, determiners and plural forms of nouns are not permitted, and although prenominal adjectives can occur, they are confined to patterns with particular prepositions (see also Jackendoff, 2008: 21). Lindquist and Levin (2009: 180-181) also note that in their English data "N_1 'to' N_1 phrases seem to be entirely immune to both singular/plural alternation and insertions of definite/ indefinite articles", but that there is a marginal possibility to insert adjectives between the preposition and the second noun (e.g. 'from hand to reluctant hand').

Searches were made in the Spanish corpus for the pattern 'plural noun + preposition + plural noun', where the preposition was *a, con, contra, en, por, sobre* or *tras*, the 7 prepositions which occurred in the N_1 P N_1 pattern. No examples with a repeated noun were found. The pattern 'noun + preposition + article + noun' was also searched for, with the same set of prepositions, and for both definite and indefinite articles, taking into account the fusion of *a el* into *al*. The only combination found was *tiempo al tiempo*, which occurred 11 times, in the expression *dar(le) tiempo al tiempo*, meaning 'to be patient', or *ganar(le) tiempo al tiempo* 'to do something rapidly, not lose time', or simply by itself, implying one of these meanings. Here, *tiempo al tiempo* is not itself a unit, since the construction can be seen simply as one in which *tiempo* fills two arguments of *dar* 'give' or *ganar* 'gain'. Searches were also made for the patterns 'noun + preposition + noun + adjective' and 'noun + preposition + adjective + noun', again with the same set of prepositions. Not a single instance of adjectival modification was found. Again, we must be aware of the small size of the database, but these results suggest that Spanish is even more restrictive than English in relation to the internal modification of N_1 P N_1 expressions.

6. 5. Triplication

Jackendoff (2008: 21) also notes the possibility of triplication, especially with 'after', as in 'week after week after (miserable) week'. A search was made for the pattern 'noun + preposition + noun + preposition + noun', with the same set of 7 prepositions. Only one example of triplication of the same noun was found: *círculo tras círculo tras círculo* 'circle after circle after circle'. Google searches (made on 29 June 2009) on pages in Spanish gave 574,000 hits for *día tras día*, 409 for *día tras día tras día* (i.e. 0.07% of the total for duplication), 1,180,000 for *año tras año*, 264 for *año tras año tras año* (0.02%). On the other hand, searches on pages in English for 'day after day' gave 3,750,000 hits, 'day after day after day' 435,000 (11.6%), 'year after year' 4,490,000, 'year after year after year' 215,000 (4.8%). Again, the data suggest that Spanish is somewhat conservative in this respect.

6. 6. Register variation

Table 7 shows the distribution of the various combinations across the four registers of the Spanish corpus (oral, fiction, news, academic), all of equal size. The total proportion of the 20 most frequent combinations is in the order fiction > news > oral > academic, and the categories of fiction and news together account for 66.3% of the total. The percentage figures in each cell of the table represent the proportion of the total number of types for that combination accounted for by a particular register.

Combination	Total	Oral	Fiction	News	Academic
día a día	137	34 (24.8%)	50 (36.5%)	45 (32.8%)	8 (5.8%)
paso a paso	72	8 (11.1%)	39 (54.2%)	20 (27.8%)	5 (6.9%)
par en par	67	3 (4.5%)	52 (77.6%)	11 (16.4%)	1 (1.5%)
año tras año	61	3 (4.9%)	26 (42.6%)	16 (26.2%)	16 (26.2%)
cara a cara	56	4 (7.1%)	31 (55.4%)	18 (32.1%)	3 (5.4%)
día tras día	41	7 (17.1%)	27 (65.9%)	5 (12.2%)	2 (4.9%)
mano a mano	29	3 (10.3%)	7 (24.1%)	15 (51.7%)	4 (13.8%)
cuerpo a cuerpo	28	6 (21.4%)	10 (35.7%)	7 (25.0%)	5 (17.9%)
punta a punta	27	5 (18.5%)	15 (55.6%)	7 (25.9%)	-
boca en boca	24	-	17 (70.8%)	7 (29.2%)	-
lado a lado	22	-	15 (68.2%)	2 (9.1%)	5 (22.7%)
mano en mano	22	-	15 (68.2%)	7 (31.8%)	-
casa por casa	21	1 (4.8%)	11 (52.4%)	8 (38.1%)	1 (4.8%)
oreja a oreja	20	1 (5.0%)	16 (80.0%)	3 (15.0%)	-
casa en casa	18	3 (16.7%)	11 (61.1%)	4 (22.2%)	-
hombre a hombre	18	4 (22.2%)	6 (33.3%)	7 (38.9%)	1 (5.6%)
tiempo en tiempo	16	2 (12.5%)	9 (56.3%)	5 (31.3%)	-
trecho en trecho	16	1 (6.3%)	15 (93.8%)	-	-
palabra por palabra	15	5 (33.3%)	9 (60.0%)	1 (6.7%)	-
punto por punto	15	6 (40.0%)	4 (26.7%)	4 (26.7%)	1 (6.3%)
Total	**725**	**96 (13.2%)**	**385 (53.1%)**	**192 (26.5%)**	**52 (7.2%)**

Table 7: Register variation in the 20 most frequent combinations

7. Conclusion

In this paper, the pattern N_1 P N_1 has been investigated in a 22.8 million word corpus of Spanish, and comparisons have been made with observations made for English by Jackendoff (2008) and by Lindquist and Levin (2009). The 20 most frequent types have been examined in detail, and it has been demonstrated that they can be classified in terms of their semantics, and that this classification correlates strongly with the presence or absence of initial *de*. Analysis of the syntactic functions of the expressions shows that although the majority of tokens are adverbial in function, some combinations of repeated noun and preposition are also used as postmodifiers of nouns, and some as nominals. Modifying uses are most common with those expressions which do not indicate movement from a source to a destination, but are not confined to such expressions. If the adverbial function of an expression preferentially uses a form with initial *de*, this is usually retained in the modifying use, but dropped in the nominal use. Spanish appears to be even more restrictive than English in terms of the internal modification of these structures, for instance by inclusion of articles or adjectives, or the use of plural nouns. N_1 P N_1 combinations are more frequent in fiction and news than in oral language, and least frequent in academic writing.

It is hoped that the results of this investigation will be of interest not only in their own right, as telling us more about Spanish and how it is similar to or different from English, but also for translators and those involved in language teaching and learning.

Notes

[1] It is a great pleasure for me to dedicate this paper to Carmen Pérez Basanta, whose interest in lexis and in corpus linguistics informs most of her work in applied linguistics.

[2] The analytical software available on the corpus website does not allow a general search for 'any noun + any preposition + any noun', because each of the individual components of the pattern occurs more than 10 million times in the corpus, so leading to computational overload.

[3] The proportion for *contra* is misleading, in that the frequencies are extremely small.

[4] The combination *punta a punta* actually appeared 28 times, but in one case the occurrence of *punto a punto* 'point to point' in the immediate context indicated very clearly that this was an error, the intended expression being *punto a punto*. This was therefore excluded from the data for analysis.

[5] Glosses are given according to the Leipzig glossing rules available at *http://www.eva.mpg.de/lingua/resources/glossing-rules.php*. Additional labels not present in the guidelines have been created where necessary for this paper: GER gerund/present participle, IMPERS impersonal, IMPPRET Spanish 'pretérito imperfecto', INDEFPRET Spanish 'pretérito indefinido', PRONOMCLITIC pronominal clitic.

[6] In collocation with *gol* 'goal', *marcar* can also mean 'score', but this is not the context in which *(de) hombre a hombre* appears.

[7] Some frequencies of the combinations are slightly different from those given by Lindquist and Levin, because of difference in the software used: they used the Zürich BNCWeb interface, whereas the results reported in *Table 3* are obtained using WordSmith Tools.

[8] In the case of *de par en par*, the movement use is the basic one, but we have seen that a derived state-descriptive is also possible.

[9] As we saw in *Section 1*, Linquist and Levin (2009: 177) postulate that the further we move along the path from adverbial to modifying use, and then to nominal use, the narrower and more specialised the meaning becomes. This certainly seems to be true of the nominal use of *punta a punta*, which in South American Spanish is associated with racing and refers to a race in which the same horse, car, etc. leads from start to finish.

Missing words:
The vocabulary of BBC Spanish courses for adults

Paul M. Meara, University of Swansea, Wales, United Kingdom
Jesús Suárez García, Barnard College, New York, USA

1. Introduction

Until very recently, vocabulary played a role in the production of language teaching materials that was very definitely a secondary one. Although inevitably present in any course book, vocabulary was generally subordinated to other elements that were considered more important to the process of learning a language. Thus, in the 1950s and 1960s, when grammar translation was the dominant approach to language teaching, the lexical content of courses was considered less important than the grammatical content of textbooks. To a large extent, the vocabulary taught was determined by the words that appeared in the works of classical authors whose texts were used for teaching purposes. Later, the structural or audiolingual methods, based on behaviourist theories subordinated the vocabulary to be taught to the linguistic structures that the student was required to automatize during the process of learning. In the 1970s, communicative approaches to language teaching began to be developed, partly as a reaction to the shortcomings of earlier methods. *Functions* and *Notions* came to be the main curricular focus for language teaching, and functional-notional approaches dominated classroom practice. The vocabulary which appears in courses that were developed with this method in mind simply reflects the vocabulary which is used in the context chosen to introduce the functions and notions which the student is required to master – *In the restaurant*, *At the airport*, *At the doctor's* to list but a few of the typical ones.

The common assumption that underlies all these treatments of vocabulary is the idea that vocabulary acquisition takes place naturally when people learn other more basic elements: learn grammar, or structures, or functions, and you will inevitably learn vocabulary. Vocabulary acquisition is something that just happens on its own. One consequence of this is that the textbooks of the period show a surprisingly cavalier attitude towards the vocabulary items that they choose to teach. Words are included almost at random, and their selection depends heavily on the intuition of authors.

2. The study

This paper illustrates this problem in a series of beginners' Spanish courses. Specifically, we analysed a set of six textbooks published by the BBC over a period of 30 years (1965-1995). These courses were all aimed at adult learners of Spanish, working on their own, and were primarily intended as a companion text for radio and television broadcasts. Inevitably, however, they were widely adopted as standard textbooks for adult learners attending classes as well. It is difficult to underestimate the influence of these courses on adult education, and it is no exaggeration to say that these courses pretty much defined the syllabus for adult learners of Spanish in the UK for a period of about thirty years.

The course books analysed and their date of publication are listed below:

- *¡Oigan Señores!* (1965)
- *Starting Spanish* (1967)
- *Zarabanda* (1971)
- *¡Dígame!* (1978)
- *España Viva* (1987)
- *Sueños* (1995)

Sueños, though published in 1995, is still available, and still widely used as support material for adult learners.

Our basic data was a list of the vocabulary items included in the glossary that each of these courses provides in the back of the course book. Our analysis consisted of a comparison of the words included in each glossary, with the intention of establishing how far the glossaries coincided and differed. We used some specially written computer programs to do this. The output of these programs was a list of words which appeared in each course. We also prepared a list of words which appeared only in one course, a list of words which appeared in two courses, a list of words appearing in three courses, and so on up to six. In English, the vocabulary syllabus has been influenced for a long time by the pioneering work of Harold Palmer and Michael West, which placed a lot of emphasis on frequency counts. For this reason, English courses – at least those published in the UK – tend to be fairly uniform in the words they choose to include in their vocabulary syllabuses. For other languages, this tendency is much less marked. We thought it would be interesting to compare these influential BBC courses with a view to establishing just how much agreement there was among the editors as to what words should be included in course materials of this sort.

Before we could carry out this analysis, it was necessary to edit the word lists for each course. This editing process is more complicated than we might expect, because the different courses treat words in different ways. Specifically, the way grammatical function words were handled was not consistent. Some courses included words like *el, la, un, una* and pronouns in their word lists, while others did not. Furthermore, the way morphological variants of words were handled was not consistent either. Some texts listed masculine and feminine forms separately, while others did not. Some texts listed irregular forms of verbs separately. Some courses also included multiword phrases such as *ir de compras* in their glossaries, whereas others did not, and these inconsistencies also needed to be treated in a uniform way. We needed to standardise the lists in order to carry out the necessary comparisons.

The changes that we implemented to achieve this standardisation mainly consisted in removing items which were not single words, or were morphological variants of other words. These included:

- multiword expressions which could not be considered as single lexical items (*hace frío, ponerse al teléfono*);
- regular feminine forms (*vieja, gorda, hermana*);
- plurals;
- non-infinitive forms of verbs;
- superlative adjectives.

In all these cases, only the base form of the word was counted. We also standardised variant forms of words which appeared in different forms in different texts, e.g. *espárrago/ espárragos, verdura/verduras*, etc. In these cases, we used a single form.

Although some of these changes are not straightforward to implement, they allowed us to simplify the word lists, and once this was done it was a relatively routine process to run comparisons between them. We also used other sources to throw light on the vocabulary of the BBC courses. These were the vocabulary lists contained in *Un Nivel Umbral* (Slagter, 1979), and *Diccionario de Frecuencias de las Unidades Lingüísticas del Castellano* (Alameda, Cuetos, 1995).

Un Nivel Umbral is a Spanish adaptation of the *Threshold Level* vocabulary developed by a team led by Peter Slagter with the support of the Council of Europe. In this list, vocabulary is taught as part of a notional and functional syllabus aimed at beginning adult learners. The aim, both in the Spanish list, and in the other languages for which a *Threshold Level* has been elaborated, is to establish a basic vocabulary which will allow a person travelling in Europe to communicate with speakers of the local language. Bearing this aim in mind, it seemed reasonable to compare the vocabulary that appears in the BBC courses with the vocabulary that is listed in the *Nivel Umbral* syllabus.

At the time we did this work, the *Diccionario de Frecuencias de las Unidades Lingüísticas del Castellano* was the most recent and the most complete work of its kind that had been published in Spanish, although a number of other word counts have appeared more recently. We used this word count to determine which levels of frequency covered the vocabulary included in each of the BBC courses, and this allowed us to determine how far frequency of use was indeed a factor in the selection of words for inclusion in these courses.

3. Results and analysis

The first analysis that we carried out was a comparison of the six textbooks against each other. The results of this analysis are reported in *Table 1*.

In *Table 1*, the first column lists the six textbooks under review, while *Column Total* shows the number of different words that each of them contains. These totals vary considerably. *¡Oigan Señores!* teaches a basic vocabulary of only 675 words, while *Sueños*, the text with the largest vocabulary, teaches a basic vocabulary of 1,956 words – almost three times as many. *Table 1* also allows us to make a comparison with the number of words listed in the lexical component of the *Nivel Umbral* syllabus (1,158 words)[1]. *Table 1* shows that two of the BBC courses have vocabularies which are considerably larger than the vocabulary in the *Nivel Umbral* list. *Dígame* aims at 1,549 words, while *Sueños* aims at 1,956 words. The other courses all have considerably smaller vocabularies.

Course	Total	A	B	C	D	E	U	P
¡Oigan Señores!	675	98	74	94	113	122	174	26%
Starting Spanish	941	98	218	189	152	135	149	16%
Zarabanda	753	98	203	143	109	99	101	13%
Dígame	1,549	98	221	231	259	286	454	29%
España Viva	951	98	196	168	165	170	154	16%
Sueños	1,956	98	218	219	240	316	865	44%
Nivel Umbral	1,158							

Table 1: Number of words in each textbook and words appearing in one or more than one textbook

We might imagine that there would be a large degree of overlap in the basic vocabulary taught by the six courses. Surprisingly, this turns out not to be the case, and we can see this in the remaining columns of *Table 1*. The numbers in this part of the table require some explanation. *Column A* shows the total number of words which appear in all six courses. Only 98 words meet this criterion – a figure which is surprisingly small. This list of 98 words is shown in *Table 2*. *Column B* shows the number of words each course shares with only four other courses; *Column C* shows the number of words each course shares with only three other courses; *Column D* shows the number of words each course shares with only two other courses; and *Column E* shows the number of words that each course shares with only one other course. *Column U* shows the number of words which are unique to each of the courses. Thus, *¡Oigan Señores!* contains 174 unique words which do not appear in the word lists provided by any of the other course books. 122 words appear in one of the other textbooks; 113 additional words appear in two of the other textbooks; 94 additional words appear in three of the other textbooks; 74 additional words appear in four of the other textbooks; and 98 words that appear in all six texts. *Column P* shows the data in *Column U* as a percentage of the total vocabulary in each text. Thus, the 174 words that are only found in *¡Oigan Señores!* make up 26% of the total vocabulary of that text.

agradable	cenar	desde	llevar	parecer	salir	tienda
ahí	cerca	dormir	luego	pasar	seguir	trabajar
avión	cerrar	empezar	mano	película	sello	trabajo
azul	cerveza	entrada	manzana	periódico	semana	tren
bailar	ciudad	habitación	marido	piso	sin	último
barato	claro	iglesia	mediodía	playa	sitio	ver
bastante	comida	invierno	mes	plaza	sobre	verano
billete	cosa	jugar	mismo	precio	sol	verdad
cabeza	creer	lado	necesitar	preferir	solo	vez
caja	cuarto	lavar	niño	pueblo	sopa	viajar
carne	cuenta	leche	novio	puerta	sólo	viaje
caro	dejar	leer	nuevo	quedarse	tercero	viejo
casi	demasiado	lejos	número	querer	terminar	volver
cena	descansar	llamar	pagar	saber	tiempo	ya

Table 2: The 98 words appearing in all six course books

Clearly, there is little evidence here of a principled selection underlying the choice of words to be taught. One is tempted to note that the list allows women to talk about their husbands, but does not allow men to talk about their wives, that blue is the only colour in the list, although the list does not contain any noun that is likely to be blue, that the list contains *semana* and *mes* but not *día* or *noche*. The presence of *tercero* (but not *primero* or *segundo*) is also surprising. This view that the list of shared words is a bit odd is reinforced by the data shown in *Table 3* which compares the *Nivel Umbral* vocabulary with the vocabulary of the six textbooks. Of the 1,158 words that appear in the *Nivel Umbral*, 157 also appear in one of the textbooks, 164 appear in two, 188 appear in three courses, 188 appear in four, 180 appear in five courses, and only 95 appear in all six. 285 words which appear in the *Nivel Umbral* do not figure in any of the six textbooks.

	Total	1 text	2 texts	3 texts	4 texts	5 texts	6 texts
N Umbral	1,158	157	164	188	188	180	95

Table 3: Where the vocabulary of Nivel Umbral *appears in the texts.*

Several additional points are worth making here. The first point concerns the very large differences in the vocabulary learning load which the different courses expect of their students. The mean number of vocabulary items is 1,136 but there is substantial variation around this figure. It strongly suggests that there is no real agreement here about what might be considered a reasonable vocabulary learning load for adult beginners. Given that the courses all apparently have the same objectives – to prepare the students to communicate in Spanish and to introduce them to the typical aspects of Spanish culture – this lack of consensus among the courses is particularly striking.

The second point that stands out is that only 98 words appear in the glossaries of all six courses. These words include a number of items which are not among the 2,000 most frequent words in Spanish – *sello* (stamp), *avión* (aeroplane), *sopa* (soup), for instance – though, of course, the relevance of these words to tourists will be readily apparent. More importantly, perhaps, the list does not contain a number of highly frequent words which we might expect to find in a list of common words. *Pequeño* (small), *ahora* (now), *hombre* (man), *mujer* (woman) are all absent from this list, despite the fact that they are listed among the 500 most common words in Spanish. Surprisingly, perhaps, of the 98 words which appear in all the textbooks, only 60 come from the first thousand most frequent words in Spanish. Ten percent of these shared words are 'unusual' words that do not appear in the two thousand most frequent words in Spanish.

The texts vary very widely in the frequency of their selected vocabulary, but in general, the vocabulary they teach does not seem to pay much attention to frequency as a selection criterion. The best text in this regard is *Zarabanda*, where 40% of the vocabulary taught falls within the 1K frequency band. For the other texts, the figures are much worse.

Criticising textbooks for not taking account of objective frequency criteria is probably a little unfair. At the time these texts were produced there were very few analyses of vocabulary frequencies in Spanish, and the tradition of counting word frequencies in English had had little impact on the teaching of Spanish, at least in the UK. The most widely available frequency count at the time was Juilland and Chang Rodríguez (1964), a text which was not widely known outside academic circles, and was in any case primitive by comparison with the standard English word lists. It was based on a very restricted set of genres – mainly fiction published between 1920 and 1940 – and the corpus on which the count was based was a relatively small one – a mere 500,000 words. The application of corpus linguistics to teaching Spanish was still a long way in the future (Sánchez et al., 1995) and would take a long time to influence Spanish teaching in the UK.

What is more surprising is that the authors of these course books seemed to be unaware of the curriculum work that was being carried out by the Council of Europe over the period of publication that we are looking at. The *Threshold Level* syllabus was explicitly developed for adult learners travelling in Europe, precisely the target audience that these BBC courses were aimed at. We might expect that there would be a considerable overlap between the words taught in these courses and the emerging functional syllabuses. Surprisingly, this does not appear to be the case.

Table 4 shows the extent of the overlap between the BBC courses and the vocabulary of the *Nivel Umbral*. Large overlapping vocabularies are found for *Dígame* and for *Sueños*, but this appears to be an accidental result of the fact that these two courses teach large vocabularies anyway. There is no real evidence that the Council of Europe material influenced the vocabulary lists of these courses, and no real evidence that the publication of the *Nivel Umbral* in 1979 marked a watershed in the production of materials aimed at adult learners.

course book	words only in course book	shared words	words only in *Nivel Umbral*
¡Oigan Señores!	338	337	821
Starting Spanish	393	548	610
Zarabanda	274	479	677
Dígame	860	689	469
España Viva	434	517	641
Sueños	1,261	695	463

Table 4: Overlap between the six courses and the vocabulary of Nivel Umbral

4. Conclusion

This brief study suggests that the lexical syllabuses adopted by the BBC in their courses for adult learners of Spanish were largely unsystematic and unprincipled. The choice of vocabulary was mainly driven by ad hoc principles, particularly the random occurrence of words that just happened to appear in a particular context. All words are treated equally, and it is not the case that highly frequent words are singled out or given special treatment.

The very small number of words that appear in all six courses suggests that this ad hoc approach to vocabulary selection may not always be successful. It raises a number of interesting questions about the sort of performance we would expect from learners who have followed each of these courses to their conclusion. What would happen if we put together six students each of whom had followed one of these courses? Would they actually be able to communicate with one another? And how would they each perform if we took them to Spain at the end of their courses, and set them loose on an unsuspecting Hispanic speaking word? Would students who had followed a vocabulary rich course (like *Sueños*) be better able to communicate than students who had followed one of the lighter courses? Indeed, we might add: are students who follow one of the vocabulary rich courses less likely to complete these courses, simply because they are being overloaded with words?

Nation (1990) identifies several reasons why a systematic approach to vocabulary selection seems worthwhile:

- whichever method of vocabulary teaching we adopt, teaching vocabulary is inevitable;
- there is a large body of research about how vocabulary can be taught effectively and which vocabulary is most suitable for learners;
- there is a lot of empirical evidence which suggests that some vocabulary learning methods are more effective than others;
- students themselves almost always report that vocabulary is their biggest single stumbling block in learning an L2.

The results of this study suggest that ad hoc selection methods do not necessarily provide a good vocabulary learning environment for students. They do, however, lead to textbooks which contain a lot of vocabulary which is of limited value, and fail to provide contexts which teach learners some of the basic vocabulary that they need.

Notes

[1] It is perhaps worth noting here that the *Nivel Umbral* list is rather smaller than the basic vocabularies we find in other versions of the *Threshold Level* materials published by the Council of Europe, which typically contain about 2,000 words. It is not clear why the *Nivel Umbral* is smaller than this typical value.

Connectors in EFL learners' essays and in course books

Rosa M. Jiménez Catalán, University of La Rioja, Spain
Julieta Ojeda Alba, University of La Rioja, Spain

1. Introduction

Connectors operate as a kind of cement that binds together different elements of discourse; their function is to join words, clauses, and sentences in a given text. They play different roles in communication and help listeners and readers to comprehend meanings and intentions in oral and written discourse; they noticeably facilitate or hinder communication. Based on the belief of their relevance for English as a Foreign Language (EFL) learners, in this study we explore Spanish secondary students' production of English connectors in a letter writing task, and their presence in the course books students are exposed to. As far as we know there is no empirical evidence either about the connectors employed by Spanish EFL learners or about the connectors contained in their course books. However, looking at these discourse elements, from the dual perspective of learners' use and exposure, may allow us to identify language learning and teaching gaps, and to ascertain the adequacy of the input learners receive through their course books.

2. Previous studies

Since the 1980s, research on the connectors used by EFL learners has come to the fore in applied linguistics. A great deal of this research is corpus-based and comparative in nature, as it draws data from corpora and contrasts the frequency of connectors in native speakers' discourse with that of foreign language learners, as well as the production of connectors by language learners of different mother tongues. The aim of this comparative research is to ascertain whether there are similarities or differences among the groups compared. In the comparative studies of native speakers versus language learners, results point to the following tendencies:

- learners overuse connectors in the target language (Evensen, 1990; Field, Yiep, 1992; Milton, Tsang, 1993; Bolton et al., 2002; Narita et al., 2004; Fei, 2006; Wei-Yun Chen, 2006; Zhang, 2007) although the specific items overused do not always coincide in these studies as the following list reveals: *and* (Evensen, 1990; Zhang, 2000; Abe, 2001); *also, besides* (Zhang, 2000); *moreover, for instance, on the contrary* (Granger, Tyson, 1996; Altenberg, Tapper, 1998); *lastly, besides, moreover, secondly, firstly, consequently, furthermore, regarding, therefore, namely* (Milton, Tsang, 1993); *for example, first, second, on the other hand, secondly, finally, firstly, last, third, on the contrary* (Zhang, 2007);

- learners present little variety in the use of connectors (Connor, 1984; Miranda, Lee, 2003);
- learners misuse connectors (Granger, Tyson, 1996; Abe, 2001; Wei-Yun Chen, 2006; Bikeliene, 2008), in particular: *besides, therefore* (Wei-Yun Chen, 2006), and *anyway* (Granger, Tyson, 1996). Misuse of connectors has proved to be a common tendency in the interlanguage of learners with different mother tongues, and this is so, even at advanced levels.

Most research on the production and use of connectors by foreign language learners is based on samples of advanced EFL university students. Apart from Evensen's (1990) study on Swedish EFL learners in secondary education and the one by Abe (2001) on Japanese EFL senior high school students, there are practically no studies on the production of connectors by beginners or low intermediate learners in secondary education. The lack of studies on these groups of learners goes hand in hand with a lack of analyses on connectors in course books. There are studies on vocabulary input in course books, from a non-corpus as well as a corpus approach, (for a review see Jiménez Catalán, Mancebo, 2008); however, as far as we know, there are no studies on connectors in course books aimed at EFL learners. Our study aims to contribute to narrowing this gap on three flanks:

- research on connectors produced by Spanish EFL learners in secondary education;
- analysis of connectors in a writing task frequently contained in the course books addressed to low intermediate EFL learners;
- exploration of the connectors contained in the course books used by the above learners.

Specifically we set out to answer the following questions:

- what proportion of EFL learners use connectors?
- How many connectors do EFL learners use on average in a letter-writing task?
- What type of connectors do they use?
- What connectors are EFL learners exposed to by means of their course books?

3. Methodology

3. 1. Working definition

In this study, we use the term *connector* in a broad sense: as an umbrella term to refer to a word or words whose main function is to connect words, clauses, sentences and paragraphs. Likewise, we use *overuse* and *underuse* in relation to the input contained in our participants' course books, although most studies have used the native speaker as the basis for comparison. After careful thought, we decided not to use this norm of reference but rather that of our learners' course books. The reason has to do with the purpose and pedagogical nature of this study: we focus on foreign language learners' performance in a writing task usually contained in most course books for level and age similar to that of our sample of EFL learners: A1 level teenagers.

3. 2. Samples

The present study is based on two kinds of samples: learner compositions and learners' course books. Compositions and course books were selected because of their importance for EFL learners in school contexts. Learning to write compositions, such as informal and formal letters, is part of the English curricula objectives in Spanish secondary education. Course books are the usual learning and teaching materials employed by teachers and learners in the Spanish educational system. Regarding compositions, our sample consists of 228 texts produced by an equal number of EFL learners. Our informants belong to four secondary schools of analogous socioeconomic backgrounds from middle-class areas of a medium-sized capital city located in the north of Spain. By the time of data gathering (Spring, 2008) informants had received an average of 770 hours of EFL tuition, and their average age was 14.

The course book sample includes four books. This gives us four different sub-groups each corresponding to each of the four schools participating in this study: Group A, Group B, Group C, and Group D. Since the four schools are of analogous socioeconomic background, the chief identifying variable is considered to be the textbook employed during the course. Group A was taught by means of the text *Challenge*, Group B by *English Alive!*, Group C by *Exchange*, and finally Group D by *Making Moves*.

3. 3. Procedures and analyses

Our sample of EFL learners completed a composition in the form of a letter to a prospective host family in England:

> Imagine you are going to live for a month with an English family (the Edwards), in Oxford. There are four members in the family: Mr. and Mrs. Edwards, and the children, Peter and Helen. Write a letter to them in English in which you introduce yourself, and tell them about your town, your school, your hobbies, and anything else of interest that you would like to add.

Before beginning the composition, the informants were given the same explicit oral instructions in Spanish. The time allowed to complete the task was 30 minutes.

Once the compositions were collected they were edited and electronically transcribed. All the Spanish words were deleted prior to quantitative counts. Next, the compositions were encoded in plain text files into the computer and subjected to the WordSmith Tools text analysis program (Scott, 2004). This program provided us with an alphabetical list of the words used by students in the letter-writing task that was adopted for the identification of connectors. It also provided us with the number of raw frequencies for each connector. For connectors of more than one word such as *for instance, for example*, or *as a matter of fact*, we proceeded in two phases: (1) identification of the keyword: *instance, example, matter, word*; (2) verification of the keyword in context. We then entered each connector together with the number of occurrences, the identification codes for each student, and the school code into an Excel file. The resulting data were submitted to a Chi-square Test, which allowed us to ascertain that the sample of EFL learners (n=228) was homogeneous and that there were no significant differences among students according to the school variable. The value of the Chi-square Test was 5.31, p 0.150 (significant at p < 0.05).

As to the compilation of the corpus from learners' course books, the procedure was similar to the one followed with the compositions, except for the electronic transcription: whereas compositions were transcribed entirely into the computer, course books were not. In this case the researchers, after reading through the content of these course books with the utmost thoroughness, proceeded to identify connectors, using dictionaries, grammar, and discourse reference books (Ball, 1986; McCarthy, 1993; Celce-Murcia, Larsen-Freeman, 1999; Richards, Schmidt, 2002). After identifying the connectors in these course books, we entered them into a file, arranged them in alphabetical order, and finally applied quantitative analysis.

4. Results

Our first research question set out to ascertain the number of students who employ connectors in their compositions. In this regard, *Table 1* shows two facts:

- most students *do* make use of connectors but often no more than two types per composition;
- nearly half of the students use only two or three connectors per composition, while the other half use only one, or even no connectors at all.

A total of 552 connector tokens were identified in the corpus of compositions produced by our sample of EFL learners. However, this overall figure indicates that, on an individual basis, students use very few connector types in their compositions. This is confirmed by the mean (2.42), minimum (0), and maximum (6), which are rather low.

Number of connectors	0	1	2	3	4	5	6
Number of students (n=228)	6	43	86	53	24	14	2
Percentage of students	2.6	18.9	37.7	23.2	10.5	6.1	0.9

Table 1: Raw number and percentages of students who use connectors

Another issue in the present study was the identification of the types of connectors used by students. *Table 2* displays the types of connectors identified in learners' texts, distributed by the number and percentage (%) of students who used each connector. The figures point to the learners' poor repertoire of connectors: only 13 types were identified in the whole corpus of compositions.

The types of connectors used by students can be classified, following Halliday and Hasan's (1976) classification of conjunctive relations (further elaborated by Celce-Murcia and Larsen Freeman in 1999) into four categories:

- additive: *and, also*;
- adversative: *but, however*;
- causal: *because, so*;
- temporal: *when, then, where, before, first, after, after that*.

As can be seen, temporal connectors clearly surpass the other three categories in number of types. However, the distribution of the different connectors per student shows that among the range of connectors contained in the corpus of compositions as a whole, only *and* is used by a majority of students. The next most frequently used connector is *but* used by over half of students. The remaining types are employed by only a few students. The most overwhelming examples of underuse are *however, first, after*, and *after that*, used by one student out of 228.

So far we have found that, apart from *and*, our sample of EFL learners hardly use connectors in their compositions and that on the few occasions they do use them they resort to a very small range. We now turn to our exploratory analysis of the input related to connectors in learners' course books.

Connectors	n=228	%
And	220	96.5
But	143	62.7
Because	83	36.4
When	30	13.2
Also	28	12.3
Then	16	7.0
So	8	3.5
Where	5	2.2
Before	3	1.3
However	1	0.4
First	1	0.4
After	1	0.4
After that	1	0.4

Table 2: Types of connectors used by EFL learners:
raw and relative frequencies

The counting of different types of connectors per course book yielded the following results: Group A (*Challenge*): 35 types; Group B (*English Alive*): 25 types; Group C (*Exchange*): 24 types; and Group D (*Making Moves*): 39 types. We note that as far as overall frequency is concerned, there are differences in the input of connectors provided by these course books: Groups A and D contain 10 and 11 types more than Groups B and C. Not only do these course books differ in the number of connectors, they also do so as regards the specific connectors they contain. The second column in *Table 3* displays the connectors included in the course books. A close look at them tells us that there are 54 types of connectors, out of which the four course books share only 14.

The shared connectors are: *after, also, and, because, before, but, finally, for example, if, later, now, until,* and *when*. However, there is a number of exclusive connectors in each course book, i.e. some connectors appear in one course book but not in the others. Regarding these non-shared connectors, we observe that the course book *Making Moves* contains more exclusive connectors than the others. The third column in *Table 3* lists the exclusive connectors in each course book.

	Number of connectors in each book	Non-shared vocabulary
Group A: *Challenge*	After (5), also (6), although (1), and (416), as soon as (2), at the end (1), at the moment (1), because (20), before (4), between (2), but (53), by the way (1), even (8), finally (3), first (4), for example (4), for the first time (1), however (4), if (26), in the end (2), instead (3), later (4), next (5), now (11), of course (1), or (53), since (6), so (21), then (40), too (8), unless (10), until (1), when (45), while (12), yet (7).	In the end, instead, for the first time, between, by the way.
Group B: *English Alive*	After (20), also (33), and (783), as well (1), at first (1), at the moment (6), because (38), before (21), but (107), finally (1), first (9), for example (2), if (58), in fact (1), later (3), next (11), now (8), or (114), so (57), such as (1), then (143), the next day (4), until (2), when (105), where (3), whether (1), while (16).	Whether, as well, the next day.
Group C: *Exchange*	After (20), also (29), and (587), at first (3), at the moment (2), because (13), before (8), but (87), even (2), finally (2), for example (1), if (45), in total (1), later (4), now (15), or (59), so (9), soon (1), still (2), then (92), though (4), too (3), until (2), when (77), where (21).	In total, soon, still, though.
Group D: *Making Moves*	After (11), afterwards (4), also (13), although (1), and (563), as if (1), as soon as (5), at first (1), at the end (2), because (17), before (11), besides (1), but (46), even (1), even though (1), finally (4), firstly (2), for example (3), however (3), if (42), in fact (1), instead (2), later (1), now (5), of course (5), on the other hand (2), or (47), since (7), such as (7), the reason why (1), then (19), therefore (1), unless (2), until (5), when (54), whereas (1), while (8), yet (6).	Afterwards, since, the reason why, therefore, whereas, as if, on the other hand besides, even though, on the other hand.

Table 3: Distribution of connectors by course book

5. Discussion

This study shows that Spanish EFL learners hardly use connectors in their compositions. Not only are connectors underused, the range of variation is also very small. Learners resort to coordination rather than to subordination, and among the former, they employ basic connectors such as *and* or *but* to connect clauses and sentences. Underuse rather than overuse is the main trend in the production of connectors in a letter-writing task by this sample of EFL learners. Overuse is only observed with the coordinated conjunction *and*. Our results coincide with those reported in Connor (1984) as well as in Miranda and Lee (2003) who drew attention to the lack of variety in the use of connectors by EFL learners. Our results do not support the common claim that overuse of connectors is a universal characteristic of learners' interlanguage.

Regarding connectors in our sample of EFL learners' course books, our results show that they are indeed contained in the four books examined but that they raise various problematic issues. In the first place, the number of connector types is not the same in the four course books. The implication is that in their second year of compulsory secondary education, the sample of Spanish EFL learners under study are not exposed to an equal number of connectors in their course books. Ten connectors more may not sound an important difference; however, it may involve higher exposure. But it is not only an unequal number of types that may make a difference, it is also whether these types are the same or different in course books aimed at the same level. As we have seen, the shared vocabulary regarding connectors among the four course books is 14 out of 59. Obviously this is a serious problem if we consider that the Spanish Ministry of Education approved these course books to be used in Spanish secondary schools. If the course books do not contain equal input, the learners' exposure to the target language cannot be the same. And if exposure is different, learners' language learning conditions will differ.

Another problem found in our exploratory analysis of connectors in course books is that the recurrence of most connectors is of almost negligible value for facilitating their assimilation by EFL learners. There are many cases in which the connector appears only once in the course book. This means that learners are not exposed to satisfactory input. As Jiménez Catalán and Mancebo (2008) note, researchers do not agree on the issue of the number of repetitions needed to learn a word, but there is agreement on the fact that at least between six and nine encounters are required to learn the word (see Krachroo, 1962; Bunker, 1988; Reyes, 1999; Rott, 1999)

The present study has demonstrated that EFL learners either underuse or omit most of the connectors contained in their course books, except for *and, but,* and *because*. Our results suggest that there is a serious gap as regards EFL learners' knowledge and use of the English connectors contained in course books. The tendency to overuse basic conjunctions such as *and, but,* or *because* as well as the small range of types of connectors used by this group of learners, compared to the input they are exposed to, may affect the quality of their writing and probably their oral and written performance in the target language as a whole.

We are aware of the fact that letter composition tasks may not require a great deal of connectors in comparison to other kinds of genres such as argumentative or expository texts. However, connectors are also needed for the smooth transition of the sentences, to express relations of different kinds such as cause, consequence or reason, to introduce new paragraphs, or simply to mark the transition between different sequences, and yet they are not found in learners' compositions.

Learners' underuse of connectors may well be due to their scarcity in learners' course books. According to Crew (1990: 31), foreign language learners' misuse of them is a universal characteristic of interlanguage: learners with different mother tongues seem to have difficulty in using them appropriately. This common tendency may be related to language transfer but other reasons may be that, in line with Granger and Tyson (1996: 23), the information on connectors contained in dictionaries and grammars is neither sufficient nor adequately explained.

We agree with both Granger and Tyson (1996) and Milton and Tsang (1993) who advocate the increase of practice of connector usage. Language teachers should include activities to develop students' awareness of the use of these discourse elements in compositions. Spanish EFL learners are not aware of the fact that some connectors are used only in formal writing. Likewise, as they go hand in hand with the type of genre, we also think that teachers should train their students in the practice and use of connectors so that students become familiarized with the prototypical characteristics of texts from different genres. It is not enough to provide learners with practice in the use of connectors; they also need to be aware of register and text type in order to select the appropriate connectors. Connectors do not stand by themselves, they are realized in discourse, and their functions may vary according to the specific text, which in turn, may vary according to genre. Intensive and extensive practice on the use of connectors in different types of discourse should be implemented in the EFL classroom, as it has been proved that increasing practice of connectors has a positive effect on the quality of learners' essays (Jalilifar, 2008).

However, increasing practice without modifying course books' input is rather ineffective. The analysis carried out on the connectors contained in learners' course books has yielded very unsatisfactory results for three reasons:

- these course books do not contain either enough connectors or exercises to practise them, if we consider that they are used by EFL learners with a considerable amount of hours of instruction (770 hours) in the target language;
- writing tasks in English are required in the transition from low intermediate to intermediate levels in Spanish secondary education, and in order to write well in English students will need a good command of a wide range of connectors;
- there is at least one written composition in English in the compulsory exam that Spanish students must take prior to university entrance.

The gap identified in the second year of compulsory secondary education (three years before entering university) is a serious one. Action is urgently needed to solve this problem. In our opinion, the situation would improve if a gradual writing programme were introduced earlier on, that is, from late primary education to the last year of secondary education. In this programme, the explicit instruction of vocabulary, and within it, the explicit instruction of connectors in relation to text characteristics, should have its place.

6. Further studies

The present study is an exploratory one. Nevertheless, given the large number of students, the homogeneity of the sample, and above all, the shared conditions with other schools in Spain (since, under current legislation, English language teaching in secondary education is subject to an equal number of hours of instruction and an equal syllabus), we may assume that our results might also serve, with caution, for English teachers in other Spanish secondary schools. Likewise, given that the letter-writing task is frequently found in course books and that the course books analyzed here are aimed at an international audience rather than a specific country, we hope that the findings obtained in this study may be useful for teachers and researchers in secondary schools in other parts of the world.

The present study suggests the need for further research at least in the following domains:

- the issue of correlation between connector vocabulary input and learners' connector production; to what extent are they related? Do exclusive connectors in course books result in exclusive EFL learners' connector production?;
- analysis of the difficulties learners face in using connectors: what are the main problems as reflected in their misuse of connectors?;
- the relation between learners' proficiency in the target language and their use of connectors: how do low and high proficiency learners use connectors? What is the connector profile of low and highly proficient language learners?

Acknowledgments

The authors gratefully acknowledge the financial support of the *Ministerio de Educación y Ciencia* and *FEDER* through Grant HUM2006-09775-C02-02, research project "El desarrollo de la competencia léxica en la adquisición del inglés como lengua extranjera".

The treatment of lexical collocations in EFL textbooks

Christián Abello-Contesse, University of Seville, Spain
M. Dolores López-Jiménez, Pablo de Olavide University, Spain

1. Introduction

This chapter focuses on the nature of *lexical collocations*, specifically on the roles such word combinations play in current textbooks published for teaching English as a foreign and/ or second language (EFL/ESL). The chapter begins with a review of the strengths and weaknesses of foreign language textbooks in general, and gradually moves on to the lexical feature under study. Various definitions of lexical collocations as found in the literature over the last 30 years are discussed and a rationale for giving greater attention to lexical collocations in teaching materials is offered from the perspectives of L2 teaching and learning. Furthermore, the most likely criteria for selecting collocations for teaching purposes are discussed. In the rest of the chapter, an empirical study is described and analyzed; the study consisted of (i) a collocational analysis based on 12 textbooks used for teaching EFL in Spain, together with (ii) a questionnaire distributed among 116 Spanish EFL teachers whose aim was to assess their perceptions of vocabulary and collocational aspects present in the textbooks they were using. The main results of the study are then discussed using both data sources (i.e., the textbooks analyzed and the responses given to the questionnaire). Finally, we advance our conclusions and related pedagogical implications.

2. L2 textbooks, vocabulary teaching, and lexical collocations

Few teachers today would seriously question the central role played by L2 textbooks as a major pedagogical resource when teaching a non-native language (L2). Over the last 30 years, L2 textbooks (hereafter TBs) have been characterized by their capacity to adapt to changing situations, such as the introduction of new technologies, new methodological trends in L2 teaching, or the increasingly demanding requirements of the publishing market. This resilience is largely responsible for the dominant influence that TBs continue to have in L2 classrooms in general and in EFL classrooms in particular.

With the advent of new technologies, TBs have become more colorful and are accompanied by supplementary materials, such as CDs, CD-ROMs, and videos. From the perspective of L2 teaching methodology, the techniques and activities that characterize the different methods and approaches tend to be evident in TBs. In the case of the structural approach, dominant in the 50s and 60s, TBs showed an emphasis on formal aspects of the L2, mainly morphology and syntax, when compared with other language components, such as the lexical and semantic areas. On the other hand, the influence exerted by the communicative approaches from the late 70s to the mid 90s led to the publication of TBs where many of the accuracy-related aspects were abandoned in order to concentrate on the verbal transmission of messages or conversational fluency. Similarly, the emphasis of these communicative approaches on learner variables is still reflected in the TBs and in the blurb, where it is sometimes claimed, for example, that the TB has been designed to meet the students' needs and interests (Masuhara, 1998). With regard to users' needs and interests, L2 TBs specialized in language for specific purposes and intensive courses began to consolidate in the publishing market in the 1990s. Likewise, the publishing market has continually increased in importance, and this has led TBs to concentrate on market demands, to the detriment of pedagogical concerns. That is why Haines (1996), when making a distinction between the underlying TB trends in past and present EFL/ESL teaching, suggests that in the past publishers tended to sell what had already been published, while now what they tend to publish is what is already known to sell in the market.

In spite of the supremacy of the TB over alternative materials, it has not been free from criticism. From the teachers' viewpoint, a frequent criticism is that the dominant position of the TB often has negative repercussions, thus limiting their responsibilities and skills, since teachers (particularly inexperienced ones) tend to delegate decisions about what and how to teach to the TB, while ignoring critical feedback as it is usually taken for granted that the TB writers' decisions are superior to their own. On the other hand, related problems such as the design of the learning activities included in many TBs, lead the teacher to assume not just an active role in the teaching process, but, more significantly, an unnecessarily dominating one, in which a remedial function between the writers and the students is adopted.

From the L2 student's point of view, there is an overall dissatisfaction with the lack of attention that TBs tend to pay to the students' local and national realities; this is partly due to the absence of contemporary topics and events in the learners' immediate world (e.g., gender violence, unemployment, underemployment, drug abuse, sex discrimination, family breakdown, electronic game addiction, etc.), thus promoting materials that turn out to be notoriously bland, safe, and trivial as well as excessively uniform in their structure. Similarly, published TBs, particularly those for EFL/ESL, do not typically include the learners' most representative features in them. In other words, the main characteristics of their native or dominant language (L1) and their native culture (C1) are most often ignored in terms of both crosslinguistic and crosscultural influences. These deficiencies are essentially the result of monetary considerations (Lawley, 2000), since it is substantially more profitable for international publishing houses to produce a single TB that can be sold in many different countries – regardless of the students' language or sociocultural backgrounds – than to design it taking into account these fundamental features, as usually happens with TBs for the teaching of Spanish or French published in English-speaking countries.

Moreover, the TB has been accused of ignoring most pedagogical implications derived from second-language learning theories and the findings of research into second language acquisition (SLA). Tomlinson (1991, 2008) claims that in the main, the exercises found in TBs are based on the manipulation of certain L2 features while communicative activities tend to be absent, thus making it difficult or impossible for students to make more extensive use of their intellectual or cognitive resources.

While the importance of the TB as a pedagogical resource in L2 teaching has remained constant, if, indeed it has not increased, over the last 3 decades, the language components on which TB writers concentrate have not always had the same weight in L2 teaching. In the mid 70s, Richards (1976: 77) clarifies that "the teaching and learning of vocabulary have never aroused the same degree of interest within language teaching as have such issues as grammatical competence, contrastive analysis, reading, or writing". In the 80s numerous researchers began to take an interest in vocabulary learning (e.g., Carter, 1987; McKeown, Curtis, 1987), although it was not until the following decade with the publication of two essential works, *The Lexical Approach* (Lewis, 1993), and *Implementing the Lexical Approach* (Lewis, 1997), that the central role of the lexical component was recognized. It was then explicitly claimed that language consists of grammaticalized vocabulary rather than lexicalized grammar (Lewis, 1993).

From the 1990s on, various areas of interest in research on L2 vocabulary learning proliferated, and researchers made the transition from skepticism to action. Questioning the relevance of vocabulary in L2 teaching led to a growing interest in pedagogical issues, such as deciding what vocabulary to teach and how to teach it. Clear examples of this trend have been the various studies on the learning of lexical collocations over the last 15 years. Among them are studies on the accuracy with which students of different L1s use English collocations (Bahns, Eldaw, 1993; Nesselhauf, 2003) and studies on the development of collocational knowledge (Zhang, 1993). Overall, the previous literature indicates the following 5 conclusions:

- there is a lack of collocational knowledge on the part of EFL/ESL learners;
- collocational knowledge does not evolve parallel to the rest of the lexicon;
- it is necessary to teach the concept of collocation and explicitly teach those collocations which are different in the students' L1 and their L2 in order to avoid mistakes caused by crosslinguistic influence in general and L1 transfer in particular;
- factors such as idiomaticity, frequency, and formality influence the development of collocational knowledge;
- deficits in collocational knowledge are attributed in part to the excessive emphasis on *traditional grammar* and the practice of *free selection* of L2 vocabulary by TB writers to the detriment of the principle of idiomaticity.

However, these conclusions are rather tentative since the authors mentioned above do not specify the selection criteria used in their studies nor do they offer methodological proposals to teach L2 lexical collocations on the basis of theoretical principles from SLA research (Higueras, 2007).

3. Definitions of lexical collocation

The different definitions of the concept of collocation provided by SLA researchers and L2 teaching methodology specialists in English-speaking countries from the 80s to the present tend to be rather simplistic as they merely touch on the features involved in the concept and simply identify collocation as frequent co-occurrences of two words (Higueras, 2004).

Gairns and Redman (1986: 37) define collocation as "when two items co-occur or are used together frequently, they are said to collocate". They point out that it is difficult to group lexical items according to their collocational properties. This is why L2 teachers and students tend to deal with them as they crop up in an isolated manner. They suggest collocations should be taught when reviewing recently-covered vocabulary as a way to expand the lexical knowledge of items that students are already familiar with.

McCarthy (1990) does not include the concept of collocation as part of *multi-word lexical items* (hereafter MWLI) and considers it a sense relation at the paradigmatic level like synonymy, antonymy, and hyponymy. He claims that collocations constitute an important organizing principle in a language's lexicon. Consequently, the notion of collocation is considered to be a fundamental feature in studying vocabulary. Nation (1990), like other authors (Gairns, Redman, 1986; McCarthy, 1990), does not regard collocation as a type of lexical item, but defines it as words that co-occur. One of Nation's (1990) most significant contributions is the broad definition he provides of what it means to *know* a word. Nation (2001) breaks the concept down into 3 main sections, namely, *form, meaning,* and *use.* Concerning use, he specifies that knowing a lexical item implies knowing what kinds of words tend to occur with it from a receptive and a productive viewpoint.

Through his *Lexical Approach,* Lewis (1993, 1997, 2000a) assigns a great deal of importance to collocations and distinguishes the following 3 types of MWLI: polywords, collocations, and institutionalized expressions. He emphasizes two main features concerning collocations, namely their arbitrariness and variation, both from a syntagmatic and a paradigmatic perspective (Lewis, 1993). Unlike institutionalized expressions that belong to the pragmatic component, collocations are related to content rather than to language/communicative functions (e.g., complaining, apologizing, requesting, etc.). Schmitt (2000) describes collocation as words that occur together, a tendency or property that is present both in free and in idiomatic combinations. He claims that expressions with less variation are the least complex in L2 learning. Thornbury (2002) defines collocation in terms of frequent co-occurrence of words, and does not include it as part of MWLIs. He places collocation on a continuum ranging from compounds, to idioms and phrasal verbs, to collocations.

More recently, McCarthy and O'Dell (2005) describe collocation as a pair or group of words that are frequently used together. In addition, they state that although such word combinations sound natural to native speakers of the target language, they require an extra effort for L2 learners.

This chapter will make use of Higueras' (2004) definition as it is one of the widest in scope, uniting different points of view, such as perspectives related to psychology, semantics, frequency of use, combination preference, and combinatory restrictions. Similarly, the idiosyncratic nature of a collocation is, according to Higueras (2007), what justifies its study when teaching L2 vocabulary since a word in the student's L1 might require different combinations when contrasted with its L2 equivalent. For example, the English collocation *weak tea* would translate into Spanish as *té flojo* and not its literal translation, **té débil*. Higueras' (2004: 71) definition is:

> a type of lexical unit [...], a psychological unit for native speakers of a language [...], constituted by two lexemes [...] that frequently co-occur, and that show a typical relationship between both [...]. Collocations are partially compositional since the base retains its original meaning; however, the collocate assumes a special meaning when appearing with the base [...]. Collocations also show combinatory preferences and restrictions imposed by usage and standardization [...]. Such preferences and restrictions might come from our world knowledge or they might be due to idiosyncratic reasons related to individual languages.

4. Reasons for teaching lexical collocations in an L2

Lewis (1997) states that since words are rarely used alone, it makes sense to teach them in the patterns in which they typically appear. Corpas Pastor (1996) shows that collocations help learners improve their comprehension and produce certain texts and registers, given that certain collocations only appear in specific L2 varieties. Hill (2000) justifies the teaching of collocations on the following 4 grounds:

- in the mental lexicon, a collocation is the strongest force in the creation and comprehension of texts;
- the lexicon is not arbitrary, that is, to a certain extent, the choice of a lexical unit is predictable. Therefore, the knowledge of certain collocations helps predict the type of words that appear together. For example, if we consider the verb *have* within the context of a liquid, the most likely combinations that might surface include *tea, coffee, milk, mineral water, orange juice*, etc., but not *engine oil, shampoo*, or *sulphuric acid*;
- roughly 70% of what we hear, decide, read, or write forms part, to a greater or lesser extent, of fixed expressions. Thus, it is not enough to know a great number of words; it is also necessary to have an adequate collocational knowledge;
- teaching collocations solves one of the main problems that many L2 students experience. Put differently, an adequate level of knowledge and use of collocations would help students avoid non-target-like lexical choices which may originate in their being unaware of the existence of collocations. This lack of collocational knowledge frequently requires students to produce longer utterances in order to express the content of the collocation that they do not know. With respect to this point, Morgan Lewis (2000) claims that collocations often express complex ideas simply and precisely, thus helping students avoid longer productions that might not reflect the same idea with the same level of precision.

4. 1. Reasons for learning lexical collocations in an L2

Nation (1990, 2001) claims that the knowledge of a word would remain incomplete for students if they are not aware of its collocational combinations. It may be argued that learning lexical collocations in an L2 would benefit students not only in terms of productive and receptive word knowledge (due to their non-compositional nature), but also in encouraging learner autonomy. The following paragraphs will provide a brief description of each of these aspects (i.e., productive and receptive knowledge as well as learner autonomy) relative to the learning of L2 lexical collocations.

First, the encoding of meaning in lexical collocations (productive knowledge) may be problematic (Hussein, 1990), as they have acquired a certain degree of idiomaticity. Castillo Carballo (2001) states that L2 learners employ target-like use of collocations when choosing the base, but show non-target-like variation with the collocate as it takes up a special meaning when it appears with the base. Lewis (1993) also stresses the important role of collocations in expressing meaning. For example, it is impossible to explain the meaning of the verb *to bark*, without referring to the word *dog*. Likewise, the meaning of the verb *to bark* is not complete only with the collocational combination *dogs bark*, but also with related collocations, such as *dogs bark, pigs grunt, ducks quack*, etc. In justifying the learning of collocations in an L2, McCarthy and O'Dell (2005) claim that collocations are often the most natural way of expressing something in a language (e.g., *smoking is strictly forbidden* is more natural than *smoking is strongly forbidden*) and they carry a greater degree of precision in expressing a notion (e.g., *It was very cold and very dark* may be expressed as *It was bitterly cold and pitch black*).

Second, the decoding (receptive knowledge) can also be problematic for L2 learners in cases of intense semantic specialization of the collocate. For example, in the English collocation *black market* the adjective refers to the illegal way by which people buy and sell foreign money and goods that are difficult to obtain, not to its color.

Third, given the arbitrary nature of collocations (i.e., collocations show preferences and restrictions due to idiosyncratic reasons related to individual languages), learning lexical collocations in an L2 plays an important role in encouraging learner autonomy (Woolard, 2000). Learning collocations in an L2, Woolard (2000: 35) argues, mostly consists of students noticing and recording them; thus, teachers should provide students with enough resources for them to explore texts for themselves.

4. 2. Selection criteria for teaching purposes

Penadés Martínez (2004) indicates that native speakers (adult, well-educated, etc.) of a language use a large number of collocations; this implies that L2 students are unlikely to learn all of them, even though they must learn to use tens of thousands.

In quite an early proposal, Brown (1974: 3) concludes that *normal* collocations should be taught before *unusual* ones since the former are seen as the basis of the latter.

She does not, however, offer criteria for distinguishing between the two types in practice. Leed and Nakhimovsky (1979) recommend that the selection and teaching of collocations should be undertaken via lexical functions arguing that the theory of lexical functions contributes both consistency and diversity while avoiding arbitrariness when designing pedagogical materials.

Yorio (1980) suggests that criteria such as students' needs, usefulness, productivity, and ease of use should be taken into account. Students' needs are identified through an analysis of the students' aims while usefulness requires an analysis of the relevance of the different combinations. Productivity is calculated by performing a study of the combinations' applicability, and ease of use relates to the notion of how easily combinations may be produced from a phonological and syntactic perspective. Meanwhile, Gitsaki (1996) proposes that the most frequently-used collocations and those with the highest degree of idiomaticity should be selected. Therefore, for example, the collocational combination *recommend highly* is more abstract than the collocation *try hard* since this latter represents a physical action. Similarly, *recommend highly*, when compared with the collocation *try hard* lacks literal meaning. Another selection criterion is that proposed by Lewis (2000c) which advises that attention be centered upon those collocations formed by frequently-used L2 nouns. Frequently-used nouns (e.g., *car*) have less lexical content than other less-frequently used ones (e.g., *telescope*) and, therefore, need a greater degree of nuance through adjectives such as *powerful, second-hand, family*, etc. (Lewis, 2000c: 144).

Like Lewis (2000c), Hill et al. (2000) suggest (making no reference to the issue of selection) that when teaching collocations, special attention should be paid to:

- frequent and useful nouns although they do not contribute much meaning and in spite of the inconvenient fact that they include a large number of collocations;
- delexicalized verbs, such as *do, make, put, keep, get, have*, etc. which many students overuse without actually knowing which noun(s) form acceptable collocations with them.

In a different chapter in the same book, Hill (2000: 63-64) favors the selection of medium-strength collocations. He distinguishes between unique, strong, medium-strength, and weak collocations. The author offers no definition for these types of collocations, but rather identifies them through examples. Therefore, *foot the bill* is a unique collocation since the verb *foot* is used only in this combination, *foot the invoice* and *foot the coffee* being incorrect. Adjectives such as *trenchant* and *rancid* in *trenchant criticism* and *rancid butter* form strong collocations since these two adjectives usually, but not exclusively, appear with the nouns *criticism* and *butter* respectively. The adjectives *long, short, cheap* and *expensive* would form weak collocations because they can be combined with a large number of nouns. Finally, collocations such as *major operation, hold/have a conversation* or *make a mistake* would fall within the classification of medium-strength collocations. Hill (2000) states that most intermediate-level students know the constituent parts of these collocations separately although they are probably unaware of the combinations they form. In other words, intermediate-level students have not stored *hold/have a conversation* as a single element, but rather as separate elements in their mental lexicon. Hill considers an intermediate level of proficiency as a starting point to teach collocations, a proficiency level where collocational teaching may focus on those lexical items the learners already know in an isolated way.

Nesselhauf (2003) states that the selection of lexical collocations should take into account frequent and acceptable ones, either in a neutral or specific register and those collocations that require an intermediate degree of restriction. For example, the collocational combination *exert influence/control/pressure/authority/power* includes a lesser degree of restriction than *fail an exam/test* due to the fact that *exert* combines with a larger number of nouns.

Gitsaki (1996) criticizes the fact that some of these criteria (e.g., usefulness, productivity, and ease of use) are arbitrary and claims that teaching collocations requires a scientific rigor with regard to which and how many collocations should be taught, how to practice them, and at what level their teaching should be introduced. Such an approach would remove the obligation upon teachers to rely on their intuition when deciding on the most useful collocations to teach.

It is worth noting that there is a widespread view among the authors mentioned above that one of the fundamental criteria to be used in selecting which collocations to teach is that there should be no direct equivalence between the learners' L1 and L2 as regards collocational usage (Bahns, 1993; Corpas Pastor, 1996). One option for applying this criterion is Newman's (1988) who proposes undertaking a contrastive study between collocations used in the students' L1 and their L2, thus avoiding errors arising from crosslinguistic influence and, especially, L1 transfer.

4. 3. Pedagogical proposals for teaching collocations in an L2

In the literature related to teaching and learning collocations, various pedagogical proposals can be found (Brown, 1974; Lewis, 1997, 2000a; Higueras, 2004). One of the most recent, Higueras (2004), based on language and language learning theories, aims to make a two-pronged approach to the teaching of collocations in the classroom by providing teachers with language training on the concept of collocation (this being one of the proposal's most novel aspects) and by helping to define the language content in the design of teaching units where collocations and other types of lexical items are to be practiced. However, the proposals advanced so far have not only been characterized by their limited scope, with no definitions concerning syllabus or course planning according to proficiency levels (Higueras, 2004), but also by a notorious absence of presentation techniques for collocations and activities for collocational practice in classroom situations where there is a need to undertake a communicative exchange. Therefore, most of the activities are characterized by their controlled nature. In other words, students are either limited to recognizing the collocation per se – a purely mechanical exercise – or are merely required to know the meanings of the words involved in order to obtain the correct collocation in a matching-type exercise. This, however, does not guarantee that L2 lexical collocations are learned due to their non-compositional nature since, as mentioned earlier, the collocate acquires certain characteristics only in the presence of the base rather than in isolation.

5. Types of lexical collocations

Different types of lexical collocations have been identified depending on the part of speech and the syntactic relationship of the constituent elements. Benson et al. (2010 [1986]) indicate the existence of 7 types of lexical collocations while Corpas Pastor (1996) and Koike (2001) recognize 6 types, and Írsula Peña (1994) only 4. The empirical study on which this paper is based made partial use of the classifications proposed by Benson et al. (2010 [1986]), Corpas Pastor (1996), and Koike (2001). Thus, for the purposes of the present study, lexical collocations have been classified as follows:

- noun subject + verb: *blizzards rage, bees sting*;
- verb + noun object (verb + preposition + noun): *squander a fortune, burst into tears*;
- adjective + noun: *weak tea, rough estimate*;
- noun + preposition + noun: *a colony of bees, a pack of dogs*;
- verb + adverb: *affect deeply, apologize humbly*;
- adjective + adverb: *sound asleep, strictly accurate*.

From a semantic perspective, this chapter has included collocations in which the collocate acquires the following characteristics:

- a semantic specialization that limits its combinations with other bases (e.g., *shrug one's shoulders*);
- an abstract or figurative meaning (e.g., *capture/catch/seize/grip one's imagination*);
- an almost grammaticalized meaning forming collocations with a delexicalized verb (e.g., *make an agreement*).

6. The study

The empirical study upon which this chapter is based included a detailed analysis of 12 textbooks (TBs) produced for teaching English as a foreign/second language at 3 different proficiency levels. Four TBs from 3 different levels (i.e., beginning/elementary, intermediate, and advanced) were selected and analyzed along with the responses to 116 questionnaires completed by experienced EFL teachers in Spain. The main goals of the study were, first, to analyze the treatment given to the selection, presentation, and practice of lexical collocations in all 12 TBs and, secondly, to compare the treatment given to lexical collocations in the selected TBs with the EFL teachers' perceptions of that treatment in equivalent TBs they were using or had recently used at their schools.

6. 1. The instruments used

All 12 TBs analyzed were aimed at young adults and adults and were published between 1997 and 2007 by major European publishers. All textbooks were designed for general and regular L2 learning (i.e., not for specific purposes or intensive language study). In order for a TB to be included as valid data source for the present study, it was required to have explicit vocabulary sections not shared with any other language components (e.g., syntax, morphology, etc.) or skills (e.g., reading, writing, etc.). A further requirement for selection was for the TBs to cover at least 3 language skills in addition to the grammatical and lexical components.

The various vocabulary exercises and activities included in the TBs were analyzed following a specific typology devised for this study that was based on the students' relative degree of control over their expected answers. The typology consisted of the following 5 activity types:

- *mechanical exercise*: explicit comprehension of lexical items is not necessary as there is only one correct answer (e.g., completing a word with the missing vowel and/or consonant letters);
- *closed exercise*: a greater degree of comprehension of the target vocabulary is needed, yet there is still only one valid answer (e.g., fill-in-the-blank exercises);
- *open activity*: students are required to understand the target vocabulary; there are two or more valid answers and there may or may not be explicit information gaps (e.g., question-and-answer activities based on the target vocabulary, giving definitions of target vocabulary);
- *communicative activity*: there is an open answer and/or a lexical choice that is required to complete the activity, along with explicit information gaps; the instructions ask students to interact with each other to achieve a predetermined final outcome which may not be reached individually (e.g., writing advertisements in pairs using the vocabulary provided);
- *ambiguous activity*: there is a single exercise or activity which contains features of more than 1 of the 4 categories described above.

The questionnaires were distributed among EFL teachers in Spanish high schools, universities, and official language schools in Seville and western Andalusia. The teachers were asked to base their answers on the one TB they were most familiar with at the time the study was conducted. These TBs were also aimed at young adults and adults, designed for non-intensive/non-specific study, and included at least 3 language skills apart from the grammatical and lexical components. The answers to the different statements on the questionnaire were measured following a frequency scale; the scale included the following 5 options:

- N/A = Don't know/does not apply;
- 1 = No/never;
- 2 = Occasionally;
- 3 = Frequently;
- 4 = Yes/always.

6. 2. Results from the analysis of the EFL TBs

As a point of departure with regard to the *selection* and *presentation* of lexical collocations in the TBs under scrutiny, it may be pointed out that only 1 of the 12 TBs (8.33%) provides the specific source from which the vocabulary included was obtained.

In terms of the explicit/implicit *presentation* of lexical collocations, as the proficiency level of the TBs increases, the percentage of TBs that introduce lexical collocations also increases (4.17% in the beginning/elementary TBs, 12.5% in the intermediate TBs, and 19.75% in the advanced TBs).

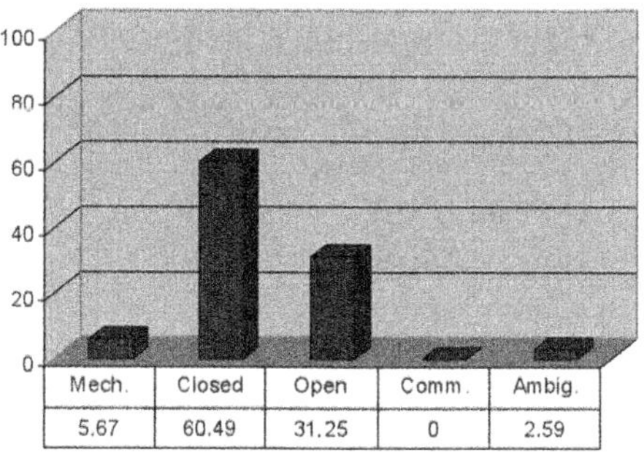

Figure 1: Explicit and implicit practice of lexical collocations: typology

With regard to the explicit/implicit *practice* of lexical collocations, there is a lower percentage of teaching units including the practice of such collocations in the beginning/ elementary TBs (45.14%) as compared with their intermediate (64.26%) and advanced counterparts (57.29%). The practice itself is mostly comprised of closed exercises (60.49%) and open activities (31.25%) (see *Figure 1*). Among the different types of lexical collocations that are covered in the practice of collocations, those that are present in a higher percentage of teaching units are limited to 2 types only: *verb + noun* (61.76%) and *adjective + noun* (48.03%) (see *Figure 2*).

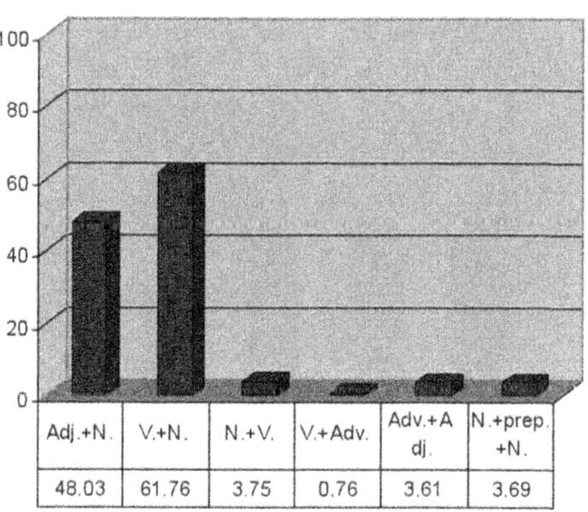

Figure 2: Types of lexical collocations

As far as the *explicit practice* of lexical collocations is concerned, the results indicate that in 83.33% of the TBs analyzed, such collocations are taught in an explicit fashion. Three of the TBs that teach lexical collocations explicitly are books that, according to their cover or title, have been adapted to the Spanish educational system. However, in their description, these 3 TBs do not indicate if the lexical collocations included were selected on the basis of the differences existing between the students' L1 and their L2. In addition, the terminology employed to identify the practice of lexical collocations varies to a certain extent; for instance, 70% of the TBs that teach collocations explicitly use the term *collocations*; 20% use the expression *words that go together*, and 10% use the word *expressions*. In 28.57% of the TBs where the label *collocation* is used, not only are lexical collocations classified as such, but also other combinations, such as compounds (*healthcare, check-list*), grammatical collocations (*on business*), idioms (*fight tooth and nail*), and non-phrasal verbs (*take*) are to be found under this label.

6. 3. Results from the questionnaires

Concerning the selection and presentation of lexical items, according to the views expressed by the EFL teachers who completed the questionnaires, the explicit criteria for vocabulary selection and sequencing are identified in only 22.9% of the TBs they were most familiar with.

As for the explicit introduction of vocabulary, the EFL teachers surveyed believe that in general the explicit *presentation* of lexical items is *frequent* in their TBs (3.17: *1=No/ never, 2=Occasionally, 3=Frequently, 4=Yes/always*). They also estimate that it is less frequent in advanced TBs (3.0) when compared with beginning/elementary (3.34) and intermediate ones (3.15).

With respect to vocabulary *practice*, the EFL teachers consider that 'enough variety' is present *occasionally*, or close to *frequently* (2.85) in the type of vocabulary practice provided in the TBs they are most familiar with (*1=No/never, 2=Occasionally, 3=Frequently, 4=Yes/always*).

In addition, the EFL teachers are of the opinion that the most frequent collocations in the vocabulary practice activities are *verb + noun, noun + verb*, and *adjective + noun* (see *Figure 3*).

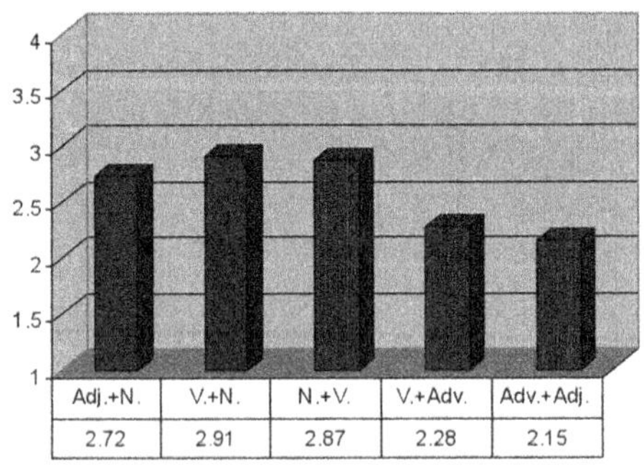

Figure 3: Types of lexical collocations

Finally, when the percentages of *N/A (Don't know/Not apply)* responses to individual statements on the questionnaire are compared, the highest percentages of such replies are to be found in the statements related to lexical collocations (the collocation types included were *noun + verb, verb + adverb, adjective + noun, verb + noun, adverb + adjective*). The highest percentages are found in response to the statements where the EFL teachers were asked to identify the relative frequency with which collocations were present in the TBs they were using. The average percentage of N/A responses to questions concerning lexical collocations was 11.23% while the average percentage of N/A responses to the rest of the questions was only 3.3%.

7. Discussion

In terms of the *selection criteria* employed in the TBs, the results of the analysis show that only 8.33% of them specify the vocabulary selection criteria used. Interestingly, the EFL teachers' views coincide with the results obtained, thus reflecting the paucity of selection and grading criteria when describing TBs. It is highly probable that in the rest of the TBs analyzed, in which the writers do not specifically state the selection or grading criteria, they performed a random selection of the new vocabulary therein.

As for the explicit/implicit *presentation* and *practice* of lexical collocations, the percentages found in intermediate- and advanced-level TBs are higher than those obtained in beginning/elementary-level TBs. There is, however, no empirical evidence concerning the suitability of starting to teach lexical collocations from intermediate levels onwards. Spanish-speaking authors such as Castillo Carballo (personal communication, 2009) and Higueras (2004, 2007) state that L2 students need to acquire word combinations from the very first moment that they begin to learn an L2. On the other hand, English-speaking authors, such as Hill (2000), advise that lexical collocations be taught from an intermediate level. With regard to the teachers' opinion on the *presentation* of lexical items, they believe presentations decrease as the TBs' proficiency level increases. These contradictory findings may imply that the EFL teachers may have expressed their views concerning lexical items in general rather than focusing on a specific type of item, namely, lexical collocations.

Within the explicit/implicit *practice* of lexical collocations, there is a higher percentage of closed exercises compared with the percentages of both open and communicative activities. Two of the reasons explaining the greater presence of closed exercises may be:

- the use of a specific definition of *communicative activity* within the typology used in this study;
- internal variation within communicative methodology since, from the mid 90s on, communicative approaches started dealing with both form and fluency in a more balanced manner, while the earlier communicative approaches of the 1970s and 80s had focused more extensively on verbal interaction and fluency. Given the fact that the TBs analyzed were published between 1997 and 2007, it is highly probable that this methodological variation was present.

As regards the presence of variation in the type of vocabulary *practice* included, the teachers surveyed consider that *occasionally* there is variation. However, this result must be treated with caution since the teachers, as mentioned earlier, answered about the frequency of the practice provided in general (i.e., both one-word lexical items and MWLIs), while the type of practice included in the TB analysis focused on the practice of lexical collocations in particular.

Within the explicit/implicit *practice* of lexical collocations, the collocation types that are dealt with in a greater number of teaching units are *verb* + *noun* and *adjective* + *noun*. It is highly likely that TB writers based their selection on their own intuition since there are no empirical studies (that the present authors are aware of) on the frequency of different types of lexical collocations in English. The teachers' opinion on the frequency of the different types of lexical collocations found in the vocabulary practice of the TBs they were using does not coincide with the results of the TBs analyzed. This suggests a relative lack of knowledge of what a lexical collocation is on the part of the teachers surveyed. This finding is also supported by the much higher percentage of *N/A* responses in the questionnaire statements related to the presence of different types of lexical collocations in the TBs' vocabulary practice.

8. Conclusions and pedagogical implications

Given that vocabulary selection and grading criteria are not identified in most of the TBs, it may be deduced that the writers' *selection* of the different types of lexical collocations is neither systematic nor pedagogically useful. This lack of criteria is pointed out by Rixon (2000: 56) who indicates that such criteria are not even mentioned in the teacher's books:

> Thus, much of the thinking and planning becomes embedded, even buried, in the materials on the page. In the teachers' books that accompany these courses, authors tend to be rather silent on the subject of the selection and ordering of the language content of their syllabuses and they say particularly little about vocabulary in this regard.

Regarding the explicit/implicit *presentation* and *practice* of lexical collocations, the greater presence of these combinations in intermediate and advanced-level TBs has little or no scientific rigor since there are no empirical studies to support the suitability of teaching collocations from intermediate levels onwards. For the most part, the types of activities upon which the practice of lexical collocations are based are *closed* and *open* activities while communicative activities are surprisingly absent. In light of these results, it can be claimed that teaching lexical collocations, specifically in the practice stage, continues to be quite traditional. Tomlinson (2008) criticizes the fact that EFL/ESL teaching materials do not reflect the L2 learning process since most of the activities only revolve around memorizing, repetition, substitution, and transformation.

Concerning the mismatch between the results of the TB analysis and the EFL teachers' views of the presence of lexical collocations in the vocabulary practice of the TBs they were using, together with the higher percentage of teachers who chose *N/A* as their choice when questioned about the presence of these collocations, it may be deduced that the participating teachers were not familiar with the concept of *lexical collocation*, a situation that might have prevented them from identifying the most frequent collocation types.

Finally, it can be claimed that the results of recent research into applied linguistics related to the teaching and learning of L2 collocations have been taken into consideration in most of the TBs analyzed. Among other findings, this research suggests that lexical collocations should be taught directly (Gitsaki, 1996). With regard to the relevance of using differences between the students' L1 and L2 when selecting the lexical collocations to be taught, (Bahns, 1993; Castillo Carballo, 2001; Laufer, 2005b), our conclusion is that in those TBs that teach collocations directly, such differences were not taken into account. In 3 of the TBs analyzed where lexical collocations are dealt with explicitly, reference is made to the Spanish educational system or it is specifically stated that the TB is a Spanish edition. However, their description does not specify if the students' L1 was, in fact, used in selecting the lexical content included.

In spite of the fact that in the last 30 years vocabulary has become an increasingly important element in L2 teaching, there are still several aspects that could and should be improved, such as the specific case of teaching lexical collocations in EFL TBs. With regard to the implications of this study for the design of teaching materials, the first piece of advice would be that TB writers indicate the criteria upon which they have based the selection and grading of the lexical collocations included, thus avoiding an arbitrary, asystematic choice that is of limited use. Secondly, in those TBs where such collocations are directly practiced, we recommend that their selection be based upon contrastive studies that recognize and apply the differences existing between learners' L1 and L2 as a practical procedure designed to counter the high number of collocational errors due to L1>L2 crosslinguistic influence. Thirdly, it is suggested that specific attention should be paid to lexical collocations in EFL TBs early on instead of artificially postponing it until intermediate or advanced levels. Last but not least, EFL TB writers are advised to strike a better balance between the more tightly-controlled practice and the less controlled practice of lexical collocations (i.e., mechanical and closed exercises versus open and communicative activities), thus avoiding the excessive presence of closed exercises and the notorious absence of communicative tasks in their TBs. As pointed out earlier, the teaching of such collocations in L2 English may well have favorable effects on learning/ using the target language not only in terms of fluency, but also in terms of higher levels of lexical accuracy and idiomaticity. For L2 learners, these are highly desirable benefits that should merit more than the merely simplistic recognition exercises found in many current EFL textbooks.

Access routes to lexical collocations in English learner's dictionaries on CD-ROM

Alfonso Rizo-Rodríguez, University of Jaén, Spain

1. Introduction

No language specialist will question the fact that "collocations" (Palmer, 1933: 7; Firth, 1957: 194), also called "unités phraseologiques" (Bally, 1951; vol. 1: 68), or "prefabs" (Bolinger, 1976: 238), constitute a distinctive feature of English. Some will even claim that these lexical co-occurrences should be given priority in the description of English (Sinclair, 2008), since statistical analysis has amply shown that language can be characterized in terms of both lexical and grammatical patterns (Fellbaum, 2007: 2; Ellis, 2008: 6; Granger, Meunier, 2008: 247), and, more specifically, that it offers the user "a large number of semi-preconstructed phrases that constitute single choices" – *idiom principle* (Sinclair, 1987: 319-320). Moreover, recent theories of language (Hoey, 2005: 4-5) claim that lexical units are stored in our mind together with their characteristic meanings, their collocational and colligational patterns, as well as their typical genre and register specifications – *lexical priming*. This psychological conception of collocations is also found in Bolinger (1976: 238, 1985: 69), Pawley and Syder (1983: 205), and Sinclair (1991: 110).

Hence, it is not surprising that nowadays, in EFL/ESL, more and more attention is being paid to this lexical phenomenon (Meunier, Granger, 2008). Similarly, much emphasis is laid on the need to promote *phraseological competence* in language acquisition (Siepmann, 2008: 185). As Granger and Meunier (2008: 249) suggest, echoing Sinclair (2008), "the centrality of the phrase in language" may well "lead to the centrality of the phrase in teaching". But a necessary prerequisite is that awareness of phraseology's significance should be raised, especially among non-native teachers (Granger, Meunier, 2008: 251).

At the same time, specialists insist that considerable support should be given to EFL/ESL students in this area "through appropriate instructional methodologies, materials, digital resources, and dictionaries" (Ellis, 2008: 9). In particular, as regards lexicographical coverage of collocations, specialists insist that phraseology should be recorded appropriately in dictionaries. For some authors, that means facilitating "a more objective and intuitive access to collocations" (Handl, 2008: 48), that is more explicit (Wible, 2008: 173), and more flexible and representative of the "full richness of the data" available (Fellbaum, 2007: 4).

In parallel with these demands, we are currently witnessing the rapid advance of electronic technologies which are paving the way for novel methods for corpus-driven lexicographical description. This entails, among other things, extensive use of vast corpora (as well as cutting-edge search software and lexical profiling tools) as well as the emergence and consolidation of digital dictionaries, accessible both online and on CD-ROM.

Accordingly, it is only natural for teachers, linguists, and lexicographers to consider how the electronic format can contribute to the description of language and, hence, to new language learning and teaching methodologies. In this sense, we fully subscribe to Granger and Meunier's views (2008: 247): "the phraseological revolution in language learning and teaching will be electronic or will simply not be".

Against this background, this article aims to review succinctly the lexicographical description of lexical collocations in five learner's dictionaries of English on CD-ROM. Differences and similarities between the digital and the printed format will be uncovered to establish to what extent these electronic works afford new, exclusive access routes to collocations. Evidence will also be gathered for an initial assessment of the five dictionaries as regards their treatment of this linguistic phenomenon.

This study ultimately belongs in the area of dictionary-using skills (Béjoint, 2000: 154; Hartmann, 2001: 30), which seek to raise an awareness of dictionary layout and content among teachers and students alike (Rizo-Rodríguez, 2004, 2008, 2009), and is inspired by a wide body of research into electronic dictionaries (Dodd, 1989; Nesi, 1996, 1999; Winkler, 2001; McAlpine, Myles, 2003; Oppentocht, Schutz, 2003, among others).

Dictionaries of English collocations proper (e.g. Kjellmer, 1994; Benson et al., 1997 [1986]; Crowther et al., 2002) fall outside the purview of this study.

2. Collocational specifications in MLDs on CD-ROM

Since collocation "is a pervasive, but, at the same time, elusive phenomenon in language" (Handl, 2008: 47), it is only logical that users should expect dictionaries to offer systematic, explicit, detailed collocational details about content words, and that lexicographers sometimes find it hard to live up to these expectations. Until now, studies of the lexicographical treatment of collocations have dealt almost exclusively with the printed dictionary (e.g. Cowie, 1981; Cop, 1988; Ivir, 1988; Benson, 1990; Bogaards, 1999; Mittmann, 1999; Siepmann, 2006, 2008; Moon, 2008; Handl, 2008). Our description will instead be focused on the electronic format. For that purpose, we will examine the latest editions of the major monolingual learner's dictionaries (MLDs) of English on CD-ROM:

- *Cambridge Advanced Learner's Dictionary*. 3rd edition. Elizabeth Walter and Kate Woodford (eds). Cambridge: Cambridge University Press, 2008. – CALD3;
- *Collins Cobuild Advanced Dictionary*. 6th edition. John Sinclair (founding editor-in-chief). Glasgow: Harper Collins Publishers. Boston: Heinle Cengage Learning, 2009. – COBUILD6;
- *Longman Dictionary of Contemporary English*. 5th edition. Chris Fox and Rosalind Combley (eds). Harlow: Pearson Education Limited, 2009. – LDOCE5;
- *Macmillan English Dictionary for Advanced Learners*. 2nd edition. Michael Rundell (ed.). Oxford: Macmillan, 2007. – MED2;
- *Oxford Advanced Learner's Dictionary*. 7th edition. Sally Wehmeier (ed.). Oxford: Oxford University Press, 2005. – OALD7.

The term "lexical collocation", borrowed from Benson et al. (1997 [1986]: xxx), is here understood, in accordance with a wide number of classic references, as a statistically-significant, conventional, restricted, arbitrary, idiosyncratic, non-idiomatic co-occurrence of two or more lexical items usually having compositional meaning (Halliday, 1961; Hausmann, 1979; Cowie, 1981; Sinclair, 1991; Fontenelle, 1994; Kjellmer, 1994; Corpas Pastor, 1996; Howarth, 1996; Handl, 2008). To examine the description of lexical collocations, we need to refer to the well-established distinction "base" and "collocatif" (Hausmann, 1979: 189), as well as to characteristic collocational patterns of content words: noun (base) + verb, verb + noun (base), adjective + noun (base), verb (base) + intensifying adverb, adjective (base) + intensifying adverb (Benson et al., 1997 [1986]: xxx-xxxiii). On close inspection, the description of these units in these electronic dictionaries relies on three main methods: varied indications in the entry text, extra elements specifically devoted to collocations, and access to these lexical co-occurrences by means exclusive to the lexicographical software (e.g. its *Advanced Search* function).

2. 1. Collocations in entry text

Close study of the microstructure of the five electronic dictionaries (EDs) reveals that the treatment of lexical collocations in their entries faithfully follows the policies found in the printed edition. The descriptive methods adopted include:

- addition in bold type of typical collocates of a head after its definition, and explicit illustration by means of example sentences:

  (MED2)
  Verdict. An official judgment made in a court.
  record a verdict: A verdict of accidental death was recorded.
  reach a verdict: The jury took 16 hours to reach a verdict.
  return/deliver a verdict: The jury returned a verdict of not guilty;

- bold type printing of collocations in example sentences:

  (OALD7)
  They **give advice** *for people with HIV and AIDS.* **Follow** *your doctor's* **advice.** *We were advised to* **seek** *legal* **advice**;

- allocation of collocates to distinct senses of a word:

  (LDOCE5)
  Favour. 1 Something that you do for someone […].
  Could you **do** *me* **a favour** *and tell Kelly I can't make it?*
  Paul, can I **ask** *you* **a favor** *?*
  I **owed** *him* **a favour** *so I couldn't say no.*
  Favour. 2 support, approval […]
  Find/gain/win favour
  In Sweden and other countries, nuclear power has **lost favor**;

- covert inclusion of collocations in definitions or in examples, i.e., no typographical means are used to point them out:

(COBUILD6)
Verdict. In a court of law, the **verdict** is the decision that is given by the jury or judge at the end of a trial.
The jury returned a unanimous guilty verdict...
Three judges will deliver their verdict in October.

Both the print edition and its digital counterpart are totally identical in this respect. However, the use of colour fonts and special layout attributes characteristic of entries in the EDs add to the readability and clarity of the collocational information provided on the CD-ROM.

As shown in *Table 1*, with the exception of the *Collins Cobuild Advanced Dictionary*, the dictionaries share significant similarities in the use of the descriptive techniques mentioned. They are usually rather explicit in the presentation of information, either by straightforwardly giving typical collocations, and even illustrating them, or marking them clearly in sample sentences. Likewise, phraseological combinations are even individually associated with specific meanings of polysemic headwords (e.g. *account, favour, defence*). Moreover, when compared with their previous editions (Rizo-Rodríguez, 2005), the microstructure of the works examined clearly contains a larger amount of collocational information.

All these features are indicative of the learner-driven, pedagogically-oriented text of these dictionaries. COBUILD6 is noticeably less attentive to the user's needs, as it only includes collocations in the definitions of headwords and in example sentences, without any explicit typographical means. This type of lexicographical practice requires a special linguistic competence on the part of the user, who has to play a more active role when identifying collocations in the entries.

	CALD3	COBUILD6	LDOCE5	MED2	OALD7
Inclusion of collocations in bold	-	-	+	+	-
Explicitly illustrated in example sentences	+	-	+	+	+
Collocations in bold in example sentences	+	-	+	-	+
Allocation to distinct senses of a word	+	-	+	+	+
Covert inclusion in definitions	-	+	-	-	-
Covert inclusion in example sentences	+	+	+	+	+

Table 1: Collocational information in entry text

If we take a closer look at the entries for content words in these EDs, we notice that the treatment of lexical collocations shows a number of shortcomings and limitations, at least from the standpoint of the conscientious learner. These drawbacks could be put down to an apparent lack of systematisation on the part of the lexicographer. For one thing, in every dictionary examined, sharp contrasts can be noticed between the rich details found in some entries and the patchy coverage in others. For example, compare the entries for *excursion* and *trip* in the same dictionary:

- (MED2)
  Excursion. "A short journey that you take for pleasure".
  My Saturday morning excursion into town.
  Excursion. "A short visit to an interesting place arranged by a tourist organization, often as part of a holiday".
  A one-day excursion to the Grand Canyon;

- (MED2)
  Trip. "An occasion when you go somewhere and come back again".
  a bus/train/boat trip: *The boat trip down the Amazon was great.*
  a business/fishing/shopping trip: *He's just returned from a fishing trip to Scotland.*
  a trip abroad/overseas: *My parents are planning their first trip abroad.*
  make/undertake a trip: *I make about 20 business trips a year.*
  go on/take a trip: *The whole family went on a trip to Florida.*
  a day trip: *a day trip to Paris.*

Moreover, these dictionaries do not seem to have adopted strict printing criteria to highlight collocates. Sometimes, collocates are not typed in bold in example sentences, and, even more misleadingly for the learner, some collocates are highlighted and others are not:

- (CALD3)
  Decrease.
  Our share of the market has decreased sharply this year.

- (CALD3)
  Increase.
  The cost of the project has increased **dramatically/significantly** *since it began.*

- (OALD7)
  Mortgage.
  to apply **for** / **take** *out* / *pay off a* **mortgage.** *Mortgage rates (= of interest). A mortgage on the house. A mortgage of £60 000. Monthly mortgage repayments.*

Another weakness identified in these EDs' entries (except in COBUILD6), is that they unsystematically mix up the various descriptive methods outlined above: the collocates of a word are sometimes explicitly included in its entry, while at times they are simply printed in bold in examples, or, for no apparent reason, they are just part of the example sentences without any special indication.

Finally, a controversial question: where are collocational details to be included, in the entries for the heads or in those for the collocates? According to semantically-based approaches to the study of collocations (Hausmann, 1979; Cowie, 1981; Cop, 1988; Benson et al., 1997 [1986]; Pérez-Fernández, 2003), the constituent elements of these lexical co-occurrences maintain a semantic relationship (Siepmann, 2005: 410, 417; Handl, 2008: 49-50): the head (or base) is usually conceived of as an autonomous element governing a specific collocate, which "ne réalise pleinement son signifié qu'en combinaison avec une base" (Hausmann, 1979: 192). This conception of collocations, also called "phraseological" (Moreno Jaén, 2009: 27), has obvious lexicographical repercussions: it is argued that collocates should be included in the entries for their heads (Benson, 1990; Fontenelle, 1994; Cowie, 1998: 18), if the collocational information is to serve encoding purposes (Bogaards, 1999: 126-127; Mittmann, 1999: 103). Heads (nouns, verbs, and adjectives) are highly instrumental units for productive tasks; as they favour arbitrary, idiosyncratic, non-idiomatic co-occurrences with certain collocates, the non-native user of English needs to refer to the entry for a head in order to learn about its collocational preferences and produce native-like utterances. In this area, MLDs are indispensable tools for the learner. Consider, for instance, the entries below, where a base is accompanied by its collocates:

- (CALD3)
  Judgment.
  to show **good**/**sound**/**poor** *judgment.*
  I don't think you have the right to **pass** *judgment (***on** *others)*
  I'm going to **reserve** *judgment (***on** *the decision) for the time being.*
  It proved difficult to **come to**/**form**/**make** *a judgment about how well the school was performing,*

- (MED2)
  Criticize.
  be strongly/**severely**/**widely**/**sharply**/**heavily criticized:** *Social services were widely criticized for not taking more action to protect children at risk.*

By contrast, in the receptive mode, collocations are usually unproblematic, since they normally have a compositional meaning and "the meaning of the whole is just the sum of the meaning of its parts" (Handl, 2008: 48). This may imply that collocational associations should preferably be placed in the entries for the heads. However, the five dictionaries examined very often include heads in the entries for their collocates, which may be of little use for production and, hence, unnecessarily space-consuming, as in the entry below, where heads like *attempt, idea, principles,* and *hope* are shown next to their collocate, *abandon.*

- (LDOCE5)
  Abandon.
  They **abandoned** *their* **attempt** *to recapture the castle.*
  Because of the fog they **abandoned** *their* **idea** *of driving.*
  They were accused of abandoning their socialist principles.
  Rescuers had **abandoned** *all* **hope** *of finding any more survivors.*

From a theoretical perspective, though, some authors claim that certain collocates (e.g. adjectives) have a higher "collocational factor", and are "collocationally stronger", than their heads (Handl, 2008: 61). This basically means that, unlike a particular head (which can be used with a wide range of words), its collocate characteristically, and almost exclusively, occurs with that head. This has also been explained in terms of "collocational direction" (Siepmann, 2006: 423) and "collocational attraction" (Handl, 2008: 61). For example, *heady* (collocate) is typically associated with a restricted number of nouns (heads), like *days, perfume, drink, combination,* or *atmosphere,* and 'attracts' them:

- (OALD7)
  Heady. "Having a strong effect on your senses".
  the heady days of youth. The heady scent of hot spices. A heady mixture of desire and fear;
- (LDOCE5)
  Heady.
  a heady combination of wine and brandy
  the heady atmosphere of the early sixties.

Admittedly, this is a sound argument in favour of displaying heads in the entries for their collocates in these cases but, in many other instances, when a collocate is not stronger than its head (as shown in the entry for *abandon* above), this type of lexicographical practice may be unjustified and rather ineffective.

2. 2. Collocations displayed in extra sections

A second device in these EDs for the description of collocations is the addition of extra sections or components specially designed to represent collocational details clearly and thus broaden the sometimes patchy information available in the entry text. Every dictionary examined, except OALD7 (which is the oldest), makes use of this type of device.

Mention must first be made of the *Collocations* boxes appended to many entries in LDOCE5, supplementing the description by bringing together a headword's most common collocations. These boxes are particularly useful as they group collocates grammatically (verbs, adjectives, and adverbs) and illustrate them appropriately. Although the print edition of LDOCE5 also contains *Collocations* boxes, they are often less detailed; moreover, not every entry featuring a *Collocations* box in the ED includes it in the printed version (e.g. the entry for *petition*). This is logical, given the large storage capacity of the DVD-ROM format exclusive to this dictionary (the other four came out on CD-ROM). This straightforward manner of presenting collocational details in boxes added to entries (only found in LDOCE6 on DVD-ROM) contrasts with the so-called "layered" type of presentation (a distinctive feature of electronic dictionaries), which enables users to retrieve at their discretion further details about a headword not supplied directly in the text of its *Definition* window (Tono, 2000: 856; Rizo-Rodríguez, 2008: 24).

Four electronic dictionaries – CALD3, COBUILD6, LDOCE5, and MED2 – have adopted this method of providing extra information on collocations. Thus, some entries contain a tab (an on-screen button labelled *collocations* in CALD3 and MED2, or *word partnership* in COBUILD6) which can be clicked to activate a pop-up window which displays a headword's common collocations. Interestingly, these tabs in CALD3 and

MED2 are associated with certain senses of a given word. An additional feature of this pop-up window in MED2 is that the EFL teacher can copy and print its content or, in CALD3, simply have it printed in order to use it, for example, in the classroom.

In MED2, a total of 506 lexical words contain a *collocations tab* (in the dictionary's *Extra Feature Search* utility). Their pop-up window (an exact replica, in its content, of its printed counterpart) offers common collocations which are not exemplified (see *Figure 1*). Many entries are devoted to nouns (e.g. *array, control, criticism*), accompanied by adjective collocates or verbs. Despite being a great help for encoding purposes, the treatment is inconsistent: adjective collocates are given for some nouns and verb collocates for others. Ideally, both types should be shown for every noun, as in the case of *advice* or *impact*. Pop-up windows for adjectives (cf. *essential, important*) may include characteristic nouns co-occurring with them, which is of little use for productive tasks, or adverbs modifying them (cf. *rich*), while those for verbs (e.g. *arise, dismiss*) offer common nouns used with them (again only effective for decoding purposes) and, sometimes, intensifying adverbs as well (e.g. *weaken*). Finally, there are some entries for adverbs (e.g. *highly, seriously*), which include adjectives occurring with them which do not help users in encoding tasks. All valuable information that could be enhanced by making it more systematic and consistent.

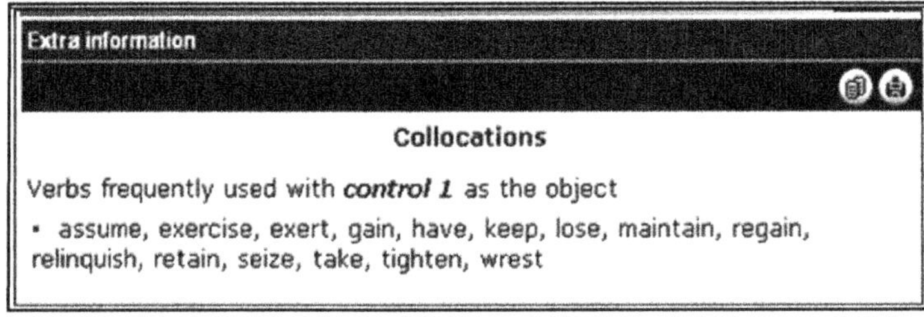

Figure 1: Sample Collocations window in MED2

Word Partnership boxes in COBUILD6 (identical in content to the equivalent box in the printed version) offer a meagre number of collocates and no exemplification. Collocates are grouped grammatically and associated to specific senses of a headword.

CALD3 is more exhaustive than COBUILD6 and MED2: it includes examples and gives a higher number of a word's collocates in its *Collocations* pop-up windows (cf., e.g., the entries for *challenge*, or *change*). Regrettably, the complete list of entries including information on collocations is not available. The information in the *Collocations* boxes in the printed version (called *Word partners*) is considerably shorter: the ED gives more collocates – e.g. for *adventure, advantage* –, classifies them grammatically, and illustrates them.

LDOCE5 features a small *Collocations* window in the top right-hand corner of its interface giving access to three links: collocations from the entry being looked up (reproducing the content of the *Collocations* box mentioned above – see *Figure 2*), from other dictionary entries, and from the *Longman Corpus Network*. This type of hyperlink access is exclusive to the digital format and helps the user navigate "across and within entries via a choice of links" (Winkler, 2001: 3). This is a unique feature of this dictionary.

Practically every content word in the A-Z list is provided with an active link in the small *Collocations* window, even those not containing a *Collocations* box in the entries as well as extensive illustrative material for each collocation. Here the electronic format shows its real potential and exposes the limitations of the printed format. Additionally, the *Phrase Bank* window in LDOCE5 displays common phrases in which a word is found. This window also includes collocates of a search term (the distinction *phrase – collocation* is not clearly established in the EDs examined). All things considered, the description provided in this dictionary proves more exhaustive than in the rest of the EDs surveyed (see *Table 2*).

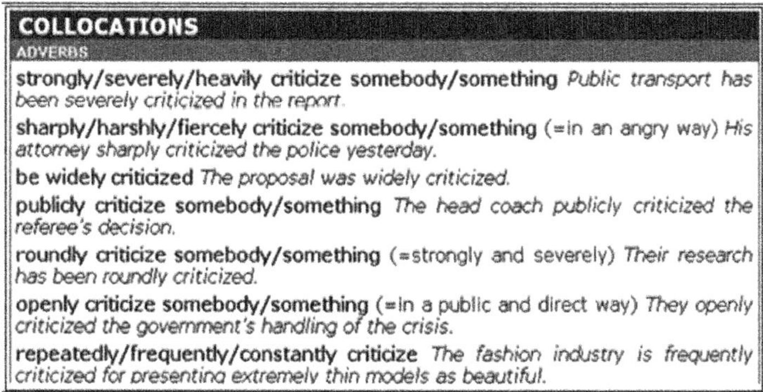

Figure 2: Sample Collocations window in LDOCE5

All these extra windows clearly enhance the description, despite some limitations. For example, why are *Collocations* boxes appended just to a particular nuance or sense of a word (not to every sense)? Similarly, no reason is given as to why certain entries for nouns, adjectives, verbs, adverbs include collocations tabs and others do not. Why *seriously* and not *severely*? Why *abandon* and not *rain*, in MED2, for instance? Probably because of the close dependence still existing between these EDs and their printed counterparts: for reasons of space, the printed version cannot devote more attention to this area, and the electronic edition simply reproduces its limitations. Thus, the *Collocations* windows in COBUILD6 and MED2 are identical to those in their printed versions. Fortunately, those in CALD3 considerably expand on the content of their printed counterparts, and LDOCE5 clearly surpasses its printed version with its phrase bank and its links to collocations from other dictionary entries, and from the *Longman Corpus Network*.

Another shortcoming is that the dictionary user sometimes finds it difficult to locate the collocational information, since very often collocates are given in the entry for their heads but sometimes heads are included in the entry for their collocates. These divergences, also noticeable in the types of units described as collocations, are probably a consequence of the current multiplicity of conceptions of this linguistic phenomenon – textual, statistical, psychological, semantic, and pragmatic (Hoey, 2005: 3-4; Siepmann, 2005: 410-11; Siepmann, 2008: 186-7) – and may well lead to "insufficient lexicographical treatment", as Fellbaum (2007: 2) suggests.

	CALD3	COBUILD6	LDOCE5	MED2	OALD7
Collocations boxes appended to some entries	-	-	+	-	-
Layered presentation in pop-up windows	+	+	+	+	-
Collocations illustrated in these windows	+	-	+	-	-
Collocations links for every content word	-	-	+	-	-
Phrase bank	-	-	+	-	-

Table 2: Collocational information in extra sections

2. 3. Access to collocations by means exclusive to lexicographical software

Like the conscientious learner, the non-native EFL teacher's effective and full use of a pedagogical dictionary with its potentially rich source of collocational details depends on the availability of various specifically-designed search options available only with software. EDs need to be designed to enable users to consult all the data in through flexible access routes (Dodd, 1989: 87-88; Nesi, 1996: 545; McAlpine, Myles, 2003: 75; Oppentocht, Schutz, 2003: 218-219). Traditional look-up methods, largely shaped by the rigid A-Z macrostructure of the printed book, have important limitations in this respect. After putting the five EDs to the test, some were found to have specific search options allowing the user to obtain collocational information in ways that differ from conventional consultations of a specific entry. Some queries require considerable linguistic command on the user's part to identify collocations, since they may not be marked as such, which is why Wible (2008: 173) considers EDs to be passive reference tools; they may not help the learner who is unaware of the fixed, collocational nature of a given lexical co-occurrence. By contrast, other search methods provide the inquisitive dictionary user with explicit collocational information quite straightforwardly. In both cases the search software demands an active role from the user. The essentials of these search mechanisms need to be summarised.

First, the *Word Search* function may directly supply collocates of a given headword typed in an ED's *Search* window. This is the simplest way of consulting an electronic dictionary and, surprisingly, it may sometimes return a reasonable number of collocational hits. For example, the search term *memory* in OALD7 produces a good list of collocations, including *photographic memory, virtual memory, hazy memory, poignant memory, be engraved/etched in/on your memory, erase the memory, refresh your memory,* etc. The EDs reviewed (except COBUILD6) produce a fair number of results, depending to varying degrees on the word consulted (sometimes only a few collocates are given). OALD7 and, curiously enough, the CD-ROM accompanying the first edition of the *Macmillan English Dictionary* (2002), stand out in this respect from the rest. For example, a search for the substantive *verdict* in MED1 gives the following search results: *open verdict, bring in a verdict, return a verdict, a majority verdict, record a verdict, reach a verdict, deliver a verdict.* By contrast, the *Word Search* function in MED2 only produces two collocations: *open verdict* and *return a verdict.* On the negative side, it must be noted that very often, the hits obtained are not explicitly presented as collocations, but are simply listed alongside other search results (as in LDOCE5), printed in a different colour (as in CALD3) or type (MED2), mixed up with idiomatic expressions (as in CALD3, MED2, and OALD7), or even misleadingly called *structures* in OALD7. Needless to say, this practice is not learner-driven; hence Wible's views (quoted above).

Second, these EDs (except COBUILD6) incorporate an *Advanced Search* option thereby surpassing what the most painstaking printed dictionary user can find. This is one of the clearest indications of EDs' potential as language learning/teaching tools. Complex lexical searches can be conducted in the entire dictionary (headwords, phrasal verbs, phrases, idioms, definitions, and examples) with the help of an elaborate system of filters, as well as wildcards (the symbols ? and *), and Boolean operators (AND, OR, BUT). This is a very powerful, effective type of tool in the hands of EFL teachers needing supplementary classroom materials (Rizo-Rodríguez, 2008: 29-30) which, when applied to searches for collocations, lends itself to various uses:

- users can type a given term (for example, a verb) in the advanced *Search* box and add a Boolean operator and a wildcard e.g. in front of *-ly* thus gaining instant access to every entry included in that search string. For example, by keying in *criticize* AND **ly*, a total of 10 matches are returned in CALD3, and 68 in MED2, including typical examples of this verb in its joint use with characteristic intensifier collocates as they occur in entries like *assail, attack, bash, castigate, denounce,* etc; thus, fixed combinations like *strongly / severely / publicly criticize* can be found in the definition text of these entries or in the example sentences; all the EDs, except COBUILD6, can be used in this way;
- this also works well with adjectives or past participles: e.g the string **ly* AND *shocked* can be typed in order to get the adverb collocates of this participle;
- a noun's adjective or verb collocates can be obtained with MED1, by keying in * noun in the basic *Word Search* function, which produces adjective or verb collocates of the noun, provided *collocations* has been selected in *Search Options*; for example, the search * *damage* produces a good number of adjectival collocates and also some verbal ones (e.g. *serious, severe, extensive, cause, do, suffer,* etc.); this type of search is only possible with MED1 and OALD7;
- searches of the type * *adjective* or * *verb* can be made if the user wants to confirm the adverb collocates of adjectives or verbs; for example, the searches * *important* or * *reduce* yield various intensifier collocates of these words (e.g. *critically, vitally important; greatly, significantly reduce*); in this function, the MED1 and OALD7 software is a clear improvement over the other EDs examined, which do not support this type of search;
- by keying in the string *-*ly* in MED1, a total of 578 collocational hits involving *-ly* adverbs combined with verbs, adjectives and past participles is obtained; interestingly, the same search string does not produce any result in MED2 or in the other EDs.

Third, further collocational details can be retrieved by conducting *searches in the text of all the example sentences* in the dictionary (see *Table 3*). This can be done by using the *Advanced Search* option mentioned above. For example, if we key in a noun (e.g. *control*) and launch a search for this term in the entire set of example sentences in the dictionary, many example sentences are automatically returned where advanced users will usually find collocations (see *Figure 3*), even though they are not marked as such. This can be done in MED2 and OALD7. In CALD3 and LDOCE5, by contrast, an advanced search for a given term does not return a list of all the example sentences where it can be found; instead, it retrieves all the entries including an example sentence where the search term occurs. The process is thus less straightforward but is based on the frequent inclusion of collocates in example sentences; little or no collocational evidence will be obtained for words poorly exemplified (e.g. *limitation* in OALD7) or whose example sentences only illustrate grammatical patterns (e.g. *accept* in MED2).

	CALD3	COBUILD6	LDOCE5	MED2	OALD7
Word Search function	+	-	+	+	+
Advanced Search function	+	-	+	+	+
Example Sentence search	+	-	+	+	+
Extra Example exploration	+	-	+	-	-

Table 3: Access to collocations by means exclusive to lexicographical software

Finally, the advanced learner and the non-native EFL teacher may refer directly to a *repository of extra illustrative examples* available on the CD-ROMs of CALD3 and LDOCE5 and thus obtain examples of the lexical collocations of a particular word. As in the previous case, detecting these lexical co-occurrences depends on the user's linguistic competence and is subject to the limitations of the example sentences themselves (commented on above). In this respect, the *Extra Examples* window in CALD3 offers only a discreet amount of illustrative material, while LDOCE5's *Example Bank* is more generous. However, both are surpassed by the plentiful linguistic evidence supplied by the *Wordbank* included in the fifth edition of the *Collins Cobuild Advanced Learner's English Dictionary* CD-ROM (2006), a five-million word corpus. Curiously, its sixth edition (2009) does not incorporate it.

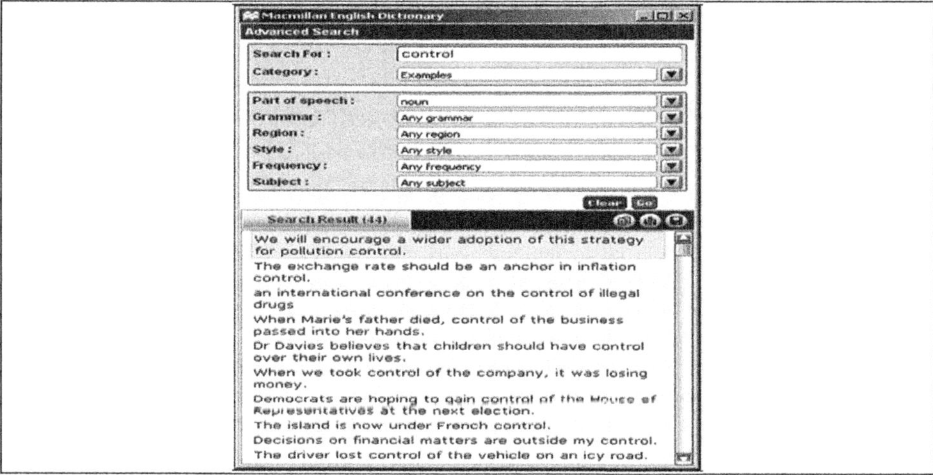

Figure 3: Example sentence search in MED2

3. Conclusions

The treatment of lexical collocations in learner's dictionaries of English on CD-ROM leads to various conclusions. First, the text of the latest of all five EDs examined still bears many similarities to their printed counterparts. In particular, the description of lexical collocations in the microstructure is identical in both formats (see *2.1.*); considerable attention is paid in the entries to lexical collocations by explicitly providing them, illustrating them in example sentences, and employing specific typographical devices to this end. However, a number of shortcomings have also been identified; practically all the EDs show inconsistent coverage, unequal distribution of information, irregular printing policies, and unsystematic arrangement of collocational details.

Hence, original contributions to the description of this area on the part of MLDs on CD-ROM must be sought elsewhere (see *2.2.*). More specifically, our study reveals that these EDs (except OALD7) make use of a layered type of presentation (by means of tabs) which facilitates customized access to extra information on collocations. Even more significant is the fact that some of these digital references (CALD3 and LDOCE5) have employed their large storage capacity to design collocation boxes which are more informative than those of their printed counterparts; they even display links to collocations in the dictionary's entire text and (in the case of LDOCE5) a large corpus. EDs definitely surpass the book format and cater for many of the user's look-up needs rather successfully.

What makes these electronic tools stand out is their powerful search functions (see *2.3.*). Their software enables a good number of exclusive complex searches for collocations not possible with the printed version. Obviously, it is in this third area that both the committed EFL teacher and the conscientious user will find new access routes to lexical collocations covering the entire dictionary. Thus, the electronic learner's dictionary, unlike its printed counterpart, characteristically fixed and static (Dodd, 1989: 87), is more dynamic and lends itself to new customized uses which enable the user to interact with its rich text and deploy the various search capabilities according to his/her needs (Rizo-Rodríguez, 2008: 34). This obviously demands dedication and linguistic proficiency on the part of the advanced user; casual browsing (or navigation, in this case) is not enough.

Finally, differences in the EDs' treatment of lexical collocations have been highlighted. *Table 1* shows that, of the five works, COBUILD6 is clearly the least attentive to learners' needs in the coverage of lexical collocations in the entries; the other four are more explicit and informative and, hence, more pedagogically oriented. As regards the inclusion of *extras* devoted to collocations (*Table 2*), LDOCE5 clearly stands out from the rest with its detailed *Collocations* boxes appended to entries, its layered presentation and, above all, its collocation links for practically every content word. By contrast, OALD7 contains no such feature, while CALD3 and MED2's *Collocations* windows are more informative than COBUILD6's. The search capabilities of these dictionaries when retrieving collocations are thus far from homogeneous (*Table 3*). While OALD7's *Word Search* and *Advanced Search* functions give fairly satisfactory results, COBUILD6 simply lacks this feature, and MED2, LDOCE5 and CALD3 are slightly less functional in this respect than OALD7. A curious finding in this respect is that the software developed for the first edition of the *Macmillan English Dictionary* is definitely more appropriate than the second.

All things considered, these CD-ROMs provide the EFL teacher and the advanced student with a wide number of exclusive access routes to lexical collocations. Hopefully, specialists will continue streamlining lexicographical software so that forthcoming editions of electronic learner's dictionaries will offer new, more flexible paths to these word combinations. This may eventually lead, in the not too distant future, to novel electronic dictionaries designed in a manner totally independent of the printed dictionary.

Acknowledgements

Research leading to this article was sponsored by the Spanish Ministry of Science and Innovation under R&D contract HUM2007-61766/FILO entitled "ADELEX: Assessing and Developing Lexis through New Technologies". The author formally acknowledges the use of sample entries and screenshots from the dictionaries on CD-ROM examined for the purposes of criticism and review.

Section II:

Applying New Corpus-based Evidence in Language Pedagogy

Introduction to Section II:
Applying New Corpus-based Evidence in Language Pedagogy

María Calzada Pérez, University Jaume I, Spain

The five chapters that make up this section explore corpus data as they apply in the L2 classroom. They spring from the age-old concern of ensuring that new data, and the new ways of looking at data thrown up by research, can be successfully passed on into the teaching system. There is obviously a danger that this process will come unstuck through bad implementation, often unfairly discrediting the research itself. The concern for quality assurance explored in *Section I* in relation to corpora functioning as validity-testing tools for coursebooks and learner's dictionaries, thus comes to be applied in *Section II* to corpus studies itself, as applied in the L2 classroom. *Section II* thus constitutes, as it were, and in its own special way, a L2 classroom survival kit for corpus studies.

Chapter 9 opens the proceedings with its ruthless investigation of DDL (data-driven learning) projects. It dissects 27 DDL studies and assesses the learning outcomes described in each in relation to general background (countries, languages, learners, corpora and software) and specific background (details of participants, duration, language focus, study design and research tools). Based, as it is, on a 'corpus' of DDL projects, Chapter 9 provides readers with a cautionary but generally optimistic framework for assessing DDL's overall classroom viability. With DDL, as with many other kinds of applied research, there is room for improvement but the fact that DDL studies keep 'marching on' is an encouraging sign.

Chapter 10 focuses on the issue of academic writing in French by English speakers, and specifically the writing of introductions to economic papers; in so doing, it explores the hypothesis that a study of certain items, based on concordances from a corpus of one-million words of academic writing in French (Chambers, Le Baron, 2007), will enhance the text-based study of the various features of article introduction. After an overview, which points out potential dangers when using corpora to teach writing, Chapter 10 focuses on how better results can be achieved, for example with students who produce original or translated economic texts, by blending qualitative aspects, such as reflection on the CARS model proposed by Swales (1990), with the quantitative aspects arising from corpus data.

Corpus-based data can also focus on *specific* lexicogrammatical features, as Chapter 11 shows with its examination of adverbs in English. However, if teachers *do* undertake such a task, they will be well advised to base it on a careful comparison of native and non-native discourse produced *in exactly the same circumstances*. Thus, Chapter 11 compares the production of adverbs by native and non-native speakers of English in an experiment that uses the same visual prompts to elicit data. The lexical incompetence often ascribed to EFL students thus needs to be seen against the actual use made by native speakers when performing the very same task, a matter which reserves a few surprises. Chapter 11, with its often witty style, thus demonstrates how important it is to ask searching questions about expected and unexpected native and non-native speaker patterns, which can only be answered when a carefully-controlled experiment has been implemented.

Chapter 12 deals with the Internet and with the capacity of corpus studies, through *web-as-multimodal-corpus* concordancing, to adapt to the needs of the direct Internet exploration of phraseology in the L2 classroom. It describes the *MWS* tool which has been designed to provide insights into the way Internet texts and genres work. *Web-as-multimodal-corpus* concordancing is, in fact, a newcomer which puts together two rising stars in corpus studies: web-as-corpus concordancing and multimodal corpus linguistics. The cornerstone of the former is the belief that the Internet, the ultimate corpus, is, pedagogically speaking, an as yet untapped opportunity for L2 learning. The latter, instead, holds that language is only one of the resources deployed in the much larger semiotic system through which society makes its meanings. Chapter 12 thus takes, as its starting point, the dual assumption that the use of linguistic resources in the web is determined and shaped by the presence of visual and spatial resources with which it interacts and that their combinations produce hierarchically-arranged *web units* and *web events* which make meaning through mutual co-contextualisations across different scalar levels, thereby generating patterns, including patterns of evolution over time, that *MWS* can (in part) detect. However, conscious of the learning curve that this involves, the *MWS* tool functions in a layered way that allows both simple web searching for beginners and more advanced web searching for expert users. Even so, its touch-of-a-button production of data-comparing charts and tables simplifies the transition from the simplest forms of web concordancing to more complex ones.

Chapter 13 takes yet another stance on the viability of corpora in the L2 classroom, this time in relation to L2 teachers' demands that corpora should support the exploration of ideological and cultural issues. It thus gives a detailed account of the OBAHIL corpus which consists of two sub-corpora, the OBAMA subcorpus and the HILARY subcorpus. In so doing, it illustrates these politicians' skilful use of lexicogrammatical items such as *It's (high/about) time*. These gifted orators produce a powerful model of discourse in English from which learners can profit. The chapter thus tackles the issue of ideology and its introduction into the L2 classroom via corpus-based methodology linked to the exploration of lexicogrammar, and in particular, the rhetorical devices that Clinton and Obama actually use. The corpus is a small one, compiled from the speeches they made during the 2008 nomination campaign and represents a step forward in the study of individual styles in the language classroom. As well as comparing the speeches' similarities and differences, the chapter also compares the effectiveness of the many software tools that allow these rhetorical devices to be characterised in terms of their incidence and functions in discourse. Thanks to the ample range of data patterns and statistics thus acquired, the chapter also investigates issues of corpus selection and compilation with reference to the value of large and small corpora within the area of corpus-based studies.

Learning outcomes from corpus consultation

Alex Boulton, CRAPEL–ATILF/CNRS, Nancy University, France

1. Introduction

Large corpora have been hailed as a veritable "revolution" in kuhnian terms for the field of language teaching (e.g. McCarthy, 2008b: 564), certainly insofar as they have influenced syllabus design, testing, and even materials. However, the effects may remain largely invisible downstream to teachers and learners, especially if they remain passive consumers of upstream work. Certainly, as Carter (1998: 64) pointed out a decade ago, there is no necessary reason why corpus description (*what* to teach) should translate into classroom practice (*how* to teach). However, it is possible for learners to explore corpora themselves, either directly via a concordancer, or mediated by other software or materials, in what has come to be known as Data-Driven Learning or DDL (Johns, 1990). DDL represents a fairly "radical" approach (Johns, 1988: 20-22), and remains generally confined to the university research environment despite efforts by many researchers to undertake a "corpus mission" (Römer, 2009: 92) to introduce DDL to a wider teaching community.

One frequently-cited problem could be the type of information available: in particular, there is very little in the way of 'off-the-peg' materials, or indeed any texts geared towards end-users, teachers and learners alike (see, for example, Boulton, 2010 in press). Furthermore, there may be literally hundreds of academic papers discussing applications of corpora in language learning and teaching, but, it is routinely alleged, very few that attempt any empirical evaluation of the approach. It is commonplace for articles in many disciplines to call for more empirical research, but this seems to be particularly the case for DDL. Among many others, one could cite Johansson (2009: 42) who has recently insisted that:

> Corpora [...] should not be used in language teaching just because we now have this wonderful tool and would like to apply it in language teaching as well. Their use is vindicated to the extent that it agrees with what we know about language and language acquisition, *and can be shown to be an effective learning tool.* [emphasis added]

Yet he goes on to lament the lack of "systematic studies testing the benefits of the approach" and calls for more "controlled experiments" (Johansson, 2009: 41). Corpus linguistics is an inherently empirical discipline, and a lack of empirical research in applying it to language learning would at best be ironic – and at worst might suggest that researchers have deliberately avoided the issue, or abstained from publishing negative findings. A lack of a solid empirical support base would thus undermine the arguments for DDL, leaving us with little more than rhetoric and ex cathedra pronouncements along the lines of *it seems… * or *it is obvious…*

A survey of empirical research in DDL published to date therefore seems appropriate. This is not a light undertaking, even as regards collecting relevant papers, as DDL itself lacks a single, watertight definition, leading to multiple interpretations (Boulton, in press). For present purposes, a broad interpretation is chosen to ensure maximum coverage, and DDL is therefore taken to refer to any use of overt corpus data for foreign or second language (L2) learning or teaching, whether the researchers claim it as DDL or not. As the focus is on empirical research, papers are included only insofar as they subject some aspect of DDL to observation or experimentation with some kind of externally validated evaluation other than the researchers' own intuition. Given these broad criteria, a search of the literature has so far brought to light at least 70 separate studies published to date in English alone.[1]

Perusing these papers, the variety of research questions becomes apparent, but they fall into a number of broad categories (some with multiple objectives into two or more at once). Firstly, there are those that attempt to test whether learners are capable of corpus investigation, and look at their behaviour using DDL. The evaluations tend to be qualitative in the main, analysing learners' productions (especially written or oral project reports) and their representations, and use instruments ranging from teacher observation to class discussion, interviews, logbooks, diary grids, and other forms of self-report protocols. The results of such studies are hugely valuable, showing the multitude of different ways corpora may be introduced successfully to the language classroom.

Secondly, a large number of papers evaluate learners' affective reactions to corpus use. Many of the same self-report instruments are used, though the most common here is the questionnaire, asking learners whether they found the activities easy, useful, enjoyable; whether they think they learned anything from them; and whether they intend to use corpora again in the future. The results are overwhelmingly favourable, the vast majority of studies finding learners (and teachers) responding positively to the approach, with very rare exceptions (e.g. Whistle, 1999). The participants' reactions are certainly very important and have to be taken into account, though of course their subjective appreciations of their own learning may not be reflected in actual learning.

A third group of studies looks at specific outcomes of corpus use, though they further divide into two distinct categories. The first examines outcomes of using corpora as a reference tool, usually for writing, error-correction, or translation. These studies do provide objective, quantitative data from a variety of tests and evaluations of written performance, with highly encouraging results — indeed, it may turn out that the main advantage of corpora for language learners is as a reference resource. However, the main focus of this paper is on learning outcomes, a question not addressed directly in the majority of these studies: while some learning probably does result from using a corpus as a reference (just as one may learn something from consulting a dictionary), this is a separate issue requiring separate analysis.

Chambers (2007) has already provided a survey of empirical studies in DDL, but the present paper adds to this in two ways. Firstly, the 12 papers in her survey included evaluations of learners' behaviour and representations, as well as use of corpora as a reference resource. These studies provide rich insights, but are included here only insofar as they also report on learning outcomes, thus specifically addressing the key questions of whether DDL works and how effective it is. Secondly, Chambers noted that the majority were small-scale, qualitative studies, and that it is "worth asking why there are not more large-scale quantitative studies" (2007: 5). Again, without denigrating the relevance of small-scale, qualitative studies, focusing on measurable outcomes should allow more specific insight into the effectiveness of DDL in different contexts.

The present paper thus represents a survey of 27 empirical studies of DDL which focus on L2 learning outcomes, a surprising amount given the repeated lament of a lack of such research – and there are no doubt more, especially published in languages other than English which are not included in the present survey. The disadvantage of such a large number is that the discussion of individual studies will inevitably be fairly succinct. To help, *Table 1* provides some basic information on the studies: the paper(s) reporting each study; the country where it was conducted, along with the mother tongue (L1) of the majority of participants; the target language; the type of institution where it was conducted, as well as the major field of study of most participants; their level, from low to advanced, passing through (lower or upper) intermediate where the information can be derived; the number of learners involved (including any control group, indicated separately); the duration of the study in hours, weeks or semesters; whether the participants used a hands-on concordancer, software including corpus data, or paper-based materials; the main research tools (including use of control items or populations); and whether some kind of statistical analysis is provided, or merely raw figures and percentages.

Section 2 describes the background context to the studies as a whole, along with research questions and design; *Section 3* briefly summarises the learning outcomes of individual studies, and examines issues of statistical significance. Finally, *Section 4* attempts to synthesise the findings to date and put them into some kind of perspective; the conclusion outlines areas for future empirical research.

2. Background

This section introduces the background to the studies – firstly the general context (countries, languages, learners, corpora and software), followed by the context specific to the research itself (participants, duration, language focus, study design and research instruments).

study	country (L1)	L2	context	level	learners	time	interface	test design/ tools	Q
Gan et al., 1996	Malaysia (Malay)	English	teacher-training (L2)	adv	48	10 wks (20h)		pre+post test, control items	stat
Cobb, 1997a, 1997b, 1999	Oman (Arabic)	English	uni (business)	low	11	1 year		pre+post test + delayed, control pop	stat
Ciesielska-Ciupek, 2001	Poland (Polish)	English	high school	low	33	?		post test + delayed	raw nos.
Cobb, Horst, 2001; Horst et al., 2001	Canada (mixed)	English	uni (mixed)	int	33	12 wks		post test, control items	stat
Cobb et al., 2001	Canada (English)	French	? (?)	int	1	14h		pre+post test	raw nos.
Curado Fuentes, 2002, 2003	Spain (Spanish)	English	uni (business)	int	20 (c=10)	2 wks		post test, control pop	raw nos.
Lee, Liou, 2003	Taiwan (Chinese)	English	high school	int ?	46	10 wks (8h)		pre+post test	stat
Sun, Wang, 2003	Taiwan (Chinese)	English	high school	int ?	81 (c=40)	1h40		pre+post test, control pop	stat
Chan, Liou, 2005	Taiwan (Chinese)	English	uni (mixed)	int ?	32	5 wks (5h)		post test + delayed, control items	stat
Kaur, Hegelheimer, 2005	USA (mixed)	English	uni (?)	int	18 (c=9?)	4 wks?		post test, control pop	stat
Tian, 2005a, 2005b	Taiwan (Chinese)	English	uni (mixed)	int +	98 (c=48)	5 wks (10h)		pre+post test, control pop	stat
Allan, 2006	Ireland (mixed)	English	lang centre (mixed)	adv	18 (c=5)	12 wks		post test, control pop	stat
Koosha, Jafarpour, 2006	Iran (Farsi?)	English	uni (L2)	adv	200 (c=100)	1 sem		pre+post test, control pop	stat
Liou et al., 2006	Taiwan (Chinese)	English	uni (?)	adv ?	varied	variable		post test + delayed	stat
Braun, 2007	Germany (German)	English	high school	int ?	25 (c=13)	4 wks (16h)		post test, control pop	stat
Cresswell, 2007	Italy (Italian)	English	uni (translat)	adv	126 (c=65)	1 sem?		post test, control pop	stat
Curado Fuentes, 2007	Spain (Spanish)	English	uni (tourism)	int +	20 (c=10)	5h		post test, control pop	stat

study	country (L1)	L2	context	level	learners	time	interface	test design/ tools	Q
Estling Vannestål, Lindquist, 2007	Sweden (Swedish)	English	uni (teachers; admin)	adv	a) 37 (c=23); b) 35	1 sem each	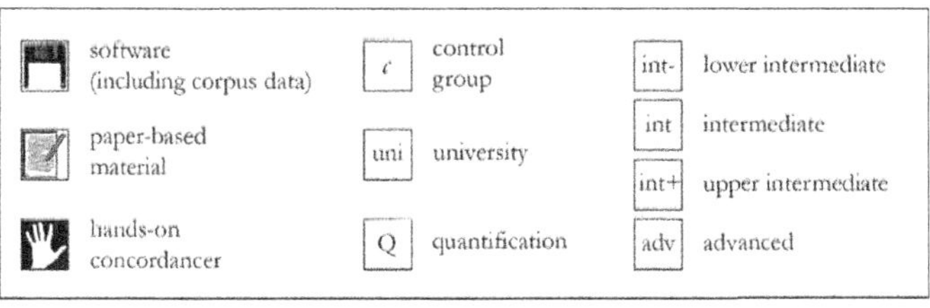	pre+post test, control pop	raw nos.
Huang, Liou, 2007	Taiwan (Chinese)	English	uni (L2?)	int	38	12 wks (out of class)		pre+post test	stat
Yeh et al., 2007	Taiwan (Chinese)	English	uni (L2)	int +	19	4 wks (1h20)		post test + delayed	stat
Belz, Vyatkina, 2005a, 2005b, 2008	USA (English)	German	uni (?)	adv	2	8 wks (4h)		pre+post test	raw nos.
Boulton, 2008, 2010	France (French)	English	uni (architect)	int -	62	1h		pre+post test, control items	stat
Johns et al., 2008	Taiwan (Chinese)	English	high school	int ?	22 (c=11)	16 wks (48h)		post test, control pop	stat
Lin, 2008	Taiwan (Chinese)	English	uni (L2)	adv	25	8 wks (13h20)		pre+post test + delayed	stat
Smith et al., 2008	Taiwan (?)	Chinese	internet volunteers (?)	int ?	25 (2 post tests)	6 wks		pre+post test	raw nos.
Boulton, 2009a	France (French)	English	uni (engineer)	int -	132 (c=64)	30 mins		post test, control pop	stat
Boulton, 2009b	France (French)	English	uni (architect)	int -	59 (c=25)	12 wks (3h)		post test + delayed, control pop	stat

Table 1: Overview of studies

Key to *Table 1*:

	software (including corpus data)	c	control group	int-	lower intermediate
	paper-based material	uni	university	int	intermediate
				int+	upper intermediate
	hands-on concordancer	Q	quantification	adv	advanced

2. 1. General context

Though DDL first appeared as a term in this sense in 1990 in a paper by Tim Johns, he had discussed applications of corpora in language teaching and learning as far back as 1984 in a book co-authored with John Higgins; Sandra McKay had independently published a paper on such uses of corpora as early as 1980; and McEnery and Wilson (1997: 12) attribute the first applications of corpora to language teaching to Peter Roe at Aston University in 1969. It is perhaps surprising then that the first empirical study of learning outcomes did not appear until 1996. Since then, at least 27 studies have appeared in various sources, over two thirds of them (19) in the last five years. Some have been the subject of more than one paper, totalling 35 separate publications. Of these, 23 have been in journals (notably six in *Computer Assisted Language Learning* and four in *ReCALL*), and nine in publications arising from conferences, whether proceedings or selected papers. Although Cobb (1997a) devoted his doctoral thesis to DDL research, and a number of books on corpus used in L2 involve some discussion of DDL (e.g. Hunston, 2002; O'Keeffe et al., 2007), there has as yet been no book-length treatment of DDL itself, much less with detailed empirical analysis.

Asia seems to be a particularly fertile ground for empirical DDL research, with 10 of the 27 studies conducted in Taiwan alone (plus one each in Malaysia, Iran and Oman); a further 10 studies were produced in European countries (three in France, two in Spain, one each in Germany, Ireland, Italy, Poland and Sweden); the remainder were in North America (two each in Canada and the USA). This suggests that learners of many different linguistic and cultural backgrounds can make use of corpora, and also that there is substantial interest in DDL in Asia and Europe in particular, although there are of course other studies exploring various uses of corpora in language teaching and learning in other parts of the world. In 23 cases, the majority of the learners spoke the local language as their L1; the other four involved speakers from mixed L1 backgrounds. It is likely that this reflects the reality of much language teaching, with learners mainly in their home environment tackling foreign rather than second languages. The target language was also fairly uniform, with 24 studies focusing on English; the remainder concerned Chinese, French and German. The dominance of English comes as no surprise due to its perceived influence today, though other factors may also be at work: corpora are more readily available in English than for most other languages; interfaces are frequently in English; awareness is likely to be higher given the number of publications in English; and it may even be that English, with its relatively reduced morphological variation, is more suitable for a corpus approach than some other languages.

Over two thirds of the studies (at least 19) involve learners in higher education, in seven cases majoring in the target language or translation studies; in eight they may be classified as advanced, in 17 as intermediate. Although it is frequently claimed that DDL may be most appropriate (or even exclusively so) for advanced, sophisticated learners, five of the studies take place in high school, and five (including four at university) explicitly claim the learners have lower intermediate levels of proficiency at best. The comparative rarity of studies in other contexts or with lower levels may be due to more prosaic factors. Universities represent the researchers' home environment where their students represent a captive audience; relatively sophisticated resources are also likely to be more readily available, not least of which is the time available for teachers and researchers, as well as greater flexibility in deciding their own programmes; and learners at university will already in most cases have spent several years studying the L2, whether they are majoring in it or need it for academic or special purposes. It would certainly seem worthwhile exploring further with younger learners in secondary education, with adults in other contexts (only a single study takes place in a language centre, one on-line), and with learners at lower levels.

It is more difficult to provide a completely accurate account of the corpora and tools used, not least because the information is not always explicit in the original articles; many also use a variety of corpora and tools in the same study. Seven use very large, often publicly available corpora, including the British National Corpus in four cases. However, the majority of studies draw on in-house corpora, often created by the researchers specifically for their students. The smallest is only 2,000 words, but there appears to be no upper limit: nine use the web as corpus with a variety of tools such as WebCorp and SketchEngine. Most of the corpora consist of 'general' language, though six are compiled from news texts, and one or two each from literary texts, course books, business documents or advertisements. Two used graded texts from the corpus; only five of them involved parallel corpora (TANGO, TOTALrecall and TeleKorp), and one a multimodal corpus (ELISA); these aspects thus reflect scope for future work if accessible software allows it.

In 14 of the studies, the learners had direct access to the corpus via a concordancer; eight use some kind of CALL program or other software which incorporates a concordancer; only eight make significant use of paper-based materials (three of the studies involving a combination). Again, the software used can be difficult to pin down, sometimes integrated to the particular corpus, sometimes written specially for the purpose or designed at the researchers' university. Other publicly available packages include WordSmith Tools, LexTutor, and Internet search tools. Most of the time, the learners accessed the data during the class or in special sessions in the computer room; occasionally this was supplemented with work outside class time or even at home. Only in Smith et al. (2008) was the whole experiment conducted elsewhere, in this case with volunteers recruited via Internet and working entirely on their own.

2. 2. Research contexts

On average, each study involved 47 learners, including control groups in 14 cases; four compared experimental and control items among the same population; 12 used a pre-test/post-test format, including seven also with a delayed post-test for longer-term retention. At the smaller end of the scale, two case studies featured only one or two learners; at the other end, three studies involved over 100 participants. These figures are sufficiently high overall to suggest that researchers have not ignored the importance of quantitative evidence for DDL. Indeed, all of the studies here provide some form of quantitative evaluation, and 21 subject their results to statistical analysis of some kind.

Different articles report the duration of the study in different ways, making comparison difficult. For those that give the minutes or hours, the average exposure to DDL is just over 10 hours. This would correspond to nearly an hour a week over a semester; indeed, those that describe the exposure in longer periods also report nearly 10 weeks of DDL. The shortest are clearly experimental in nature, with perhaps a single contact with corpus data (one study lasting only 30 minutes); however, 10 studies run for one or two semesters. The difference is apparent in a number of ways in the articles themselves: the studies based on shorter time-scales tend to begin with a research question and create an experimental situation to answer it; the longer ones typically begin with a course that is in place, and introduce research questions to assess some aspect of it.

While some of the corpora and tools used in the older papers may appear rather dated now, the methodologies employed have tended to remain fairly stable. Most studies used more than one research tool, including classroom observation, discussion, interviews, tracking, and most frequently questionnaires, although these were frequently for additional questions concerning learners' attitudes. For issues explicitly related to learning outcomes, a large variety of different tools were used for testing purposes, usually several in each study. Some are quite open and lead to a qualitative assessment (of writing, oral presentations, creating dictionary entries, etc.), but most require learners to complete fairly closed tasks (such as cloze, matching, sentence completion, substitution, error-correction, translation, or reading comprehension). Occasionally external tests were used, such as the *Vocabulary Knowledge Scale* and the *Vocabulary Levels Test*, as well as general exams not designed explicitly to test the items covered by the experiment – though most that did so acknowledge a number of problems inherent in this.

The majority of studies tend to have a fairly specific language focus, although some of the longitudinal data covers a range of features. Unsurprisingly, these mostly revolve around lexical aspects, as they are comparatively easy to search for in a corpus. The vocabulary may be of a particular type, such as connectors or items from Coxhead's (2000) *Academic Word List*, each featuring in two studies. The concordancing often includes induction and retention of meaning, but generally with a focus on larger units including compounds, clusters and collocations; this correlates with Johns' insight that DDL is most effective "on the 'collocational border' between syntax and lexis" (2002: 109). Although four studies do tackle wider themes of syntax and grammar directly, most are closer to the dividing line of *usage*, i.e. how words behave in different contexts, genres or text types. Some studies avoid a specific linguistic focus, including three that concentrate on reading skills, and one on noticing.

3. Learning outcomes

Although most of the studies surveyed here also feature some analysis of attitudes and behaviour, the present discussion will be limited to learning outcomes alone. As the majority focus on advanced adult learners using hands-on concordancing, we will first concentrate on the minority that look at younger or less advanced learners, or use of paper-based materials. Design problems are indicated at times, but space does not permit detailed discussion of individual studies, and the reader is referred to the original papers.

3. 1. General outcomes

Firstly, five of the studies feature teenage learners in secondary schools. Ciesielska-Ciupek (2001) supplemented course books with Internet materials and concordance print-outs. Tests on language items covered were positive, and maintained four weeks later with no further revision; the testing procedures are not entirely transparent, however, and no statistical analysis is provided. The experimental group in Braun's (2007) study used a unit of her ELISA video corpus, scoring higher on the follow-up computer-based tasks, although there was no overall difference with the control group in the final test on the unit as a whole. Learners with an inductive preference scored higher in Lee and Liou's (2003) study, and all levels improved following the DDL sessions, with the differences between them being reduced; although these differences are not statistically significant, they are taken to show that concordancing is of particular benefit to lower-level learners. In a study on collocations, Sun and Wang (2003) report that the inductive group showed significantly greater improvement than the control group, especially for the apparently easier items tested. Finally, Johns et al. (2008) find that the experimental group performed significantly better than the control group in the post-test for reading comprehension, and had double the reading speed; they also performed significantly better in the end-of-term exam, suggesting improvement extending beyond the specific tasks covered.

Another four papers claim to implement DDL with lower-level learners in higher education. In his doctoral thesis and two other papers, Cobb (1997a, 1997b, 1999) reports learners in the experimental treatment scoring significantly higher on vocabulary learning overall, in terms of both meaning and use in new contexts; the advantage was maintained in delayed tests for longer-term retention. The other three studies were all conducted in France. In the first (Boulton, 2009a), the experimental groups performed significantly better in an immediate post-test, especially from KWIC concordances as opposed to complete sentences; however, no difference was found between groups in the delayed post-test, suggesting that corpus data may be most useful as a reference resource for lower levels of language ability. In the second (Boulton, 2008, 2010), learners improved most on items in the experimental treatment, although the difference with the control treatment is not significant; the lower-level students narrowed the gap using DDL, while the more advanced ones maintained their advantage using the traditional approach. In the final study (Boulton, 2009b), learners who had experienced hands-on corpus exploration were later found to perform better in a test of noticing skills than the group undergoing traditional teaching, although the difference was not statistically significant.

Two other papers discuss implications of level, although neither claims to be dealing exclusively with lower levels. Chan and Liou (2005) find no significant correlation between level and post-treatment scores. DDL led to significantly greater improvement in both the immediate and delayed post-tests; the pattern of results is argued to show that an inductive DDL approach takes time to produce its maximum effect. Similarly, Tian (2005a, 2005b) reports no correlation with proficiency, and although both DDL and traditional teaching are successful, DDL is found to be significantly more useful for work on grammar and text type, but not significantly so for the usage points tested.

In total, eight studies make substantial use of paper-based materials. In three cases this is in combination with hands-on concordancing or other software, including the paper by Johns et al. (2008) discussed above. In Belz and Vyatkina (2005a, 2005b, 2008), following paper-based and hands-on treatment from native-speaker and peer-produced corpora, learners' on-line productions showed the target items being used more frequently and appropriately than before, although no statistical analysis is available as much of the study focuses on qualitative analysis of two learners only. Estling Vannestål and Lindquist (2007) report trials of experimental materials for grammar learning, although learning outcomes were only evaluated in one semester. No difference was detected between the experimental and control groups, perhaps because the post-test seems to have covered a wider range of items than those dealt with explicitly in the course.

Other papers involving printed materials include Ciesielska-Ciupek (2001), Boulton (2009a) and Boulton (2008, 2010) reported above. In addition to these, Koosha and Jafarpour (2006) compared treatments for prepositional collocations from paper-based materials only, the statistical analysis finding that the experimental group scored significantly higher in the use of the target language. A detailed paper by Allan (2006) shows the experimental group making significantly greater gains than the control group. Intriguingly, the advantage remained even for items not covered in the study, which is taken as evidence that the benefits of concordancing include strategies that can carry over to other language items.

Like Johns et al. (2008) mentioned above, the paper by Cobb et al. (2001) makes use of a single novel as a corpus, although this is a case study of only one learner, ruling out any statistical analysis. Nonetheless, the immediate post-test shows substantial gains being made in vocabulary, and retained in a delayed post-test. Smith et al. (2008) also report a small-scale study – inadvertently so, as they started out with 25 volunteers recruited via the Internet. Only 2 completed the post-test, one of whom had achieved the maximum score on the pre-test; however, the other did double his score following the treatment. Lin (2008) encounters a similar problem deriving from very high scores on the pre-test, but the *Vocabulary Knowledge Scale* showed depth of knowledge improving significantly following the experiment. Additionally, analysis of the participants' written productions revealed substantial increase in productive use of the target items, which declined only slightly in the delayed post-test.

Future teachers showed significant improvement on experimental items in Gan et al. (1996), despite extremely limited computer skills to start with. Cobb and Horst (2001; also Horst et al. 2001) find DDL helping with definition writing. Concordancing was the most important factor behind significant gains in vocabulary overall, although these were small, which the researchers attribute to the evaluation tools used: these publicly-available tests measured general lexical ability but were insufficiently sensitive for the specific items covered during the experiment. The learners in the study by Liou et al. (2006) showed significant improvement on the various items covered, as well as in inductive learning, although it is clear that the various elements in this paper are intended mainly as pilot studies of the tools rather than rigorous experimental analyses of DDL.

The learners in Cresswell's (2007) paper used concordances either inductively or deductively depending on learning style preference; both groups were generally successful, with some caveats – in particular, the overt knowledge of connectors derived from corpus consultation was not found to translate well into use in essays, as the DDL group performed only very slightly better than the control group. On the other hand, Yeh et al. (2007) report that use of the target items did improve in learners' written productions; there was also significant improvement in immediate and delayed post-tests for collocations of over-used adjectives. Similarly, in Kaur and Hegelheimer (2005), learners used the target items significantly more frequently and more accurately in the final written assignment. The post-test also showed the experimental group performing better, though not significantly so, with no apparent correlation between concordance use and results. An analysis of videoed data in Curado Fuentes (2002, 2003) showed the experimental group making more errors, but also considerably more effective use of the target points in their oral presentations. In a separate study, Curado Fuentes (2007) reports the experimental group performing significantly better than the control group in reading related to their corpus work with tourist advertisements. Huang and Liou (2007) used graded texts with lexical items colour-coded according to the number of presentations, with limited results: although learning improved as the words were met more frequently, some words encountered up to 15 times were still not learned.

The studies which use a pre-test/post-test design suggest that learning does take place after corpus consultation; in other words, the approach can be *effective*. However, given exposure of some kind, one might be forgiven for supposing that some learning will take place whatever the approach. It is therefore crucial to evaluate whether or not DDL is *efficient*. This is explored in the studies that compare experimental and control groups (or experimental and traditional treatment for language items), which on the whole give the advantage to DDL. Such a general statement of course needs to be supported by statistical analysis, the topic of the following section.

3. 2. Statistical significance

The sheer diversity of research questions and designs makes a formal meta-analysis of the results above difficult, and probably impossible. However, a certain number of general observations do seem to present themselves. Firstly, the overall body of empirical research in DDL provides overwhelmingly favourable reactions to DDL on the part of the learners; the very few exceptions include Estling Vannestål and Lindquist (2007) discussed above. As regards learning outcomes, the majority of the studies surveyed here are similarly encouraging, although detailed analysis suggests a slightly more mitigated picture, partly because even experienced researchers in applied linguistics may not be at ease with quantitative methods (Rasinger, 2008), leading to problems in design or analysis. In particular, six of the studies limit themselves to raw figures and do not (or, given the design, cannot) present serious statistical analysis of the main learning outcomes targeted (Ciesielska-Ciupek, 2001; Cobb et al., 2001; Curado Fuentes, 2003; Estling Vannestål, Lindquist, 2007; Belz, Vyatkina, 2008; Smith et al., 2008). Tellingly, of the 21 that do, none report DDL to be less effective than traditional teaching practices. Of course, it might be that negative results are less likely to be written up as they stand, though they may lead to modified research which does produce the desired results and which is then published. Certainly, it seems probable that the majority of researchers behind the papers in this survey are enthusiastic about the potential of DDL, and are therefore unlikely to be seeking actively to disprove its merits, however (un)scientific this may be. On the other hand, five do report findings that fall short of the usually accepted levels of significance ($p<0.05$), although they may at times come close, and the results should therefore not be disregarded altogether (Lee, Liou, 2003; Kaur, Hegelheimer, 2005; Cresswell, 2007; Boulton, 2008, 2009b).

Some of the reportedly significant results also need qualification in the light of the experiment design. The paper by Liou et al. (2006) is evidently a series of pilot studies of work in progress and does not provide full description of the research design (e.g. the number of learners involved) or the results (e.g. the entire set of results from the delayed post-test). The results in Tian (2005a, 2005b) may be compromised by the different question formats for each type of language item in the pre- and post-tests, making direct comparison problematic. A similar concern may arise with the early study by Gan et al. (1996), as learners were apparently allowed to choose the items to study; this is not discussed further, and it is not clear how the common post-test catered for this. Allan (2006) attributes the carry-over of positive effects to untreated items as a sign that DDL promotes varies strategies; an alternative may lie in the design of the experiment itself – in particular, there is substantial variability between the learners regarding the work completed, and the small control group of only five learners scored substantially higher in the pre-test than the experimental group, and thus had less room for improvement. Similarly, the learners in the study by Lin (2008) began with high scores on the vocabulary test, so only depth of lexical knowledge could be tested (though with significant results).

A number of other studies also report positive findings only for some of the research questions. Sun and Wang (2003) find a significant advantage for the experimental treatment only for the two easier collocation patterns tested and not the harder ones, while Boulton (2009a) and Braun (2007) each produce outcomes significantly in favour of corpus use in the immediate post-tests, but not in the delayed tests. The results reported in Huang and Liou (2007) and Cobb and Horst (2001) are significant, but the researchers report that they are nonetheless disappointingly small.

This leaves a total of six studies with unambiguously positive findings that meet the normal requirements of statistical significance, all published in peer-reviewed journals or books (Cobb, 1997a, 1997b, 1999; Chan, Liou, 2005; Koosha, Jafarpour, 2006; Curado Fuentes, 2007; Yeh et al., 2007; Johns et al., 2008). That is not to say that these researchers are blinded by enthusiasm: they typically qualify their findings with a variety of hedging devices (*overall, on the whole, in general, by and large, on average*, etc.); are careful not to overgeneralise their conclusions to wider populations in other circumstances for different language points; point out limitations of their study, especially in regard to uncontrolled variables; and, without exception, call for further research to validate their findings.

4. Discussion

The results as presented here may appear somewhat pessimistic – often with mitigated outcomes, small or not statistically significant results, problems of research design, and so on. But there are grounds for cautious optimism. A comparison can be made with corpus linguistics as a whole, where it is a basic principle that a single piece of data (such as an individual concordance line) may be interesting, but needs to be interpreted with caution: only with a large number of cases can one begin to have confidence in the underlying patterns that emerge. The same is broadly true of empirical studies: individually the results are often promising, though inconclusive; but taken together, they can be highly encouraging. Statistically, a small amount of data is likely to produce results that are not significant, but pooling the results increases their value tremendously. This is usually the domain of meta-analyses, but as mentioned above, such an undertaking would currently seem to be unrealistic given the fragmented nature of the studies in this survey with their disparate research questions, designs and data reporting. However, were anyone to have access to the full data sets and the necessary tools and skills to combine them into a formal meta-analysis, it is difficult to imagine that size effect would not take the overall significance of the studies well beyond the usual levels of acceptability.

Furthermore, we should perhaps not expect absolutely clear-cut results from individual studies in any case – indeed, there might be reason for suspicion if this were so. The number of factors to take into account makes it virtually impossible to isolate a single variable absolutely, especially over longer periods. This underlines a problem inherent in most quantitative analysis, as the tendency is to base the findings on average outcomes, as if the learners constituted a "monolithic group rather than [...] idiosyncratic individuals" (Yoon, 2008: 32); or as Estling Vannestål and Lindquist (2007: 336) put it:

> If a new idea is tested and it turns out not to be successful for everybody in the experimental group all the time, it is easy to draw the conclusion that the new methodology is not successful at all, even if it is perhaps successful for some people sometimes, which may in itself be a positive outcome.

Work on learning styles may be able to shed some light on this (Boulton, forthcoming), but there is no reason to suppose this is a problem unique to DDL. The overarching modern paradigm in language teaching and learning for the past three decades has been the communicative approach, which has encountered similar problems and has not necessarily found it any easier to produce convincing empirical research into learning outcomes (cf. Rasinger, 2008: chap. 1). Yet the communicative approach certainly did not wait for the evidence to be in before it began to spread. If it has come to prevail, it is rather because it has a broad theoretical basis supported by promising (rather than conclusive) individual studies that break the larger issues down into manageable research questions to reveal overall tendencies.

The same seems to be true of DDL, which has substantial theoretical support and, as seen here, empirical evidence that it can work in a variety of contexts. However, simply showing that it is effective may be playing to the sceptics, who are quick to point out a number of objections, especially in terms of logistical barriers – for example, that DDL can be tedious, mechanical and time-consuming, with learners drowning in unnecessarily complex data; that it depends on advanced ICT skills and entails extensive training for both learners and teachers; that it requires computer rooms full of expensive and complex technology which, even if available, is prone to breaking down; that only the most advanced, sophisticated and motivated learners can make sense of the complex data and truncated KWIC concordances; and so on (see Boulton, 2009c, for a fuller discussion). The studies here go to great pains to show that learners can gain benefits from corpus consultation and overcome these barriers; and while most of them may indeed focus on advanced, sophisticated adult learners with training in hands-on concordancing and access to sophisticated equipment, there is also an increasing number showing that simple incarnations of DDL (e.g. with paper-based materials or more controlled activities) can lead to immediate benefits even for lower-level learners with negligible training and limited resources.

But these are largely side-issues given the main advantages attributed to DDL – amongst other things, that it promotes a range of cognitive skills, and increases sensitisation and ability to deal with authentic language; that the interactive, discovery-based approach fits with the current constructivist view of language learning; that induction of patterns and regularities is a more 'natural' approach than the intellectually rigorous rule-based approach characteristic of much traditional teaching; that it can increase motivation where learners are allowed to pursue their own queries, leading to greater autonomisation and life-long learning; and so on. Countless articles discuss such theoretical considerations and promote these arguments as the real advantages of DDL. However, few of the papers in this survey address such considerations, which tend to be ignored or glossed over in empirical studies – in part, no doubt, as all such long-term, general skills are extremely difficult to assess. The exceptions in the present study include Boulton (2009b), which finds some evidence that corpus training enhances noticing skills (Schmidt, 1990); and Johns et al. (2008) and Allan (2006), who both find that DDL learners score higher than controls on items not covered explicitly in the course, suggesting incidental benefits and increased learning ability. Five of the seven studies that use delayed tests also find that DDL is more effective than traditional treatment for longer-term retention.

5. Conclusion

This survey has covered a number of studies that aim to evaluate learning outcomes from corpus consultation. Although it falls short of conclusive proof of the effectiveness of DDL, it does provide grounds for optimism. Firstly, there is substantially more empirical research into the learning outcomes of corpus consultation than is frequently alleged: 27 separate studies to date. If there are repeated complaints about the alleged lack of research, it may be partly because corpus linguists are more demanding of empirical studies than researchers in the field of language teaching and learning as a whole. Secondly, the overwhelming majority of studies produce encouraging results, even if they are not always statistically significant on all research questions. The evidence may not be totally foolproof, but this is true of many widely-held tenets in applied linguistics; crucially, what there is points to the usefulness of corpus consultation for language learning in the short term, and possibly enhancement of language sensitivity and learning ability. The studies here show that DDL can be usefully employed for learners of many different language backgrounds and in different situations when appropriately adapted, whether using sophisticated equipment or the simplest of materials, in pursuing individual language interests or in tightly controlled activities, for high and low levels alike.

Inevitably, research needs to continue, and a number of areas are in urgent need of further investigation, not least multimodal, spoken or parallel corpora. Other issues comparatively understudied include, as mentioned above, lower-level learners using simple tools and techniques for basic language questions – in other words, "ordinary teachers and learners in ordinary classrooms" (Mauranen, 2004a: 208). These of course include paper-based materials (Boulton, 2010 in press) which require little if any training to use, and which might be suitable for bringing DDL to a wider audience, beyond the university environment to younger learners in state schools, as well as to adults in language centres and continued education, and indeed outside the formal educational context altogether. As Chambers (2007: 13) puts it:

> If corpus consultation […] is to become a common activity for learners across the broad spectrum of language studies (general language learning, literary studies, languages for specific purposes, translation, etc.), it would seem necessary for developments to take place in a broader context than that which has been examined here, namely the classrooms of researchers with expertise in corpora and concordancing. […] It is perhaps outside the classroom that the next important step in research in this area will take place.

More is also needed on variables between different learners, including attitudes, motivations and learning styles (cf. Boulton, forthcoming). This might help to counter the problems of treating all learners equally in quantitative studies, where low average results may conceal a variety of different outcomes for individual learners. At the same time, the findings would need to be off-set against evaluation of the usefulness of generic materials, as most of the papers here create their own activities from scratch, any reuse being confined to other learners in the same institution. Johns himself (1990: 36) proposed there should be available a bank of reusable "ready-made DDL materials"; so far Hadley (2002) is the only one to have reported on their use (specifically, the *COBUILD Samplers*: Goodale, 1995), but his paper concentrates on learner behaviour and attitudes rather than learning outcomes. Developments such as these would help to take DDL out of the hands of expert teacher-researchers and make it accessible to ordinary learners.

The current state of empirical research into learning outcomes from DDL is, as this survey has shown, more extensive than frequently claimed. Sceptics are likely to seize on the inconclusive results from many individual studies, though it has been argued that little more could reasonably be expected. On the contrary, the overall weight of evidence is encouraging, implying that teachers should not hesitate to introduce DDL to their learners in a variety of contexts, though empirical research should of course continue.

Notes

[1] The full current list and summary information can be found on the website accompanying this book (*http://mcaweb.unipv.it:8080/mcaweb/EEL/VOL1/chap9.html*) and on the author's homepage (*http://arche.univ-nancy2.fr/course/view.php?id=967*). There are no doubt more than 70: I would be grateful for any leads to other empirical DDL papers.

Combining text-based and corpus-based approaches in the learning and teaching of academic writing in French

Angela Chambers, University of Limerick, Ireland

1. Introduction

Academic writing, and in particular research articles, have been the subject of a considerable and increasing body of research, motivated largely by the need for research to underpin the needs of non-native speakers of English wishing to study and publish in that language. Swales (1990), Hyland (1996, 1998) and others have analysed both the structure and the characteristic linguistic features of the research article in English, emphasising the coexistence of adherence to accepted norms and the creative combination of characteristic features to produce original texts. In French research by Béacco (1995), Condamines (2000) and others focused on areas such as the expression of the author's opinion and on the role of prepositions in scientific writing. Carter-Thomas (2007) takes a comparative approach, analysing medical research articles in English and French, while Carter-Thomas and Rowley-Jolivet (2001) compare features of spoken and written academic discourse in English. Such research, based on the analysis of a significant number of texts, informs what is taught to learners, although in a language class the focus will generally be on the study of the linguistic aspects of a single text, showing how the use of features such as anaphora, argumentative devices, references to the author and to other researchers, connectors and negation contribute to the overall fabric of the text.

This paper aims to bring together these two approaches to the study of texts, namely the analysis of a large number of texts or the study of a single text, in the context of language learning and teaching. The hypothesis is that a concordance-based study of certain items can enhance the text-based study of the features of an article introduction. While published research in corpora and language learning focuses mostly on English, it is argued here that the findings of such research may also be applicable to the study of similar genres in other languages, in this case French. After situating the study in the context of corpus-based and text-based approaches to academic writing with particular reference to language learning and teaching, one article introduction in the discipline of economics is studied (see *Appendix 1*). This is followed by a concordance-based study of some of the features highlighted in the article introduction, using a corpus of one million words of academic writing in French (Chambers, Le Baron, 2007). This will enable us to see to what extent the combination of these two approaches has the potential to enhance the learning and teaching environment in academic writing.

2. Academic writing: From research to teaching and learning

While a number of corpora of academic writing have been made available to researchers, for example the KIAP corpora (Fløttum et al., 2006), research in this area is not dominated by a quantitative approach, but combines quantitative and qualitative aspects. Indeed, as Lee (2007: 88) notes, a combination of qualitative and quantitative analysis makes up the vast majority of corpus-based research, contrary to stereotype. In research on academic writing in particular, even researchers such as Hyland (1996), who has at his disposal a large corpus of research articles, adopts a qualitative approach, selecting a relatively small number of texts to study, 26 in this case, treating the texts as a resource for finding examples of the many functions of hedges which he identifies, rather than creating tables quantifying the number of occurrences of a particular function. Carter-Thomas and Rowley-Jolivet (2001), on the other hand, while undertaking what is also mostly a qualitative study of a small corpus of nine presentations at an international conference in physics and the corresponding articles published in the proceedings, take quantitative data as their starting point. Comparing, or rather contrasting, their own written and spoken data quantitatively not only with each other, but also with a more general corpus of academic discourse and a corpus of conversations, they conclude that the presentations are closer to conversations than to academic prose.

While studies such as those mentioned above (Hyland, 1996; Carter-Thomas, Rowley-Jolivet, 2001) are clearly motivated by the need for non-native speakers of English to master the conventions of academic discourse in English, the pedagogical applications of their findings are not developed in any detail in the publications. In other studies, however, the focus is not on the analysis of the corpus data but rather on the ways in which they can be used with students. A substantial and increasing body of research in this area has developed since the mid 1980's, initially inspired by Johns (1986), who used printed concordances with his students of English, what he termed data-driven learning and Tribble and Jones (1990), who popularised the use of concordances in the English language classroom. O'Sullivan and Chambers (2006) gave their students direct access to a small corpus of academic and journalistic writing in French on the subject of the French language, and studied their use of the data to correct errors in an essay which they had written on an aspect of the history of the language. Like other researchers in the area (Stevens, 1990), they had specially created the corpus to be relevant to their students' needs. Lee and Swales (2006) report on a project in which postgraduate researchers in a number of disciplines are encouraged to create their own specialised corpus in English, which they then use as a resource for academic writing.

The use of corpora as a resource in academic writing in French raises a number of issues. Firstly, the dominance of English in the research literature raises the issue of whether the research findings relating to English can be applied to other languages. In the area of corpora in language learning in general, publications on German by Dodd (1997) and on Italian by Kennedy and Miceli (2001) investigate the potential of resources in these languages. O'Sullivan and Chambers (2006) focus on academic writing in French at undergraduate and postgraduate level, once again with generally positive results. There is, however, a need for more research on these and other languages to provide language teachers, language teacher educators, and materials developers with data and analysis which they can apply in their work.

The question also arises as to whether Swales' "moves" (1990: 141), or the structure which he has identified in a large number of scientific research articles, can be applied to languages other than English. His CARS model (Create a research space) is summarised below:

- establishing a territory: claiming centrality, and/or making topic generalizations, and/or reviewing items of previous research;
- establishing a niche: counter-claiming, or indicating a gap, or question-raising, or continuing a tradition;
- occupying the niche: outlining purposes or announcing present research, announcing principal findings, indicating RA structure.

As we shall see, the article introduction being studied here corresponds to this structure. It is beyond the scope of the present chapter to investigate whether the CARS model is characteristic of articles in English only. It is certainly true that in the corpus used here it is not difficult to select articles in French corresponding to the CARS model, but it is impossible to know whether this is because it has also developed in research cultures in French independently of its use in English, or whether it is as a result of the dominant influence of English in research circles.

It is clearly also beyond the scope of this study to undertake an exhaustive study of the recurring features of introductions in French corresponding to these moves. By consulting a corpus a teacher or learner can, however, search for additional examples of a word or expression used in a similar way in other introductions in French. Aston (2001: 75-76), referring to a sub-corpus of academic discourse in the British National Corpus, warns against the danger of over-generalising on the basis of a limited number of examples.

> There are nearly 50 lectures overall, on a wide range of topics and by a fair variety of lecturers, and it has proved a useful collection from which to retrieve examples of particular discourse phenomena for teaching purposes and from which to generate hypotheses about the ways that lectures seem to work. Useful, that is, as long as you don't try to interpret it as a 'representative sample' allowing reliable generalizations about lectures as a genre.

It is this use of examples for teaching purposes, and not general conclusions about article introductions, which is intended here. The simpler application involves the teacher preparing additional materials to complement a text studied in a class. In a more sophisticated application, the learner would be able to consult the corpus directly using concordancing software.

Another issue which is raised by this study, or indeed by any study involving the use of corpus data in language learning, is whether concordance lines can be of any use to learners as they have been described as devoid of context, what Widdowson (2000: 7) calls decontextualised language. In this particular case, where the corpus contains only research articles, the learners' knowledge of the genre creates a situation where they are not totally ignorant of the context. In addition, Charles (2007: 298) notes that, as language classes often make use of extracts, this lack of context is not peculiar to corpus data, which have the advantage over the traditional study of extracts that a learner with direct access to a concordancer can access the full context simply by clicking on the computer mouse. As we shall see, consulting a corpus can quickly provide multiple examples of the use of a word or expression, and with a concordancer such as WordSmith (Scott, 2004) it is easy to identify at what point in the text each occurrence is situated, for example in the introduction. It is also easy to discover if the word or expression is used in the same way as in the text in which it was first observed. This is often clear from the concordance line itself, although it may be necessary on some occasions to consult the broader context of the sentence or paragraph.

3. From text to corpus

The corpus used for this study is the Chambers-Le Baron Corpus of Research Articles in French (Chambers, Le Baron, 2007), consisting of 159 research articles taken from twenty freely available peer-reviewed online journals, 1,045,872 words in all. The articles were published between 1998 and 2006, and belong to ten categories: media/culture, literature, linguistics and language learning, social anthropology, law, economics, sociology and social sciences, philosophy, history, and communication. Given the small size of the corpus and the limited number of online journals in some categories, it was not possible to include articles from a large variety of journals. Two journals are represented in each category, and the ten categories are similar in size in the corpus.

The choice of the article introduction to be studied (Boubel, Pansard, 2003, reproduced in *Appendix 1*) was not random; rather it was selected to correspond as closely as possible with Swales' structure (1990: 141). As Samraj (2002) and Ozturk (2007) observe, alongside the similarities noted by Swales, considerable variation can be found in the structure of research articles, across disciplines and even within a single discipline. While the absence of large corpora of academic writing in French makes it difficult to make confident claims about the representativity of the CARS model in French, it is interesting to note that it is well represented in the introductions to the 50 Economics articles in French in the KIAP Corpus (Fløttum et al., 2006). A teacher might thus choose either the more specialised KIAP Corpus or the broader academic focus of the Chambers Le Baron Corpus, depending on the interests and the needs of the learners. The three paragraphs of the introduction to Boubel and Pansard's article can be seen as corresponding to the three moves in the CARS model. In the first paragraph the territory is established, as the authors describe a rapidly changing situation, contrasting different roles in different geographical locations and highlighting the importance of the "pays anglo-saxons".

The second paragraph establishes the niche for the study, listing the issues which arise and clarifying that the article focuses on one particular issue in the United Kingdom and the United States of America. Finally, in the third paragraph the structure of the article is outlined. This chapter will focus mainly on the potential of features in the first paragraph for the learning and teaching of French combining text-based and corpus-based approaches.

In a study of this text alone, the French language teacher may signal, or preferably encourage the learners to discover a number of features. Firstly, in the opening sentence, the verb *connaître* is used to describe the current situation, a function of this verb with which the learners may not be familiar:

> Les systèmes financiers des pays industrialisés ont connu d'importantes modifications
> aux cours des dernières décennies.

Secondly, adverbs and adverbial phrases, namely *certes*, *bien entendu* and *en particulier*, play an important role in this paragraph as clear signposts for the direction of the authors' argument. *Certes*, for example, opens the second sentence:

> Certes les banques demeurent toujours au centre de la sphère financière, mais
> le métier de l'intermédiation financière bascule de plus en plus aux mains des
> investisseurs institutionnels.

Other features might include, for example, the use of anaphora and of the first person plural and the verb *aborder* to produce a clear statement of the focus of the article: "C'est cette dernière problématique que nous abordons ici", or the use of *après* plus noun phrase to refer to the preliminary definitions in the structure of the article at the start of the final paragraph. As a study of these features in the article and in the corpus would be beyond the scope of this chapter, it will illustrate how concordance data from other research articles can complement the study of *connaître*, *certes* and the first person plural in the article. Clearly the use of *connaître* and *certes* is not limited to article introductions, so the teacher can encourage the learners to notice how they are used both in the introduction and in the text of the articles.

It is difficult for the researcher, teacher or learner to carry out a scientific analysis of the linguistic features of introductions using this corpus as the articles do not all clearly label the introductions as such. In the case of many articles it is clear where the introduction begins and ends, either because it is labelled or clearly separated from the following sections. In a significant number of articles, however, this is not the case. Where the number of occurrences is limited, as in the case of *connaître* and *certes*, this problem can easily be overcome, as the concordancer makes it possible to view the position of the word in the text, and occurrences in introductions can thus be discovered. In the case of the first person plural, where the number of occurrences is very large, this would be more time-consuming.

Running a concordance of all occurrences of the lemma *connaître* reveals 81 occurrences. All are used in the sense in which the word is used in Boubel and Pansard's introduction, namely for something to be experienced rather than for an individual to be acquainted with another person. Examples are provided below:

- la conception de produits connaît des transformations sociotechniques importantes, dont la plus marquante est l'augmentation de la cooperation entre les acteurs du cycle de vie du produit (Darses, 2002). [first sentence];
- le tournant en faveur de la délibération qu'a connu la philosophie politique récente a ses racines tant dans la théorie que la pratique [first sentence];
- depuis la chute du mur de Berlin en novembre 1989, les politiques d'asile des Etats membres de l'Union européenne ont connu d'importantes mutations;
- entre 2002 et 2003 près d'un million de personnes sont devenues membres de ce mouvement religieux qui connut un taux de croissance de 8%;
- la Pologne et la Hongrie ont obtenu, à partir de 1993, des taux de croissance positifs et élevés alors que la République tchèque a connu des taux moyens et quelquefois négatifs;
- au cours des années quatre-vingt-dix, les modalités de financement international des pays émergents ont connu un certain nombre de mutations.

The absence of context in these lines is not a major disadvantage to the learners, as the context which they are studying is the introduction to Boubel and Pansard (2003), and the full text of the article is available either in the corpus or on the web. Rather the extra concordance lines help to promote 'noticing' (Schmidt, 1990) by the learners, as well as giving them other examples of other lexical items which occur with *connaître*, for example *mutation*, or the possible inversion of subject and verb in the second example. In other words, the concordance has the potential to enhance the learning experience, by providing additional attested examples of occurrences in the same genre and disciplinary area as the article being studied.

Of the adverbs and adverbial phrases used in this first section of the introduction, it is *certes* which provides the most interesting results in the concordance. There are 83 occurrences of the adverb, 22 of which appear in introductions. Examples are given below:

- au sens où le pouvoir – de marché, certes, mais il s'agit bien d'un pouvoir – peut y être contesté;
- quelques aspects certes périphériques au regard de la politique de la concurrence elle-même mais néanmoins cruciaux dans l'arsenal des politiques de croissance;
- les espaces produits en discours l'ont été par l'attribution de traits divers certes à des formes linguistiques, aux locuteurs de ses formes, mais encore à;
- qui concernent le corps et sa puissance d'agir apparaissent comme des étapes, certes nécessaires, mais non suffisantes, dans la compréhension de la béatitude;
- la question de la réforme des Nations Unies n'est certes pas une question nouvelle. On pourrait évoquer à son sujet le «monstre» de Loch Ness et en un certain sens nous aimons bien Nessie;
- dans les pages qui suivent, je tracerai (sommairement, certes) les contours de ce lieu à partir de trois personnages.

In four of the six examples – and in many more in the 81 occurrences – *certes* is followed by *mais*, which leads to the conclusion that, although its meaning implies certainty, this certainty is very likely to be eroded a few words or a few lines later. Even in the examples where *mais* is not used, there is an implied negation of the certainty. Thus in the last example we are told that something will be outlined, but only very briefly. The concordance is a very useful enhancement of the single occurrence of *certes* in the text being studied, as it makes it clear to the learner that this use of *certes*, accompanied by the negation of the certainty, in other words with a negative "semantic prosody" (Louw, 1993: 157) is not rare in academic writing.

The question arises as to whether this use of *certes* is peculiar to academic writing or is found in other genres as well. It may thus be of interest to the teacher and learner to compare its use in corpora of other genres. Condamines (2002) points out that patterns may be identified for one corpus only, for corpora of the same genre, or (very rarely), for all corpora. As we shall see, patterns may also be common to a number of genres. Using only freely available online corpora, a teacher could quickly discover that there are 183 occurrences of *certes* in a corpus of journalistic discourse (Chambers, Rostand, 2005) similar in size to the corpus of academic writing, with *certes* commonly preceding *mais*. In an online corpus of 24 interviews with teenagers in French (SACODEYL), on the other hand, there are no occurrences at all. While remembering Aston's (2001: 75-76) advice on the importance of avoiding generalisations on the basis of small collections of data, young learners might decide to be wary of using *certes* in informal spoken French, at the very least not before they hear native speakers using it. It could be argued, of course, that a corpus is not necessary to discover that *certes* is used with this negative semantic prosody, as a corpus-based dictionary could provide the information. It is interesting in this respect to consult both a non-corpus-based dictionary and a corpus-based dictionary. Mansion (1940 [1934]), which is not corpus-based, provides the following brief definition:

Certes, adv. Most certainly. *Oui certes! yes indeed! to be sure!*

By 1997, the year of publication of the second edition of the corpus-based *Oxford-Hachette French Dictionary* (Corréard, 1997), more attention is devoted to the adverb, and the negative semantic prosody is emphasised, with even the positive meaning of 'indeed' being illustrated with a negative example.

Certes adv.
1. (en signe de concession) admittedly
ce ne sera certes pas facile, mais / admittedly it won't be easy but…
certes, je me suis trompé, mais / admittedly I made a mistake but…
il est seduisant certes, mais prétentieux / he is good-looking, certainly, but he is conceited

2. (assurément) indeed
C'est une question d'honneur? - Certes non! / is it a question of honour? - certainly not!

Given the decades between the publication of the two dictionaries, it may be possible that the negative semantic prosody is a development, but it is not difficult to find examples in Proust, including the well-known phrase which describes Swann's initial reflection on Odette, and which he remembers again at the end of their affair: "elle était apparue à Swann non pas certes sans beauté, mais d'un genre de beauté qui lui était indifferent" (Proust, 1913: 234). This is not to imply that, either in Proust or in academic or journalistic writing, all uses of *certes* have negative connotations, but rather that occurrences are sufficiently numerous that it would be misleading not to make learners aware of them. Furthermore, while a learner can discover that *certes* is used in this way from a dictionary, studying occurrences in a single text, complemented by a genre-specific corpus provides a richer learning environment, encouraging the learner to notice not just the use of the word or expression, but also other lexical items and grammatical structures which occur alongside the word.

In any investigation of the potential of corpora in language learning, it is important not to paint too rosy a picture. A number of the publications which report on learner reactions to corpus consultation reveal that while learners appreciate the benefits, namely access to multiple examples which are relevant and up to date (Bernardini, 2002: 179; Chambers, 2005: 120), they also find the process of analysing large numbers of concordances time-consuming, laborious and tedious (Cheng et al., 2003: 181; Yoon, Hirvela, 2004: 274; Chambers, 2005: 120). Swales (2004: 144) also notes that analysing concordances can be tiring for learners. Teachers, however, are the main topic of this study, although published research, such as that referred to above, tends to focus on the reactions of learners rather than teachers.

In the case of the concordances of *certes* above, for example, the examples presented were chosen because they illustrated the negative semantic prosody clearly, and because even a brief concordance line contained a clue to the context. An example which would have been more challenging for learners involves a sentence where *mais* occurs 118 words and two sentences after *certes* (Gadet, 2003).

> Certes, au plan formel comme au plan sémantique, l'argot suit les procédés généraux de formation en vigueur dans la langue (Calvet, 1994) : suffixation (dite parasitaire quand il s'agit de variétés dépréciées) ; troncation finale (assoce, biz, délib) ou plus rarement initiale (leur, blème chez les jeunes) ; métaphore (se dégonfler, galère) et métonymie (casquette pour « contrôleur ») ; séries synonymiques, calembour et remotivations étymologiques, mots expressifs (suffixes dépréciatifs, métaphores ironiques) ; emprunts (anciennement, à la faveur des guerres et des conquêtes ; récemment, aux langues de l'immigration, arabe, langues africaines, créoles antillais, et à l'anglais ; mots tziganes-marav, ou prétendus tels – pourav, graillav). Soit, une forte continuité dans les procédés, et une indéniable diversification quant aux produits. Mais dans l'argot traditionnel comme dans la langue des jeunes, l'effet des procédés héréditaires ne se module guère que par la fréquence : la langue des jeunes intensifie les emprunts et diversifie les sources.

Although some learners may fail to discover that this example fits in the same category as those quoted above, the large numbers of concordance lines where the negative connotations are evident even in the truncated line make it likely that learners with direct access to the data will have the possibility of observing the pattern.

The second principal move in Swales' model, establishing a niche, provides less interesting results than the first, confirming Ozturk's emphasis on variation in the structures of research articles. Had citations been used, for example, they would have provided an opportunity for the teacher to alert the learners to citation practices, finding additional examples in other articles by using simple techniques of using the bracket symbol as a search item. Boubel and Pansard include no citations in the introduction, although the literature review of their article includes ample citations. Rather they include general phrases to refer to existing research, such as "des réflexions sont menées" and "de multiples questions sont posées". The use of *question* has been studied in both academic and journalistic writing in French (O'Sullivan, Chambers, 2006; Chambers, Wynne, 2008), illustrating how concordances can provide learners with useful data showing how it is used in a number of ways in French which have no direct equivalent in English. It will not be further investigated here, not because it is not relevant; like *connaître*, it has an important role to play both in introductions and in the body of the article. Of more importance in the context of the introduction, however, is the use of *nous* to present the plan of the article, which, as we shall see, is an important characteristic of the introduction studied here.

Occupying the niche, the final move in Swales' CARS model, is well illustrated in the third paragraph of this introduction, where the authors give the plan of their article, clearly signposted in the final sentence of the second paragraph. The use of the first person plural is of interest here, particularly as the teacher can use the additional concordance data to point out to the learners that the plural form is also commonly used in articles authored by a single person in French, and that the use of the first person is rare. While the use of *nous* by single authors is clearly not limited to introductions, it is particularly relevant in the part of the introduction where the structure of the article is given. In this context, Boubel and Pansard's introduction includes three occurrences of *nous*:

- c'est cette dernière problématique que nous abordons ici;
- après une présentation des formes d'intermédiation financière en vigueur nous cherchons à mieux cerner le rôle des dispositifs de retraite;
- le second constat que nous dressons est que les choix réalisés, au sein de ces deux pays, par les pouvoirs publics en termes de dispositifs d'épargne retraite ont influencé de manière significative le partage du marché de l'épargne.

Nous occurs very frequently in the corpus, 3,326 times in all. While it fulfils a number of roles, its main function is clearly to enable the author or authors to inform the readers of how they intend to structure what follows. While analysing 3,326 occurrences is a major undertaking, a relatively brief search will enable the teacher or learner to select other examples of *nous* used in this way. One particular advantage of this is that it provides examples of verbs used in this way by authors, providing a much greater variety than those in the three examples:

- dans un premier temps, nous aborderons brièvement la notion d'égalité en rapport avec les concepts de;
- pour expliciter les termes de la discussion, nous allons d'abord situer dans le temps le phénomène commémoratif au Québec;
- nous allons repérer ces scènes au fil des oeuvres avant de nous interroger sur;
- le second niveau, que nous allons tenter de définir dans les pages suivantes;
- nous allons considérer les rapports existants (ou ayant existé) entre les systèmes;
- cette question à laquelle nous allons tenter de répondre se double d'autres questions sur la complémentarité;
- dans le cadre de cet article, c'est le rapport que l'homme entretient avec l'objet que nous analysons;
- en nous appuyant sur des témoignages d'artistes qui les pratiquent, nous examinerons;
- nous nous attacherons par conséquent avant tout à montrer la continuité d'un genre;
- puis, nous nous attarderons sur trois facteurs qui, au sein de ce régime pédagogique, permettent;
- à la suite de négociations complexes sur lesquelles nous ne nous attarderons pas;
- nous avons décidé de nous concentrer sur des entreprises proposant des sites Web;
- nous avons retenu ces trois cas pour diverses raisons. En premier lieu;
- pour mieux saisir cette interaction, nous avons choisi de nous pencher sur la communauté de Saint-Roch-de-l'Achigan.

The examples given above were selected from a concordance of the 3,326 occurrences, sorted according to the word on the right of the search word, *nous*. This enabled the verbs used commonly with *nous* to be easily noticed. Alternatively, the 3,326 results could be randomly reduced to a smaller, more manageable number, 300 for example. The major advantage of data such as these is that they provide teachers and learners with attested examples of use, rather than relying on the teacher's intuition. In the area of Language for Specific Purposes, they have a much more important role to play than in general language teaching contexts, as the teacher will in the vast majority of cases not have the relevant experience on which to draw for the use of acquired knowledge of the language or native speaker intuition.

4. Conclusion

In the context of Language for Specific Purposes, an approach based on the study of a single text in class is limited in a number of ways, Firstly, the teacher's lack of expertise in the subject area limits the potential of native speaker intuition or the knowledge acquired through learning the language. Cobb (1997b: 313) points out that language classes alone do not provide enough time to encounter enough examples to promote learning, or 'noticing'

(Schmidt, 1990). The advantage of concordances is that, if appropriate corpora are available (which is not always the case), they are a source of multiple attested examples of naturally occurring discourse, providing both teacher and learners with information about language use in the specialist area. In a broader context, where students may be required to master other genres in their future careers, specialised corpora also have a role to play, and introducing learners to them in their degree programme thus potentially provides them with a useful transferable skill. In other words, learners can be introduced to the existence and use of specialised corpora and also to the *ad hoc* compilation of these corpora. The ability to write successfully in a given genre is important in many areas. Swales (2004: 4) emphasises "an increasing genrification of administrative and academic life", noting also how concordances can play an important role in one particular area, namely academic writing (2004: 144):

> The use of corpus-concordance packages for teaching research English is still in its early stages but, with suitable doctoral student training and the imaginative development of manageable student tasks, it will doubtless come to play an increasing part in our mix of research and teaching activities as we move further into the new century.

While this potential is highlighted in the context of English, it would seem counter-intuitive not to assume that, given suitable resources, it is also applicable to other languages, including French. The imaginative development of manageable student tasks is also clearly necessary at levels below that of doctoral student. The study of an individual text, or part of a text, is firmly ensconced in language learning. As we have seen, concordance data have the potential to enhance this in a number of ways, but if this is to become a reality in the language classroom a number of developments are necessary. Vast reference corpora cannot solve the needs of all learners. Chambers and Wynne (2008) suggest that a systematic approach to sharing resources could help to create a situation where the types of specialist corpora which would be relevant to many university courses could be made freely available. These could form the basis for the type of pedagogic research which has been undertaken so far with small, specially created corpora which are not always generally publicly available. In other words, there is still considerable scope for future research in the application of corpora in language learning and teaching.

Appendix 1: Les investisseurs institutionnels et l'épargne retraite - Aurélie Boubel et Fabrice Pansard

Économie internationale 96 (2003), p. 43-62.
www.cairn.info/load_pdf.php?ID_ARTICLE=ECOI_096_0043

Les systèmes financiers des pays industrialisés ont connu d'importantes modifications aux cours des dernières décennies. Certes les banques demeurent toujours au centre de la sphere financière, mais le métier de l'intermédiation financière bascule de plus en plus aux mains des investisseurs institutionnels, ce mouvement s'opérant parallèlement à la montée en force des marchés de titres (Rybczynski, 1997 ; Byrne et Davis, 2002). Bien entendu, ces tendances ne se présentent pas de manière uniforme dans chaque pays, et de fortes disparités demeurent. En particulier, le processus d'institutionnalisation de l'épargne est beaucoup plus avancé dans les pays anglo-saxons, du fait de leur adoption de longue date de systèmes de retraite par capitalisation.

Dans la plupart des pays d'Europe continentale, des réflexions sont menées pour mettre en place à grande échelle un mode de financement complémentaire des dépenses de retraite fondé sur la capitalisation. De multiples questions sont posées par l'instauration de ce type de mécanisme. Si certaines ont une teneur sociale, portant notamment sur la problématique de l'équité, d'autres, comme le rôle que joueront les différents intermédiaires (compagnies d'assurance, sociétés de gestion…) dans les dispositifs en discussion, interpellent plus directement l'industrie financière. C'est cette dernière problématique que nous abordons ici, en prenant comme base d'analyse les expériences menées par les États-Unis et le Royaume-Uni.

Après une présentation des formes d'intermédiation financière en vigueur dans les principaux pays de la zone euro ainsi qu'aux États-Unis et au Royaume-Uni, nous cherchons à mieux cerner le rôle des dispositifs de retraite dans la structuration de l'industrie financière au sein de ces deux derniers pays. Le premier constat est que l'instauration de fonds de pension s'est réalisée de manière très diverse dans les pays ayant opté pour ce type de système, et que derrière cette appellation générique se cache une réalité qui n'a rien d'uniforme. Simples enveloppes fiscales, fonds à part entière (fonds de pension) ou produits offerts par les compagnies d'assurance, les produits d'épargne retraite ont de multiples facettes aux États-Unis et au Royaume-Uni. Le second constat que nous dressons est que les choix réalisés, au sein de ces deux pays, par les pouvoirs publics en termes de dispositifs d'épargne retraite ont influencé de manière significative le partage du marché de l'épargne entre les différents investisseurs institutionnels, avec comme conséquence des modèles américains et britanniques sensiblement différents.

The death of the adverb revisited:
Attested uses of adverbs in native and non-native comparable corpora of spoken English

Pascual Pérez-Paredes, University of Murcia, Spain

> University education should concentrate more on vocabulary
> development [...] (Pérez Basanta, 2005: 560)

1. Introduction

I was daunted by the opening lines of Anatoly Liberman's blog entry "Do it real quick: or the death of the adverb", in his OUP USA *The Oxford Etymologist*[1]. In this column, Liberman makes the point that the line between adjectives and adverbs is becoming blurred, and that eventually adverb endings are likely to disappear: "Individual cases are hard to explain, and valid generalizations are hardly earned, but the tendency is obvious: adverbs are on the retreat in Modern English". Certainly, that has been the English way in the past. Liberman's statement about the 'death' of the adverb made me curious about the use of adverbs. However, even more shocking was the fact that we can all too easily, maybe too 'easy', make generalizations about language use based on our perceptions or personal experiences, contact with a language or plain introspection.

Adverb acquisition has been reported as being a problematic area for non-native advanced speakers of English. In some studies, this view is based on non-natives' over-use or under-use of degree adverbs such as *very* (Philip, 2008). My study takes a slightly different path, surveying the actual use of adverbs in contemporary spoken English in two distinct groups of young adult speakers, British English native speakers of English, and Spanish learners of English as a Foreign Language (EFL) who carried out the *same* speaking task. In doing so, I have tried to play up the comparability of the two corpora, as both groups were not only asked to speak about the same topic but were also presented with exactly the same visual prompts. Similarly, I 'downgraded' the elicitation task by asking native speakers to perform a communicative task which is common in the field of foreign language teaching, rather than asking non-native speakers to 'upgrade' and perform communicative tasks alien to their practice and knowledge. In this way, my approach to corpus data complies with the notion of *authenticity* outlined by Widdowson (1996) and, in a wider context, with a position which calls for re-thinking of the relationship between corpus linguistics and applied linguistics (Pérez-Paredes, 2010 in press).

The research question I have tried to answer is as follows:

- If upper-intermediate learners of English use adverbs differently from native speakers, how does this use differ (a) quantitatively and (b) qualitatively?

2. Literature review

Pérez Basanta (2005) has shown her concern for the low lexical competence of EFL Spanish university learners, a conclusion supported by Sánchez-Hernández and Pérez-Paredes (2005) in English for Academic Purposes (EAP) in the field of psychology. More specifically, the use of adverbs by learners of English, or non-native speakers of English, has been thematically neglected in applied linguistics (Philip, 2008). This is an area where Spanish learners of English have similarly underperformed (Pérez-Paredes et al., forthcoming).

The learner corpus bibliography[2] available at the Centre for English Corpus Linguistics, University of Louvain, Belgium, updated on July 22, 2009, contains only two bibliographical entries where the use of adverbs is explicit. Altenberg and Tapper (1998) focused on the analysis of conjuncts. The authors compared, in the main, the uses of conjuncts in essays of advanced Swedish learners of English (n=86) against the essays written by English native speakers (n=70). Although the total tokens considered is the same (50,000 words), the average length of the essays differed considerably, 580 in the case of the Swedish learners and 1,000 in the case of the English native speakers. The results of the study show that, in general, Swedish learners underuse conjuncts as compared to their English peers, and, in particular, resultive and contrastive conjuncts. Some conjuncts are overused, the case with *furthermore, still* and *for instance*. The study by Altenberg and Tapper presents important affordances in the field of contrastive learner/native languages, as it spotlights the need to use comparable data obtained in identical, or at least similar, communicative settings, using, at the same time, data collection procedures which are far from being unknown to EFL learners.

Osborne (2008) analyzed adverb placement in post-intermediate learner English. This study differs from Altenberg and Tapper (1998) and is more in keeping with the thriving field in contrastive studies which deals with optionality theory (Lozano, 2008). In analyzing thematic verb raising and verb-to in non-native grammars, Eubank et al. (1997) and Eubank and Grace (1998) also treated the placement of adverbs in a marginal way. Osborne (2008) found that speakers of French, Italian and Spanish preferred a non-native Verb-Adverb-Object arrangement much more distinctively than speakers of Germanic languages, mainly Dutch, German and Swedish speakers. The corpora used in this study included both native and non-native essays, in particular the different subcomponents of the ICLE corpora (Granger, 1993).

These two studies point to the fact that native and non-native speakers use adverbs differently. This finding is corroborated by research in learner language, which has pointed out that the use of adverbs seems to be a problem area for Dutch learners of English (de Haan, 1999), French learners of English (Granger, 1998; Osborne, 2008), Italian learners of English (Philip, 2008) as well as for Germans (Lorenz, 1999). Most of the time, this statement is based on the frequency of use of a particular adverb (Hsue-Hueh Shih, 2000), syntactic properties (Lorenz, 1999) or proficiency level. De Haan (1999), for example, found that the use of adverbs increases with the proficiency level of the learners. Gilquin et al. (2007) report overuse of adverbs expressing a high degree of certainty and underuse even in very common hedging adverbs in academic writing. Using the same methodology research as the one advocated here, Pérez-Paredes et al. (forthcoming) have investigated the use of adverbial hedges in a sample of Spanish and British speakers of English. They found that, given the narrower range of uses of the adverbial hedges in the Spanish speakers, rhetorical awareness of the hedging device as manifested by adverbials (*sort of*, *kind of*, *maybe* and *almost*) is much lower, which may result in poor persuasive language skills and a different projection of the affective interpretations that the interlocutors are engaged in.

3. Methodology

3. 1. Informants

This study uses two different sources of data. The first is a learner corpus, the Spanish component of the Contrastive Analysis of Orality in Spoken English (CAOS-E) corpus[3], made up of interviews with EAP learners, with a mean age of 19.6 (n=59), all of them native speakers of Spanish, with an average 8.8 years of study of English prior to university. All the students were enrolled in the first year of the Degree in English Studies at the University of Murcia, Spain. The total number of words, considering only the informants' production, not the interviewers', is 45,558[4], and the mean word count is 772.16 per contributor. The interviews were recorded in the 2004-2005 academic year.

The second corpus is the British component of the CAOS-E corpus made up of interviews with British students of Modern Languages (ML), all native speakers of English, with a mean age of 22.25 (n=28). The total number of words considered in this corpus is 21,509, with a mean word count per contributor of 768.17. The interviews were recorded in the Manchester Metropolitan University, in the 2005-2006 academic year.

One of the reasons underlying this choice of informants was the use of comparable data from speakers with similar profiles in Spain and the UK, thus minimizing some of the problems involved when analysing vocabulary (Pérez Basanta, 2005). The CAOS-E corpora were POS-tagged and processed for Multidimensional Analysis (Biber, 1988) by Douglas Biber at the Corpus Linguistics Research Program at Northern Arizona University, USA.

3. 2. Task

The CAOS-E interviews followed the same 3-part format of The Louvain International Database of Spoken English Interlanguage (LINDSEI) corpus (De Cock, 1998; Brand, Kämmerer, 2006). Speakers were first given three topics for discussion, namely, an experience that had taught the speaker an important lesson, a country that had impressed the contributor or a film or play that had attracted the attention of the speaker. A small part of the interview was then devoted to interpersonal communication. Finally, students were given four pictures which represented a story and were asked to describe them and offer an account of what was going on. The pictures gave speakers the chance to elaborate on individual interpretations of a situation where a woman is having her portrait taken, but seems to be dissatisfied with the painter's first attempts.

Given the identical nature of the spoken task involved in the third part of the interview in both groups of speakers, this is precisely the data that will be considered in this study[5]. The total number of words in the British speakers' corpus, considering only the informants', and not the interviewers', production, is 4,455, and the mean word count is 159.1 per contributor.

3. 3. Discrete elements analysed

Even in recent grammatical accounts of the English language (Biber et al., 1999: 552-560), adverbs have been divided into the traditional categories of place, time, manner, and degree. Among the latter, we find a further subdivision into amplifiers and diminishers or downtoners (Biber et al., 1999). Adverbs of manner, time or place are usually labelled as circumstantial adverbs. This survey looks at the occurrence of amplifier adverbs (*absolutely*, *completely*, etc.), downtoner adverbs (*nearly*, *only*, etc.), emphatic adverbs (*just*, *really*, etc.) and adverbs functioning as discourse particles (*well*, *anyway*, etc.). The group of adverbial hedges has been previously analysed (Pérez-Paredes et al., forthcoming), so they will not be included here. General adverbs (*quite*, *perhaps*, etc.) will be looked at, although their multipurpose nature in Biber (1988) makes it difficult to provide anything other than quantitative accounts. By comparing the normalized frequencies of use of these sets of adverbs, I will attempt to provide further insights into the extent of the use of the items analysed in both corpora.

The second, qualitative, aspect of the research question posed above in *Section 1* will be answered by looking at the output of multidimensional analyses performed on the two corpora of this study. Multidimensional Analysis (MA) involves the use of statistical techniques to study register variation in attested uses of language. Biber (1988) carried out factor analysis to explore the distribution and clustering of different linguistic features across registers in English. Each group of co-occurring features becomes a dimension at whose extremes register types are found which show a remarkably different mean score for this particular dimension. The interpretation of this data leads us to the assumption that features appearing very frequently in a particular register, i.e. official documents, are usually rare in another, i.e. broadcasts in the case of Dimension 3 – situation-dependent versus elaborated reference – (Conrad, Biber, 2001).

MA differs from other corpus methods in important practical ways. The focus of MA shifts the researchers' attention from mere comparison between two or more corpora to the notion of language variation as a continuum, foregrounding major functional trends that go beyond the individual analysis of particular linguistic features, i.e. hedges or nominalization. Using this statistical procedure, puts us in a better position to assess the influence of adverbs in the overall picture emerging from the factor analysis which has been used to account for the different functions of texts.

4. Results

The following paragraphs (*Sections 4.1.* to *4.5.*) present both the absolute frequencies observed for the items analyzed as well as their relative frequencies per 1,000 words. Also included is a normalized ratio of the speakers who used the different items analyzed. One sample is given for every item and corpus. *Section 4.6.* presents some of the properties of the data analyzed, while *Section 4.7.* outlines MA results of these corpora.

4. 1. Amplifier adverbs

In the learner corpus, 4 occurrences of amplifier adverbs were found: 2 occurrences of *obviously*, one occurrence of *absolutely* and one of *actually*:

- C1-3: her her friends .. but it's {ABSOLUTELY} different mm the portrait   and   she...;
- C1-5: think this is about .. well {OBVIOUSLY} a painter that it has...;
- C1-18: it again but .. better .. but .. {ACTUALLY} .. is like .. the picture is...

The relative frequency of this set of adverbs vis-à-vis the total number of tokens in the third part of the corpus was 0.8, while the relative frequency of users of this adverb category, per 1,000 individuals, was 67.7.

27 occurrences of amplifier adverbs were found in the native speaker corpus: 16 occurrences of *actually*, 10 occurrences of *obviously*, and one occurrence of *absolutely*:

- C2-12: would suggest that they don't {ACTUALLY} erm .. feel that it's a ...;
- C2-3: way she looks .. and he's {OBVIOUSLY} gone and changed it .. to ...;
- C2-8: in this final one she's {ABSOLUTELY} .. ecstatic and over the moon ...

The relative frequency of this set of adverbs vis-à-vis the total number of tokens in the third part of the corpus was 6.06, while the relative frequency of users of this adverb category per 1,000 individuals was 535.7.

4. 2. Downtoner adverbs

Only one occurrence of a downtoner adverb, the adverb *basically*, was found in the learner corpus:

- C1-27: she's telling things .. she's angry {BASICALLY} .. in the third one he's...

There was no trace of adverbs such as *merely* or *slightly* in the spoken production of the 59 informants. The relative frequency of this set of adverbs vis-à-vis the total number of tokens in the third part of the corpus was 0.2, while the relative frequency of users of this adverb category per 1,000 individuals was 16.9.

In the native speaker corpus, 3 occurrences of amplifier adverbs were found: 2 occurrences of *slightly* and one occurrence of *basically*:

- C2-4: asking her to .. even move {SLIGHTLY} or .. like she has moved …;
- C2-20: what she doesn't like .. she {BASICALLY} looks .. quite miserable .. erm .. boring…

The relative frequency of this set of adverbs vis-à-vis the total number of tokens in the third part of the corpus was 0.6, while the relative frequency of users of this adverb category per 1,000 individuals was 107.14.

4. 3. Emphatic adverbs

12 occurrences of amplifier adverbs were found in the learner corpus: 10 occurrences of *really*, one occurrence of *just* and one of *so*:

- C1- 3: made her very beautiful .. and {REALLY} she's not yeah yeah okay…;
- C1-11: that paint the painter er {JUST} to have her portrait you …;
- C1-8: me I'm like this I'm {SO} beautiful .. well I think she…

The relative frequency of this set of adverbs vis-à-vis the total number of tokens in the third part of the corpus was 2.4, while the relative frequency of users of this adverb category per 1,000 individuals was 152.5.

In the native speaker corpus, 9 occurrences of amplifier adverbs were found: 5 occurrences of *really* and 4 of *just*:

- C2-27: so he says alright I'm {REALLY} sorry .. I suppose if you …;
- C2-23: hand side .. bottom left .. he's {JUST} made an adjustment .. erm to…

The relative frequency of this set of adverbs vis-à-vis the total number of tokens in the third part of the corpus was 2.02, while the relative frequency of users of this adverb category, per 1,000 individuals, was 285.7.

4. 4. Discourse particle adverbs

29 occurrences of amplifier adverbs were found in the learner corpus: 21 occurrences of *okay* and 8 of *well*:

- C1- 1: mal no sé que decir {OKAY} er .. there is a girl …;
- C1-8: like this I'm so beautiful .. {WELL} I think she .. yes .. that …

The relative frequency of this set of adverbs vis-à-vis the total number of tokens in the third part of the corpus was 5.8, while the relative frequency of users of this adverb category per 1,000 individuals was 305.08.

In the native speaker corpus, 33 occurrences of amplifier adverbs were found: 28 occurrences of *okay* and 5 of *well*:

- C2-4: think they're doing erm .. oh {OKAY} I see .. erm .. well the…;
- C2-3: mhm .. erm .. {WELL} he's drawing .. her in this …

The relative frequency of this set of adverbs vis-à-vis the total number of tokens in the third part of the corpus was 7.4, while the relative frequency of users of this adverb category, per 1,000 individuals, was 607.1.

4. 5. General adverbs

28 occurrences of general adverbs were found in the learner corpus, including 6 occurrences of *a little*, 5 occurrences of *finally*, and one of *probably*:

- C1- 38: and the .. the woman are {A LITTLE} .. disagree of the .. picture .. and …;
- C1-2: but .. erm more beautiful .. and {FINALLY} the the girl or the …;
- C1-4: don't know .. I don't know {PROBABLY} .. the .. the woman .. ask the …

The relative frequency of this set of adverbs vis-à-vis the total number of tokens in the third part of the corpus was 5.6, while the relative frequency of users of this adverb category per 1,000 individuals was 322.03.

In the native speaker corpus, 42 occurrences of amplifier adverbs were found, including 9 occurrences of *quite*, 6 of *probably*, 3 of *pretty* and 2 of *exactly*:

- C2-4: is .. erm .. he doesn't look {QUITE} happy about that but he …;
- C2-5: next one so what he's {PROBABLY} done is he's tried to …;
- C2-13: erm .. he seems to be {PRETTY} good actually .. so it's probably…;
- C2-20: C2-20: and erm obviously it's not .. {EXACTLY} her but .. she likes it…

The relative frequency of this set of adverbs vis-à-vis the total number of tokens in the third part of the corpus was 9.4, while the relative frequency of users of this adverb category per 1,000 individuals was 535.7.

4. 6. Data frequency properties

Table 1 summarizes the distributional data for the five types of adverbs considered in this study. Mean frequency scores (*Figure 1*) show that the British speakers outdid their Spanish peers in all five adverb counts: 3.1 times higher in the case of general adverbs, 13.7 times higher in the case of amplifiers, 5.5 times higher in the case of downtoners, 1.6 times higher in the case of emphatic adverbs and, lastly, 2.4 times higher in the case of adverbs used as discourse particles. Overall, the L2 learners used 1.2 general, amplifier, downtoner, emphatic and discourse particle adverbs in the speaking task while the natives used 4.07.

Data sets		General adverb	Adverb + amplifier	Adverb + downtoner	Adverb + emphatic	Adverb + discourse particle
EAP learner Corpus	Individuals	59	59	59	59	59
	Mean	0.47	0.07	0.02	0.20	0.49
	Minimum	0	0	0	0	0
	Maximum	4	1	1	3	4
	Range	4	1	1	3	4
	Std. Deviation	0.878	0.254	0.130	0.550	0.878
	Kurtosis	7.401	10.818	59.000	12.379	4.075
	Std. Error of Kurtosis	0.613	0.613	0.613	0.613	0.613
	Skewness	2.532	3.529	7.681	3.299	2.002
	Std. Error of Skewness	0.311	0.311	0.311	0.311	0.311
	Sum	28	4	1	12	29
	% of Total Sum	40.0%	12.9%	25.0%	57.1%	46.8%
Native Speaker Corpus	Individuals	28	28	28	28	28
	Mean	1.50	0.96	0.11	0.32	1.18
	Minimum	0	0	0	0	0
	Maximum	8	4	1	2	6
	Range	8	4	1	2	6
	Std. Deviation	1.991	1.319	0.315	0.548	1.335
	Kurtosis	2.892	0.058	5.614	1.581	5.153
	Std. Error of Kurtosis	0.858	0.858	0.858	0.858	0.858
	Skewness	1.638	1.113	2.686	1.516	1.863
	Std. Error of Skewness	0.441	0.441	0.441	0.441	0.441
	Sum	42	27	3	9	33
	% of Total Sum	60.0%	87.1%	75.0%	42.9%	53.2%

Table 1: Data distribution of all 5 adverb types analysed

Lower kurtosis distributions are only found in the mean scores for adverbs used as discourse particles (4.075) and general adverbs (7.401) in the learner corpus, as well as in adverbs used as amplifiers (0.058) and adverbs used to express emphasis (1.581) in the native speaker corpus. This shows that none of the five distributional series is normal in the learner corpus, while only two are normal in the case of the native speaker data set (kurt < 2). The skewness statistics confirm this tendency.

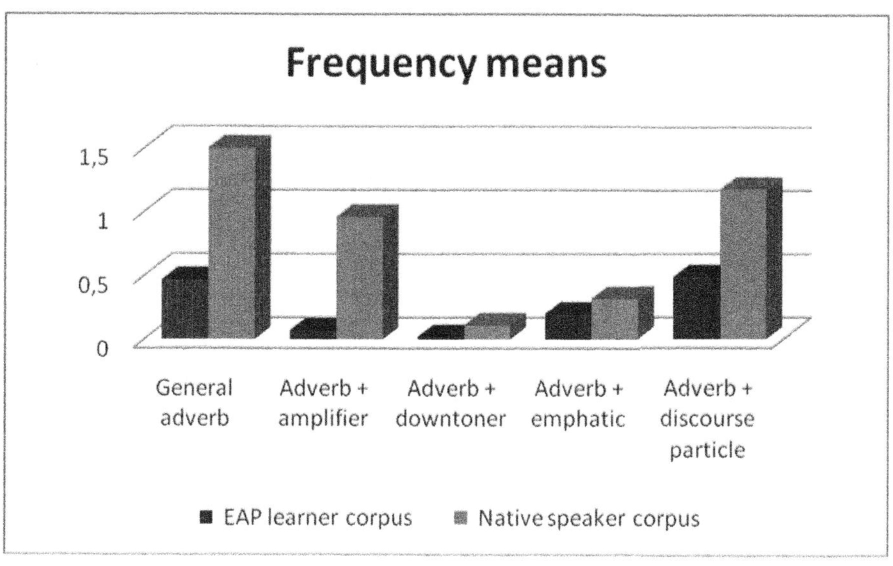

Figure 1: Frequency means

4. 7. Multidimensional profile

Text registers can be profiled through MA, giving linguists the chance to further analyze and characterize language according to dimensions of use. For every dimension, a particular set of texts representing a register creates a dimension score which can be contrasted with the dimension scores for other sets of texts and registers. In this way, the choice of discrete linguistic features such as the one analyzed here can be seen in conjunction with other features as conforming registers. For the purposes of this study, only Dimensions 1 – involved versus informational production – and 3 – elaborated reference versus situation-dependent reference – appear to be affected by the frequency of use of the adverbs considered in my analysis (Biber, 1988; Conrad, Biber, 2001). Adverbs used as downtoners and adverbs used as particles played no significant role in the configuration of any of the main factors or dimensions isolated by Biber (1988).

In Biber's (1988) seminal study, the overall score for general adverbs was 65.6, 71.8 in the case of the interview register, 86 in the case of face-to-face conversations and 65.4 in the case of spontaneous speech. The speakers in the learner corpus achieved a mean score of 28.2, while the mean score for British speakers in the native corpus was 31.4 (*Figure 2*).

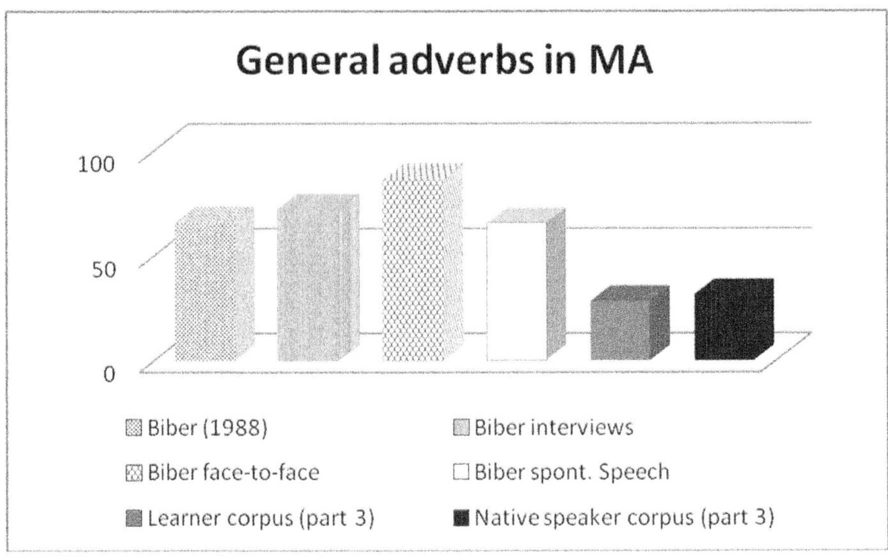

Figure 2: MA overall scores of general adverbs

The overall score for emphatic adverbs (*Figure 3*) was 6.3, 9.7 in the case of the interview register, 12.2 in the case of face-to-face conversations and 5.8 in the case of spontaneous speech. The speakers in the learner corpus achieved a mean score of 2.9, while the British speakers in the native corpus achieved a mean score of 2.5.

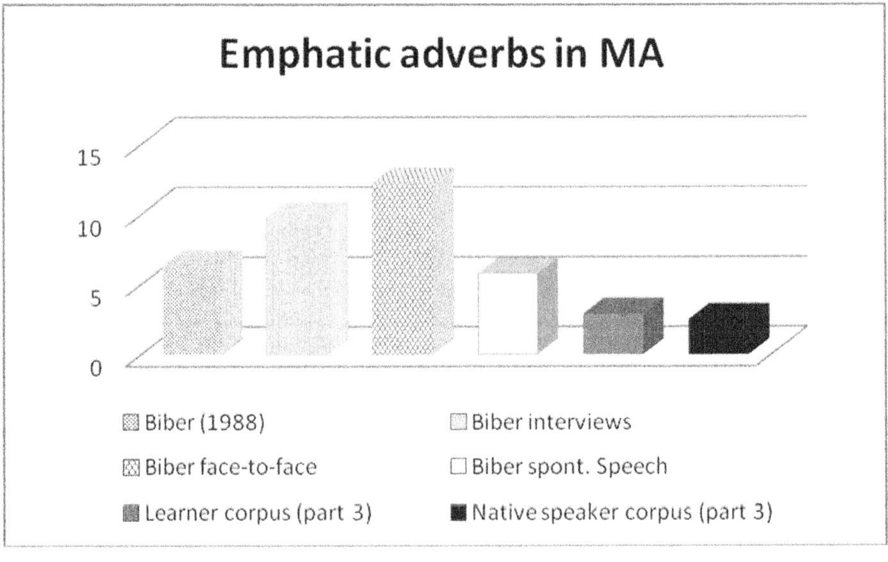

Figure 3: MA overall scores of emphatic adverbs

The overall score for amplifier adverbs (*Figure 4*) was 2.7, 6.8 in the case of the interview register, 6 in the case of face-to-face conversations and 5.1 in the case of spontaneous speech. The speakers in the learner corpus achieved a mean score of 12.6, while the British speakers in the native corpus achieved a mean score of 9.5. General adverbs is the most relevant linguistic feature on Dimension 3, further up the list before nominalizations, scoring 19.9.

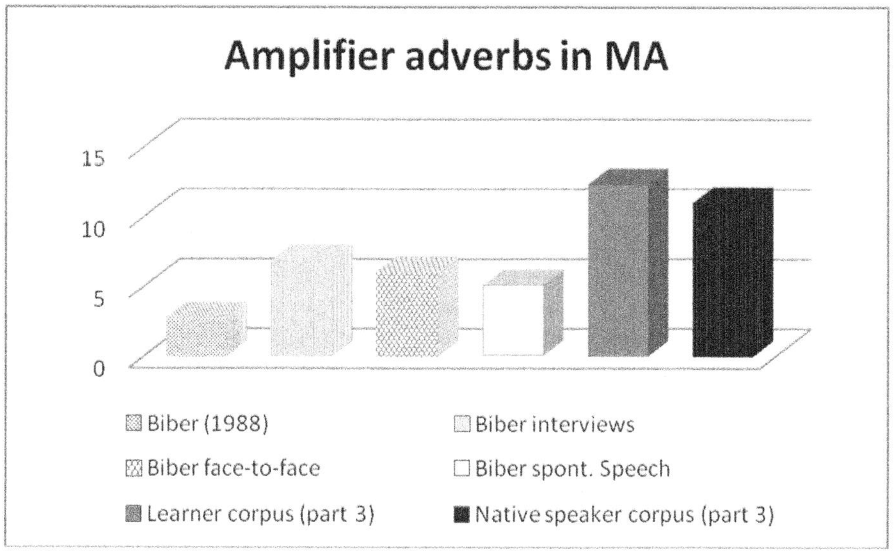

Figure 4: MA overall scores of amplifier adverbs

Table 2 summarizes these results and, in brackets, provides the mean scores for all three adverb types considered in the three parts of the corpus (see *Section 3.1.*):

	General Adverbs	Emphatic Adverbs	Amplifier adverbs
Biber (1988) overall score	65.6	6.3	2.7
Biber (1988) interview register score	71.8	9.7	6.8
Biber (1988) face-to-face conversation register score	86	12.2	6
Biber (1988) spontaneous speech register score	65.4	5.8	5.1
Learner corpus	28.26 (29.9)	2.99 (5.2)	12.3 (12.6)
Native speaker corpus	31.4 (41.5)	2.5 (14.06)	11 (9.5)

Table 2: Scores in different corpora

5. Discussion

The research questions in this study need to be understood within the scope of efforts to maximize the comparability of corpora (Ädel, 2006) and as a way to make up for the well-known problems present in any corpus study, no matter how large a corpus is or how well it claims to represent a particular language, group of speakers or genre (Gilquin, Gries, 2009; Gries, 2010 in press). In particular, this study sheds light on the uses of a group of adverbs by native and non-native speakers of English asked to give an account of a cartoon story, very much in keeping with 'standard' EFL oral proficiency tests. In this sense, I have not, primarily, tried to establish a comparison between native speakers' use of adverbs as manifested in principled corpora, but rather I have done so in terms of the *actual* language that native speakers used when fulfilling a task, one which is not likely to be represented in principled corpora at all but which is almost certainly one language learners will have faced in the course of their formal EFL instruction. This approach thus seeks to overcome methodological problems that may occur when data is not comparable in this way. A case in point is Park and Lee (2005), who used the type-token ratio of adverbs, found in Japanese and Korean learners of English taking part in cyberspace interaction, and compared it with data from the *Collins COBUILD English Dictionary for Advanced Learners of English*.

The results outlined in *Section 4* confirm that the Spanish learners of English in this study use adverbs in a different way to the British university students who contributed to the native speakers' corpus analyzed. However, on closer examination, the data also shows that native speakers do *not* outperform or perform differently from non-native speakers in a systematic way, simply because they are more proficient. The whole set of amplifier adverbs (see *Section 4.1.*) was only used 0.8 times per 1,000 tokens, while native speakers used them 6.06 times. When the number of users is normalized, only 67.7 over 1,000 upper-intermediate Spanish learners of English use amplifiers, which compared to 535.7 per 1,000 British speakers makes it very clear that the amplifier adverb is not part of the active spoken lexical repertoire of these Spanish learners. This is confirmed by Pérez Basanta (2005), who analyzed the vocabulary of learners with an identical profile.

Downtoner adverbs (see *Section 4.2.*) are virtually neglected by both groups of informants, as one speaker in the learner corpus and three in the native speaker corpus used either *basically* or *slightly*. For a corpus linguist, this is a clear indication that important features of a language may be absent from the general count, an argument for the use of 'the-larger-the-better' approach to corpora. However, for the applied linguist, interested in pedagogical applications, there is an important lesson to be learned, namely that this particular task was not sensitive to the range of meanings usually found in the use of downtoner adverbs. However, we were only in a position to appreciate this *once* we had recorded, transcribed, tagged and retrieved the information from a comparable native corpus. This raises an important issue for those carrying out research in language evaluation, namely, how to accommodate the expected appearance of linguistic features in the discourse of learners. In other words, language assessment has traditionally been reactive to learner's speech: evaluators assess learners' language and identify signs of proficiency there, including language features. The data in this study does not support this approach. Native speakers, at least within the range of the adverbs analyzed here, *do not* systematically outperform non-natives in *quantitative* terms. Although the problem deserves further attention and specific research, I am tempted to affirm that a careful investigation of the properties of the register, or sub-register, used for testing or evaluation purposes would enable language educators to design more robust and valid tests. This is an area where MA may prove useful.

The set of emphatic adverbs (see *Section 4.3.*) is used by learners 2.4 times per 1,000 tokens, while native speakers use it 2.04 times. When the number of users is normalized, 152.5 per 1,000 upper-intermediate Spanish learners of English use emphatic adverbs, which, compared to 285.7 per 1,000 British speakers, points to the fact that the speaking task used to collect the data certainly did not spark much need to express emphasis through adverbs. In this respect, the position of emphatic adverbs is similar to that of downtoner adverbs.

The set of discourse particle adverbs (see *Section 4.4.*) was used by learners 5.8 times per 1,000 tokens, while native speakers used it 7.4 times. When the number of users is normalized, 305.08 per 1,000 upper-intermediate Spanish learners of English use discourse particle adverbs, which compared to 607.1 per 1,000 British speakers points to the fact that, despite its presence in the active spoken lexical repertoire of the Spanish learners, the use of discourse particle adverbs in *quantitative* terms lags far behind that of young British speakers. The pervasiveness of *okay* needs to be pointed out both in the Spanish speakers corpus, and, perhaps even more strongly in the British corpus where 28 out of 33 occurrences of this type of adverb can be attributed to this particle, possibly an indication of low lexical density language among young speakers, even when they are, respectively, EAP learners and Modern Language students in tertiary education. There is no attested use in the corpus of a discourse particle adverb other than *okay* and *well*, not even *now*, in this function.

The set of general adverbs (see *Section 4.5.*) was used by learners 5.6 times per 1,000 tokens, while native speakers used it 9.4 times. When the number of users is normalized, 322.03 per 1,000 upper-intermediate Spanish learners of English use emphatic adverbs which compared to 535.7 per 1000 British speakers points to the fact that, despite its presence in the spoken active lexical repertoire of the Spanish learners, the use of general adverbs lags quantitatively far behind young British speakers who, not surprisingly, use a wider repertoire, including adverbs such as *moderately*, *quite* or *rather*, not found at all in the learner corpus.

In our data, 29 out of 59 informants used no general, amplifier, downtoner, emphatic or discourse particle adverb whatsoever, which explains the different mean scores for frequency used (see *Section 4.7.*). The following is a transcription of one of the speakers in the learner corpus (C1-9):

> mm I think it's um: a girl .. who wants that .. um a very famous .. mm .. painter er draw um
> a picture of her .. but I think she: ... .. she: try to: em draw her: very beautiful but he: ..
> bueno da igual she: thinks that he sorry she thinks that the picture is not: so much em like
> her .. and: um because of in that girl ask   h e r
> friends if they think   the woman in the picture is .. like her (CAOS-E, Corpus 1, C1-9).

This transcription confirms Pérez Basanta's (2005) findings about the low-level performance of Spanish EAP learners, as well as de Haan's (1999) finding that proficiency levels correlate with the use of adverbs. However, I believe that these statements need further exploration. In the British speakers' corpus, 7 out of 28 informants, i.e. 25%, used no general, amplifier, downtoner, emphatic or discourse particle adverb whatsoever. The following is a transcription of one of the speakers in the British corpus (C2-2):

> there's a man there, painting a picture..he's looking at a woman there erm.. studying it..in
> the second picture it's just, you know.., she eh.. doesn't like the painting very much, so
> she's getting angry with him, and I think in the third picture, he's painted her a lot better
> than she: looks herself..in the fourth picture, she's   showing her friends, and she's
> very impressed with it.. (CAOS-E, Corpus 2, C2-2).

The speaker approaches the task very straightforwardly, in a matter-of-fact way, no flowery prose or further insights into what could be possibly going on is given. So, for some native speakers using the types of adverbs under scrutiny seems to be simply unnecessary. Is this a signal of under-competence? Obviously, the question is rhetorical and designed merely to underscore an apparent clash between expectancies in terms of proficiency assessment (de Haan, 1999) and real, attested use of language.

Does this difference in the use of adverbs affect the nature of the register? This second research question can only be answered after looking at the data in *Section 4.7*. However, it is difficult to respond to this question in absolute terms as we need a new factor analysis which takes into account the language variation continuum emerging from the analysis of the interviews in our corpora in terms of a different register. Looking at the differences between the native and non-native speakers, we can only appreciate slight quantitative differences in all the three scores considered, (general, emphatic and amplifier adverbs).

Amplifier adverbs, largely underused by non-native speakers as compared to native speakers, appear to move away from the mean scores in Biber's (1988) analysis, more dramatically when we take all the texts and text typologies analyzed into account (*Section 4.7.*). This may be attributed either to the spoken nature of the data or the distance in time between the texts in Biber (1988) and those in CAOS-E, recorded in 2004, 2005 and 2006. The mean score associated to amplifier verbs is, even so, high, even higher in the case of learners. The face-to-face conversations and spontaneous speech texts in Biber (1988) show a different tendency as far as the use of amplifier adverbs is concerned. If we consider the scores in Biber (1988), our informants' use of amplifier adverbs approaches the interview register (mean score of 6) rather than, for example, that of official documents (mean score of 0.9) or academic prose (mean score of 1.4).

The situation is reversed in the case of general adverbs, where both native and non-native speakers seem to output low mean scores, 28.2 in the case of learners and 31.4 in the case of native speakers, which are, nevertheless, very far from the 65.6 mean score for general adverbs in Biber (1988), 86 in the case of face-to-face conversation. When we consider the scores in Biber (1988), our informants' use of general adverbs is more in line with that of official documents (mean score of 43.7), professional letters (mean score of 49.8) and academic prose (mean score of 51.8).

Finally, the situation with emphatic adverbs is more difficult to assess. While it is true that the mean scores of both native speakers (2.5) and learners (2.9) are below those of the mean score for emphatic adverbs in the registers analyzed in Biber (1988), we cannot overlook the fact that registers such as spontaneous speech yield a mean score of 5.8 for this type of adverb. Others, however, are much farther away, such as face-to-face conversations (12.2), or interviews (9.7). When we consider the scores in Biber (1988), our informants' use of emphatic adverbs is more in line with that of academic prose (mean score of 3.6), official documents (mean score of 4) and general fiction (mean score of 4.9).

6. Conclusions

The use of MA methodology confirms my previous findings (see *4.1.* to *4.6.*) on the differences in learners' use of the adverbs analyzed here when compared to standard, principled corpora. However, this difference works in different ways and levels. First, it applies to both non-native and native speakers of English, who seem to come closer to Biber's (1988) *mainstream* mean scores in the case of general adverbs and amplifier adverbs than learners do, but who remain equally distant from expected mean scores for emphatic adverbs. These three adverb types seem to streamline their uses in different ways. Second, while the use of amplifier adverbs in the corpora analyzed is extraordinarily high, the uses of emphatic adverbs and general adverbs actually resemble frequency patterns which square with other registers, sometimes as divergent as academic prose (in the case of empathic adverbs) or official documents (in the case of general adverbs). A multivariable analysis seems to be required to assess whether these differences can, *inter alia*, be attributed to the collection-time variable. Third, when compared against the text registers in Biber (1988), I have found that the informants in the native and non-native corpora use a divergent frequency pattern, which is difficult to square with a single register. However, under the light of MA, and when compared, the data from the native and the non-native speakers' corpora show significant similarities. This finding tentatively leads us to affirm that the pedagogical interview register, represented here by the CAOS-E corpora (Pérez-Paredes et al., forthcoming) and the LINDSEI corpus (De Cock, 1998; Brand, Kämmerer, 2006), may be characterized by important peculiarities which differ from standard registers in principled corpora. If this finding is further confirmed, it will invalidate straightforward native/non-native language comparisons with corpora where this register is not represented.

Ädel (2006) explains linguistic differences between learners and native speakers on the grounds of register awareness, cultural conventions, general learner strategies and genre comparability. The use of MA has proved useful in showing that a bigger picture based on register variation reveals that the significant differences in terms of frequency, found in *Sections 4.1.* to *4.6.*, disappear when we look at adverbs used in other *mainstream* registers. Further research should try and explore whether my findings apply to other linguistic features. A new MA analysis of the whole LINDSEI corpus and a comparable native language corpus may help shed further light into the actual register types found in the realm of the pedagogical interview.

Acknowledgements

The research leading to this article was funded by Fundación Séneca-Agencia de Ciencia y Tecnología de la Región de Murcia under II PCTRM 2007-2010 (contract 11091/EE1/09).

Notes

[1] Retrieved September 20, 2009 from *http://blog.oup.com/2007/08/adverb/*
[2] Retrieved September 25, 2009 from *http://cecl.fltr.ucl.ac.be/learner%20corpus%20bibliography.html*
[3] More information on *http://www.um.es/docencia/perez-paredes/labels/CAOS-E.html*
[4] The total count is higher if we include the interviewer's questions, backchannelling and comments. For the purposes of this research I have decided to include only the tokens produced by the students.
[5] Picture retrieved September 25, 2009 from
http://www.fltr.ucl.ac.be/fltr/germ/etan/cecl/Cecl-Projects/Lindsei/pictures.bmp

A web-as-multimodal corpus approach to lexical studies based on intercultural and scalar principles

Anthony Baldry, University of Messina, Italy

> *semi-automatic genre/topic categorization is a treat by itself, opening up numerous alleys for research (e.g., comparative studies of the language of sports vs. politics, of the rhetoric of comment vs. news articles, training domain-specific language models, etc.).*
>
> (Baroni et al., 2004: 1774)

1. Introduction

This chapter is concerned with research into diversity-aware explorations of the web undertaken within the *Living Knowledge (LK) Project* (Giunchiglia et al., 2009) and specifically with exploring the new field of *web-as-multimodal-corpus concordancing* using *MWS*, part of the suite of concordancing and annotation programs developed at CVML, University of Pavia (Baldry, Coccetta, 2010 in press; Baldry et al., 2010 in press). The major focus of the research presented here is how and why we should carry out direct online concordancing of higher-level web units and how and why we should explore the links between these units and lexical items as an alternative to corpus linguistics that is primarily based on the use of lemma-based techniques. As such, the research is very much part of multimodal corpus linguistics (Baldry, Thibault, 2001, 2006a, 2006b, 2008; Baldry, Coccetta, 2010 in press).

The working hypothesis is that unearthing lexical patterns, and characterizing their properties, needs to be undertaken in relation to the evolution of the web itself, and, in particular, the evolution of the structure of web genres and web page 'layout'. Thus, while clearly supporting the traditional goals of corpus linguistics, the chapter clearly pursues a different goal as compared to the study of lexicogrammatical patterns, the more usual objective of concordancing whether of the *web-as-corpus* type (Aston et al., 2004; Baroni et al., 2006; Hundt et al., 2007) or more traditional types (Sinclair, 1991; Aston, 1995; McEnery, Wilson, 1996; Johansson, Oksefjell, 1998).

In the furtherance of this objective, *Section 2* presents a scalar model of web pages that builds on these previous studies and explains the need for the focus on mini-genres, taken as examples of higher web units detectable in, for instance, online newspaper genres and their subgenres. *Section 3* further characterises *MWS* mini-genre analysis as a first step in the development of concordancing systems capable of incorporating scalar models of multimodal genre analysis and briefly describes the links between traditional KWIC concordancing and genre detection together with a brief look at some of the technical aspects of this linkage. While neither the *LK Project*, nor the *MWS* suite, is directly concerned with pedagogy, *Section 3* also sketches out possible ESP applications for undergraduate and postgraduate students mainly with reference to the potential benefits of manual and semi-automatic techniques in web searching-cum-concordancing activities. Within the overall discussion of the goals of multimodal genre analysis made possible by this new type of concordancing, *Section 4* describes further pedagogically-oriented applications of *MWS* designed to encourage reflection on the interplay between micro-web structures, such as lexical features, and macro-web structures, not just mini-genres but also higher units in the light of their significance when examining the intercultural and socio-political aspects of websites. Overall, the chapter illustrates the appropriateness, for example, within university ESP courses, of examining and comparing opinions as expressed in web texts in the belief that one of the major spin-offs of *web-as-multimodal-corpus* concordancing is a greater capacity to measure trends, conflict, opinions and bias in specific thematic domains such as immigration or climate change, issues which are touched on at various points in the chapter and underscored in the concluding remarks as a way of illuminating and re-interpreting corpus-based lexical studies.

2. Concordancing based on web unit and web genre analysis

What are mini-genres and what are the links between them and web-based concordancing? A scalar model of the web page is a good starting point when attempting to answer these questions and when (re)designing concordancing techniques to fit the needs of web genre analysis. The term *web unit* as used in *Table 1* refers to the individual visual/verbal objects and genres that make up a web page. This term is preferred to others such as *multimodal texts, website/web page meaning-making units* or *web content*. In particular, the term *unit*, in contrast to others such as *content* or *text*, underscores the view that a web page functions, from both sociosemiotic and cognitive standpoints, by making its meanings through the interaction of separate layers of meaning. Thus, the term *web unit* helps promote the idea that a web page is made up of sets of interacting and co-contextualising structures that co-exist on the same meaning-making level, each of which is typically subordinate in its composition to units on higher (inter)semiotic levels but also superordinate to other units on lower meaning-making levels.

TEXT LEVELS	Level 5	Level 4	Level 3	Level 2	Level 1	Level 0
Web units as specific instances	Pagelet	SuperCluster	Cluster	Micro-cluster	SubCluster	Basic resources: language, colour, lines, shapes, spatial disposition etc.
Web genres (i.e. web units as generalised types)	Hypergenre	Genre	Mini-genre	Micro-genre	Genrelet	
Functions of levels	Thematic systems where abstract meanings are made		User interaction and interpretation			

Table 1: A scalar model of a web page

Further interactions and co-contextualizations take place across these levels so as to build up, as it were, a *web of meanings* – not quite the usual meaning associated with the term *web*, when applied to the Internet, but nevertheless aptly describing one of its fundamental properties. In theory, there is no limit to the number of possible levels of web units in a web page; in practice, the model presented in *Table 1*, assumes that, in any given page (assumed to be Level 6) four or five will be typically present but some are likely to be conflated, at various points and in different ways on the same web page. The basic unit with which the web user interacts is the *cluster*. Many clusters have evolved into recurrent objects, or *mini-genres*, e.g. search engines, logos, headlines, subheadlines, captions, photos, videos, menus, indexes. (For mini-genres in printed and digital texts, see Baldry, Thibault, 2006a, 2006b; for a study of mini-genre evolution in university web pages, see Baldry, O'Halloran, in press).

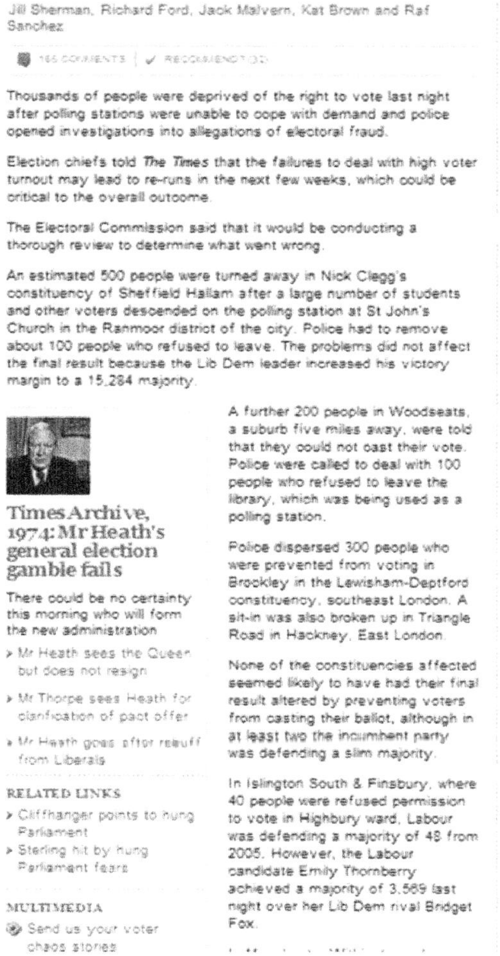

Jill Sherman, Richard Ford, Jack Malvern, Kat Brown and Raf Sanchez

Thousands of people were deprived of the right to vote last night after polling stations were unable to cope with demand and police opened investigations into allegations of electoral fraud.

Election chiefs told *The Times* that the failures to deal with high voter turnout may lead to re-runs in the next few weeks, which could be critical to the overall outcome.

The Electoral Commission said that it would be conducting a thorough review to determine what went wrong.

An estimated 500 people were turned away in Nick Clegg's constituency of Sheffield Hallam after a large number of students and other voters descended on the polling station at St John's Church in the Ranmoor district of the city. Police had to remove about 100 people who refused to leave. The problems did not affect the final result because the Lib Dem leader increased his victory margin to a 15,284 majority.

A further 200 people in Woodseats, a suburb five miles away, were told that they could not cast their vote. Police were called to deal with 100 people who refused to leave the library, which was being used as a polling station.

Police dispersed 300 people who were prevented from voting in Brockley in the Lewisham-Deptford constituency, southeast London. A sit-in was also broken up in Triangle Road in Hackney, East London.

None of the constituencies affected seemed likely to have had their final result altered by preventing voters from casting their ballot, although in at least two the incumbent party was defending a slim majority.

In Islington South & Finsbury, where 40 people were refused permission to vote in Highbury ward, Labour was defending a majority of 48 from 2005. However, the Labour candidate Emily Thornberry achieved a majority of 3,569 last night over her Lib Dem rival Bridget Fox.

Times Archive, 1974: Mr Heath's general election gamble fails

There could be no certainty this morning who will form the new administration

- Mr Heath sees the Queen but does not resign
- Mr Thorpe sees Heath for clarification of pact offer
- Mr Heath goes after rebuff from Liberals

RELATED LINKS

- Cliffhanger points to hung Parliament
- Sterling hit by hung Parliament fears

MULTIMEDIA

Send us your voter chaos stories

Figure 1: Voting in 2010 and 1974

Subclusters (*Table 1*) are the point in the text-making process where resources – language, colours, lines, shapes and so on–are 'mixed together' to create specific meanings. Each subpart will have a characteristic function; a search engine, for instance, usually consists of two parts, the first, a search box in which to type the search word(s), the second, a search-enacting item, typically an arrow or, alternatively, a word such as *Go* which, when clicked, will carry out a web search. Thus, for example, the embedded panel containing the *Times Archive* in *Figure 1* is a web unit functioning at the *supercluster/genre* level; its subunits or *clusters*, are typically marked off by lines or different fonts. The photo and the wording "Times Archive 1974: Mr. Heath's general election gamble fails", for instance, form a *cluster*, a functional unit made up of two *micro-clusters* marked off from the rest of the text by position, cross-reference to Mr. Heath and font size. The second of these is, in its turn, made up of two parts (*Subclusters*) divided by a colon.

Other examples of *micro-clusters* include the many instruction-oriented micro-genres (cf. *Figures 2* and *3* in this respect) made up of two specular visual/verbal micro-clusters, usually an icon followed/preceded by a word such as *Share, Print, E-mail, Submit* and, occasionally, a couple of words such as *Text Size* followed/preceded by one or two icons. At the other end of the scale are higher units, *genres* and *hypergenres*, which represent the more abstract levels of organisation of web pages and about which we still know relatively little and whose forms and functions in many cases seem to be in state of flux, partly as a result of the fact that web genres are evolving, more often than not, quite rapidly (see Baldry, Thibault, 2006a: 136-46; Baldry, Coccetta, 2010 in press). A good example of the existence of higher textual units in both printed and online newspapers are what might be called *co-articles*, juxtaposed texts which are co-present, both formally and functionally. Thus, while readers perceive the relationship in the example given in *Figure 1* as a relationship between an article and a panel-cum-index consisting of hypertext links to articles in 'archival' pages, in actual fact, what is being created is a single overarching web unit enacting the *hypergenre* of *then-now* evolution, relating, in this case, the current political state-of-affairs in the UK to one 36 years before.

Table 1 thus describes functional, rather than formal, units. This extends to the relationship between the instance level and the genre level. In this respect, *Table 1* is a working hypothesis about the probable relationship between specific and typical uses of web units, one that multimodal corpus linguistics seeks to clarify. We may note in passing that there are many cases where *Level 2* is conflated either with *Level 1* or *Level 3* in the texts analysed in this chapter; the distinction between a mini-genre and a micro-genre is thus one of local function rather than overall categorisation. A photo, for example, typically seems to be construed by a user as a mini-genre, even where it is actually functioning at a different level, whether higher or lower. To what degree, *micro-clusters* and *subclusters* need to be categorised as recurrent subparts (i.e. *micro-genres, genrelets*) that are functionally and frequently distinct from mini-genres is an open research issue.

Web users are not normally aware of a web page's scalar patterning. This is partly because the existence of separate levels is obscured by local conflations. Moreover, as eye tracking suggests (Baldry et al., 2010 in press), web users are less aware of the higher web-page units that make up web pages than they are of the intermediate mini-genre level typically expressed through photos, captions, diagrams and tables. This is hardly surprising: many mini-genres derive from verbal and visual literacies that pre-existed the days of digital genres and digital mediacy and are thus familiar to current users thanks to literacy skills acquired through years of experience with printed media. The mini-genre level is thus the level through which web users typically interact with, and act upon, web pages through keyboard typing or the use of a mouse or a touchpad. Whether web literacy will remain this way, or whether higher levels such as *hypergenres* will increasingly emerge, or whether icon-based *micro-genres* will emerge as a markedly separate layer of meaning are further research questions that the tools being developed at CVML are designed to fathom.

Figure 2: A mini-genre analysis of a page from the Independent *in 2009*

Figure 3: A mini-genre analysis of a page from the Daily Telegraph *in 2010*

3. Design features of MWS

As indicated in *Section 1*, the goal of the current stage of *MWS* research within the *LK Project* is to implement the scalar model of the web page given in *Table 1* in terms of mini-genres. Thus, by providing a comparative mini-genre analysis of a *Daily Telegraph* web page on the *Chelsea Flower Show* in 2010 with one from the *Independent* in 1999, an awareness of the web page structure that is hidden from view begins to emerge. The *MWS* mini-genre analysis given at the top of the page (*Figures 2* and *3*) accurately summarises the genre features of two articles detected through a concordance for *Chelsea Flower Show* and identifies the absence in the first article, but presence in the second, of a photo (*Image prompt*) and hence of a *Caption*. This semi-automatic analysis is a first step in detecting the evolution that web pages have typically undergone in the span of a decade vis-à-vis ratios in their verbal, visual and interactive make-up and thus begins, in a very preliminary way, to make this relationship explicit.

As described in more detail below, *MWS* detects *html* patterns in web pages so that, for example, the analysis identifies search words in terms of their distribution in the mini-genres that make up web pages. The latest version of *MWS* extends the prototype possibilities for mini-genre analysis shown in *Figures 2* and *3*, by providing the user (teacher, researcher and so on) with the means to define their own mini-genre templates capable of capturing the 'new' mini-genres represented in *Figure 3* by the *tag-share* (centre), *related articles* (bottom left) *most-viewed* (bottom right) clusters (absent or less prominent in *Figure 2* due to differences in house style and the web's technological and sociosemiotic evolution in the last 10 or so years). This *make-your-own-mini-genre-template* and *do-it-yourself mini-genre analysis* activity permits skilful users to detect Web 2.0 mini-genres (often linked to advertising) that have been added retroactively to web pages (e.g. the *Twitter* advert in *Figure 2* which, since *Twitter* was founded in 2006, indicates a subsequent, automatic advertising add-on).

Hidden in the two reports analysed in *Figures 2* and *3* is an example of bias: while the first article is clearly pro-vegetable, the second is, as it were, pro-flower. The result of editorial policy or simply chance? Charts generated by *MWS* provide the answer in a split second: the 600-odd hits (*Figure 4*, Table bottom left corner) show that flowers have a slight edge over vegetables (*Figure 4*, bottom right: *MultiWord Chart*). An identical search carried out for each of the two newspapers separately (but not reported for reasons of space) gives almost identical results. It also confirms the higher incidence of articles on this thematic in the *Daily Telegraph* (*Figure 4*, top right: *Per Site Chart*) but no special pro-vegetable bias in either of the two newspaper websites searched. So, rest assured, the *Chelsea Flower Show* need not be renamed the *Chelsea Vegetable Show* – not just yet at least!

The *MultiWord Chart* data are the result of a 'multiword' search (*Figure 4*, top left) of the type *flower*vegetable*flower*vegetables* – where * is a separator-cum-instruction to search for these words separately in sequence – in the context of the *Chelsea Flower Show*. Thus, the term 'multiword search' is used in this chapter exclusively to indicate a search consisting of units made up of one or more words separated by an asterisk. Work is in progress to incorporate diagrams and/or charts that correlate the overall distribution (shown in the *MultiWord Chart*) with changes over time (*Figure 4*, bottom centre: *Date Chart*) so as to track the ratio of changes over time in different newspapers and, on this basis, make predictions about future likely trends.

With the exception of titles (a search function already available in *Google*), *MWS* cannot, in its current release, carry out a direct search in the web to find the incidence of the word *flower* or *vegetable,* or indeed any other word or word unit, in relation to *specific* mini-genres (subheadlines, captions, first lines, image prompts and so on). But it *can* do so *indirectly* thanks to the *MGAFilter* tool (*Figure 4*, left) which carries out a second search (*secondary searching*) of the first 'trawl' (*primary searching*). In this way, it is possible to achieve a higher degree of accuracy when assessing the relevance to the meaning of the individual web page articles that *MWS* retrieves through primary searches. For example, the *CompareChart* (*Figure 5*, right), shows the incidence in the *Daily Telegraph* of the 30-odd mentions of the year 2009 in the overall set of almost 400 *Chelsea Flower Show* concordances but identifies just 4 dateline mentions and hence accurately dates 4 articles to 2009.

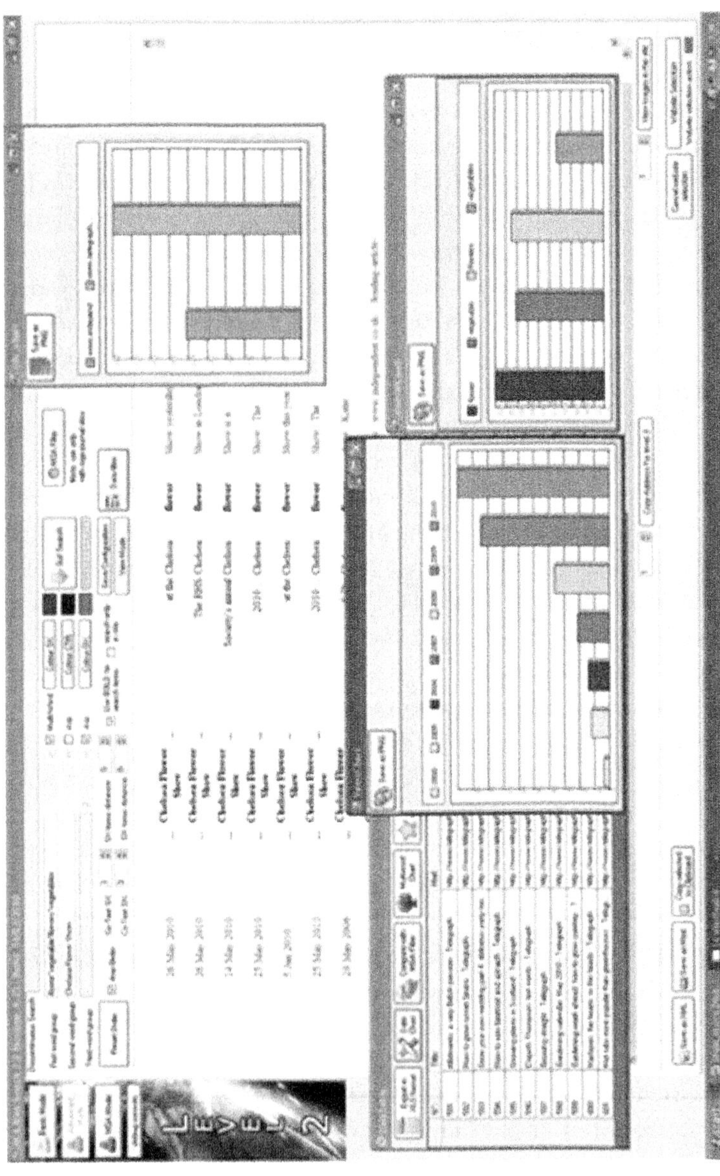

Figure 4: Visual concordancing: Flowers or vegetables at the Chelsea Flower Show?

Valuable and motivating as it may be for users, whether researchers, teachers or students, to be able to convert web data almost instantly into such tables and charts, their measurements require cautious assessment. An obvious problem is that *flower* unlike *vegetable*, is a verb in English. In addition, the search merely requires that one of the search words be co-present on the same page with the wording *Chelsea Flower Show* – hardly an indication of the true relevance of *flower* and *vegetable* in the *Daily Telegraph*'s and *Independent*'s articles. Fine tuning is thus required, using devices, such as the *MGAFilter* mentioned above, which make it possible to search for data in terms of specific mini-genres (see *Figure 5*).

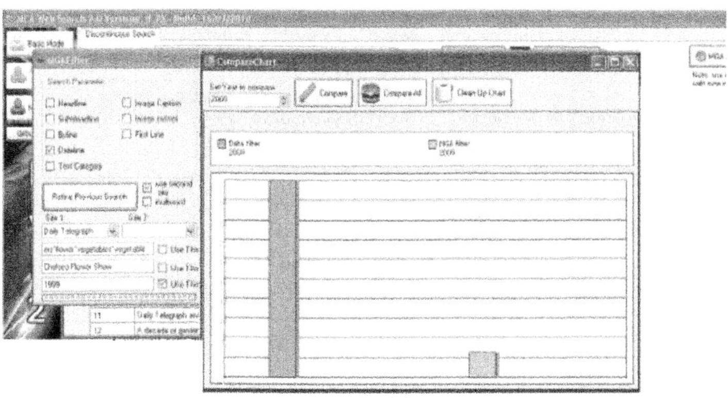

Figure 5: Secondary searching with MGAFilter *plus* CompareChart *date distributions*

Given that the research work, using *web-as-multimodal corpus* techniques, of understanding how web pages work semiotically is only just beginning, how can a research instrument like *MWS* possibly be of use to students, for example, first-year undergraduate students? Part of the answer lies in the fact that, unusually, for a concordancing program, *MWS* has different levels of analysis. *Level 1* (or *Basic Mode*) resembles traditional concordancing systems with its focus on words and word combinations: it retrieves a set of KWIC (*Key Word In Context*) concordances i.e. lines of written text in the web that distinguish the target search words from their *co-text*. As with other such systems, *MWS* uses a colour system to identify leftward and rightward co-texts from the target words. With its focus on traditional aspects of concordancing, this level provides basic training for first-time users. Even so, like *Level 2*, it gives access to the *website selection* tool (*Figure 6*: bottom right and inset top right) which allows an unlimited number of websites to be specified and hence searched; this is a clear improvement, in keeping with the overall tradition of corpus linguistics, vis-à-vis forms of web searching that impose searches *either* throughout the entire Internet (*Google, Yahoo* etc.) *or*, at the other extreme, searches of just one website (i.e. based on individual website search engines).

As part of its multimodal training function within *MWS*, *Level 1* also includes an *image tool* concerned with transcending the narrowly-focused and rather limiting assumption that web searches only return lists of words detected in running text rather than in descriptive labels such as captions.

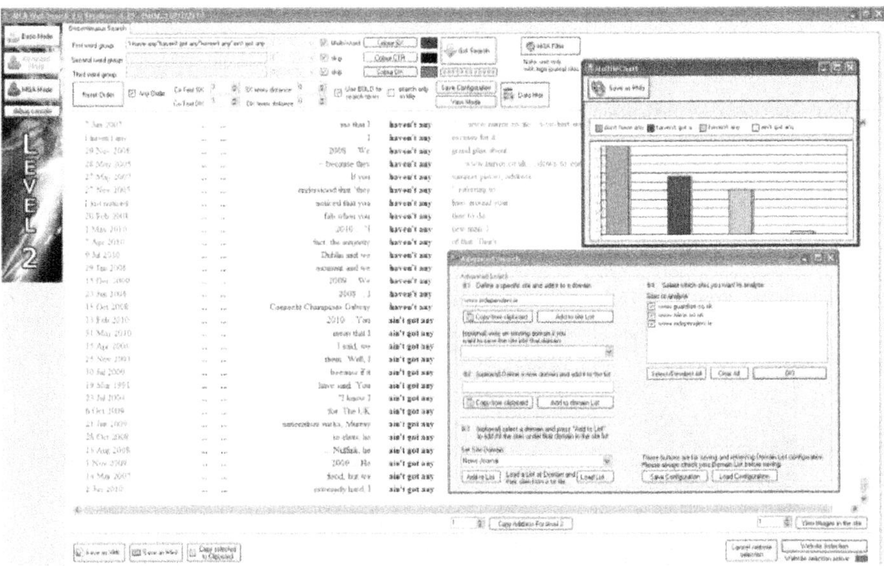

Figure 6: don't have any vs. haven't got any vs. haven't any vs. ain't got any

Most users soon migrate to *Level 2*, illustrated in *Figure 6*, given its greater potential for comparison thanks to its implementation of both primary *and* secondary searching. Primary searching can be carried out at this level in terms of (a) a *discontinuous* search function i.e. searches which retrieve and relate words in specific documents despite the (possible) presence of other intervening words; (b) the multiword function which allows a word or set of words to be separated by an asterisk and thus deemed, as appropriate, to be synonyms, antonyms or wordsets related in other ways (including, of course, multilingual wordsets); (c) chart-and-table-based reporting of the distribution of words directly exportable to other media (e.g. *Prezis* or *PowerPoints*). The *MGA Filter* allows the user (currently only in an embryonic way) to carry out *secondary searching* in relation to specific mini-genres thus obtaining more precise data as the search is carried out in relation to a headline, subheadline, first line or image caption (or combinations thereof).

One example of research that first-year undergraduate students, e.g. of political science, journalism or linguistics, might wish, or might be asked, to tackle relates to lexicogrammatical variety in different world newspapers. *Figure 6* (right) shows that using the *MultiWord* option will confirm the relative frequency (from most to least) of *don't have any* vs. *haven't got any* vs. *haven't any* vs. *ain't got any* in three culturally different newspapers from the British Isles (*Guardian online, Mirror online* and (Irish) *Independent online*). When the same search is applied to 30, rather than 3, English-language newspapers from many parts of the world, the same pattern of distribution (not shown for reasons of space) is returned (in about a minute) albeit with sharper differences between the incidence of each form. Chart-and-table quantification is particularly valuable when, as in the latter case, thousands of concordances are returned as it allows immediate comparative lexis-driven visualisation to be made that explores cultural diversity along many parameters: diversity of *topic* (politics, gardening) diversity of *text mode* (written, spoken, written to be spoken) diversity of *genre* (blogs, news, comments) as well as *cross cultural diversity* involving differences in geographical location and different points in time.

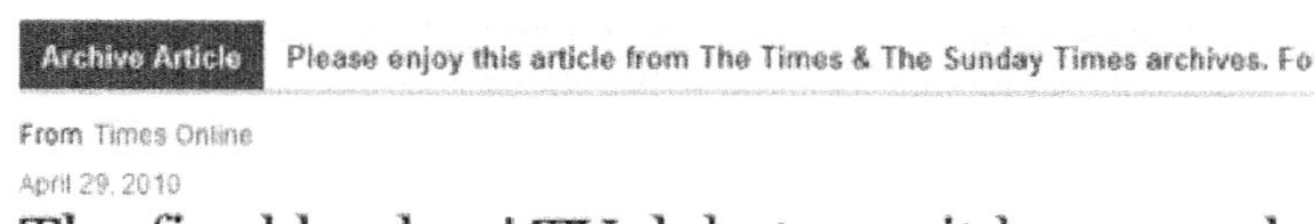

Figure 7: *Top: an* As-it-happened *report. Bottom: first 10 Search hits in* DataTable

Not surprisingly, *Level 3* is directed towards the identification of culturally-oriented ways of retrieving data from the web, which includes recourse to users' latent but often unarticulated knowledge of genres. As hinted at above in *Section 1*, in the current stage of development, *Level 3* identifies combinations of byline, headline, subheadline, dateline etc. and thus helps explore hypotheses about the distributional significance of these mini-genres, i.e. whether they help distinguish a newspaper article based on a *Press Agency* report from other web genres such as *By our own correspondent* articles or Blogs.

A combination of primary and secondary searching will, for instance, help bring home to first year undergraduates, the significance in online newspapers of the emergent *As it happened* subgenre of online newspaper reporting, often assumed to relate to sporting events but which, in fact, as *Figure 7* (top part) shows, is of particular significance in the political arena. The type of article reproduced in *Figure 7* is, as it were, back-to-front in the way that it reports events, i.e. not a traditional article reporting events *after* they have happened but instead *live* reporting in which written updates on what has been said or done are provided every few minutes or so. This type of article, emblematic of our Information Society, is read in two ways. First, there is the live mode which follows the FIFO (*First In First Out*) principle. Second, there is also an *after-the-event mode* whereby, when all has long been said and done, the reader can read the report following the FILO (*First In Last Out*) principle: what happened last, is read first, and what happened first, is read last. The matter is further complicated by the fact that some articles are not live reporting but *after-the-event mode* simulations intended to look as if they were genuine *As it happened* reports!

Regardless of one's personal opinions about this subgenre, it is an innovation which throws out many long-standing expectations about newspaper articles and is an infinite source of classroom debate, discussions about definitions and expectations about how newspapers and newspaper reporting works in the Internet age, ranging from explorations of the participants mentioned, the tenses adopted to the absence or presence of expected textual and lexical features – in a word, a paradox which is an endless source of classroom investigation. *MWS's DataTable* (see *Figure 7*, Bottom) gives a strong clue as to the growing significance of this genre: *all* the headlines (the first 10 in the search report) mention either the wording *As it happened* or *Live blog* (or both). The four major quality UK newspapers (*Guardian, Times, Independent, Telegraph*) in particular, seem in their online versions to have privileged the use of this genre (e.g. as compared with 4 other sites searched: *www.economist. com, news.bbc.co.uk, www.independent.ie, online.wsj.com*) recording 270 out of 332 hits for a search structured as: First line: *As it happened*; Second line: *political*; Third Line: *2010*.

Underlying *MWS's* primary and secondary search methods of retrieving words in the context of specific web units and specific websites is a combination of pattern matching and tagging techniques. The latter are based on the assumption that a specific web genre *html* code is likely to identify a specific web unit e.g. for a newspaper article *headline, subheadline, byline (author), date, subgenre, running text* and *photo*. While there may be some variation in the *html* pattern, it will not be sufficient to undermine the viability of searches based on this principle. Once known, web unit tags and styles can be used to locate these web units in websites. Though different websites adopt different design strategies (including, for instance, the many differences in the online newspaper genre), common factors exist which help generalize the process of extracting web units from the source code. For example, a headline is practically always marked by the <title> html tag, or a subset of it. Analogously, running text is typically placed inside one or more <p> ("paragraph") tags immediately after the headline, while a photo is usually identified by an <img> tag. This method cannot always be adopted: the date, for instance, requires some kind of pattern matching; a trade-off thus needs to be found in the deployment of the various detection techniques, a matter affected by decisions about whether to privilege searching carried out in specific sets of websites, or searches performed on a broader basis, the former being more precise, the latter being more universal but probably less precise.

4. Multimodal genre analysis

Let us summarise what we have stated or assumed so far. This chapter is a record of work in progress being carried out within the *Living Knowledge Project* by the UniPv partner in relation to multimodal semiotics and the contribution that multimodal genre analysis can, in particular, make to the development of diversity-aware approaches to information and knowledge detection in the Internet. Multimodal genre analysis has an important role to play in understanding and, perhaps, shaping the ties that link website engineering to social and semiotic evolution, sometimes called semiotic engineering (De Souza, 2005). In addition to being an improvement on manual pen-and-paper techniques of website analysis and, in particular, the speed with which web annotation can be carried out, the *MWS* suite of tools, through an essentially semi-automatic approach, contributes to the overall theoretical insights that guide the project by focusing, in particular, on the integration and interplay between linguistic, visual and spatiotemporal resources that exist in web pages and by suggesting how such insights can be incorporated into more fully automated detection procedures.

In this respect, we have shown how the hierarchical structure of web pages, as represented in the scalar model of the web page given in *Table 1*, can be incorporated, at least in part, into a semi-automatic software system that combines advanced forms of web searching with traditional concordancing and with visual (chart-and-table) reporting. In so doing, the chapter suggests the considerable user empowerment (e.g. for students, teachers and researchers) associated with the ability to link up textual structures on different scalar levels. The approach is ultimately designed to ensure that lexical studies can be effectively linked up with intercultural and multimodal aspects of texts while ensuring that the software techniques involved are within the grasp of the vast majority of users. As with all forms of concordancing and web searching, the data obtained reflect the individual user's skills and creativity, one reason why *MWS* has been built to reflect the different needs and skills of different users.

The scalar model in *Table 1* also carries with it the implication that the higher up the scale we go, the more likely we are to encounter increasingly abstract textual structures and the expressions of cultural diversity associated with them. One way of proceeding in these uncharted waters is in terms of thematic systems with polar characteristics, or to see the matter from a slightly different perspective, cultural expressions of potential conflicts, for example, *the young (children) vs. the old (their parents)* generation conflict (Baldry, Thibault, 2006: Section 3.8.1; see also Baldry, Thibault, 2007) or the *now vs. then* thematic system expressed in *Figure 1* above. A further example of a thematic system relevant in many pedagogical circumstances is the climate-change conflict between 'interventionists' and 'non interventionists' respectively showing bias towards the belief that climate change *is/is not* the result of human behaviour and thus *requiring/not requiring* corrective measures.

Intuitively, such a conflict can, and will, be expressed, for example, in online newspapers or journals, in terms of a specific instance such as a photo of a coal-fired power station belching out smoke and a verbal caption of the type "Is this the legacy you wish to leave for your children?" However, we need to find techniques that will provide a more accurate description than this intuitive model. Within the model given in *Table 1*, the combination of photo + caption is a relation between two clusters that form a *SuperCluster*, one which provides a basis for solving this particular problem (see Baldry, Coccetta, 2010 in press). It is the linkage between the two clusters (technically a covariate tie see Baldry, Thibault, 2006a: 139) that makes it possible to index (i.e. 'evoke', 'have in mind', 'think of', 'be aware of') the underlying thematic system. Thematic systems are typically intertextual and more abstract than the specific meanings of specific texts. That is, they are implied meanings. The overt meaning in this hypothetical example is something like: "we shouldn't have power stations like this". The implied meaning is something like: "a conflict exists between interventionists against non-interventionists and you, the reader, are being recruited as a potential interventionist/non interventionist". This latter meaning is intertextual, that is we build it up from our experience of many texts on similar thematics; we do not (normally) build it up from a single text.

In the web, thematic systems are typically intersemiotic (i.e. multimodal) as compared with many (but by no means all) printed texts, whence the role of multimodality and, in particular, multimodal annotation of web pages in the *LK Project* to discover how such systems with their underlying ideological potential (bias/persuasion) can be detected. Typically, they will be linked to other such systems and will partially overlap with them e.g. the potentially associated conflicts between young/old generations, new/old technologies, left-wing/right-wing political affiliations. This stage of the research is not easy to grasp and pin down. But, when reached, it will provide some basic input for the understanding of how intertextual thematic systems are realised in terms of web units, e.g. in climate change websites (see Baldry, Coccetta, 2010 in press).

At this point, we need to ask once again where does the first-year undergraduate student, for example, stand in all this? One answer is that s/he can begin to take a few steps down the road that leads to full understanding of intertextual thematic systems by using *MWS* to explore and compare political leader's ideological positioning. By blending corpus linguistics' concordancing techniques with web searching techniques, *MWS* adapts them to the goals and needs of detecting cross-cultural phenomena and makes it possible to compare, for example, the incidence of statements on immigration, made by, or about, leading political figures and to turn them into easily comprehensible charts.

A simple example is what current/previous world leaders have to say about immigration or what is said about them in this context. Such a query can be set up as: First line: *Berlusconi*Prodi*Obama*Bush*Cameron*Brown*Sarkozy*Chirac*. Second line: *immigration*. The search is designed to compare the incidence of four countries where immigration issues have been a major issue in recent years and to find out in which country the matter is, currently, a really burning issue. *Figure 8* gives the results (for over 10,000 'hits') for this search in the following 40 newspapers: UK: *thesun.co.uk; mirror.co.uk; dailystar.co.uk; thetimes.co.uk; newsoftheworld.co.uk; dailyexpress.co.uk; dailymail.co.uk; observer.co.uk: thesundaytimes. co.uk; telegraph.co.uk; guardian.co.uk; timesonline.co.uk; independent.co.uk;* online websites of TV stations: *www.cnn.com; news.bbc.co.uk; financial newspapers or magazines: www.ft.com; www.economist.com; online.wsj.com; www.afr.com;* US newspapers: *www.washingtonpost.com; www.latimes.com; www.nytimes.com; www.usatoday.com; www.nydailynews.com;* English language newspapers from other parts of the world: (Australia) *www.theage.com.au; www.theaustralian.com.au; www.smh.com.au;* (Canada) *www.theglobeandmail.com; www.thestar.com;* (Ireland) *www.independent.ie; www.tribune.ie;* (South Africa) *iafrica.com;* (New Zealand) *www.nzherald.co.nz.* French and Italian newspapers: *www.lefigaro.fr; www.liberation.fr; www.humanite.fr; www.leparisien.com; www.lemonde.fr; www.corriere.it; www.repubblica.it.*

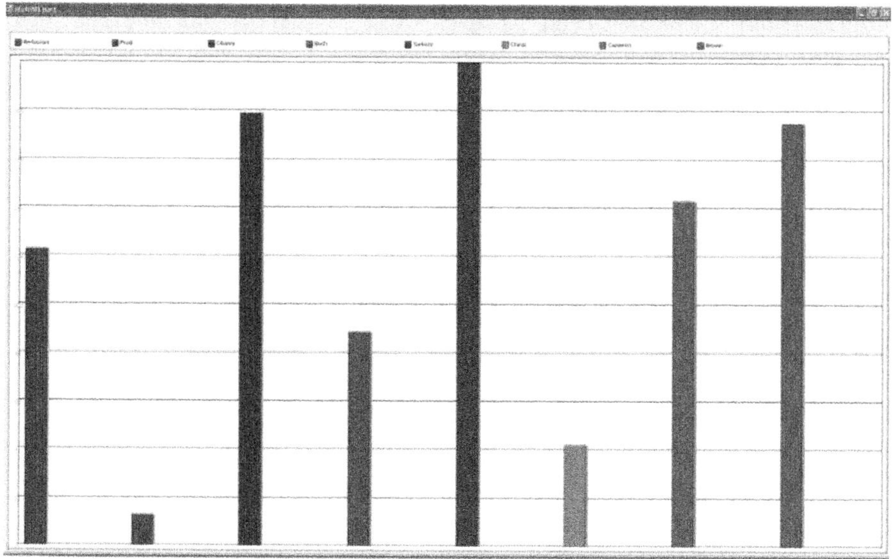

Figure 8: Who said most about, or was most linked in the press, to immigration

The results given in *Figure 8*, perhaps somewhat surprisingly, show Sarkozy rather than Obama, as being most linked to immigration. This suggests various related phenomena are at work: the multilingual nature of the search and the inclusion of a good number of French newspapers; the increase in the quantity of web reporting with every year that passes (a matter confirmed by many other searches); the high probability that statements on immigration are picked up by the media only when leaders are in power and its corollary that the opinions of those out of power are soon discarded (NB. in the case of Cameron/Brown, the search was carried within a few weeks of handing over power). Precisely the fact that changes in incidence vis-à-vis this kind of subject tend to be very rapid may help explain why Sarkozy outstrips Obama on this issue (despite the latter's election promise to deal with this issue). In other words, this kind of search measures very temporary and fluctuating states – precisely what many web users (politicians, political commentators, businesses sensitive to political winds) really need from the web and, so far, have tended not to get from the current generation of websearch tools.

With the provisos mentioned, students and teachers can thus study immigration as reported in newspapers on a comparative basis, producing charts that can be incorporated into their documents e.g. for exam and conference presentations, dissertations and so on. But, as the caption to *Figure 8* suggests, primary searches needed to be followed up by more precise searches.

The examples could go on endlessly, all leading to insights that help to formulate better tools for web-unit detection and a better understanding of the web's constantly evolving textual nature and social functions. While *MWS* helps explore hunches about (inter)semiotic patternings that reflect cultural diversity, thanks to its semi-automatic procedures, it also helps transcend the hard work of manual encoding and 'manual' searching (i.e. searching of each individual website through each site's search engine). One of the ultimate objectives of the *LK Project* is, of course, to develop ways of detecting cultural diversity in a fully automatic way. But perhaps one of the ironies of the *LK Project* is that it has also encouraged the more specific, but nevertheless valuable, goal of semi-automatic analysis within a research process that supports and speeds up the process of manual encoding of texts.

5. Conclusions

This chapter raises the question as to how readers interact with web pages, combine information from the various sources, share it with others while, at the same time, creating and maintaining coherence. The co-contextualising nature of web units is a property that determines the function and meaning of each web unit within a web page and which governs the ways in which users extract, and act on, website information and opinions, whence the focus on incorporating a scalar model of web textuality into *MWS*.

MWS is thus not designed to emulate or outperform *web-as-corpus* concordancing tools, such as *WebCorpLive (www.webcorp.org.uk/wcadvanced.html)* (Renouf et al., 2007), or even to resemble them. Rather, the underlying goal is to detect web units, as defined above, and improve on techniques for their reporting. In this respect, a distinctive feature of *MWS* is its hybrid concordancing-cum-websearching-cum-web-interpreting nature: it combines *html tag* searches with *lemma* searches so as to be able to explore the web page as a textual structure *tout court* and to assist the work of understanding how the highest levels of textuality affect the lowest and vice-versa.

Given contemporary society's general concern with understanding and adjusting to cultural diversity, predictions about the future, bias and opinion and their evolution over time, multimodal genre analysis is, in our belief, of particular social and research significance beyond the *LK Project*, within which these tools were conceived. Since genres of all types are supremely cultural artefacts and expressions of specific cultures as well as of the shared ground between societies with different languages, the development of semi-automatic instruments like *MWS*, which improve on pen-and-paper methods in the detection of expressions of cultural diversity by directly interrogating the web, will speed up the acquisition of datasets that are fundamental for the development of fully automated search procedures.

However, central to the vision of websites presented in this chapter is the belief that the compositional structure of Internet – Halliday's textual metafunction (Halliday, 1978; Halliday, Matthiessen, 2004) – is in a state of flux to the point where new forms of web literacy will emerge that go beyond the level of the recurrent objects of traditional literacies such as headings, subheadings, running text, photos and captions and so on, characterised here as mini-genres. This process will, instead, dictate the need to detect, in particular, the higher level meaning-making units that will increasingly determine users' interactions with, and between, a web page's subparts, thereby ensuring that lower-level web units are not read, viewed or shared in isolation to each other.

In terms of web research, the working hypothesis being put forward by the LK UniPv team at CVML is that, as time goes by, and in ways detailed above and elsewhere (Baldry, Coccetta, 2010 in press; Baldry et al., 2010 in press; Baldry, O'Halloran, 2010 in press), a diversity-aware approach to web searching will encourage a process that is already underway, namely the integration of web searching with other activities such as reporting methods, annotation and concordancing. This chapter's underlying contention is that, as opposed to a language-only approach, a multimodal approach, and in particular a *web-as-multimodal-corpus* approach to web genres, web events and web activities facilitates a clearer perception of this process. In this respect, *MWS,* within a specialist approach, is beginning to tackle the work of semi-automatic genre/topic categorization, from the comparative standpoint mentioned in the opening quotation.

Overall, we may conclude this chapter by saying it constitutes an indirect critique but interpretative appreciation of the current goals and methods of corpus linguistics from both a pedagogical and research standpoint. While concerned with lexical studies and, in particular, lexical distributions in the web, the chapter illustrates the potential of a *multimodal-web-as-corpus* approach when interpreting, for example, the evolution from printed to online newspapers in both L1 and L2 text studies in a variety of social and research contexts, some, but not all, concerned with pedagogy.

Finally, in its appreciative critique of corpus linguistics from a specialist standpoint, the chapter points to the crucial contribution that combined concordancing, web searching and visual forms of data reporting can play in critical text analysis, all the more so when the focus of interest is shifted from a single level of analysis, currently often the case in lemma-based corpus linguistics, to an examination of the interplay between micro textual units and higher levels of textual organisation. As the chapter attempts to suggest, one benefit is the potential for greater classroom awareness of the multimodal, intercultural and scalar nature of contemporary websites, in a word, better understanding of what a web page is.

Acknowledgements and notes

The following newspapers are thanked for permission to reproduce the following: *The Daily Telegraph* (Figure 3), *The Independent* (Figure 2), *The Times* (Figure 1) *The Sunday Times* (Figure 7). The research leading to these results has received funding from the European Community's *Seventh Framework Programme* (FP7/2007-2013) under grant agreement n° 231126 *LivingKnowledge: LivingKnowledge – Facts, Opinions and Bias in Time*. Details of this project can be found on the *LK* website: *http://livingknowledge-project.eu/*. Special thanks go to the *Living Knowledge* (*LK*) partners for advice about this chapter and, in particular, to Fausto Giunchiglia (overall *LK* co-ordinator) and Vincenzo Maltese (coordinator of *LK* Work Package 1), both working at the University of Trento. Many thanks to Virginio Cantoni, the director of CVML, (*Computer Vision and Multimedia Laboratory*) part of the *Dipartimento di Informatica e Sistemistica,* University of Pavia and Marco Porta and Alessandro Gaggia who, with the author, carried out the design and implementation stages of *MWS* and *MWB* at CVML. Thanks also go to Eleonora Campi, Valeria Cassola, Francesca Coccetta and Ivana Marenzi who have all, at various stages, worked on their development and dissemination. The *MWS* and *MWB* and other programs that make up the *MWS* suite are freely available to researchers, teachers and students on the *mcaweb.unipv.it* website. Further releases and new programs are envisaged in the course of the second year of research in keeping with *LK Project* desiderata.

Learning from Obama and Clinton:
Language classroom corpora relating to individuals

María Calzada Pérez, University Jaume I, Spain

1. Introduction

Corpus linguistics has been defined as "the study of language based on examples of 'real life' language use" (McEnery, Wilson, 2004: 1). A corpus, for its part, is described as "a large collection of authentic texts that have been gathered in electronic form according to a specific set of criteria" (Bowker, Pearson, 2002: 9). The study of electronic corpora dates back to at least the 60's when scholars such as W. Nelson Francis, Henry Kucera, Geoffrey Leech, John Sinclair and others started carrying out what were then considered "lunatic" (Sinclair, 1991: 1) research projects that consisted in the hitherto unheard of compilation of massive collections of texts. Despite some early teething problems, compilations initially contained 1 million words (e.g. the Brown Corpus) and gradually grew up to 100 million words and beyond (e.g. BoE, BNC, etc.). By the 90's the motto was already 'the larger the corpus, the better' or as Sinclair puts it elsewhere (in Ghadessy et al., 2001: ix): "No data like more data". Corpora were then mega-corpora or, as Flowerdew calls them, "giga-corpora" (see Flowerdew, 2004: 12) and were preferably used for language description and lexicographic tool design. The turn of the century brought with it a very different view of the topic. ELT, ESP, EFL and Translation Studies (TS) became seriously involved in corpus-based work leading to "the return of the micro-corpus" (Flowerdew, 2004: 12) complying with the definition above (i.e. a corpus is 'a large collection of texts') but now containing from 20,000 to 200,000 words 'only'. Micro-corpora are commonly linked with genre studies and much of the research carried out with small corpora to date revolves around the features of specialised genres (a methodology which is particularly useful for ESP and TS).

In a volume dedicated to small corpora and ELT (Ghadessy et al., 2001), Paul Nation (2001b: 31) explains that work along these lines requires

> a set of good research questions that can be answered by study of a corpus, a corpus to provide a source of data, and the computer programmes that can facilitate the task of organising the data from the corpus.

With so much data we run the risk both of asking too many questions, or, the reverse, mesmerised by the data, we may end up lingering over a (minor) point for far too long (and produce all the data that verify this point). Our questions may be too predictable or too innovative and bold. And when these questions have to do with teaching and learning, instability may set in. We may start with Question A and end up analysing Question B (echoing Bernardini's learning methods based on serendipity).

Deciding on the corpus (or corpora) to study is no easy task either. This is why most of the publications regarding corpus-based research devote a relatively large portion of their work to explaining the material they have chosen to study. Discussion of criteria for selection and compilation abounds (e.g. Laviosa, 1997; Bowker, Pearson, 2002; Biber et al., 2004; Olohan, 2004) and there is no serious work on the area without a carefully deployed analysis of the reasons for choosing the corpus that was chosen.

The tools of analysis may initially be seen as a slightly easier issue. We 'all' use WordSmith Tools as it is informative, user-friendly and convenient. Its basic functions are good enough for raw text, and its rather more complex functions accommodate (xml-) tagged corpora. And yet there is a wider range of options out there, potentially just as informative, user-friendly and convenient. Furthermore, tools may be developed (and are being developed) for specific needs. Tools are being used (and some of them are even being shared freely) for corpus-based analysis. Maybe this third issue is not as straightforward as it originally seemed. *Section 2* discusses the research questions being posed in it. *Section 3* presents the corpora chosen for analysis and pedagogical applications while *Section 4* presents the tools used and *Section 5* exemplifies some of the analyses that may be carried out with the corpora and tools proposed to answer the questions posed. *Section 6* brings the paper to a close with a brief conclusion.

2. The questions

2. 1. Is there anything to be taught via corpora of individual linguistic production?

So the current trend seems to be to learn languages and improve translating skills via a specialised (i.e. generic) corpus, which De Beaugrande (2001: 11) characterises as "a small corpus, delimited by a specific register, discourse domain, or subject matter". Teachers may use this small, specialised corpus by itself or they may compare it against larger, general corpora in order to identify the peculiarities of the specialisation under study. As De Beaugrande (2001: 10) sees it, the reasons for doing this are indisputable:

> Comparing data from large corpora of general discourse with data from small corpora of specialised discourse is a useful tactic for exploring vital differences among general and specialised meanings of important terms, such as language. Paradoxically, the shift of a term from general usage to specialised usage may not bring a direct gain in precision or clarity, but in fact a margin of uncertainty and obscurity. Students of language should be aware and wary.

Illustrative examples of this *genre approach* (see Gee, 1997) to corpus work are Tribble (2001) and Henry and Roseberry (2001). Tribble analyses web-published leaflets (and, more specifically, web leaflets promoting MAs in applied linguistics) carrying out typical studies on wordlists, keywords, text-pattern or textualisation (via concordancing) and structural interpretation. Henry and Roseberry propose research where "early human intervention (EHI)" (Sinclair, 2001: xi) is particularly relevant and compile a corpus of introductions to guest speakers and then identify and manually tag sections and moves for each introduction, taking into consideration that different moves pursue different purposes. Thus armed, they single out the sections and moves identified grouping them into subsidiary corpora. Having accomplished all this, they then analyse linguistic behaviour in the subsidiary corpora and compare it against the whole corpus and other comparable corpora. These analyses are the source of lesson material. The spirit of their study (Henry, Roseberry, 2001: 97) is summed up below:

> Unless students are shown clearly how language cojoins with purpose and how purpose is related to moves, it is not likely that students will easily learn how to make the appropriate language choices for the different moves of a genre.

Both papers show that much is to be gained from a thorough, descriptive analysis of generic corpora, the results of which are then taken into the classroom. As De Beaugrande (2001: 26) argues, after the generic description:

> The next stage would be to turn our teachers and learners loose on some small corpora and to interface their users with activities such as reading and writing in English.

Although it acknowledges the importance and usefulness of the genre approach, the present paper seeks to go a step further and examine the possible value of individual linguistic production in teaching/learning situations. That is, apart from learning from the system (i.e. the genre), can we also learn from what a single person does, from what individuals do? And if we can, why don't we do so in the classroom? Or are we to disregard individuality and idiosyncrasy altogether as an invalid source of teaching/learning material?

The field of TS, and specifically Corpus-based Translation Studies (CTS), may inspire us to pose and reflect upon these questions. CTS was born around the mid-90s when Mona Baker (1993, 1995, 1996) started to tinker with a corpus-based methodology in order to describe prototypical translational behaviour. Baker and others (see for instance work by Kenny, Laviosa, Olohan) started with the system and initially placed their attention on (and posed their questions around) the 'generic' features of translated (as opposed to original) texts. After all, translated texts are created within particular contexts (in particular discourse communities with access to particular genres). And these contexts (discourse communities and genres) may differ from those where the original texts emerge. This line of research has been very fruitful and has led to the discussion of translational norms and universals. But, by the end of the 20th century, CTS scholars, and notably Baker herself (see Baker, 1999, 2000), went back from the system to the individual. They were actually doing nothing new. Itamar Even-Zohar (the father of the polysystems theory) (see Even-Zohar, 1990) had already set his eyes not just on the (poly)system but also on the agent (1997) and Morven Beaton (2005) had complemented *ideology* with the notion of *axiology*. Much of TS research seems to be moving back towards the individual, but this time scholars are carrying with them the systemic lessons learned in their journey back and forth. So if (corpus-based) TS is revisiting the individual, why can't (corpus-based) teaching do the same?

2. 2. Shall we go beyond lexico-grammar in the corpus-based classroom?

The second question we are posing in this paper has to do with the nature of language teaching itself. In the past, learning a language meant the acquisition of "a closed set of formal rules which precisely determine the well-formed strings" (De Beaugrande, 2001: 11). With corpora (and certain approaches to corpora, especially those proposed by Sinclair, amongst others), researchers did not rely on *a priori* rules as much as before and teachers became mediators of open repositories where grammar and lexis merged. These may be considered major breakthroughs. However, the question we pose here goes a step beyond: Are ideological features also eligible as part of the language-learning process?

This question has been answered by Critical Discourse Analysis (CDA) advocates (see, for instance, Fairclough, 1992), who believe teaching/learning may be empowered by ideological awareness. But CDA proponents veer towards a case-study methodology and tend to avoid corpus-based research, with some notable (mainly descriptive rather than pedagogical) exceptions (e.g. Garzone, Santulli, 1998; Partington, 1998, etc.). Corpus linguists, for their part, have been interested in 'awareness' for some time now, but most of them see awareness as the conscious understanding of the functioning of linguistic (i.e. grammatical and lexical) features by learners (Bernardini, 2004) and by teachers (Tsui, 2004). Ideology is not normally on the agenda.

3. The corpus

So with these two questions as our starting points, we now need to choose a corpus from which to teach – a "learnable small corpus" (De Beaugrande, 2001: 15). The corpus we have chosen for analysis here (the OBAHIL corpus) consists of two subcorpora comprising the speeches delivered by Barack H. Obama (the OBAMA subcorpus) and Hilary R. Clinton (the HILARY subcorpus) during the 2008 nomination campaign in the United States. The time span of the speeches compiled ranges from 3rd January 2008 (when the Iowa Caucuses took place) to 9th June 2008 (when Obama had won the Democratic primaries and Clinton publicly acknowledged his victory). The whole corpus contains 85 speeches (i.e. 49 speeches by Obama and 36 by Clinton) totalling 233,955 words according to AntConc (i.e. 117,199 by Obama and 116,756 by Clinton) and 242,608 words according to WordSmith Tools 4.0 (i.e. 124,608 by Obama and 117,722 by Clinton).

Bowker and Pearson (2002), Olohan (2004) and Flowerdew (2004) are among the long list of researchers who discuss corpus selection and compilation. Flowerdew (2004:

25-27), in particular, maps the process with very revealing questions, which we will use to explain (and justify) our compilation process. According to Flowerdew, before choosing to compile a specific corpus, the first question a researcher (cum-teacher) is to ask him/herself is: 'What is the purpose behind building a corpus?' In our case, as has been stated above, we want to compile a corpus which provides material to test

- whether individual production can be used to teach linguistic (lexical and grammatical) features;
- whether ideological traits may be suitable for the language classroom.

We believe the corpus chosen provides unbeatable material to fulfil our purposes. On the one hand, it provides individual linguistic production of the highest quality. Both Obama and Clinton are particularly well known for their oratory techniques and also for the outstanding results they have achieved with them. So if students are to learn from 'individuals', they might as well learn from undoubtedly great speakers. On the other hand, both Obama's and Clinton's speeches are distinguished by a strong ideological streak. If we want to discuss ideology in the classroom, we might as well do it with material where ideology is not only clearly present but also to be expected (by students).

Flowerdew (2004) poses a second question for the selection and compilation process: 'What genre is to be investigated?' This chapter replaces a generic approach with an individual focus. The study of political speeches has indeed much to offer the academia. And the present paper may be followed by a comparison of Obama's and Clinton's language production with that of the prototypical features of the political speech genre. But, as has already been explained above, this is not the purpose of our corpus building.

Flowerdew (2004) also poses a third question that would aid researchers in selecting and compiling their corpora: 'How large is the corpus supposed to be?' A corpus of speeches by US nominees during a nomination campaign can only be a small corpus, i.e. anything ranging from 20,000 and 200,000 words (Flowerdew, 2004: 19). As stated above, our corpus has a total of 233,955 words according to AntConc and 242,608 words according to WordSmith Tools 4.0. The corpus could be much larger and contain all the speeches delivered by both speakers. But as explained above, the turn of the century brought with it the return of the micro-corpus, which has since proved useful on many an occasion. Indeed, in its present state, the comparability of both subcorpora is notable, almost impeccable (speeches are delivered during the same period, in a similar context and for very comparable purposes). Though a larger corpus of speeches would be useful for language learning, this small corpus has much to offer the language learner. Flowerdew (2004) continues with two very practical questions: 'How will the data be collected?' and 'How will the [...] corpus be tagged/marked up?' The OBAHIL corpus is particularly appealing for language teachers because it is reasonably easy to compile. Speeches are simply downloaded from the following websites and then saved in a .TXT format:

- *http://www.presidency.ucsb.edu/2008_election_speeches.php?candidate=44* (for Obama)
- *http://www.presidency.ucsb.edu/2008_election_speeches.php?candidate=70* (for Clinton)

With basic computing knowledge, XML-tagging is also possible and has in fact been carried out automatically with the use of regular expressions. XML certainly enhances the teaching possibilities of the corpus. For example, the speeches downloaded here often incorporate reactions by the public in capital letters and brackets, in this manner:

> Well, first of all, I want to congratulate Senator Clinton on a hard-fought victory here in New Hampshire. She did an outstanding job. Give her a big round of applause.

> <public>(APPLAUSE)</public>

> You know, a few weeks ago, no one imagined that we'd have accomplished what we did here tonight in New Hampshire. No one could have imagined it.

Following Guerini et al. (2008, in press), tags about public reactions are indicators of hot-spots of persuasion dynamics. And this has undoubtedly much to teach language learners. But for this paper, the catchword was simplicity. After all, teachers ought to 'keep it short and simple'. Flowerdew (2004) asks researchers to reflect on a final consideration: 'What kind of reference corpus would be suitable to contrast with the (specialised) corpus?' In our case, our subcorpora may be directly compared with the BoE or even the BNC. Previous corpus-based experiments could also work as (semi-) comparable material for replication. Thus, we would be working with the small-large corpus methodology that De Beaugrande (2001) advocates. However, we could equally remain 'small' and compare each subcorpus against the other. *Section 5* below shows how this may yield interesting results.

4. The tools

Working with a corpus-based methodology requires an efficient electronic toolkit. And amongst popular monolingual toolkits there is none like WordSmith Tools (*Figure 1*). As widely known, Mike Scott's programme offers an ample range of plug-ins which, amongst other things, generate wordlists, keywords and concordances. It uses stop and lemma lists (and also allows manual lemmatisation), it converts text encoding, it has XML-reading facilities and it is even robust enough to host the BNC corpus. In its new version (WST 5.0) it incorporates follow-up concordance searches, an improved file viewer utility, a corpus corruption detector and a new concgram facility. It converts .PDF or .DOC, and removes all mark-ups and lemmatising. It can also be installed onto a removable drive, which means you can take it with you everywhere. As Mike Scott argues on his website (*http://www.lexically.net/downloads/version5/HTML/index.html?whatsnewinversion5.html*) "WordSmith is organic software". Indeed it is growing in a non-stop, organic fashion.

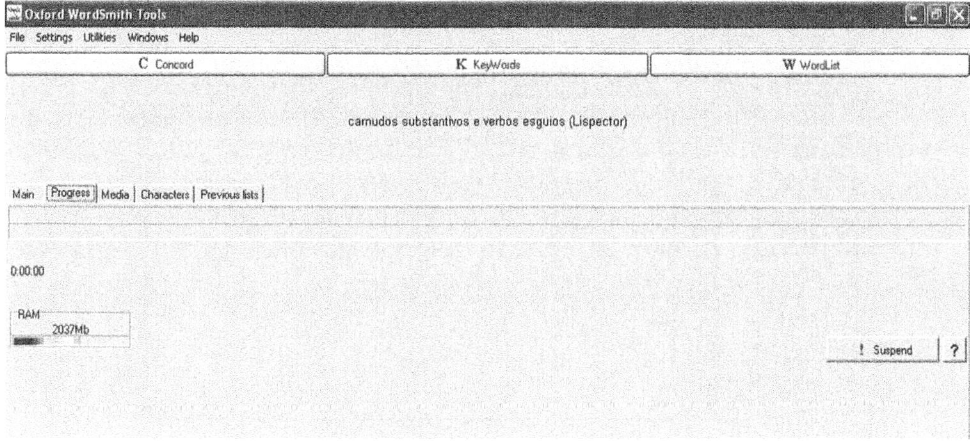

Figure 1: WordSmith Tools at work

It comes as no surprise, then, that a great deal of reliable corpus-based work has been carried out using WordSmith Tools (Scott refers to some of them in a list posted at *http://www.lexically.net/wordsmith/corpus_linguistics_links/papers_using_wordsmith.htm*). Yet, WordSmith is not the only electronic toolkit on Earth. And it is not even the best toolkit for all purposes. There are other interesting programs which go almost unnoticed within the academic community and which deserve some attention. And the reason they deserve attention is because they can do things WordSmith does not do (at least nowadays!) and this may have an impact on the kind of research being performed. They also deserve attention because they often produce (slightly) different results to those generated by WordSmith. This difference is not normally of a statistically significant relevance but shows things can be done otherwise. Asking for a 'second opinion' seems to be a good policy in life, which (surprisingly enough) is hardly ever put into practice by corpus linguists. WordSmith is an indispensable tool but it is not the be-all-and-end-all of corpus linguistics. This is why we have decided to work with both WordSmith and other less well-known tools such as AntConc, VocabProfile, Range and WMatrix.

AntConc may be seen as a simplified version of WordSmith Tools. Yet it is a very intelligent simplified version. It is true that there are many ways in which Antconc cannot compete against WordSmith Tool. It has no XML-reading facilities, for instance. But it contains all the basic (wordlist, keyword and concordancing) facilities of an electronic toolkit. Plus, it is much easier to handle and interpret than WordSmith, it runs under Windows, Linux/Unix and Mac platforms (WordSmith was originally designed for Windows)… and it is free of charge! Hence, when a teacher is considering using a tool in the classroom, AntConc can be a very appealing potential option, especially when its new upgrade is released and some of its limitations (see Laurence, 2004) have been overcome (*Figure 2*).

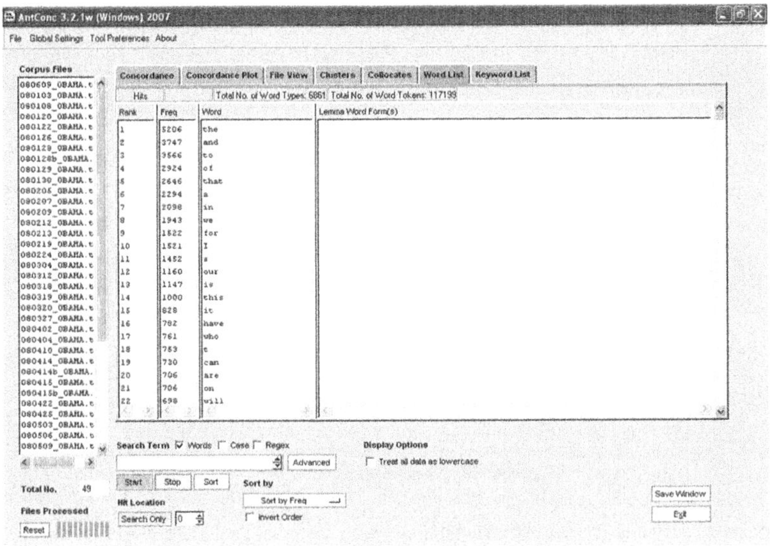

Figure 2: AntConc deals with .TXT documents

VocabProfile and Range are freeware available at *http://www.lextutor.ca/*. Technically "VocabProfile break texts down by word frequencies in the language at large" meaning that it can be used to compare corpora against vocabulary lists (based on Laufer and Nation's Lexical Frequency Profiler). The corpus word-input is divided into four categories: words pertaining to the first and second thousand levels, academic words and the remainder, or 'offlist'. It shows the percentage of the corpus-words covered by the 1,000 or 2,000 most frequent words or by academic English or by the 'offlist'.(*Figure 3*).

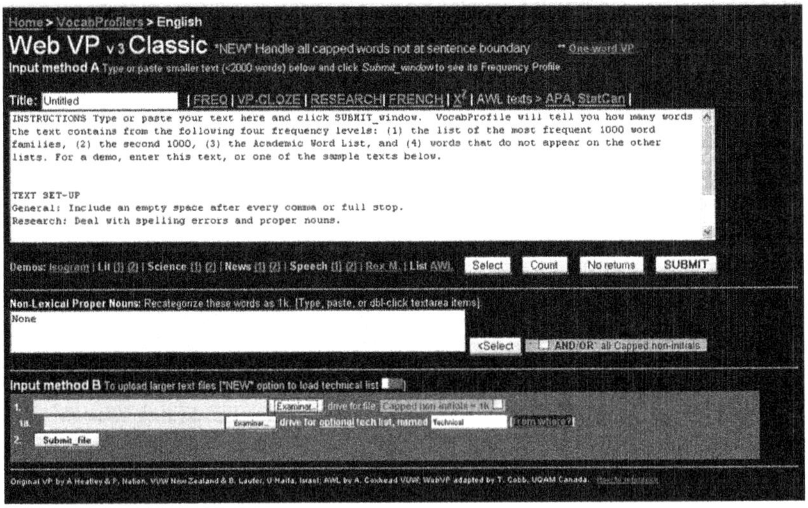

Figure 3: VocabProfile Input Page

VocabProfile uses BNC 20 word levels for analysiss so that the degree of word complication ('lexical elitism') employed by the texts can be analysed. Range, on the other hand, studies the distribution of words (or other lexical units) across a set of two or more texts. The texts can be comparable corpora or subdivisions of a corpus, or a set of texts supplied by a user. Both VocabProfile and Range give information not automatically recoverable in WordSmith which may also be of interest to students and teachers alike. Additionally, Range has a 'Text-Lex Compare' plug-in especially designed to produce classroom material.

Finally, Wmatrix (*Figure 4*) is a web interface that can be accessed via web browsers such as Firefox or Internet Explorer. It was initially developed by Paul Rayson in the REVERE project, was extended as part of the researcher's PhD thesis, and has been (and is still) updated regularly since then. It partially overlaps with WordSmith Tools and AntConc, generating a corpus wordlist, keywords and concordances. But it differs from other toolkits in that it provides corpus POS and SEMANTIC annotation. In fact, it is actually a gateway to the USAS and CLAWS corpus annotation tools. Thus it extends the keyword method to grammatical categories and key semantic domains.

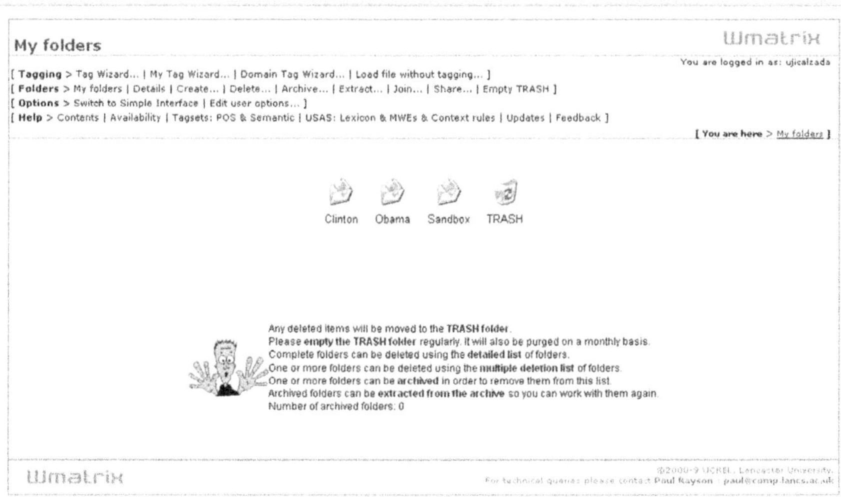

Figure 4: Wmatrix welcomes users

5. The analysis

5. 1. Statistics

When starting corpus-based analyses, the first thing scholars can do is examine statistics. This is a good beginning because they start to become acquainted with the material they will be using in class later on. Furthermore, presenting these data to students (in a simplified fashion) may also be a good way of introducing the corpus to the students.

Regarding statistics, AntConc is pretty basic and only tells researchers the overall number of word types and tokens in the corpus. In our case, AntConc shows that the OBAMA subcorpus has 117,199 tokens and 6,861 types whilst the HILARY subcorpus contains 116,756 tokens and 7,343 types. The only conclusion that may be drawn from these figures is that Clinton's input – though smaller in number of tokens – seems to be more varied as far as word types is concerned.

Text file	Overall Obama's stats	Overall Clinton's stats
File size	694,837	654,132
Tokens (running words) in text	124,608	117,722
Tokens used for word list	123,966	116,941
Types (distinct words)	6,759	6,811
Type/token ratio (TTR)	5.452301502	5.824304581
Standardised TTR	40.38570786	39.14757156
Standardised TTR std.dev.	58.93914795	60.4899292
Standardised TTR basis	1,000	1,000
Mean word length (in characters)	4.362308979	4.310626507
Word length std.dev.	2.426482439	2.426116228
Sentences	5,906	5,962
Mean (in words)	20.98986816	19.61442947
std.dev.	14.39872742	12.70244884
Paragraphs	50	36
Mean (in words)	2,479.31958	3,248.361084
std.dev.	1,313.966797	2,370.26416

Table 1: Obama's and Clinton's stats by WST

WordSmith Tools is very informative as far as statistics are concerned. *Table 1* reproduces data for the OBAMA and HILARY subcorpora. Data produced by WordSmith Tools differ slightly from the information provided by AntConc. The figures change and these changes are due to differences in the way AntConc and WordSmith define the term *word*. Now Obama's speeches add up to 124,608 tokens and 6,759 types whilst Clinton's comprise 117,722 tokens and 6,811 types. But the conclusion is similar. Clinton uses more word types than Obama. Hence her overall linguistic input seems to be more varied. However, WordSmith offers additional information which helps focus the picture. The standardised type-token ratio is actually higher for Obama than for Clinton, meaning that when you compare overall number of types against overall number of tokens, Obama's input is more varied on the whole. As was said above, it is always good to have a second opinion and when it comes to statistics, it is WordSmith Tools that refines the information provided by AntConc. *Table 1* also tells us that, as far as vocabulary is concerned, Obama's speeches (taken one by one) deviate (from each other) less broadly than Clinton's. This may mean that Obama can be seen as being slightly more consistent in his use of words throughout the whole of his linguistic production.

VocabProfile further clarifies the picture portrayed by WordSmith Tools. It tells analysts a bit more about the way in which types and tokens differ within and between the OBAMA and HILARY subcorpora (*Table 2*). By grouping word production into four main kinds (1,000 most frequent words; 2,000 most frequent words; academic English and 'offlist'), it shows that Obama uses less words from the 1-1,000 most common words group (83.42% vs 84.50%). And in this group, it is Clinton who prefers Anglo-Saxon linguistic items. Obama also uses a slightly smaller number of words from the 1,001-2,000 range than Clinton (4.22% vs 4.31%), but he prefers a larger input of Academic English items (3.93% vs 3.51%). Also Obama's behaviour is more often in the 'offlist' than Clinton's. All this may be taken to mean that although quantitatively similar, Obama's lexical use seems slightly less mainstream or Anglo-Saxon. Results by VocabProfile seem to be consistent with those by WordSmith. Obama's lexicon seems more 'select' and varied on the whole than that of Clinton. Nevertheless, his behaviour remains constant throughout his production to a slightly greater extent than Clinton's.

	VocabProfile stats for Obama				VocabProfile stats for Clinton			
	Families	Types	Tokens	Percent	Families	Types	Tokens	Percent
K1 Words (1-1000):	903	2273	103,352	83.42%	923	2251	98,777	84.50%
Function:	…	…	(64,757)	(52.27%)	…	…	(61,126)	(52.29%)
Content:	…	…	(38,595)	(31.15%)	…	…	(37,651)	(32.21%)
Anglo-Sax:								
=Not Greco-Lat/Fr Cog:	…	…	(22,158)	(17.89%)	…	…	(22,606)	(19.34%)
K2 Words (1001-2000):	546	932	5,228	4.22%	564	954	5,037	4.31%
Anglo-Sax:	…	…	(2,354)	(1.90%)	…	…	(2,225)	(1.90%)
1k+2k				(87.64%)		…	…	(88.81%)
AWL Words (academic):	396	784	4,872	3.93%	407	779	4,098	3.51%
Anglo-Sax:	…	…	(247)	(0.20%)	…	…	(240)	(0.21%)
Off-List Words:	?	2568	10,438	8.43%	?	2672	8,977	7.68%
1845+	?	6557	123,890	100%	?	6656	116,889	100%

Table 2: VocabProfile stats for Obama and Clinton

5. 2. Learning lexico-grammar with corpora

Individual linguistic production corpora may be helpful to illustrate the (successful) use of difficult lexico-grammatical items for language learners. *It's (high/about) time…* is an example of how this can be done with the OBAHIL corpus.

Non-native speakers of English find this expression difficult to grasp and language teachers, the British Council and even the BBC (amongst others) devote longer or shorter chapters to it, as may be seen at websites such as:

- *http://mbonillo.xavierre.com/httpdocs/gramatica/itstime.html*
- *http://www.britishcouncil.org/learnenglish-central-grammar-other-areas-its-high-time.htm*
- *http://www.bbc.co.uk/worldservice/learningenglish/grammar/learnit/learnitv347.shtml*

The BBC is, in fact, prompted to clarify the expression in a message posted by "Rashid from Saudi Arabia", which confirms that learners are unsure about its structure, meaning and usage. However, grammar books such as Butt and Benjamin (1994), Thornbury (1999) and Hewings (1999) provide no explicit information about it. At any rate, this is the way the structure *It's (high/about) time* is taught at a secondary school in Spain (see *http://mbonillo.xavierre.com/httpdocs.gramatica/itstime.html*), where it is seen to denote impatience and is said to be followed by three language structures:

- *It's time* + infinitive

    It's time to go to work.
    (*Ya es hora de que vayamos a trabajar.*)

    It's time to start playing.
    (*Ya es hora de que empecemos a jugar.*)

- *It's time for* + object + infinitive

    It's time for him to go to work.
    (*Ya es hora de que se vaya a trabajar.*)

    It's time for the teams to start playing.
    (*Ya es hora de que los equipos empiecen a jugar.*)

- *It's time* + subject + past

    It's time we went to work.
    It's about time we went to work.
    It's high time we went to work.
    (*Ya es hora de que vayamos a trabajar.*)

    Isn't it time the teams started playing?
    Isn't it about time the teams started playing?
    Isn't it high time the teams started playing?
    (*¿No es hora ya de que los equipos empiecen a jugar?*)

A quick look at concordances from the OBAMA and the HILARY subcorpora exemplifies the 'instruction' reproduced above and provides further pedagogical data:

1. Both speakers definitely prefer to use *It's time* without *high* or *about*. Of Obama's 115 uses, 102 are in its 'plain' format (i.e. without intensifiers) while, of Clinton's 32 uses, 27 are in its 'raw' version. Thus Obama:

- it's time we had a President who didn't choke saying the word *union*. It's time we had a Democratic nominee who didn't choke saying the word *union*;
- it's time we stood up to the drug and insurance companies who've been blocking reform for too long and tell them enough is enough;
- they believe it's time we provided real relief to the victims of this housing crisis.

Clinton:

- now it's time to fulfil those dreams;
- I say it's time to cover every single American with health insurance. And I say it's time to freeze foreclosures for families most at risk of losing their homes, including our soldiers who are in harm's way…;
- I think it's time the American people had a President again.

2. Both use the intensifiers mentioned by the books. Obama uses *about* once ('And I don't know about you, but I think it's about time we made college affordable for every young person in America') and Clinton uses both intensifiers but only once for each case:

- so, it's high time we stop talking about our problems and start solving them and that is what my campaign is all about;
- after seven years of inattention, neglect and denial, this Monday night, President Bush may well actually discuss the serious economic problems we face. And it's about time.

3. Items with few concordance entries (including *hapax legomena*) are sources of pedagogical information. However rarely, Obama and Clinton use other intensifiers not normally found in the teaching references. Obama, for instance, looks backwards (i.e. *It's + (long) past + time*) to highlight the urgency of the action introduced by this expression:

- and it's long past time to amend bankruptcy laws that were written to protect banks and lenders instead of working people;
- it's past time that Congress passed this bill.

Clinton prefers to underline the immediacy of the present when she combines *It's time* with *now*, producing *It's now time*:

- the Democratic Party is a family, and it's now time to restore the ties that bind us together and to come together around the ideals we share, the values we cherish…;
- it's now time for equally aggressive action to help families avoid foreclosure and to keep communities across our country from…

Furthermore, Obama goes for *It is also time* on nine occasions and Clinton produces a variant of the latter when she utters:

- it's also a time we put an end, once and for all, to the no-bid contracts that squander taxpayer money while lining the pockets of the…

Obama also resorts to *It is finally time*. On the one hand, *also* (and *finally*) shows that the language unit under scrutiny here forms an important part of the speakers' rhetorical strategies. *It's time… It is also time… It is finally time…* create persuasive forms of parallelisms. On the other hand, adding *a* between *It's also* and *time* occurs in a sentence where there are other emphatic features (e.g. *once and for all…*). Students may infer that the indefinite article is used here also with intensifying purposes.

It might be argued that these 'unexpected' expressions (*past, now, also, finally*, plus time, which are ignored in the theoretical explanations consulted) are not very popular amongst the then candidates. But the fact is that they use them, and that by using them they deviate from the ('plain', 'raw') (quantitative) norm to enrich the quality of their lexicon, thus increasing their type/token ratio. These statistically non-significant, individual uses contribute to give language learners a wider picture of *It's time*.

4. As well as the three structures given in books, the OBAHIL corpus shows other combinations are possible. Apart from *It's time + to/for/subject + past, It is time THAT* is also adopted. Since Obama and Clinton are 'successful speakers', students may be willing to consider this 'new' structure and may eventually conclude that it is, in fact, a variant of *It is time + subject…* By analysing examples produced by the concordancer with their teacher's help, students may realise that two variants of the same structure gives more possibilities in interaction. For instance, Obama chooses *It is time THAT* in the following to create parallelisms that make his speech more cohesive, powerful and evocative:

- but they believe it's finally time THAT we make health care affordable and available for every single American; THAT we bring down costs for workers and for businesses; THAT we cut premiums, and stop insurance companies from denying people care or coverage who need it most.

When examining Clinton's production, students will gather plenty of authentic material to illustrate how *It is time THAT* is followed by both past and present tenses:

- it's time that we make trade work for working families;
- it's time that we moved from good words to good work, from sound bites to sound solutions.

Since *It is time THAT + subject* equals *It is time + subject*, when students now analyse the latter, they will realise that this can also be followed by the present and past tenses, thus finding evidence that contradicts 'the rule' (stated in the theoretical explanations consulted) which claims that *It's time + subject* is always followed by the past tense:

- maybe it's time we ask Americans if they want to play a part in rebuilding America. (Clinton)

Clinton's use of hypothetical 'maybe' as compared with Obama's constant use of *It's time + subject + past*) adds a further dimension to the analysis. And possibly so should we (language teachers). In short, these are only a very few pedagogical advantages of using individual production corpora to learn lexico-grammar in the language classroom.

5. 3. Discussing ideology in the language classroom

M.A.K. Halliday's *Functional Grammar* (1994) has been used both to teach linguistic aspects of English (e.g. cohesion) and to obtain an ideological profile of speakers. As is well known, throughout his research, Halliday distinguishes three linguistic realms: the ideational, the interpersonal and the textual. The former – the main focus of this section – is concerned with the expression of what is popularly known as *content* and primarily conveys experiential meaning "of some kind of a process, some event, action, state, or other phenomenal aspects of the real world" (Halliday, Hasan, 1989: 18). Together with processes (events, actions and states), experiential meaning also encompasses the participants in these processes. Students have virtually no linguistic problems with the functioning of participants (often proper nouns and pronouns). And yet, examining the way in which these are used by prominent politicians (such as Obama and Clinton) may provide ideological information that will round off learners' communicative skills.

The proper nouns speakers refer to give us an idea of their active worldview. Like WordSmith Tools, Wmatrix provides frequency lists of the corpora analysed. With them, we can manually create a list of those proper nouns which Obama and Clinton have used more than 10 times in their speeches (*Tables 3a* and *3b*). Analysis of Obama's proper nouns (*Table 3a*) shows his ideational world is populated by:

- *America* and *the USA*;
- the world at large: *Iraq, Israel, the Americas, Iran, China, Colombia, NAFTA, Cuba*;
- political opponents: notably *John McCain*, and Obama's predecessor – *George W. Bush*;
- some US states and cities: Obama mentions up to 11 (excluding *Washington*);
- the node of political power which he encapsulates as *Washington*;
- the node of financial power: *Wall Street* and *Main Street*;
- democratic beacons: *Dr. King, the Kennedies*;
- *God*.

If we analyse Clinton's proper nouns (*Table 3b*), further interesting conclusions can also been drawn. Clinton's ideational world is populated by:

- *America* and *the USA*;
- American States and cities: She refers to up to 19 states and/or cities;
- Clinton's opponents in her way to the presidency, most prominently *Obama*. *McCain* is regarded as a second rate opponent;
- the node of political power, which she encapsulates as *the White House*;
- the world at large;
- her family (*Chelsea*: by looking at concordances for *Chelsea* we see this often appears as *Bill and Chelsea*).

Obama		
proper noun	**freq.**	**%**
America	323	0.36
Washington	185	0.20
John_McCain	100	0.11
United_States	99	0.11
Iraq	98	0.11
Obama	91	0.10
Senator	87	0.10
George_Bush	73	0.08
Israel	72	0.08
Barack	42	0.05
McCain	40	0.04
Wall_Street	36	0.04
Americas	34	0.04
King	33	0.04
Chicago	28	0.03
New_Orleans	26	0.03
Dr.	24	0.03
Iran	24	0.03
China	24	0.03
South_Carolina	23	0.03
Main_Street	21	0.02
Illinois	21	0.02
Kennedy	21	0.02
Michigan	19	0.02
Houston	17	0.02
New_Hampshire	16	0.02
Pennsylvania	14	0.02
Kansas	13	0.01
Virginia	12	0.01
God	11	0.01
Bush-McCain	10	0.01
Wisconsin	10	0.01
Colombia	10	0.01
NAFTA	10	0.01
Cuba	10	0.01
Ted_Kennedy	10	0.01

Clinton		
proper noun	**freq.**	**%**
America	311	0.34
Ohio	105	0.11
Iraq	102	0.11
White	77	0.08
Governor	72	0.08
Hillary_Clinton	68	0.07
United_States	60	0.06
Bush	57	0.06
Obama	55	0.06
Israel	49	0.05
New_York	47	0.05
Pennsylvania	45	0.05
Michigan	45	0.05
Florida	43	0.05
China	30	0.03
West_Virginia	29	0.03
Clinton	29	0.03
Hillary	28	0.03
Dr.	23	0.02
McCain	23	0.02
New_Hampshire	23	0.02
Kentucky	21	0.02
George_Bush	20	0.02
California	18	0.02
King	18	0.02
Wall_Street	17	0.02
Strickland	17	0.02
Puerto_Rico	17	0.02
U.S.	16	0.02
Afghanistan	15	0.02
Connecticut	15	0.02
Wisconsin	14	0.02
South_Carolina	14	0.02
Chelsea	13	0.01
Indiana	12	0.01
Zanesville	11	0.01
Texas	10	0.01
South_Dakota	10	0.01
NAFTA	10	0.01
Youngstown	10	0.01

Table 3 (a and b): Obama's and Clinton's use of proper nouns

So, from the data, we may conclude that, in order to become the Democratic nominee for the US presidency, both Obama and Clinton count heavily on America's nationalism. In fact, if we use Range to examine – at random – 25 speeches by Clinton and 25 speeches by Obama, (the maximum number of speeches Range accepts for analysis) we find that both of them mention *America* in all of the documents analysed:

001. America (word)   545 (total freq.)   25 (speeches)   1(BNC word level)

T_0   T_1 T_2 T_3 T_4 T_5   T_6   T_7   T_8   T_9
T_10   T_11 T_12 T_13 T_14 T_15 T_16 T_17 T_18 T_19
T_20   T_21 T_22 T_23 T_24 (Clinton)

001. America (word)   543 (total freq.)   25 (speeches)   1(BNC word level)

T_0   T_1   T_2   T_3   T_4   T_5   T_6   T_7   T_8   T_9
T_10 T_11 T_12 T_13 T_14 T_15 T_16 T_17 T_18 T_19
T_20 T_21 T_22 T_23 T_24 (Obama)

The data above include the word under study (i.e. *America*), its total frequency in the 25 speeches chosen at random (i.e. 545 for Clinton vs 543 for Obama), the number of speeches in which the word appears (*America* appears in 25 speeches, that is, in all speeches by Clinton and by Obama), the BNC vocab level the word belongs to (*America* pertains to BNC word level 1, that is, it is among the most common words in English) and finally the exact texts in which the word appear (starting from Text 0 up to Text 24, which is the way in which Range counts texts).

Obama and Clinton also agree in distancing themselves from George W. Bush and they coincide in highlighting the issue of *Iraq* as part of their agendas. Range shows that, out of the 25 speeches analysed at random, 18 contain a reference to Iraq.

003. Iraq (word)   124 (total freq.) 18 (speeches)   7 (BNC word level)

T_0   T_1   T_2   —   —   T_5   —   T_7   T_8   T_9
T_10 T_11 T_12 T_13   —   T_15 T_16 T_17 T_18   —
 —   —   T_22 T_23 T_24 (Clinton)

012. Iraq (word)   68 (total freq.) 18 (speeches)   7 (BNC word level)

T_0   T_1   —   —   T_4   —   T_6   T_7   T_8   T_9
 —   T_11 T_12 T_13 T_14 T_15 T_16 T_17   —   —
T_20   —   T_22 T_23 T_24 (Obama)

So the linguistic data show a number of similarities in the politicians' ideologies. However, there are also clear differences between them and these are reflected by their use of proper nouns. While Obama turns abroad more frequently, Clinton looks inwards (to US states and cities) to a greater extent. Being a Senator for quite a while, Clinton sees the White House as the real node of power rather than Washington. It is well known that, during the elections, Obama presented himself as an outsider to Washington, which he attacked fiercely. This is, in principle, confirmed by *Table 3b*. Clinton regards Obama as her main adversary; Obama, on the contrary, focuses on McCain as the one to beat. While Clinton resorts to the notion of the nuclear family (Bill and Chelsea), Obama seems to enlarge his reference world to his Democratic family (the Kennedies), human rights activists (Martin Luther King) and even God. We all know what happened next and what American people voted for.

Another very popular way, amongst researchers, of assessing speakers' worldviews is through the study of their pronouns. Indeed the use of pronouns is one of the first things learners are taught when they study English. However, not many learners realise that pronouns are an important means of expressing ideology. As is well known, *I* may logically denote a more subjective, individualistic and self-centred stance. *You* addresses the audience directly, as if the speaker was communicating with each of the listeners almost on their own. *We* may be part of a collective and inclusive strategy, where speakers place themselves in the same category as the listeners. On the contrary, *they* may be part of exclusive strategies, where opponents are singled out and identified.

When comparing corpora, Wmatrix displays overused and underused POS-items very clearly. Wmatrix in fact suggests that Obama and Clinton use pronouns differently. *Table 4* shows the pronouns Obama overuses (+) and underuses (-) vis-à-vis Clinton.

POS-item	Meaning	Obama's Freq	%	Clinton's Freq	%	Under /over	Log Likelihood
PPIS1	I	1255	1.39	2217	2.39	-	248.60
PPY	You	596	0.66	1160	1.25	-	171.78
PPIS2	We	2049	2.26	2053	2.22	+	0.44
PPHS2	They	570	0.63	509	0.55	+	4.98

Table 4: Obama and Clinton use pronouns differently

These results may lead us to the conclusion that Clinton is more individualistic than Obama. She especially distinguishes between two independent interlocutors (*I* and *you*). According to previous research (see Duman, Locher, 2008), when choosing *I*, Clinton emphasises her unique status as presidential candidate. Here are some examples from the HILARY subcorpus:

- I am as ready as I can be after having had this incredible experience here in Iowa;
- I have set big goals for our country;
- I want to make it absolutely clear I intend to restore America's leadership;
- I am not going to leave anyone out.

Duman and Locher (2008) also argue that Clinton uses *you* especially when she addresses her viewers in their capacity as voters. Again our data confirms this conclusion:

- when you go to vote on Tuesday, you are voting not only your own interests, your own needs, your own values;
- well, you are not invisible to me;
- over the last week, I listened to you and, in the process, I found my own voice;
- I am here today because of you and because the work that Dr. King started and the work he was doing when his life was cut short is directly related to your cause;
- if you are scared, keep going. If you are hungry, keep going. If you want to taste freedom, keep going;
- I hope you will go to and support this campaign because it is your campaign;
- I think it's time we had a president who stands up for you and I will be that president.

Obama is a more 'gregarious' (i.e. collective) speaker. He does not address the audience directly as much as Clinton but aligns himself with (and distances himself from) them to a greater extent than she does. Duman and Locher (2008: 211) argue that Obama uses the first person plural *we* to identify with the viewer "as a victim of negative agents". The OBAMA subcorpus comes to reinforce Dunam and Lorcher's statement:

- you said the time has come to tell the lobbyists who think their money and their influence speak louder than our voices that they don't own this government, we do;
- this was the moment when the improbable beat what Washington always said was inevitable. This was the moment when we tore down barriers that have divided us for too long;
- for many months, we've been teased, even derided for talking about hope;
- we know the battle ahead will be long. But always remember that, no matter what obstacles stand in our way, nothing can stand in the way of the power of millions of voices calling for change. We have been told we cannot do this...

Duman and Locher (2008: 211) also claim that Obama uses *we* to share with the audience a very active role in the future transformation of America. Here are some examples from the OBAMA subcorpus along these lines:

- we're choosing unity over division;
- we are choosing hope over fear;
- and whether we are rich or poor, black or white, Latino or Asian, whether we hail from Iowa or New Hampshire, Nevada or South Carolina...;
- ... we are ready to take this country in a fundamentally new direction.

Like Duman and Locher (2008), we also find data that support the fact that Obama uses *they* to refer to opposing lobbies, who victimise American people. Interestingly enough, *they* is often associated with Washington (see also above):

- … they said this day would never come;
- and they will only grow louder and more dissonant in the weeks and months to come;
- … with Republicans that lobbyists are part of the system in Washington. They're part of the problem;
- now, I know those kind of antics might make sense in Washington, but they don't make much sense anywhere else, and they certainly don't make sense for working families who are struggling under the weight of their debt;
- Washington lobbyists haven't funded my campaign, they won't run my White House, and they will not drown out the voices of working Americans when I am President;
- … then they go back to Washington when the campaign's over, and nothing changes.

Again, we know what happened next. We know which strategies got the support of American people.

6. Conclusion

Very briefly, after the analysis carried out in the present paper, we would like to encourage teachers to use individual linguistic production corpora in their language classrooms. We believe the special prominence of certain (very successful) speakers (such as Obama and Clinton) may be an asset to inform students of the real use of difficult grammar points. We also believe that an explanation of ideological features in the classroom provides complementary knowledge that makes learners more aware of the (hidden) power of language. Finally, throughout the paper, we have particularly insisted on using various corpus-based tools (i.e. AntConc, VocabProfile, Range, Wmatrix) and not just the better-known WordSmith Tools. Although WordSmith is a very powerful kit to study language, there are other computer programs that offer additional possibilities. They are worth having a look at.

Acknowledgements

This paper is part of the R&D Project "Ampliación y profundización de ECPC y de ConcECPC 1.0: avances teórico-descriptivos e innovaciones tecnológicas" (Ref: FFI2008-01610/FILO), financed by the Spanish Ministry of Science and Innovation.

Section III:

ADELEX: From Theory to Practice

Introduction to Section III:
ADELEX: From Theory to Practice

María Moreno Jaén, University of Granada, Spain

Pedagogical implementation is the focus of this third and final section of a volume dedicated to the exploration of new paths in language pedagogy. Specifically, the *From Theory to Practice* design focuses on the Spanish learner of English coming to grips with the role of lexis in discourse. Comparison and contrast, together with raising learners' general metacommunicative awareness and specific capacity to monitor discourse in terms of contrasting L1 and L2 form-function relationships, are thus keywords in Section III. The individual authors relate the more general background and principles of L2 lexis learning to a specific scenario, the need for Spanish learners of English to focus on the 'rules' of discourse in face-to-face oral interaction. Special focus is thus placed on traps for the unwary, above all the different functions of 'comparable' lexical items in English and Spanish discourse, as is highlighted by the analysis of *snake-in-the-grass* words like *very* (Chapter 14) and *please* (Chapter 17) whose apparent harmlessness belies their actual insidiousness. Comparison and contrast is further underscored in the highly concentrated, awareness-raising contexts found in online forms of testing (Chapters 15 and 18) which *de facto* constitute *lexis-in-action* simulators.

Predictably, in the course of time such online interaction will increasingly take the form of sophisticated *adventure game-cum-simulation* modules that test out students' lexical skills in 'realistic' virtual scenarios. In this respect, Chapters 14 and 17 lay the foundations for identifying, pre-empting and correcting lexical miss-hits and misfires, potentially at ever earlier stages in the L2 learning process. Chapters 15 and 18 lay the foundations for their measurement while Chapters 16 and 17 complete the picture by linking these issues to the world of digital films and multimodal/multimedia scenarios, thereby taking research in ADELEX a few steps towards the exciting world of 3D *lexis-at-work-in-real-life* simulations. We may thus see the chapters in this section as pointing to the conception of virtual worlds concerned with fine-grained data-driven lexis-learning and their realisation within portable and wearable technologies. In an age of tablet technology, foreign language phrasebooks and city-and-country guidebooks have already come a long way. As part of the new world of *on-the-road* L2 learning, their separate worlds are destined to collide and merge with other genres such as street-level maps and journey planners. These are all matters where research is urgently needed and where specialists in lexis and its role in interaction should take the lead.

While heading in this direction ADELEX certainly started life in a more humdrum way. So what is it that drives ADELEX? The basic answer to this question is, as hinted above, its capacity to base lexical learning and assessment on new technologies and techniques, *in primis*, corpora. However, the perspective adopted, as in the previous sections, is highly variegated with different resources functioning in ADELEX's online repositores in different ways. The chapters in this section demonstrate how ADELEX has turned into an open-ended project, coping with issues of burgeoning interest such as the study and implementation of lexical patterns and multi-word units, multimodal approaches to conversation, multimedia resources for language teaching and second-generation vocabulary assessment.

In this respect, Chapter 14 carries out a contrastive discourse-function analysis of the word *very* in predicate adjective constructions from the standpoint of ELT classroom implementation. In a similar vein, Chapter 15 focuses on the corpus-based investigation of university learners' collocational competence that develops tools for measuring student performance vis-à-vis corpus-based pre- and post-course collocation tests; like Chapter 18, in so doing, it provides an online learner-centred approach to testing.

Chapters 16 and 17 both explore the use of films in the ELT classroom, the first with an emphasis on corpus-based approaches to conversational grammar, the second in relation to the extended contextual awareness that films as multimodal texts provide when minding your linguistic p's and q's. Both chapters contribute to the theme of creativity, motivation and enjoyment in L2 vocabulary learning characterising many of the chapters in this volume and this section, in particular. Chapter 16, in this respect, makes a careful assessment of the value for ELT of film transcripts, while Chapter 17 assesses the dynamic nature of context in digital films and how this can function as an asset in the ELT classroom.

The final chapter, Chapter 18 brings the volume back to where it started with the notions of balance in learning vocabulary and the idea that the deeper and more thoughtful the processing is, the better the learning. Only in this case the application of these principles is carried out in relation to CAT (Computer-adaptive testing), a computer approach which introduces 'new' testing criteria. As well as respecting traditional criteria such as reliability and validity, CAT also has the potential to carry out the evaluation of university L2 students' lexical skills in relation to other criteria such as the student's need for creativity, efficiency and motivation. Thanks to its ability to adapt constantly to learner input, testing can, through CAT, become a source of positive enjoyment and gratification. Further details on ADELEX are given in the Appendix on pages 315-316 of this volume.

'Very' in predicate adjective constructions:
A contrastive (English-Spanish) discourse-functional approach towards its pedagogical implementation

Judith A. Carini Martínez, University of Almería, Spain

1. Introduction

Quirk et al. (1985: 447) opened up a fruitful field in degree modification research when – though perhaps not in a totally convinced or convincing way (see Scheibman, 2002: 58) – they hinted at the differences between the *degree* and *force* of adjectives. This has led to an ongoing scholarly debate about the characterization of adjectives in terms of their gradability or otherwise: if they are gradable, to what extent is this the case. A further issue relates to the semantic and pragmatic inferences that can be drawn from findings (see Quirk et al., 1985; Dixon, 1991; Biber et al., 1999; Huddleston, Pullum, 2002, inter alia). In particular, discourse-functional studies still remain a somewhat neglected area of research as regards this specific issue and specially so from a cross-linguistic standpoint. The objective in this paper is thus to respond to this need. The focus will be on the most *basic* intensifiers in English and Spanish: 'very' and *muy*, in basic predicate adjective constructions of the type given below:

1. Ron was *very subdued* all through the class. (H.P.1: 431)
    Ron estaba *muy apagado* durante toda la clase. (H.P.2: 429)

We intend to prove how they can both be considered intensifying discourse devices in an approach which transcends the limits of the mere propositions they are included in, and which aims at signalling the contrastive similarities and differences between them from a discourse-functional perspective. This will further enable us to construe teaching materials in accordance with the results obtained.

A word of caution is now necessary. When we speak here of *basic*, we do not mean *simple*. In fact, our observations on centering our attention on this basic structure has led us to go far beyond its limits to be able to comprehend in full the discourse-functional facets triggered by, or implicit in, the use of these degree modifiers. And once stated this crucial point, we again return to the issue of contention raised by distinguishing between the *degree* and the *force* of adjectives. Assuming that both 'very' and *muy* can contribute to the *force* of predicate adjectives by means of scalar intensification, this process is promoted by the speaker's intention to express and convey intensification in the ongoing discourse by other means than the sole use of degree modifiers – that is, the speaker builds up intensification using a series of accumulative information-structural devices, strongly cohesive, only one of which is degree modification of adjectives proper.

This paper then will be structured as follows. Firstly, we will present the data of our study and comment upon the results both quantitatively and qualitatively. Secondly, we shall extend the results obtained from our previous classifications and observations towards a discourse-functional approach. Finally, this will be followed by some pedagogical advice of interest for the Spanish university context of EFL learning and teaching.

2. Methodology

A bottom-up usage-based approach has been adopted (Bybee, Eddington, 2006), relying on naturally-occurring data from two extant recent bestselling novels, representing respectively both British English (BrE) and American English (AmE) standard varieties: *Harry Potter and the Half-Blood Prince* (Rowling, 2005), henceforth H.P.1; and *The Da Vinci Code* (Brown, 2003a), henceforth D.C.1, together with their Spanish translations (Rowling, 2006; Brown, 2003b) and henceforth H.P.2 and D.C.2, respectively. Given the extremely similar length of both novels, balanced sampling was assured.

A usage-based model is a model of language use which aims to account for how linguistic knowledge is both represented and stored in the minds of speakers for any particular construction. Type/token frequency of language use is one of its basic conceptual components. A bottom-up approach is highly favoured in this model.

The examples were manually tagged and the tokens were selected with the proviso that at least one of the modifiers ('very' and/or *muy*) was attested in the two languages contrasted, leading ultimately to a bidirectional contrastive scrutiny. The decision to limit our study to predicate adjective constructions sprang both from the need to limit the dispersion of data to avoid overly broad generalities and concluding generalizations, thus enhancing specificity, and from the conviction that the chosen bottom-up approach on carrying out a first study, solely considering the most basic constructions, provides a more convenient starting point for further research into more complex discourse-functional patterns.

3. Analysis and discussion of the data

The totals in both varieties are the following:

- 'very' (H.P.1): 303/104 (34.32%)
- 'very' (D.C.1): 82/27 (32.92%)
- *muy* (H.P.2): 420/91 (21.66%)
- *muy* (D.C.2): 223/46 (20.06%)

Overall, the total number of tokens of 'very' tagged in the English originals were 303 tokens in H.P.1, and 82 in D.C.1. Of these, 104 (34.32%) and 27 (32.92%), respectively, correspond to predicate adjective constructions with basic copular verbs ('be', 'seem', 'look' and 'appear'), the constructions we are considering here. These are very high percentages, if we consider the multiplicity of remaining patterns/functions in which 'very' can appear:

- 'very' in predicate adjective constructions with copular dynamic verbs implying a change of state ('get', 'become', etc.);
- 'very' in predicate nominal constructions;
- 'very' as modifier of adverbs;
- 'very' as an adjective.

In the Spanish versions, the total number of tokens of *muy* are 420 in H.P.2 and 223 in D.C.2. The predicate adjective constructions with basic copular verbs (*ser*, *parecer* and non-locative *estar*) total 91 (21.66%) and 46 (20.06%). If we consider not only the number of other constructions that include *muy*, but also the fact that Spanish is able to substitute the degree modifier proper for the morpheme *-ísimo/a/os/as* added to the adjective (e.g. *muy bueno = buenísimo*), the percentage of *muy* tokens of the construction as compared to the total number of *muy* tokens in the corpus might also be considered quite high. The remaining patterns/functions are summarized as follows:

- *muy* in predicate adjective constructions with copular dynamic verbs (*volverse, ponerse*, etc.);
- *muy* in predicate nominal constructions;
- *muy* as modifier of adverbs;
- *muy* modifying a past participle.

3. 1. Type/token frequency of 'very' and *muy* in predicate adjective constructions

Table 1 shows the number of bidirectional contrastive tokens coded in the corpus. A plus sign indicates presence, and the minus sign absence, in the corresponding translation.

VERY/MUY	H.P.1	D.C.1	H.P.2	D.C.2	Total
+very/+muy	59	17			76
+very/-muy	45	10			55
+muy/-very			91	46	137
+very	104	27			131
+muy			150	63	213

Table 1: Bidirectional contrastive tokens

From *Table 1*, it can be seen that the total number of tokens of 'very' present in the corpus amounts to 131, and as regards *muy*, 213. The figures also show that globally considered there is an imbalance between the two items in the translation, so we cannot talk of a one-to-one correspondence, a fact which will be discussed below. Nearly half of the contrastive examples stemming from 'very' (45 out of 104) are not rendered in the

Spanish version by *muy* in H.P., and in D.C. there is a gain in the correspondence but 'very' (27 tokens) is still significantly higher than *muy* (17 tokens). A number of constraints are responsible for the presence or absence of this correspondence between 'very' and *muy*, a selection of which follows:

+very/-muy
Use of alternative inflected intensifier *-ísimo*:

2.   Ginny and Gabrielle will look *very sweet* together. (H.P.1: 126) (sic)
Ginny y Gabrielle quedarán *monísimas* juntas. (H.P.2: 131) (sic)

Collocational restrictions in Spanish:

3.   The gun in his hand was a concealable, small-caliber, J-frame Medusa, but it would be *very deadly* at close range. (D.C.1: 475)

El arma que llevaba en la mano era de calibre pequeño y fácil de disimular, aunque su disparo, en las distancias cortas, era *mortal*. (D.C.2: 531)

Idiomatic preference:

4.   Girls were *very strange* sometimes. (H.P.1: 293).
A veces *no había manera de entender* a las chicas. (H.P.2: 295)

Constraints on the metaphorical use of adjectives:

5.   Yes, I saw the initials P.S. once. When I was *very young*. (D.C.1: 157)
Sí, las vi una vez. Cuando era *pequeña*. (D.C.2: 169)

We also found it interesting to type/token those cases of *muy* which did not correspond to with 'very' in the original novels, so as to take into consideration the possible constraints which were blocking it, the most noticeable seen below:

+muy/-very
Collocational preference:

6.   Es *muy competente*, hace el doble de trabajo que el resto de los… (H.P.2: 24)
He's *highly efficient*, gets through twice the work the rest of them (H.P.1: 22)

Idiomatic incompatibility:

7.   —Ya lo sé —la consoló Hermione—. Es *muy creída*. (H.P.2: 94)
'I know,' said Hermione, dropping her voice. 'She's *so full of herself*.' (H.P.1: 90)

Idiomatic preference:

8.   … pero Dumbledore lo ha impedido una y otra vez, lo cual es *muy comprensible* … (H.P.2: 323)
… but Dumbledore has – *most understandably*, as I say – prevented this. (H.P.1: 320)

Colligational preference:

9.   —Ostras, *no parecen* muy contentas, ¿no? (H.P.2: 440)
'Blimey, they *don't look* happy, do they?' (H.P.1: 442)

Moreover, 'very' is much more frequent in the BrE standard variety sub-corpus than in the AmE one, at least as far as predicate adjective constructions are concerned. In general, we have observed that marked or explicit intensification appears more in H.P. than in D.C., as the narration in the latter is written following journalese linguistic conventions, one of which is the controlled use of adjective intensification for the sake of brevity. An additional reason for this is that H.P. has much more dialogue, and intensification is much more prone to appear in oral exchange accounts than in descriptive or narrative texts. In fact, the *Longman Grammar of Spoken and Written English* (Biber et al., 1999: 561) states that 'very' is "the only degree adverb that shows equal statistics of use in BrE conversation, AmE conversation and Academic prose", that is, an intensifier with "wide range", in Nation's (2001: 16) use of the term.

To conclude this section, it might just be added that 'very' as a degree modifier can stand on its own in an utterance, and we have found instances of this use in our corpus, thus showing a high degree of subjectivity in process, and accordingly leading to a grammaticalisation of 'very':

> 10. 'Has it been busy at the Ministry?'
> '*Very*,' said Mr Weasley. (H.P.1: 310)
>
> –¿Hay mucho trabajo en el ministerio?
> –*Muchísimo*. (H.P.2: 312)

Although we have not found any entry in any dictionary corresponding to this isolated use of 'very', we have traced an entry of the expression 'not very', of an idiomatic nature, in the *Oxford Wordpower Dictionary*.

Note also the increasing grammaticalisation of 'very' in conversation, as in the following example from the ICE-GB Corpus, where 'very' either stands alone as a verb (accounting for the fact that 'into' can only be governed by verbs) or is considered so obvious as regards intensification and subjectivity that the verb has been omitted:

> 11. He's *very into* magical realism and all that sort of crap you know… (sla-045-275)

3. 2. Type/token frequency of source language copular verbs

The subjective stance of 'be', its evaluative nature displaying internal universal perception, triggers more frequency in the number of tokens found, running parallel to the subjectivity inherent in 'very'. On the other hand, the 'permanent' value ascribed to *ser* (Clements, 1988: 780) specifying "a class norm where the subject can choose to frame a given situation", readily corresponds to a higher number of *muy* tokens. As 'look' is more sensory and objective as regards external evidence, it naturally clashes with subjective 'very', as attested by the low frequency obtained. Ellipsis of the verb renders neutral the subjective-objective dichotomy, therefore enhancing a rise in the appearance of 'very' once more. It is also worthy mentioning the overlap in translation of the verbs 'seem' and 'look' into Spanish *parecer*, at least from a literal standpoint.

Table 2 shows the stemming copular verb for the three classified correspondences (ellipsis of the verb also considered):

VERB	H.P.1	D.C.1	VERB	H.P.2	D.C.2
BE	60	23	SER	44	25
SEEM	3	1	PARECER	8	8
LOOK	5	0	ESTAR	26	9
APPEAR	0	0	------------		
ELLIPSIS	36	3	ELLIPSIS	13	4

Table 2: Stemming copular verbs

3. 3. 'Very' and *muy* at the *word* level

'Very' is an intensifier which is commonly classified as a degree modifier in the construction under study. The term *degree modifier* itself is a convenient term which avoids controversial issues as regards its inclusion either within the lexicon, that is, as a lexical category, or within grammar, as a grammatical category. *Degree* or *grade* is primarily a grammatical feature for some authors and a semantic feature for others (Quirk et al., 1985: 404), and *degree modifiers* are even nowadays considered to fall under the grammatical class of adverbs, which was criticised by Trask (1993: 74) who labels them as a distinct lexical category. In Spanish, *muy* is an intensifier similarly termed *modificador gradativo* and is invariably referred to as an adverb (Kovacci, 1999: 779; Bosque, 1999: 226). However, the term *intensifier* has been described by Bolinger (1972: 179) as an element "that scales a quality, either up or down or somewhere between the two".

Intensifiers are primarily divided into two classes, amplifiers and downtoners, scaling upwards and downwards from an assumed norm, respectively; that is, emphasizing and restricting. Both 'very' and *muy* are generally classified as amplifiers, not downtoners, though it is sometimes difficult in practice to distinguish between amplifying and downtoning expressions because "the orientation or ordering along the scale is usually determined by pragmatic, not linguistic, factors" (Sánchez López, 1999: 1090, my translation).

Apart from degree modifiers, Quirk et al. also consider another set of intensifiers, the emphasizers, which add to the *force*, not the *degree* of adjectives (Quirk et al., 1985: 447), a semantic distinction which, according to Scheibman (2002: 58), becomes "murky" because of the "natural subjectivity of expression in English conversation". As a result Quirk et al. did not draw a well-defined borderline between the two. Subjectivity will be further discussed in the next section.

3. 4. Description and discussion of data at the phrase level

In this section we will focus on 'very' and *muy* as modifiers of the accompanying adjective. The classification of adjectives follows Dixon (1991: 78-79), though we have not considered all adjectives monosemous, but have assigned metaphorical extensions of some of them to a type more appropriate to the meaning provided by the context in which they appear. The list below does not follow alphabetical order, but strictly the order of appearance in the corpus. Numbers next to any entry signal subsequent repetition(s) in the co-text.

3. 4. 1. List of adjectives

(i) +very / - muy:

- D.C.1: tired, suave, resilient, common, prominent, big, hard, special, pretty, young, important, large, pleased, direct, sacred, glad, wise, intent, good, glad, convincing, deadly, busy, sorry, young, eager, (not) good, (27);

- H.P.1: sorry, sorry, kind, busy, weak, secret, angry (2), angry, difficult, good, clear, pleasant, admirable, brave, gracious, busy, amusing, tense, frightened, pleased, unlikely, sweet, surprised, conscious, pleased, good (2), irritating, broad, good, good, difficult, important, surprised, clever, amusing, crowded, irresponsible, (not) busy, tall, thin, important, hard, astute, slim, strange, red, busy, popular, thoughtful, interested, protective, pink-faced, rude, (not) happy (2), touched, nosy, guarded, lucky, odd, careful, handsome, relieved, annoyed, agitated, nice, important, good, fond, similar, good, subdued, pretty, difficult, pleasant, valuable, sorry, nice, strong, brave, funny, dark, good, ingenuous, wrong, good, good, kind, careful, unfortunate, small, good, white, good, gratifying, neat (2), lucky, handsome, fond, important, hungry, (104).

(ii) +muy / - very:

- D.C.2: probable, distinta, oscuras, lenta, amable, (no) convencida, bonito, convencida, importante, adecuado, pálido, antigua, visible, iluminadas, adecuado, (no) resistentes, clara, cuidadoso, afectada, (no) convencido, probable, difícil, breve, perjudicial, antiguo, alterado, sólidas, fina, fina, callada, ingenioso, (no) concreto, serio, desgastadas, asustado, preocupado, afectado, claro, ocupado, ocupada, afectado, posible, sorprendido, amable, frío, curioso, (46);

- H.P.2: soliviantados, sorprendido, inepto, baja, satisfecho, competente, probable, considerado, satisfecho, sencilla, generoso, mayor, ingenioso, satisfecho, orgulloso, demacrada, reciente, creída, (no) risueña, deprimido, (no) convencida, curioso, útil, elevado, guapa, propio, ufano, conocida, ocupado, corto de luces, agitada, risueñas, amable, 'adjetivo elíptico', rara, ocupado, avanzada, debilitada, deprimente, interesante, importante, divertida, contento, alterada, bonitos, enterada, simpática, guapa, diferente, viejo, bonita, natural, elegante, comprensible, subjetivo, disgustados, misterioso, divertido, probable, cansado, ocupado, enfadada, anciana, despistada, mayor, susceptible, delgada, contentas, enfurruñado, duros, apenado, satisfecho, amable, duro, estricto, descuidado, sospechosa, especial, satisfecho, desagradable, doloroso, quieto, ingenioso, inteligente, inusual, largo, débil, fea, guapa, compungido, lista, (91).

3. 4. 2. Type/token list of source language predicate adjectives

(i) Very:

- VERY + ADJ. DIMENSION
  H.P.: broad, small, tall, thin
  D.C.: big, large;

- VERY + ADJ. PHYSICAL PROPERTY
  H.P.: hungry, strong, weak
  D.C.: deadly, tired;

- VERY + ADJ. AGE
  D.C.: young (2);

- VERY + ADJ. COLOUR
  H.P.: pink-faced, red, white;

- VERY + ADJ. VALUE
  H.P.: admirable, brave, busy (2), (not) busy, crowded, dark, funny, good (12), gracious, gratifying, handsome (2), important (4), ingenuous, irresponsible, lucky (2), neat (2), nice (5), odd, popular, pretty, secret, slim, strange, sweet, thoughtful, unfortunate, valuable
  D.C.: busy, convincing, good, (not) good, important, pretty, prominent, resilient, sacred, special;

- VERY + ADJ. DIFFICULTY
  H.P.: difficult (2), hard
  D.C.: hard;

- VERY + ADJ. QUALIFICATION
  H.P.: (not) clear, wrong
  D.C.: common;

- VERY + ADJ. HUMAN PROPENSITY
  H.P.: agitated, astute, amusing (2), angry (3), annoyed, careful (2), clear, clever, conscious, fond (2), frightened, guarded, (not) happy (2), interested, irritating, kind (2), nosy, pleasant (2), pleased (2), protective, relieved, rude, sorry (3), subdued, surprised (2), tense, touched, wise
  D.C.: direct, eager, glad (2), intent, pleased, sorry, suave;

- VERY + ADJ. SIMILARITY
  H.P.: similar.

(ii) Muy:

- MUY + ADJ. DIMENSION
  H.P.: largo;

- MUY + ADJ. PHYSICAL PROPERTY
  H.P.: avanzada, débil, delgada, quieto
  D.C.: breve, fina (2), frío;

- MUY + ADJ. SPEED
  D.C.: lenta;

- MUY + ADJ. AGE
  H.P.: anciana, mayor (2), reciente, viejo
  D.C.: antigua, antiguo;

- MUY + ADJ. COLOUR
  D.C.: claro, iluminadas, oscuras;

- MUY + ADJ. VALUE
  H.P.: baja, bonita, bonitos, curioso, comprensible, cansado, debilitada, demacrada, desagradable, deprimente, elegante, (no) especial, fea, guapa (3), (no) guapa, importante, interesante, misterioso, natural, (no) elevado, ocupado (3), (no) propio, (no) resistentes, sospechosa, subjetivo, útil
  D.C.: adecuado (2), bonito, curioso, desgastadas, importante, ocupado, ocupada, perjudicial, serio, sólidas, visible;

- MUY + ADJ. DIFFICULTY
  H.P.: duro, duros, sencilla
  D.C.: difícil;

- MUY + ADJ. QUALIFICATION
  H.P.: conocida, inusual, probable (2), rara
  D.C.: posible, probable (2);

- MUY + ADJ. HUMAN PROPENSITY
  H.P.: agitada, alterada, amable (2), apenado, asustado, competente, compungido, considerado, contentas, contento, (no) convencida, corto de luces, creída, deprimido, descuidado, despistada, disgustados, divertida, divertido, doloroso, enfadada, enfurruñado, enterada, estricto, generoso, inepto, ingenioso (2), inteligente, lista, orgulloso, propio, (no) risueña, risueñas, satisfecho (5), soliviantados, sorprendido, susceptible, ufano, simpática
  D.C.: afectada, afectado (2), alterado, amable (2), callada, claro, (no) concreto, convencida, (no) convencida, (no) convencido, cuidadoso, ingenioso, pálido, preocupado, sorprendido, simpática;

- MUY + ADJ. SIMILARITY
  H.P.: diferente
  D.C.: distinta.

The classification clearly shows that both *muy* and 'very' followed by *Value* and *Human Propensity* adjectives outnumber the remaining types. Undoubtedly, intensification as a process in which the speaker emphatically evaluates a state of being or affairs (*Value*), or expresses an emotional reaction, state of mind or personal ability (*Human Propensity*) is suitably enacted by these more human-driven, vague, subjective kind of adjectives. Metaphorical uses of the most concrete or objective adjectives are also largely preferred, falling then into the subjective categories (as for example, 'large' and *elevado*). In short, what we find here is a preference of both 'very' and *muy* to intensify adjectives which display "semantic subjectivity" (De Smet, Verstraete, 2006: 385), in concordance with the use of degree modification, a use which in itself is speaker-related.

4. Towards a discourse-functional approach

Having approached the presence and absence of 'very' and *muy* within the predicate adjective constructions, the following still remain open issues:

- the use of 'very' and *muy* to encode processes of intensification and subjectivity in relation to their propositional and discursive co-text and context;
- what realizations and constraints can we encounter from the discourse-functional perspective?

The statistical facts emerging from our corpus-based analysis show that more often than not the discourse-functional facet is essential to properly understand the use of 'very' and *muy* as degree modifiers. Compelling evidence for this claim arises from the fact that the items under analysis here frequently co-occur with a disparate type of coordinate and subordinate clauses expressing contrast, concession, etc. as listed below, which have thus proved to be highly explicit in these open issues:

Contrast – contrary to expectation (descriptive):

12. Symbols are *very resilient, but* the Pentacle was *altered* by the Early Roman Catholic Church. (D.C.1: 62)

    Los símbolos son *muy resistentes, pero* la primera Iglesia católica romana *alteró* el significado del pentáculo. (D.C.2: 62)

Contrast – contrary to speaker's previous experience:

13. I *never* saw a key like that. It was *very pretty*. (D.C.1: 155)
    Nunca he visto una llave como ésa. Era *muy bonita*. (D.C.2: 167)

Contrast – contrary to addressee's expectation:

14. 'You will *not* be able to open it.'
    'My teacher is *very wise*' the monk replied… (D.C.1: 368)

    –No podrá abrirlo.
    –Mi Maestro es *muy listo* –replicó el monje… (D.C.2: 411)

Contrast – downtoning effect of favourable evaluation:

> 15. – *Muy ingenioso* –admitió Dumbledore–. *Pero debe de ser...* (H.P.2: 73)
> 'Ingenuous,' said Dumbledore. 'But it sounds...' (H.P.1: 69)

Contrast – irony – amplifying effect:

> 16. *Very astute*, Harry, *but the mouth-organ* was *only ever a mouth-organ*. (H.P.1: 260)
> *Muy astuto*, Harry, *pero la armónica sólo* era una *armónica*. (H.P.2: 264)

Contrast – emphatic reformulation:

> 17. *–No* está *tan* mal... *Aunque* es *muy fea* –se apresuró a añadir al ver que Ginny arqueaba las cejas... (H.P.2: 586)
> 'She's *not that* bad, [...]' '*Ugly, though*,' he added hastily, as Ginny raised her eyebrows... (H.P.1: 591)

Restricted condition – contrary to speaker's expectation

> 18. Into it? *Only if* we are *very unfortunate*. (H.P.1: 525)
> ¿Meternos? *Sólo si* nos van *muy mal las cosas*. (H.P.2: 521)

Heightening – emphasis (intensifying question tag)

> 19. *Hello...* you're very pretty, *aren't you?* (H.P.1: 435)
> *Hola, encanto...* Eres muy guapa, *¿verdad?* (H.P.2: 432)

Heightening – emphasis

> 20. *I thought* I made it clear to you *how very important* that memory is. Indeed, *I did my best...* (H.P.1: 401)
>
> *Creí* que habías *comprendido cuán transcendental* es ese recuerdo. En nuestro anterior encuentro *puse especial empeño...* (H.P.2: 399)
>
> 21. Harry felt *slightly* resentful at this: *if* their lessons were *so very important*, why had there been *such a long* gap... (H.P.1: 244)
>
> El muchacho se sintió contrariado ante esa última frase: *si* sus clases particulares eran *tan importantes*, ¿por qué había habido un lapso *tan largo...?* (H.P.2: 249)

In *Examples 12* to *18*, it can be observed that contrast, whether of an adversative, concessive, or conditional-concessive nature, purveys many instances where both 'very' and *muy* appear in the flow of discourse. Contrast is *per se* subjective and intensive, and therefore adjectives that show up in its discursive structure have a strong tendency to be accompanied by degree modifiers.

In *Example 13*, for instance, the intensifier 'very' + adjective, as well as the corresponding *muy* + adjective, is triggered by the contrast conveyed by the speaker's contrary-to-expectation evaluation, signalled at the beginning of the utterance with the frequency adverb 'never' or *nunca*. The omission of the degree modifier would undoubtedly render the utterance unnatural, odd and incomplete, as it would not be in accordance with the overall meaning carried through by the speaker, that is, the speaker intention of stressing surprise on confronting the unexpected.

In *Example 19*, an intensifying question tag at the end of the utterance also results in a necessary presence of the degree modifier both in English and Spanish.

Both in *Example 15* and *Example 17*, the fronting of the adjective in English ('ingenious' and 'ugly', respectively) is an intensifying grammatical device that blocks further intensification by 'very'.

In *Example 20*, the utterance is suitably marked by a pause (in writing, a stop), dividing it into two parts, building up from a less factual to a more factual colouring of the meaning in both English and Spanish, though in the Spanish translation there is a lexicalization of the intensification (*trascendental*), pre-modified by a quantifier (*cuán*), and ending in an intensifying subjective expression (*puse especial empeño*) serving the same purpose.

20 (bis) I thought   I made it clear to you   how very important that memory is.
       definite   + *definite*   ++ *definite*

       Indeed,   I did my best... (H.P.1: 401)
       amplifier   *superlative*

       Creí que habías comprendido cuán transcendental es ese recuerdo. En nuestro anterior encuentro puse especial empeño... (H.P.2: 399)

5. Towards a discourse-functional pedagogical implementation of 'very'

In spite of its status as one of the first 1,000 lexical entries in well-known basic English word lists (West, 1953, onwards), 'very' in its disparate usage is an item whose learning, so to say, has been generally left to itself. Most particularly as a degree modifier, it has even been continuously discouraged, pedagogically and stylistically favouring other intensifiers in its place, such as 'extremely' and 'really' amongst others. This has been reinforced by the idea that 'very' belongs to that class of words pejoratively termed *teddy bear words* or *dustbin words* (see Crystal, 1987: 92; inter alia), though the comment arose from its abuse in written formal English considered as a native language, and not in the range of English in speech or as a foreign language, worthy to be dwelt on from a pedagogical point of view. Nevertheless, the recommendation of controlling its use has extended to these two last discursive types, so that there have been very few textbooks and workbooks addressed to the EFL learner covering it explicitly through pedagogical grammar notes and exercises.

An interesting exception to this is found in Thornbury (2004: 174-175), where two facing pages are entirely devoted to 'very'. The first page presents its grammar patterns, collocations and set phrases. The second page consists of exercises with further descriptive and prescriptive notes supplied as guidance. Significantly, although all the possible basic patterns of 'very' are presented (such as 'very' + NP), the author concentrates on 'very' as a degree modifier, so that all the exercises deal with this particular usage. Moreover, the vast majority of the sentences in the exercises bear the stative basic copular verb 'be', apart from one example with 'seem'. This preference is in accordance with the statistical analysis of our corpus, as the percentages showed that 'very' as a degree modifier in basic copular patterns with stative verbs are comparatively much higher than with dynamic copular verbs and even more with respect to other possible remaining patterns, both as degree modifier and otherwise (see *Section 3* above). The practice page ends with ten sentences requiring the learner to decide whether they are correct or not, and if incorrect, to rephrase acceptably. This type of exercise is widely recommended as a convenient revision of the competence or proficiency acquired in the completion of the preceding types of exercises.

Naturally, the author devises his guidance and practice of 'very' following a bottom-up approach to the teaching/learning of the item, using loose sentences. This "ease of access" (Harder, 2007: 318) inherent in bottom-up approaches is considered to be *useful* also at the level of production. But at a higher level of comprehension/production, there is the need and the convenience to devise exercises showing the discourse and pragmatic facets of a given item, in this case 'very' contrastively presented with *muy* following similar lines of building-up and discussion as those we have presented above, and filtering them into the making of teaching/learning materials, once the student has completed the basic stage of learning.

Although in this study we have only directed our attention towards one of the structural patterns of 'very', and therefore a complete account of its various grammatical, discursive and pragmatic realizations is lacking for the moment, nevertheless we may forward the following general pedagogical suggestions, at a level of comprehension:

- presentation of short utterances to the learners, with the corresponding Spanish translation, taken from a variety of sources, that may range from jokes to novels, press reports, or transcription of speech from films. The selection should manage to keep as low as possible any extra effort of comprehension as regards vocabulary and structure not serving the purpose;
- signalling of the key words they should concentrate on in order to analyse from a discourse-functional perspective the utterance where 'very' appears. Guided questions at first would be necessary;
- contrast with Spanish, highlighting any observable differences;
- follow-up, discussion and correction;
- assignment requiring them to search for any other similar utterance they may find from any source that may render a similar analysis, and asking them to signal and explain the key words that have led them to consider it so;
- follow-up, discussion and correction.

6. Concluding remarks

Theory is said to precede practice, and the major contribution of our study, to our minds, lies in highlighting the thus far neglected discourse-functional facets of 'very' and *muy* beyond the level of the sentence. In this paper, we furnish a finer-grained analysis of the salient semantico-pragmatic features of 'very' and *muy* in its most basic pattern as a necessary step towards the application of its findings in the Spanish EFL university classroom, for which we have already been able to present pedagogical suggestions. To provide our advanced students with teaching/learning materials emerging from the results of this and further analyses, accounting for the disparate functions/uses we have just begun to describe and discuss, is a must that should not be undervalued if we wish them to attain proficiency.

Acknowledgements

Research leading to this article was sponsored by the Spanish Ministry of Science and Innovation under R&D contract HUM2007-61766/FILO entitled "ADELEX: Assessing and Developing Lexis through New Technologies".

Developing university learners' collocational competence: an empirical corpus-based investigation

María Moreno Jaén, University of Granada, Spain

1. Introduction

That multi-word units, and particularly collocations, are an integral part of a native speaker's knowledge of language is largely unquestioned today (Nesselhauf, Tschichold, 2002). Following this line of argument, in the last two decades many authors have highlighted that collocations are an essential component of non-natives' lexical competence, and consequently, an aspect deserving special attention in the foreign language classroom (Bahns, 1993; Fontenelle, 1994; Lewis, 2000a; Fan, 2009).

The reason why collocations are so crucial, to the point where they have even been considered as "the single most important kind of chunk" (Lewis, 2000b: 8), is that, together with their high frequency, the impact these ready-made combinations have on students' accuracy and fluency is undeniable (Wray, 2002; Woolard, 2005). If as recent research has empirically proven (Gyllstad, 2007; Moreno Jaén, 2007, 2009), collocations are problematic for L2 learners, then the teaching of these combinations ought to be well covered. But, in fact, in most L2 teaching scenarios, collocations continue to be a marginal aspect too often addressed in an incidental and unplanned way (Nesselhauf, 2003; Higueras, 2004).

In response to these issues, we designed, implemented and evaluated a virtual module providing a systematic and effective approach to the teaching and learning of collocations. What follows reports on this experience, focusing primarily on results obtained from a small-scale study carried out from the standpoint of course validation.

2. Designing an online module for teaching collocations

The module we developed to improve learners' collocational competence was conceived as one of the units in the ADELEX programme, an online modular course for assessing and developing learners' lexical competence, designed at the University of Granada (Pérez Basanta, 2004; Moreno Jaén, Pérez Basanta, 2010). This course, first implemented through the ILIAS platform and recently transferred to a Moodle platform, is a digital programme which is part of the Andalusian Virtual Campus (*www.campusandaluzvirtual.es/node/202*) and thus designed for students of English studying in the ten universities in Andalusia.

Our main concern when designing this course was to produce a theoretically sound and pedagogically useful module. The notion of collocation was carefully considered as the foundation on which a methodology, involving such issues as selection of contents and design of a well-structured and systematic set of online materials would be based. These aspects are briefly discussed in the following paragraphs, which concentrate on the findings and effectiveness of this teaching and learning experience.

2. 1. Theoretical framework: the notion of "collocation"

Depending on the perspective and the methodology adopted, collocations have been approached in different ways by different authors. This has traditionally caused considerable controversy and is the main reason why, even today, the definition of collocation needs to be addressed in a study devoted to these combinations.

Two main strands emerge in this field of study: the lexicographical or phraseological approach, and the statistical or frequency-based approach (Nesselhauf, 2005). Recent studies have noted the emergence of a third view, a mixed approach, combining aspects from both (Gyllstad, 2007; Granger, Paquot, 2008).

In this paper, we support the mixed approach to the study of collocations, in the firm belief that both positions, the statistical and the phraseological, "have a great deal to gain from a rapprochement" (Granger, Paquot, 2008: 41). In our view, collocations can be defined as arbitrary and semantically compositional combinations of two or more words which tend to co-occur frequently in the language, while other combinations which are equally acceptable from the grammatical and semantic point of view are seldom or never used to express the same idea. Examples of this would be expressions such as *run into problems*, *fully aware* or *serious illness*. Collocations are, therefore, different from free word combinations (like *eat an apple*, *surprisingly small* or *nice car*), which show no arbitrariness in their co-occurrence, and from idioms (like *spill the beans* or *turn a blind eye*) and compounds, which are not semantically transparent or compositional. Obviously ours is, in essence, a phraseological definition of collocations. However, in line with the mixed approach, we believe that complementing this phraseological view with frequency-based techniques is likely to be highly beneficial as the latter offer operative and systematic methods for the identification and analysis of collocations which the former lacks. From the pedagogical point of view, it is at the second stage of the process, when we move from purely theoretical considerations to more practical issues concerning content selection and material design that corpus-based tools and techniques prove to be of immense value. This is the stage to which we now turn.

2. 2. Methodological procedures

Research on collocations has shown (Philip, 2007; Shin, Nation, 2008; Walker, 2008) that corpus linguistics can potentially provide answers both in terms of what collocations to teach and how to teach them and in the vital task of equipping students with the strategies they may find useful for the permanent and autonomous development of their collocational competence. In this respect, various authors (Hunston, 2002; Bernardini, 2004) have stressed the value of corpora as language-awareness tools. They promote students' encounters with authentic language and help them discover the way words co-occur in real contexts through a heuristic learning process that goes by the name of data-driven learning (DDL). In keeping with these positions, we believe that the corpora available nowadays are the best resource we, as teachers, have at our disposal to select relevant contents and design effective teaching materials.

2. 2. 1. Selection of contents: the compilation of a frequency list of collocations
The first step in the design of our pedagogical treatment was the selection of contents, i.e. the specific collocations to be included in the module. Since one of our goals was to teach students those collocations which are of particular significance for them given their frequency, we carried out a corpus-based selection of collocations. The combinations included in our online module are those made up of the most frequent English nouns and their most frequent nominal, verbal or adjectival collocates. The starting point in our selection process was to extract the 412 nouns included in the first 1,000 words of López-Mezquita's (2007) frequency list, a very reliable word count which is the result of a number of comparative analyses of data provided by the BoE, the BNC, and the Longman Corpus Network. After listing both the singular and plural forms as two different search words, we obtained a list of the 803 most frequent nouns of the English language to be used as the bases of our collocations.

The next stage in our compilation process was the search for the most frequent nominal, verbal and adjectival collocates of our bases. This search was performed by running the program *Sketch Engine* for the exploration of the BNC, as well as *jLookup* (recently updated and renamed as *Wordbanks Online*) for the exploration of the BoE and using t-score as the statistical measure of association. We thus established a cut-off point of 6 in the t-score index and extracted those nouns, verbs and adjectives which formed significantly frequent combinations with our nouns.

However, given that statistical analyses alone do not seem to be sufficient for collocation identification since not all lexical co-occurrences which are statistically significant are phraseological or arbitrary in nature, the results provided by corpus-based software had to be manually analysed to identify and reject frequent combinations which do not constitute interesting collocations from a pedagogical point of view. In our case, and bearing in mind our definition of collocation, we finally selected those collocations which met the following criteria:

1) collocates were arbitrarily restricted in their 'commutability' and/or 'combinability' and thus, required learners to store them as single units (as opposed to free combinations of words such as *young people* or *important question*);
2) they were semantically transparent (as opposed to expressions such as *to have a word* or *the bottom line*, classified as idioms given their non-compositionality);
3) their inner structure is formed by two different members, each of which adds to the general value of the combination (as opposed to compounds which form a semantic unit and behave as single words as is the case of *fast food* or *welfare state*),
4) they were used in a wide range of texts types and contexts (very specialised or subject-dependent collocations such as *marginal cost* or *registered land* were rejected).

The resulting frequency list, totalling 2,688 collocations, formed the database we used for the selection of contents in the construction of our module on collocations.

2. 2. 2. Design of teaching materials

Drawing on the list of collocations gathered, we designed a set of materials to implement this content in our virtual course, ADELEX. The objective of our online module was two-fold. On the one hand, we wanted to improve our learners' knowledge of collocations by focusing on the contents included in our frequency list. On the other, we wanted to help students acquire and develop strategies to promote processes of autonomous learning, an essential aspect if we consider the huge amount of collocations L2 speakers need to learn. Our design procedure placed strong emphasis on DDL as an efficient approach to collocational instruction in keeping with the principles outlined above: relevant input, prominence given to collocational patterns, enhancement of learners' reflection on language and promotion of constant, autonomous learning (Bernardini, 2004).

Following Nation's (2001) suggestions for vocabulary teaching, further represented in this volume, and the principles outlined above, we devised an online module consisting of four different stages. Stage 1 offers an introduction to the notion of collocation as well as corpus-based learning and corpus consultation techniques. This initial section, based on inductive learning procedures, is concerned with making learners aware of the existence and relevance of collocations. This is a necessary task if we consider that, unlike other multi-word units such as idioms and proverbs, these combinations tend to go unnoticed by learners since they do not pose problems from a receptive point of view (Wray, 2002). On the other hand, aware that "corpus skills constitute a learning task in themselves" (Mauranen, 2004b: 99), this introductory section also contains activities that guide students in the use of concordancers as learning tools.

Stage 2 is mainly devoted to helping students spot and identify collocations from L2 input achieved mainly through awareness-raising activities which require students to browse corpora and obtain information needed to complete various controlled activities (reformulating sentences, correcting miscollocations, etc.). Thus, another objective here is to train students in the use of corpus consultation strategies which enhance their knowledge of collocations and their long-term resources for autonomous learning.

In Stage 3 our main concern is practice and recycling. Based on the widely accepted hypothesis that repeated encounters are necessary for vocabulary learning to take place (Jenkins, Dixon, 1984), and also noting that the learning burden increases considerably when working on multi-word units (Lindstromberg, Boers, 2005), this section offers further practice on lexical combinations already tackled in Stages 1 and 2.

Finally, Stage 4 focuses on developing learners' written production of collocations, as well as enhancing the use of various corpus-based programs and consultation techniques to further develop autonomous learning processes. At this stage, and with the goal of producing a written essay, learners are encouraged to use different concordancers and perform a number of exploratory and open-ended searches, where they need to show their ability to obtain and implement the information gathered from their queries.

Space does not allow a thorough examination of the processes of content selection or the development of teaching material. A more detailed account of course design principles and procedures adopted can be found in Moreno Jaén (2008, 2010). The entire module can be accessed online through the ADELEX website accompanying this volume (*http://www.ugr.es/local/inped/exploringnewpaths*).

3. The present study

The main purpose of this study was to test empirically the efficiency of a corpus-based module of collocations designed within the ADELEX project. Although the potential benefits of applying a systematic corpus-based methodology for the teaching of collocations have been sufficiently acknowledged in the last few years (Nesselhauf, Tschichold, 2002; Chan, Liou, 2005; Walker, 2008), only a small number of studies have provided empirical accounts of the results obtained from practical experience on this issue (see Boulton, this volume). Hence the pilot study we have carried out which has tried to answer the following research questions:

- Are the materials efficient, i.e. do they improve learners' collocational knowledge in a statistically significant way?
- Does this module help students improve their strategies and resources to learn and search for collocations autonomously?
- What are learners' opinions about DDL techniques and resources?

3. 1. Method

Data were collected from a group of participants (N=21) who followed the ADELEX course during the 2007-8 academic year and who, consequently, completed the collocations module as part of the course. The subjects in this exploratory study were all English Philology students from seven Andalusian universities: 10 students were in their third year, 8 in their fourth year and 3 learners were in their fifth year of studies. Their native language was Spanish and their level of competence in English ranged from B1 to B2, as measured by their performance in previous tasks in the course.

The online collocations module was implemented (using the original ILIAS platform) over a period of three weeks and students were asked to complete all the activities included in the four stages described above. The instruction was sequenced to make tasks available when and for as long as the teacher desired. In our experiment, learners were allowed five days to complete and submit the quizzes and assignments in each of the module's four stages. After each stage, activities were corrected by the teacher and sent back via ILIAS with corrections and all the necessary feedback for students.

During the three weeks the module was running, ILIAS communication tools (mainly e-mails and discussion forums) were used extensively as students were required to give their opinion about a number of aspects relating to the nature and the acquisition of collocations, and to ask for help when they had any problem or queries during the learning process. Research work is just beginning to establish the implications of this form of online interaction (Pérez Basanta, 2004; forthcoming) but, in our experience, computer-mediated communication (CMC) is highly beneficial, as it maintains all participants (teacher and learners) in constant contact and students feel they are being guided and helped during their learning process.

3. 1. 1. Quantitative data collection

For quantitative data collection we used a collocation test, taken before and after the instruction. In an attempt to create a valid and reliable yardstick which assessed students' receptive and productive knowledge of collocations as well as their ability to identify them and the corpus-consultation strategies and techniques they would hopefully acquire, we designed a measuring system consisting of 7 different tasks. Thus, Tasks 1, 2 and 3 were devoted to receptive skills. The first two were *yes/no* tests measuring learners' recognition of collocations while Task 3 asked them to identify the collocations in a text. Tasks 4 to 7 addressed productive knowledge: Task 4 required learners to correct miscollocations, Task 5 to translate L1 into L2 combinations, Task 6 to reformulate, i. e. provide more accurate or elaborate adjectives than those given and, finally, Task 7 was a gap activity where students provided the collocates for a number of nouns. In Tasks 2, 6 and 7 learners were encouraged to use any resource they might find useful (such as dictionaries, concordancers, search engines, etc.) in order to complete the test, and were asked to report the specific resource used to answer each question – a procedure designed to measure the extent to which students were aware of, and able to use, concordancers before and after the course. Thus, these three tasks contained collocations also drawn from our frequency list but not included in the online module, since participants were not likely to use any resource in the post-test if they had already learnt the particular collocations presented in it. As regards the test formats used in the different sections of the measure (multiple choice, identification of elements, error correction, translation, reformulation and filling gaps), these were selected for the objectivity of scoring they allowed as a means to ensure reliability.

Finally, delivering a test through a virtual platform is a questionable procedure given that students cannot be watched by the teacher and therefore cheating can practically be taken for granted. In our experience, however, if time is well measured and allotted by the teacher, students will not have enough time to cheat by checking the answers in advance because this takes up too much time. The time factor is thus a good resource for teachers to design reliable online tests. In this particular study, all the tasks were allotted a certain amount of time which was specified in each of the rubrics.

3. 1. 2. Qualitative data collection

A questionnaire was used to collect data that assessed the effect of the pedagogical treatment as perceived by the participants in this experiment. It was also a good opportunity to identify strengths and weaknesses in the teaching material. The questionnaire consisted of 15 items which can be divided into 3 main topics:

- *Questions 1, 2 and 10 to 13*: Gathering information about the efficacy and usefulness of the collocations module.
- *Questions 3 to 9*: Gathering information about DDL methodology, i.e. the role and management of concordances and corpus-based techniques for language learning.
- *Questions 14 and 15*: Gathering information about learners' attitude, reactions and their general perception of the module.

19 out of the 21 students who completed the module filled in the questionnaire during the week after they took the course.

4. Results

4. 1. Results from quantitative data

As shown in *Table 1*, students' obtained a mean score of 48.01% in the pre-test, while the mean of correct responses increased to 67.97% in the post-test. Standard deviation was moderate in both pre- and post-tests, suggesting a relatively homogeneous group.

	Pre-test	**Post-test**
Mean	48.0159	67.9743
S.D.	11.17704	11.30978
Minimum	28.25	46.83
Maximum	70.40	89.52
N	21	21

Table 1: Descriptive statistics: pre-test and post-test

But in order to obtain a more accurate picture of students' scores, we need to analyse the results from each particular section in the test. First the pre-test data. *Table 2* shows that results were better in Tasks 2, 6 and 7, being the only ones in which they got beyond the 50% cut-off point. As to the rest of tasks, the most difficult one for students seemed to be Task 1, where they only scored 39.52%, while in Tasks 3, 4 and 5 the results ranged from 43.8% to 46.4%.

When the results of the post-test are examined (*Table 2*), a noticeable and very encouraging improvement can be observed in all tasks, with students scoring up to 29 points higher in the case of Task 1 (from 39.5% in the pre-test to 68.5% in the post-test). In Task 3 learners scored a minimum 57.14%, a higher mark than any obtained in the pre-test. Again, Tasks 2 and 6 yielded the best results although, in this case, Task 1 scores were higher than Task 7 scores, as opposed to the results of the pre-test.

	N	Pre-test		Post-test	
		Mean	**S.D.**	**Mean**	**S.D.**
Section 1	21	39.5238	14.30950	68.5714	14.58962
Section 2	21	54.7619	16.61898	77.6190	16.09496
Section 3	21	46.4286	23.80059	57.1429	17.13624
Section 4	21	44.4444	22.77100	62.9630	16.97250
Section 5	21	43.8095	17.74153	65.7143	19.63961
Section 6	21	52.8571	18.47779	77.1429	22.61479
Section 7	21	54.2857	22.03893	66.6667	25.16611

Table 2: Scores in individual sections of the pre-test and post-test

As a further step in the analysis of our data, a t-test was run to compare both pre-test and post-test scores and in order to ascertain whether there was a statistically significant difference. Tasks 1, 2, 4, 5 and 6 showed a significant difference between the pre-test and post-test performance given that their p-value was under .05 (p= .000 in all cases except for Task 4, with p= .005), whereas Tasks 3 and 7 did not (p= .102 and p= .098 respectively). But if there is one aspect which deserves special attention in this analysis, it is the fact that the t-test comparing the pre-test and post-test general means (where both tests are taken as a whole) confirms that the difference between them is significant (p= .000).

As regards the analysis of the types of resources used in the pre- and post-test (*Figures 1a* and *1b*), we can see a considerable increase in the use of corpus-based resources in the post-test (concordancers were used in 6.8% answers in the pre-test while this figure increased to 37.1% in the post-test). This came at the expense of dictionary use, the most popular reference tool in the pre-test, whose use dropped from 36.3% to 11.9%. A final word of caution, however, seems necessary with regard to these results. It should be noted that learners chose not to use any external resource in 55.1% answers in Tasks 2, 6 and 7 of the pre-test, a percentage which decreased to 50.8% in the post-test.

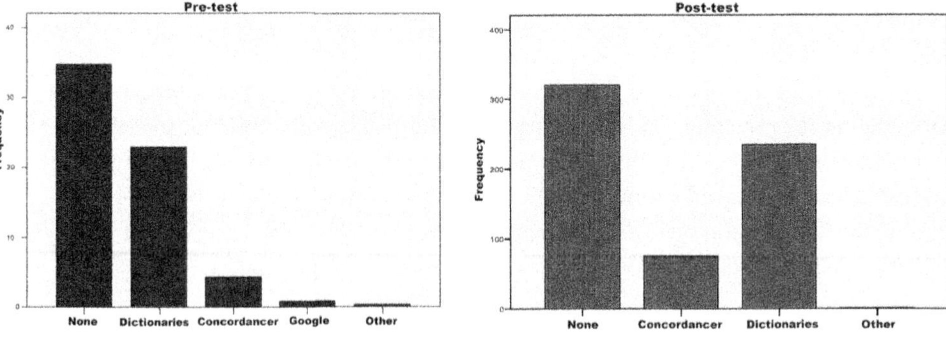

Figures 1a and 1b: Resources used in Tasks 2, 6 and 7 of the pre- and post-test

4. 2. Results from qualitative data

Turning now to the results obtained from the qualitative analysis, our goal was to establish what the general opinions of our learners were at the end of the module. As regards Section A (Questions 1, 2 and 10 to 13), the results were the following:

Question 1: Were you familiar with the concept of collocation before starting this module?

Yes, absolutely	Yes, but with some doubts	Yes, but I only had a slight idea	Not at all
5.26%	57.89%	31.58%	5.26%

Question 2: Do you think after having completed this module you have a clear notion of what a collocation is?

Yes, absolutely	Yes, but with some doubts	Yes, but I only had a slight idea	Not at all
57.89%	42.11%	0.0%	0.0%

Question 10: How many collocations do you think you have learnt in this module?

Many	Quite a few	A few	Very few	None
0.0%	84.21%	15.79%	0.0%	0.0%

Question 11: The collocations you have learnt are .... for the real-life English that you need outside the classroom.

Very useful	Useful	Not very useful	Useless
47.37%	52.63%	0.0%	0.0%

Question 12: Do you think you have acquired strategies which will help you to learn more collocations in the future? I have acquired ....

Many strategies	Some strategies	Few strategies	No strategy
10.53%	68.42%	21.05%	0.0%

Question 13: Knowing and being trained in using concordancers will make you more autonomous from the teacher in the future?

Much more autonomous	A bit more autonomous	There will be no difference
47.37%	47.37%	5.26%

Regarding Section B, this was designed to evaluate methodological procedures, in an attempt to answer our third and last research question. The data obtained regarding this aspect (Questions 3 to 9) were the following:

Question 3: Did you know what a concordancer is? Had you used them in other subjects before starting this module?

Yes, and had used them often	Yes, but used them rarely	Yes, but had not used them	No, and had not used them
10.53%	31.58%	10.53%	47.37%

Question 4: You found the *Collins Cobuild Sampler* concordancer ...

Very easy to use	Easy to use	Difficult at the beginning	Difficult to use	Very difficult to use
47.37%	21.05%	31.58%	0.0%	0.0%

Question 5: In your opinion, using a concordancer when learning collocations is ...

Very appropriate	Appropriate	Not very appropriate	Inappropriate
68.42%	31.58%	0.0%	0.0%

Question 6: As compared to traditional learning (where you have to process and apply general rules previously explained in class, etc.) using concordancers (where there is an inductive learning process based on your own observation of real language data) is, to you, ...

Much more useful	More useful	No difference	Less useful	Much less useful
21.05%	68.42%	0.0%	10.53%	0.0%

Question 7: Did you find the information you needed to complete the activities in the module using the concordancer?

Yes, always	Often, but not always	Sometimes	Rarely	Never
15.79%	73.68%	10.53%	0.0%	0.0%

Question 8: Using concordancers to learn collocations is .... than other resources (dictionaries, textbooks, etc.).

Much more useful	More useful	No difference	Less useful	Much less useful
5.26%	63.16%	26.32%	5.26%	0%

Question 9: Do you think concordancers will be of any help in other subjects in your future learning?

Very often	In certain subjects	Sometimes	Seldom	Never
78.95%	21.05%	0.0%	0.0%	0.0%

Together with these issues, learners also answered two more questions, of a more general scope, in Section C:

Question 14: In general, you found the collocations module:

Very useful	Quite useful	Not very useful	Of no use
52.63%	42.11%	5.26%	0%

Question 15: Would you add, change or eliminate anything in the module to improve it? Give us your ideas or suggestions to make it a more useful and interesting unit.

In answering this open-ended question, learners gave a number of varied answers which can be divided into three different types:

- many students commented on the vast amount of work this module involved, although in the long run we should admit that this bears on deeper and longer learning;
- some learners also considered some activities were quite repetitive and recommended that some of them should be eliminated to make the module more entertaining and appealing. Our goal of getting learners to work with concordancers as much as possible in an effort to introduce them to as many collocations as possible, may have created an overload;
- some learners felt that the difference between collocations, free word combinations and idioms had not been made clear enough and argued that as this is a very woolly area which is undoubtedly difficult to grasp at first, more time should have been devoted to this matter in the module.

5. Discussion

Starting with the results obtained from our quantitative analysis, if students' overall performance both in the pre-test and post-test is compared, we see that the mean of correct responses increased substantially, something which would initially seem to suggest a positive result from the treatment proposed. When we analyse the results obtained in each task, this satisfactory impression is further confirmed. Focusing first of all on the pre-test data, the results were better in those tasks where learners were allowed to use external resources when answering the questions (Tasks 2, 6 and 7). While this seems to suggest that learners were able to perform searches and find the information they needed successfully, this ability is nevertheless relative if we take into account the fact that the highest mean score obtained in any task in the pre-test was 54.7%, not a particularly good performance. It is perhaps even more self-explanatory to consider that the remaining 4 tasks in the pre-test yielded scores below the minimum 50%. Bearing in mind that all the collocations presented in this test were drawn from a list of frequent collocations, and that the test items were carefully constructed to include clear instructions and familiar formats for learners, these results can only be attributed, in our opinion, to the student's poor initial collocational competence.

The general improvement that can be observed in all tasks when comparing the results from the pre- and post-tests further supports the view that our teaching experience was successful. The fact that in Task 3 learners scored better than in the pre-test, seems to be a further indicator of the progress made. Once more, tasks where learners were allowed to use extra resources produced the best results although, in this case, Task 1 produced higher scores than Task 7, where external consultation was allowed. Taking into account, however, the high standard deviation in Task 7 (amounting to 25.16%), we believe that the heterogeneity of answers in this last task (perhaps partly due to candidates' tiredness) may explain why, on average, learners' scored lower than in Task 1. In general, we may observe that there was greater progress in terms of learners' strategic competence for searching collocations in an autonomous way than there was in terms of collocational competence based on the collocations they learnt in the module. In our view, this would seem to indicate that our learners will be able to cope with collocations in their future learning and will be equipped with the strategies and resources required to learn collocations autonomously.

A final case in point in the appraisal of the results obtained from our descriptive statistical analysis is the high standard deviations existing in most tasks (with the possible exception of Task 1, where the smaller standard deviation may indicate a common difficulty for learners in recognising collocations in the pre-test, and a generalised improvement in the post-test). For us, this high variation, which shows a greater level of heterogeneity than the general statistical analysis had revealed (*Table 1*), indicates that looking into different tasks and skills when measuring collocational knowledge (recognition, identification in context, production with and without access to reference material, etc.) reveals the complex and multifarious nature of this competence. Thus, and as with all other lexical elements, because collocational knowledge encompasses a number of different abilities, it shows a wider variety of levels of competence. This has, to our mind, a clear implication in terms of pedagogy: teaching collocations is a demanding task inasmuch as we need to cater for a wide range of skills if we want to build up a solid competence.

In the light of the previous evaluation it would seem that our pedagogical treatment was clearly successful. In order to be more confident about this finding we ran a t-test, which proved that all tasks showed a significant difference between the pre- and post-test performance, except for Tasks 3 and 7. Task 3, where learners were prompted to identify collocations in a text, produced the poorest results in the post-test (57.14%). We concluded that there were insufficient activities designed to train students to identify collocations and discriminate them from free word combinations. This represents, in our view, an aspect which needs to be tackled in the future as it is of paramount importance for students to be able to spot collocations.

Task 7 shows a high degree of variation, particularly in the post-test, and we suggest that tiredness and lack of attention on the part of the test-takers might have played a role in this case. However, if we consider that learners scored considerably better in Task 6 than in Task 7, which had the same goal but different format, we also think that the gap-filling format employed in the last task might be inappropriate as it tends to prompt free word combinations which form correct sentences but do not show learners' collocational competence. Hence, it seems advisable to modify this test method in future testing by adopting a different format that will make it possible to check whether this is one of the reasons why it did not bring about a significant difference in learners' performance.

Finally, the highly significant differences between the overall results obtained in the pre-test and the post-test give an answer to the question as to whether the teaching material designed is efficient and whether it contributes to improving learners' collocational competence in a statistically significant way. In the light of the results reported above we tentatively conclude that the pedagogical treatment proved to be effective in general terms, although the identification of collocations is an aspect which needs to be further developed and improved.

The second research question addressed in this pilot study asked whether our collocation module helps students to acquire the necessary strategies and resources to enable them to learn and search for collocations autonomously. The analysis of the types of resources used in the test showed a considerable increase in the use of corpus-based resources in the post-test, as opposed to the use of dictionaries, which were more often used in the pre-test than in the post-test. To our mind, this seems to imply that the module was effective in that learners were made aware of corpus-based resources and were equipped with sufficient strategies and techniques to be able to use them efficiently. Taking these findings a step further, if we consider that there was a clear improvement in learners' performance in those sections where the use of these resources was allowed, it would seem that our results confirm the general assumption that corpus-based approaches are beneficial for collocation learning, a matter which needs, of course, to be further tested out in future studies.

It should be noted, finally, that the fact that in those tasks where learners were allowed to use external resources, approximately half of the population did not make use of this option obviously means that our findings concerning the beneficial effects of our module for strategic learning cannot be taken as conclusive as they are based on too small a data set. Furthermore, the high proportion of unaided answers in the post-test seems to reveal that not all students acquired sufficient knowledge or confidence to use concordances autonomously, suggesting that three weeks is too short a time to provide all students with the necessary skills to perform autonomous searches.

Turning to the data obtained from our qualitative study, we may note that, to a large extent, these support the findings based on the quantitative analysis. As results from Section A show, 100% of students considered they had obtained a reasonably clear idea of what collocations are (although 42.11% of them reported having some doubts, a figure which clearly correlates with the poor performance in Task 3 of the test, where some learners showed serious difficulties in identifying the collocations in the text). Moreover, while 84.21% of learners considered they had learnt quite a lot of collocations, all the students found the collocations included in the module were useful or very useful for their real needs, and 78.95% considered they had learnt at least some strategies which they could use in the future to continue learning collocations. Learners were quite satisfied with the collocations they had learnt by completing this module and felt their collocational competence had been significantly improved thanks to it.

The data obtained in Section B shows that 68.42% of students found the concordancer easy or very easy to use (the remaining 31.58% said it was difficult to use but only in the beginning). On the other hand, concordancers were regarded as adequate or very adequate tools for learning collocations by 100% of learners, 89.47% considered DDL to be more useful or much more useful than traditional learning when dealing with collocations and 100% said concordancers would be useful for them on many occasions or in particular courses in the future. Generally speaking, it seems that after completing the module, learners had developed a remarkably positive attitude towards corpus-based resources and were clearly willing to apply these techniques in other subjects. Self-evidently then, in the learners' opinion, DDL seemed to be a useful and adequate approach to collocational learning.

As regards results from Section C, learners evaluated this new teaching experience very positively and their remarks are important for further research. Statistical results show that students expressed a high level of satisfaction with regard to both content and methodology, since all the questions were answered positively by over 65% of subjects. Question 14 seems to be a very revealing indicator of the strong agreement students showed concerning the usefulness and relevance of the module, since 94.74% of them (i.e. 18 out of the 19 students) felt it useful or very useful. To sum up, findings from this small-scale, descriptive study lend support to the initial hypothesis that corpus-based techniques and procedures are appropriate for teaching collocations. Indeed, the principles and knowledge we have gained from this experience underpin the new online materials we are designing in the ADELEX course, in this case based on the collocational patterns identified in multimodal texts (Rodríguez Martín, Moreno Jaén, 2009).

6. Conclusion

In spite of the plethora of studies advocating the need to improve learners' collocational competence by means of explicit instruction (Howarth, 1996; Nesselhauf, 2005), very few attempts have hitherto been made to put this suggestion into practice (Lewis, 2000a; Woolard, 2005). In our view, there are compelling reasons to believe that raising students' awareness vis-à-vis the role of collocations in lexical competence together with some teaching interventions might be highly beneficial. In order to contribute to the development of this crucial aspect of language pedagogy, we have designed and evaluated a corpus-based online module for teaching collocations, as an integral part of the development of learners' lexical competence. Since corpora are one of the most reliable and representative tools at a teacher's disposal, corpus-based data represent the backbone of the procedures used in the design and implementation of our current and future modules. In short, the goal of this learning experience was to develop students' awareness of the very notion of collocation, to train them in the inductive exploration of language to detect patterns of lexical co-occurrence and in the use of online concordancers which could help them develop processes of autonomous learning.

This pilot study also represents an initial attempt to assess the effectiveness of a corpus-based learning experience by gathering and analysing data on pre-test and post-test performances as well as students' opinions about their learning preferences, an aspect which needs to be further developed in the field of data-driven learning. The number of students taking part in this study makes it only generalizable to a narrow population, but this can be used as a starting point for further replication in studies of a similar nature shedding new light on the controversy as to whether teaching collocation explicitly and overtly might be useful within different educational scenarios and even different language backgrounds.

In the final analysis, the innovative study reported here is a step forward at a time when the advantages of corpus-based pedagogy are becoming widely documented, but comparatively very little hands-on work with corpora has been developed and empirically investigated in teaching scenarios (Braun, 2007). Moreover, this study is also an attempt to bring together quantitative and qualitative data in a single approach, thus placing the emphasis on the student's performance and opinion about his/her own learning experience. What this chapter reports is just a first step in the development of this unified approach, but one which has proved essential as regards discovering new possibilities in the teaching and assessment of L2 collocational competence.

Acknowledgements

I would like to express my deepest gratitude to Dr Carmen Pérez Basanta my mentor, guide and model over the years. This paper is dedicated to her. Thanks also to Dr Graeme Porte for his insightful comments on a previous draft of this paper.

Research leading to this publication has been funded by the Spanish Ministry of Innovation and Science under research project "ADELEX: Assessing and Developing Lexical Competence through New Technologies" (HUM2007-61766/FILO).

Exploring conversational grammar through films in the ELT classroom: A corpus-based approach

M. Elena Rodríguez Martín, University of Granada, Spain

1. Introduction

Our aim in this paper is to offer a corpus-based approach for exploring conversational grammar through films in the ELT classroom. However, before delving into the pedagogical exploitation of films for the enhancement of speaking competence, we address the issue of the differences between speech and writing. Next, we focus on definitions and pedagogical approaches to conversational grammar. This will serve as the basis for the analysis of the authenticity of film language and its relationship to real conversation. This relationship is explored through the findings of three previous corpus-based studies (Rodríguez Martín, Moreno Jaén, 2009; Rodríguez Martín, 2010 in press, forthcoming) which compare key conversational processes in the British National Corpus (BNC) (spoken component: face-to-face conversations) and a micro-corpus of film transcripts using Rühlemann's (2007) situational framework for conversation. These studies provide us with empirical evidence to support the use of film extracts for teaching conversation. We will use Rühlemann's (2007, 2008) register approach as the underlying model in our analysis of screen dialogue for pedagogical exploitation.

2. Speech and writing

In his book *English in Speech and Writing* (1996: 6), Hughes explains the difference between written and spoken language using two metaphors. According to her, "[w]riting shares many characteristics with a mountain: permanent, clearly delineated and readily available for inspection". On the other hand, when we consider speech "rather than a physically unchanging mountain, the more appropriate metaphor is that of the ocean: mutable, shifting, and difficult to capture and define". These two metaphors illustrate perfectly the most important divergences between these two modes of communication.

In a later work, Hughes (2002: 9-11) clearly delineates the distinctive features of speech against writing, taking into account two parameters: aspects of production and social aspects. In relation to the first, she argues that spoken discourse is context dependent, unplanned, transient, oral/aural and dynamic, whereas written discourse is decontextualised, planned, non-transient, visual/motoric and static. Considering the second parameter, she outlines some of the typical attitudes to speech focusing on the distinctive functions of spoken and written discourse in literate societies. In this regard, speech is considered to be a locus of change, interpersonal, informal, stigmatised, rhetorical and primary while writing is regarded as conservative, contractual, formal, prestigious, logical and secondary.

Although a detailed contrastive study between speech and writing is beyond the scope of the present paper, we believe that setting the most salient differences in contrast might provide us with an invaluable basis upon which we can build our research on conversation. As Hughes (2002: 13) states, "[t]he vast bulk of spoken material is spontaneous, face-to-face, informal conversation". Thus, it is of the utmost importance to understand the nature of spoken and written language and the differences between them (Crystal, 2001: 25) in order to fully grasp the subtleties of conversational language.

In a previous study (Pérez Basanta, Rodríguez Martín, 2006a: 780-781), we outlined the differences between speech and writing following Byrne (1988) and Crystal (1995, 2001):

- speech is time-bound, dynamic, and transient // writing is space-bound, static, permanent with more time to think;
- the pressure to think while talking promotes looser construction such as hesitation devices and pauses, repetition, rephrasing, and comment clauses // writing allows repeated reading and close analysis and promotes the development of careful organization (cohesion and coherence);
- because of face-to-face interactions, participants rely on paralinguistic features (facial expressions and gestures) // lack of contact means that participants cannot rely on context;
- the lexicon of speech is often characteristically vague, using deictic expressions, nonsense words and slang // the lexicon is more technical with specialized vocabulary;
- lengthy coordinate sentences are normal (parataxis) // there are multiple instances of subordination (hypotaxis) in the same sentence, with elaborate syntactic patterns;
- information is less-packed, full of formulaic expressions // information is densely-packed, with sentences carefully constructed and organised to form a coherent and cohesive text;
- speech is well suited to *phatic* functions (e.g. small talk) expressing social relationships, and personal opinions and attitudes // writing is suited to the recording of facts and the communication of ideas;
- errors in spoken language cannot be withdrawn // errors and inadequacies can be eliminated in later drafts;
- unique features of speech include most of the prosody: rhythm, nuances of intonation, tempo, loudness, pauses, etc. // unique features of writing include pages, lines, capitalization, spatial organization and punctuation;
- there are speech varieties in terms of dialect, accent and style // there are different written genres; some contain tables, diagrams, notes, etc. which cannot be read aloud efficiently but have to be assimilated visually.

This comparison will serve as the starting point for a detailed study of conversational grammar in the remainder of this paper.

3. Conversational grammar: definitions and pedagogical approaches

3. 1. What is conversational grammar?

Rühlemann (2008: 672) claims that the analyses of large spoken corpora have exponentially improved the linguistic knowledge of conversation in recent years. Similarly, Hughes (2002: 18) argues that the growth of spoken corpora together with technological advances for storing and analysing these corpora has resulted in "a growing potential for generalisable conclusions to be made about patterns of speech and speech behavior". As Rühlemann (2008: 672) points out, two major corpus-based grammars, *The Longman Grammar of Spoken and Written English* (Biber et al., 1999) and *The Cambridge Grammar of English* (Carter, McCarthy, 2006), have challenged "dearly held conceptions about the nature of the grammar of English".

The Longman Grammar of Spoken and Written English devotes a full section to the study of the grammar of conversation. Biber et al. (1999: 1038) consider conversation "a variety of language deserving particular attention in its own right". These authors believe that the grammatical features which characterise conversational language need to be investigated and compared with those in other registers. In order to explain these salient grammatical characteristics, they first identify several external (social, psychological, and physical) factors of conversation (Biber et al., 1999: 1041-1051):

- conversation takes place in the spoken medium;
- it takes place in shared context;
- it avoids elaboration or specification of meaning;
- it is interactive;
- it is expressive of politeness, emotion, and attitude;
- it takes place in real time;
- it has a restricted and repetitive repertoire;
- it employs a vernacular range of expression;
- lack of functional explanation.

In *The Cambridge Grammar of English*, Carter and McCarthy (2006) devote a section to grammar and spoken language, claiming that typical items and structures of spoken language had not been thoroughly described until recently (2006: 164). The reason for this dearth of detailed descriptions of spoken discourse may be that "[m]ost grammars of English have had a bias towards the written language". Because of this, they include in their work a chapter focused on spoken English based upon the four key features of spoken language (Carter, McCarthy, 2006: 164):

- spoken language happens in real time and is typically unplanned;
- it is most typically face to face;
- it foregrounds choices which reflect the immediate social and interpersonal situation;
- spoken and written language are not sharply divided but exist on a continuum.

Thus, the Longman and Cambridge Grammars try to offer a description of the features of spoken discourse. As Rühlemann points out (2008: 673),

> [p]rincipled attempts have been made to introduce and establish what has been termed, respectively, 'spoken grammar' (e.g. Carter, McCarthy, 1995) and 'conversational grammar' (cf. Biber et al., 1999; Rühlemann, 2006).

This author prefers the term *conversational grammar* because *spoken grammar* is a notion which equates mode with register (see Rühlemann, 2006). Conversation, he argues, is "the major situationally defined variety of the spoken language" and, in order to be adequately described, it requires concepts and terminologies based on the situational factors which determine conversational exchanges (2006: 385). In order to fully describe the linguistic features of conversational grammar, Rühlemann (2007) proposes a situational framework for conversation. We believe that this framework is one of the most recent and interesting contributions to the issue of conversational language and consequently deserves detailed explanation.

3. 2. Rühlemann's situational framework for conversation

The nature of conversation has been studied by many linguists who have accounted for its primary role in human communication. Pridham (2001: 1) points out that the methods used to analyse conversation are shown to be based on the notion that conversation exists within a social context which not only determines the purpose of the conversational interaction but also shapes its features and structures. This idea of context is central to Rühlemann's (2007: 2) analysis of conversational processes. His proposal of a situational framework for conversation is a valuable contribution to the field and is based on the adaptedness hypothesis:

> [...] a situation-based description of conversation can show how conversational language is adapted to certain needs arising from specific types of constraints on speakers in conversational situations.

He thus explores five factors which he considers typical of the conversational situation: shared context, co-construction, real-time processing, discourse management and relation management. Rühlemann's work provides a detailed analysis of these factors, examining some of the conversational features related to each of them using the demographically sampled subcorpus of the BNC.

First of all, Rühlemann (2007: 35) considers *shared context*: "The setting in which conversation typically takes place is characterized by a wealth of context that is shared between the participants". In this vein, he explores one major area of shared context which is linguistically manifested in the following pieces: person, place and time deixis (2007: 59).

The second factor in Rühlemann's framework is *co-construction*. He claims that one of the fundamental differences between writing and informal conversation "stems from the fact that authors normally construct their text *alone*, whereas conversationalists invariably construct conversation *interactively*" (2007: 37). This interactive aspect of conversation is manifested in turn-taking and adjacency (2007: 87) and is mainly related to question tags, backchannels and co-constructed utterances.

The following factor determining the conversational situation is *real-time processing*, that is, "conversationalists are fully exposed to the pressures of planning and processing in real time" (2007: 43). Thus, the fundamental constraint is described by Rühlemann as a scarcity of time, or the resources speakers make use of in order to deal with this limitation: silent and filled pauses and formulaic language, restarts and substitutions, headers and tails, and contractions and grammatically reduced forms (2007: 11).

In terms of *discourse management phenomena* he explains that since conversation is a spontaneous and interactional process it requires "a great deal of management" and, therefore, participants need to make use of management devices "to indicate what course upcoming discourse is intended to take in relation to prior discourse" (2007: 115). These management devices mainly consist of discourse markers.

Finally, Rühlemann focuses on *relation management phenomena*. He studies two dimensions within this factor: how speakers relate to their conversational partners (*participant-relation*) and how they relate to what they are saying (*proposition-relation*). Concerning the way speakers manage participant-relation, Rühlemann makes reference to the notions of social deixis, empathetic deixis and involvement, together with the linguistic features related to them. In this sense, he refers to the use of first-names, endearments and familiarizers, and the use of introductory *this* and historic present as a means of involving audiences in conversational narratives (2007: 181-189). On the other hand, he also examines the linguistic feature associated with proposition-relation management, or what he calls "tails" (2007: 196).

On the whole, Rühlemann offers a relevant framework which tries to systematise conversational processes and strategies. Rühlemann (2007: 216) hopes that this underlying situational-functional approach will explain the conversation construct "in a Hallidayan sense, in the context of its situation". We believe that his approach to the analysis of conversation is a useful contribution which might inform the teaching of conversational grammar in the ELT classroom.

3. 3. Teaching conversational grammar

As explained in our initial contrastive survey of speech and writing, analyses in general corpora have shown that written and spoken language present distinct linguistic patterns. However, although this distinction has received a lot of attention on theoretical grounds, it has been vastly overlooked in the second language scenario (Pérez Basanta, Rodríguez Martín, 2006a). In Mukherjee's words (2009: 205), although spoken grammar is a concept widely accepted in corpus-linguistic circles and beyond, "this concept has been widely neglected in language pedagogy until very recently". According to Carter and McCarthy (1995: 141), the teaching of speaking skills "should be based upon the grammar of spoken language, and not on grammars which mainly reflect written norms".

Hughes (2002: 134-135) explores the implications of the nature of spoken discourse on teaching speech and declares that the complex nature of spoken interaction makes it difficult, even for advanced students, to take part in informal conversations in the target language. In order to help students improve their speaking skills, she points out that it is necessary to raise awareness of the fundamental features of spoken discourse through the implementation of language awareness activities which focus on the rules of face-to-face interactions.

The importance of using conversational grammar as "the underlying model in teaching speech" has been highlighted by Rühlemann (2008: 672). He offers a register approach to teaching conversation and claims that we should reconsider the role of Standard English in order to teach conversational grammar effectively in the ELT classroom. In this regard, he believes that Standard English can no longer be regarded as "the one-and-only variety" but should be reduced to "a core variety" which would be used when teaching writing skills. This means "shifting the emphasis in EFL from a monolithic view of language to a register-sensitive view which acknowledges the fundamental functional diversity of language use" (2008: 672). Hence, in teaching conversation ("the core spoken register"), Standard English is not considered to be an appropriate model because its grammatical features differ too much from conversational grammar. This implies "a move toward allowing authentic conversation and its language into the classroom" (2008: 680).

The question now is how teachers can illustrate this register in the EFL classroom. In this respect, Rühlemann (2008: 684-685) claims that corpora are the richest source of authentic conversation and, therefore, they should be used to illustrate conversational grammar. However, he is aware of the fact that using corpora in the classroom is not an easy endeavour. On the other hand, it is also necessary to clarify what methodologies should be used for teaching the grammar of conversation. Rühlemann thinks that a reasonable methodological proposal is offered by Timmis, who argues that spoken texts should be listened to wherever possible (Timmis, 2005: 119). Nevertheless, corpora "present text, written or spoken, only in the written form" (Rühlemann, 2008: 686).

This problem has been previously noted by other authors. For instance, Hughes (2002: 170) claims that corpus linguistics tends to isolate speech data from their original oral/aural channel and from the context of the discourse. However, it should be noted that, as Mauranen (2004b: 92) explains, "[g]iven that overcoming the technical obstacle of sound concordancing in synchrony with the transcript is being conquered, speech corpora will soon provide richer representations". Thus, as Rühlemann highlights (2008: 686), this will allow us to put into practice Timmis' proposal. We believe that Timmis' methodological proposal could be improved if the texts were not only listened to, as he suggests, but also viewed. This could be achieved through the use of multimodal corpora. In Thibault's words (2000: 311), multimodal texts

> combine and integrate the meaning-making resources of more than one semiotic modality – for example, language, gesture, movement, visual images, sound, and so on – in order to produce a text-specific meaning.

In our opinion, the possibility of not only listening to but also viewing the spoken text will facilitate access to conversational grammar in context. As Moreno Jaén and Pérez Basanta claim (2009: 288), "teachers cannot teach conversation, which is by nature multimodal, with monomodal materials". They offer a proposal for developing conversational competence through language awareness and multimodality using a bank of DVD clips. We will follow this approach together with Rühlemann's situational framework for conversation in order to explore conversational grammar through films in the ELT classroom.

However, before undertaking this exploration, we need to focus on the use of films in ELT and the opinions in favour of, and against, film language authenticity. Thus, we will examine the relationship between screen dialogue and conversational grammar.

4. Screen dialogue and conversational grammar

There are many positive aspects related to the pedagogical exploitation of films in the ELT classroom (see Rodríguez Martín, 2006: 231). However, although the use of films for teaching English has proved to be a pedagogically rewarding experience, several disadvantages have been associated to this practice. One of the criticisms made of films as a resource for language teaching has to do with authenticity. Several authors argue that film language is not *the real thing*. They base their assumptions on the scripted nature of film conversation. Gregory and Carroll (1978; quoted in Taylor, 1999: 1), for instance, portray the language included in films and TV scripts as "written to be spoken as if not written". In the same vein, Walker (1999) claims that exchanges in movies may not be exactly like the unstructured, spontaneous language of everyday use. Likewise, Taylor argues (2006: 1) that film language must be considered "an entity in itself" which differs from authentic conversation. He even talks about *filmese* (film language) as "a real phenomenon" (2006: 3).

The scripted nature of screen dialogue has led some authors to focus on the differences between real life conversation and film language. Pavesi (2008) is of the opinion that the linguistic differences between natural speech and screen dialogue can be explained taking into account the tasks that speech performs in films. She argues that the differences "between spontaneous and simulated interactions are reinforced by temporal constraints which control the unveiling of the characters' relations and the unfolding events" (Pavesi, 2008: 80). As a result, two major requirements should be taken into account when writing film dialogues: "representation of orality on the one hand and time-constrained narration on the other" (Pavesi, 2008: 80).

Regarding the representation of orality, Taylor (1999: 3) believes that "[m]any factors work against the writer's efforts". For example, he points out that in everyday talk "much language use is formulaic, humdrum and banal, (…) whereas the time and space constraints of films require highly pertinent, dramatic or intriguing exchanges". However, he adds that in order to portray social realism films need to use realistic language and this has "resulted in the creation of many examples of genuine-sounding products".

In fact, many authors claim the authenticity of film language and draw attention to the advantages of using movies for teaching conversation (Stoller, 1990; Baddock, 1996; Canning-Wilson, 2000; King, 2002; Keene, 2006; Pérez Basanta, Rodríguez Martín, 2007; Moreno Jaén, Pérez Basanta, 2009). As King (2002: 510) states, films

> present colloquial English in real life contexts rather than artificial situations, and they expose students to a wide range of native speakers, each with their own slang, reduced speech, stress, accents, and dialects.

Notwithstanding the opinions in favour of the authenticity of film language, we thought it was highly recommendable to undertake several empirical studies in order to explore to what extent film language is similar to real life conversation (Rodríguez Martín, Moreno Jaén, 2009; Rodríguez Martín, 2010 in press, forthcoming). Our aim was to offer a preliminary analysis and comparison of conversational processes and strategies in the BNC and a micro-corpus of movies. The purpose of the comparison was to explore the similarities and differences between real spoken language and screen dialogue in order to provide empirical evidence to support two research projects which focus on the use of films for the development of speaking competence (Pérez Basanta, Rodríguez Martín, 2007; Moreno Jaén, Pérez Basanta, 2009). Our exploratory studies intended to offer evidence which would help us to answer the question: is film language authentic enough to be taught as an example of real life conversation?[1]

The first study (Rodríguez Martín, 2010 in press) compared conversational processes in the BNC (spoken component: face-to-face conversations) and a corpus of film transcripts using Rühlemann's situational framework for conversation (2007) as the basis for comparison. The BNC is a "grammatically tagged corpus", which is both "large and representative of many varieties of both written and spoken English" (Leech et al., 2001: xi). The spoken component of the BNC contains approximately 10 million words. It is divided into two subcorpora: The *context-governed* subcorpus (collected in different contexts) and the *demographically sampled* subcorpus (informal, spontaneous, face-to-face conversations). We decided to use the demographically sampled subcorpus as the reference or normative corpus in our studies. The micro-corpus of film transcripts was created for a research study published in 2007 (Pérez Basanta, Rodríguez Martín). It contains 10 film transcripts with a total of approximately 100,000 words[2].

In order to carry out the comparison, two software tools were used: WordSmith Tools (Scott, 2004) and Wmatrix (Rayson, 2003, 2009). First, we created a frequency wordlist of the micro-corpus of movies using Wmatrix. Next, we compared the 50 top items in the list with the 50 most frequent items in the spoken component (face-to-face conversations) and the written component of the BNC. We then focused on the comparison of the most frequent 50 items of movies and face-to-face conversations in the word frequency lists in order to study in detail the extent to which they were similar and to highlight also the differences. Finally, we generated frequency wordlists of our corpus of movies and the face-to-face conversation corpus using WordSmith Tools 4.0 and made a keyword list in order to compare the keywords in both corpora. Finally, we commented on those keywords we considered relevant in terms of their relation to conversational features and strategies following Rühlemann's framework. The results showed some tendencies which we summarised as follows: 1) Most common conversational features appear in movies if we analyse them in terms of Rühlemann's situational framework for conversation; 2) the 50 most frequent items on the list show a great similarity between movies and face-to-face conversational occurrences against those found in written English; 3) there are also differences between the two corpora (overused and underused features in our corpus of movies).

In the light of the results of this study, the second empirical research (Rodríguez Martín, Moreno Jaén, 2009) took a step further as regards exploring key conversational processes and collocations in both corpora. The goal of this corpus-based comparison carried out by means of WordSmith Tools 4.0 was to analyse whether there were relevant differences between the reference corpus (face-to-face conversations) and the customised corpus of film texts. First, we focused on some key conversational features included in Rühlemann's framework: pronouns, deictic expressions referring to place and time, backchannels, conversational contractions, grammatical reduction, presented-discourse markers and endearments. Most of these features had not been analysed in detail in our previous study. Second, following Shin and Nation's ideas (2008), we specifically dealt with the issue of collocations insofar as they might shed light on the way the two corpora diverge. The results of the comparison showed that, although there are overused and underused features in the film transcripts, most paradigmatic conversational characteristics are found in movies. Similarly, several of the most frequent collocations in spoken English also appear in our corpus of movies. Thus this study provided us with significant data that pointed in the direction that there are no relevant differences between the two corpora as regards conversational features. The findings revealed that movies make use of a wide range of conversational strategies and devices and, as a consequence, film extracts could be good input for teaching conversation in the ELT classroom.

The third study (Rodríguez Martín, forthcoming) attempted to take a further step comparing the two corpora in terms of parts of speech and semantic domains by means of Wmatrix (Rayson, 2009). Our intention was to add a new contribution to our empirical research as these two aspects (parts of speech and semantic domains) were being analysed for the first time. The results of this comparison provided us with more data to reveal the similarities and differences between real life conversation and film language. We concluded that the majority of conversational features appear extensively in movies. As a consequence, we stated that film language is useful input for teaching conversation in ELT. We believe that some of the detected differences can even be considered an advantage for learners as screen dialogue is sometimes more canonical showing a greater variety of paradigmatic conversational features such as speech acts.

Since these are exploratory studies based on a micro-corpus, we cannot claim we have conclusive findings, but we very strongly believe they show some tendencies which should be taken into consideration to support the potential of films for teaching conversation. The three studies show that movies make use of a wide range of conversational strategies and devices. Consequently, film extracts might lend themselves well to the design and implementation of classroom activities and they can be very useful for raising learners' awareness of how native speakers go about making and interpreting meaning. As Kozloff claims (2001: 27), "[t]o some extent, films teach viewers how to talk" and "[o]f all the components of a film, dialogue is the most portable, the easiest for a viewer to extract and make his own". Thus, films can be beneficial for pedagogical purposes since they can be used to make learners aware of key conversational processes.

5. Exploring conversational grammar through films in the ELT classroom: analysis of film extracts for pedagogical exploitation

As has been noted when examining the issue of teaching conversational grammar, "most textbooks and materials have failed to take on board the real features of informal interactive talk" (Pérez Basanta, Rodríguez Martín, 2006b: 190). Thus, instead of offering samples containing the features of real conversation, textbooks include "artificial scripted dialogues based on someone's intuitions about what people are likely to say or in most cases drawn from written language" (Moreno Jaén, Pérez Basanta, 2009: 287).

Although descriptions of spoken grammar are now more detailed, the question of how we should teach the features of spoken language has not been clearly addressed (Timmis, 2005: 117). McCarthy and Carter (1995: 217) have proposed "a 'three Is' methodology" (Illustration, Interaction and Induction). However, as Timmis points out (2005: 117) they did not consider this to be a comprehensive or definitive methodology. Timmis holds that the first question before developing materials for the teaching of spoken language should be the following: "in what shape or form should we introduce spoken data into the classroom?" In this regard, he argues that as conversational features are "crucially discourse-sensitive", they should be "embedded in a text". The selection of texts should be driven by two criteria: "1 Does the text have the potential to engage the students' interest? 2 Is the text plausible as natural interaction?" (Timmis, 2005: 118).

In our opinion, films provide us with the types of texts Timmis is looking for. They motivate students and, as has been suggested by our empirical studies, they are good for teaching natural interaction. Moreover, films allow us to experience conversational exchanges within a particular context of situation and, therefore, show the discourse-sensitive nature of conversation. Hence, we claim that film extracts should be used as texts to illustrate the key features of conversational grammar[3].

In *Appendix 1*, we offer an analysis of a film extract in terms of conversational grammar following Rühlemann's (2007) situational framework for conversation and Biber et al.'s ideas (1999). The film chosen is *About a Boy* (2002), one of the movies included in our corpus of film transcripts[4].

The next step in our research will be the design and implementation of activities based upon the analysis of the key features of conversational grammar in different film extracts which will be viewed by students in an online environment. The activities designed can be found in the ADELEX website accompanying this volume (*http://www.ugr.es/local/ inped/exploringnewpaths*).

6. Conclusions

Although the authenticity of film language has been criticised from different quarters, we have argued that movies are highly beneficial for teaching real life conversation, providing empirical evidence based on three corpus-based studies. These studies confirm the fact that conversational features appear extensively in movies and are, therefore, good input for teaching conversation in ELT.

We follow Rühlemann's (2008) register approach to teaching conversation and believe that conversational grammar must underlie the methodological approaches for the development of speaking competence. However, the lack of authentic samples of conversational exchanges in most textbooks points towards the need to provide teachers with appropriate materials for teaching conversation. In this regard, films can be used to explore conversational grammar in the second language classroom as replicas or imitations of real life conversation. Thus, the pedagogical exploitation of film extracts might contribute to a better understanding of spontaneous speech behaviour.

Acknowledgements

I am deeply indebted to Dr. Carmen Pérez Basanta for her guidance and encouragement. Without her continuous support, help and generosity, this paper and my research over the last seven years would not have been possible. I would also like to thank Dr. Graeme Porte for his useful comments and for proofreading. This research is part of an R&D Project (Ref: HUM2007-61766/FILO) entitled "ADELEX: Assessing and Developing Lexis through New Technologies", financed by the Spanish Ministry of Innovation and Science.

Notes

[1] We acknowledge the existence of a previous study in the field of Translation Studies which compared British and American films and TV scripts with spoken corpora (see Taylor 2004, 2006). Although we value the contributions of this project, we believe that the range of conversational features analysed is too limited (discourse markers). Moreover, the corpus used is not made of film transcripts but of film scripts. Our empirical studies are based upon the premise that what needs to be analysed is the actual spoken transcript.

[2] *Notting Hill* (1999), *About a Boy* (2002), *Truly, Madly Deeply* (1991), *Bridget Jones's Diary* (2001), *Two Weeks Notice* (2002), *Sabrina* (1995), *Sleepless in Seattle* (1993), *You've Got Mail* (1998), *Guess Who's Coming to Dinner* (1967) and *While You Were Sleeping* (1995).

[3] The copyrights of the films must be taken into account. In this regard, the use of short film extracts for teaching conversation can be justified following what *The Fair Use Act* specifies about "the use of copyrighted materials for educational purposes" (see Moreno Jaén, Pérez Basanta, 2009: 287).

[4] *About a Boy* (2002). Directed by Chris Weitz. Starring Hugh Grant and Nicholas Hoult. Screenplay based on Nick Hornby's bestseller.

Appendix 1: Analysis of conversational grammar in a film extract

EXTRACT FROM ABOUT A BOY (2002)

Dialogue:
CHRISTINE: Will, this is Imogene. You can hold her if you like.
WILL: I suppose…okay. Yeah. Got her. Lovely. Yeah, she's, um…delightful, isn't she?
CHRISTINE: I know. Isn't she?
WILL: To tell the truth Chris, I'm being a bit crap with her. You better take her back. Oh.
CHRISTINE: Hey, just think she could've been yours if you got your act together.
WILL: Just think of that, yeah. So, the place is looking…um, really nice.
JOHN: Barney, Barney, Barney, Barney. Oops, say hello to Will, Barney.
WILL: Hello, Barney. How are you?
JOHN: He's lovely.
WILL: Yeah.
JOHN: And what about you, Will? Any desire for a family of your own yet?
WILL: Not really. I'm sort of all right as I am.
CHRISTINE: Oh, please, Will.
WILL: What does that mean? Oh, "Please" what?
CHRISTINE: Look at yourself. You're 38 and…you've never had a job or a relationship that lasted longer than two months. I wouldn't exactly say you were okay. I mean, I would say you were a disaster. I mean, what, what, is the point of your life?
WILL: Bloody hell. Um…you're probably right. There's probably no point to my life but thank you for bringing it up.
JOHN: Will, the reason we wanted you to come here today was we…we wanted to ask you …
CHRISTINE: …how would you like to be Imogene's godfather?
WILL: Seriously?
CHRISTINE: Seriously.

Conversational features (Rühlemann's situational framework, 2007):
SHARED CONTEXT:
- Person deixis: first, second and third person pronouns (*you, I, she, her, he, your, yourself*).
- Place deixis: *So, the place is looking…*; *to come* here *today*.
- Time deixis: *to come here* today.
CO-CONSTRUCTION:
-Turn-taking and adjacency:
Greeting-Greeting:
JOHN: *Barney, Barney, Barney, Barney. Oops, say hello to Will, Barney.*
WILL: *Hello, Barney. How are you?*
Question-Answer:
JOHN: *And what about you, Will? Any desire for a family of your own yet?*
WILL: *Not really. I'm sort of all right as I am.*
WILL: *What does that mean? Oh, "Please" what?*
CHRISTINE: *Look at yourself…*

Invitation-Response/Question-Answer:
JOHN: *Will, the reason we wanted you to come here today was we…we wanted to ask you* …
CHRISTINE: *…how would you like to be Imogene's godfather?*
WILL: *Seriously?*
CHRISTINE: *Seriously.*
-Questions tags: *Yeah, she's, um…delightful, isn't she?*; *I know. Isn't she?*.
-Backchannels: Yeah (JOHN: *He's lovely.* WILL: *Yeah.*); I know (*I know. Isn't she?*).
REAL-TIME PROCESSING:
-Silent pauses: *You're 38 and…you've never had a job.*
-Filled pauses: *Yeah, she's, um…delightful*; *So, the place is looking…um, really nice*; *Um…you're probably right.*
-Self-repetitions: *I mean, what, what, is the point of your life?*; *we…we wanted to ask you.*
-Contractions:
  Negative contraction: *isn't, wouldn't.*
  Verb contraction: *she's, I'm, could've, he's, you've, you're.*
  Conversational contraction: *Yeah.*
-Grammatical reduction:
  Substitutions: pro-forms (pronouns).
  Omission: ellipsis (*Got her*).
DISCOURSE MANAGEMENT:
-Discourse markers: *I suppose, okay, so, I mean.*
RELATION-MANAGEMENT:
-First-names: Imogene, Barney.
-Familiarizing first-name forms: Will for William, Chris for Christine.

Other conversational features (Biber et al., 1999):
-Interjections: *Oh*; *Oops.*
-Attention signals: *Hey.*
-Taboo expletives: *Bloody hell.*

The use of DVD films as multimodal texts to raise contextual awareness in the acquisition of polite words in English: The case of 'please'

N. Ignacio López Sako, University of Granada, Spain

1. Introduction

Although some scholars have pointed out that "rich authentic input is not as prevalent as it should be and may even be missing altogether" in today's language classrooms (Tschirner, 2001: 306), and that "the teaching of conversational competence has mainly concentrated on output processing" (Moreno Jaén, Pérez Basanta, 2009: 283), the use of films in the foreign language classroom – either in the old VHS format or in more recent DVD versions – to enhance conversational skills and raise cultural awareness among advanced learners is well documented (Altman, 1989; Joiner, 1990; Garza, 1991; Voller, Widdows, 1993; Tschirner, 2001; King, 2002; McVey-Gill et al., 2002; Shawback, Terhune, 2002; Stewart, Pertusa, 2004; Bueno, 2009).

However, one area in which the use of films has remained rather unexplored is in the acquisition of markers of politeness such as 'please', 'sorry' or 'thanks', which are said to be pervasive in English. Although these words, so important for smooth interaction, are introduced early on in many textbooks (see, for example, Bowker, Lodge, 1997; McCarthy, O'Dell, 1999; Oxenden et al., 2004), a review of some major series (Cambridge's *English Vocabulary in Use*; Heinemann's *Accelerate*; Oxford's *New English File* or *Landmark*) has revealed that they are rarely explored in depth from a pragmatic point of view.

The case of 'please' is particularly noteworthy. Although in all the textbooks reviewed this word appears with a relatively high frequency at the beginners' level, it most often does so to serve as context for other learning objects (e.g. speech acts of request) and it literally disappears at more advanced levels. Questions about its combinatory potential, co-texts and contexts of use are almost non-existent. It seems to be assumed that 'please' is a word that is easy to master and that no further instruction is needed.

However, as House and Kasper (1981) found, the use of 'please' in context does not necessarily coincide with its equivalent word in other languages, and this mismatch could cause cross-cultural pragmatic failure and misunderstanding which might affect interpersonal relationships (Thomas, 1983, 1995). Moreover, 'please' typically occurs in conversation. Studies in interactional sociolinguistics and conversation analysis have shown that conversation is rule-governed (Sacks et al., 1974) and that context needs to be dynamically conceived as something created by the participants in it (Duranti,

1992; Goodwin, Goodwin, 1992; Gumperz, 1992; Rühlemann, 2007). Finally, studies in multimodal analysis have emphasised the importance of non-verbal and non-vocal communication in language learning (Baldry, Thibault, 2006a).

In light of these findings, the primary goal of this chapter is to highlight the importance of the explicit instruction of contextual features in the acquisition of the politeness marker 'please'. A second but far from secondary goal is the promotion of the idea that students' exposure to DVD films as multimodal texts is useful to raise their awareness regarding the key role played by contextual configurations for the correct production and interpretation of this target word.

2. 'Please': definition, acquisition and context

The *Oxford Dictionary of English* (2003 [1998]) gives the following definitions of the word 'please': Adverb used (1) "in polite requests or questions", (2) "to add urgency and emotion to a request", (3) "to agree politely to a request", and (4) "in polite or emphatic acceptance of an offer". Alternatively, 'please' can be used to ask someone to stop doing something about which the speaker disapproves. From a discourse perspective, 'please' is defined as a politeness marker, "an optional element [which is] added to a request to bid for cooperative behaviour" (Blum-Kulka et al., 1989: 283). It is classified under the category of "[l]exical and phrasal downgraders", which "serve as optional additions to soften the impositive force of the request by modifying the Head Act internally through specific lexical and phrasal choices" (Blum-Kulka et al., 1989: 283).

All these different uses of 'please' are seldom mentioned in English textbooks and much less explicitly addressed in learning tasks. This is understandable at a beginners' level, since the aim should be to introduce the word and allow for some initial practice of the most prototypical uses such as the first sense given above. The problem arises at more advanced levels, mainly because the word is not further practised. It seems to be assumed that 'please' is just a simple word which has its equivalence in other languages (*por favor*, in Spanish; *bitte*, in German; *onegai shimasu* or *sumimasen*, in Japanese, etc.) and the only thing a student needs to learn is its position in an utterance and its pronunciation. A competent and fully-fledged use of 'please' is taken for granted, and therefore no formal instruction of its different uses (or non-use) depending on the co-text and context is provided.

However, previous studies have shown that the picture is not so simple. For example, 'please' and its semantic equivalent in other languages seem to behave differently cross-linguistically. House and Kasper (1981) found that, in everyday request situations, "the German marker *bitte* was used more frequently and differently than the equivalent English marker 'please'" by the native speakers of each language (House, 1989: 97). In turn, House (1989) shows that German learners of English tend to overuse 'please'. This cross-cultural difference in the use of 'please' makes it necessary to bring the learners' attention to the fact that it might not be used in the same contexts.

Additionally, the frequency distributions of 'please'/*bitte* in House's study showed great variation depending on the type of request strategy used (strategy choice) and the situation or setting in which requests were performed (situation type). In relation to strategy choice, 'please' was most frequently used with Imperatives and Query Preparatory Conventionally Indirect Strategies (*Can/could you do P?*) whereas hints (Non-Conventional Indirect Strategies) never carried this politeness marker (House, 1989: 102). Regarding situation type, House (1989: 107) claims that 'please'/*bitte* are preferably used in what she calls *standard situations*, in which

> the speaker has a social right to utter [a] request, in which the hearer is perceived as having a social obligation to comply with it, and in which the posing of the request is not associated with social or communicative difficulty.

In such cases, negotiations of meaning are reduced and interactants tend to use formulaic or standardised expressions (such as Imperatives + 'please' or the Query Preparatory Conventionally Indirect Strategies + 'please'). In short, "'please' seems to be licensed when the situation implies a standardised allocation of roles, rights, and obligations for the participants" (House, 1989: 108).

Thus, we can say that the use of 'please' is highly affected by cross-cultural, co-textual and contextual (situational) factors that make its full acquisition not as simple as one might have expected. But there is one more issue that needs to be taken into account. So far, *context* has been conceived as a *situation* or setting in which an activity takes place, but, as we will see below, context is much more than that.

3. Context as given vs. context as renewed and created

In House's (1989) study, context is operationalised in terms of situation types such as asking for information, asking for an extension in the deadline for the submission of an assignment, and the like. However, the context of situation is in fact a much more complex configuration of various elements, which are partially captured by what Halliday and Hasan (1989 [1985]) call the *field*, *tenor* and *mode* of discourse. Following the above trichotomy, Moreno Jaén and Pérez Basanta (2009: 290-293) provide a fine summary of all the contextual variables that speakers need to take into account in conversation. Field comprises the subject matter and the overall purposive role of an interaction, including the topic of conversation; tenor refers to the relationship between the participants in terms of relative status, power, distance, the role represented (e.g., a person can be a husband to his wife or a doctor to his patient at the same time), the history of the relationship, and the expectations of possible future relationships; finally, mode makes reference to the medium through which communication is achieved, such as auditory stimuli – including features of spoken discourse, background noise, music, etc. – and visual stimuli – involving paralinguistics (gesture, gaze, proxemics, etc.) and other non-vocal information (e.g., colour, images, spacing, etc.).

Even so, this is still not the whole picture. Scholars working within interactional linguistics, ethnomethodology and linguistic anthropology have stressed the fact that context is not something that is just 'out there' prior and during an interaction, but something that can be constantly acknowledged, respected, recreated or manipulated in the course of interaction, either through language or otherwise. As Duranti (1992: 80) puts it,

> words do not simply reflect a taken-for-granted world 'out there', they also help constitute such a world by defining relations between speaker, hearer, referents, and social activities.

Particularly in conversation, context is jointly constituted by the participants on a turn-by-turn basis by systematically sustaining "publicly displayed and continuously updated intersubjective understanding" of the situation at hand and the interaction they are engaged in (Goodwin, Goodwin, 1992: 153). Such a display can be carried out within one single turn of talk or across several turns, and interactants are constantly looking for verbal and non-verbal contextualisation cues (Gumperz, 1982: 131; 1992: 231-232) for the correct interpretation of the interlocutors' utterance and overall behaviour. Non-verbal cues, which can be realised via vocalisations – such as laughter, crying, sighing, together with kinesic elements like gaze, facial expressions, head and hand movements and proxemics (Rühlemann, 2007: 35) – make up the 'micro-contexts' that inform, modulate and potentially modify verbal content (Arndt, Janney, 1987: 364, cited in Rühlemann, 2007: 35). The dynamic and interrelated nature of context as occurring *within* a single turn is described by Goodwin, Goodwin (1992: 182, emphasis added) in the following terms:

> In order to co-participate [in an activity] in an appropriate fashion at an appropriate moment, recipients track in fine detail the unfolding structure of the speaker's utterance, paying close attention to not only the projective possibilites made available by its emerging syntactic structure (e.g. the type of unit that is about to occur), but also the precise way in which it is spoken (e.g. lengthening of sounds within words and intonation changes). The detailed organization of the talk occurring *within a turn* thus constitutes a most important aspect of the context that participants are attending to, both to make sense out of what is happening at the moment, and as a resource for the organization of their subsequent action.

This 'tracking process', which is realised locally at the turn level, is used by the hearer to carry out an inferencing process at three different levels of generality (Gumperz, 1992: 232-233):

- the reception and categorisation of communicative signals, both auditory and visual;
- the assessment of the communicative intent of the speaker;
- the framing of the activity by virtue of which the hearer may have "expectations about what is to come at some point beyond the immediate sequence to yield predictions about possible outcomes of an exchange, about suitable topics, and about the quality of interpersonal relations" (Gumperz, 1992: 233).

In other words, in order to be able to *frame* an activity correctly and co-participate in it in an appropriate and timely manner, participants in a conversation need to be constantly looking for auditory and visual contextualisation cues that allow them to keep up with the new environments that are dynamically created as conversations unfold (Goodwin, Duranti, 1992: 5; Rühlemann, 2007: 36).

Summing up, when speakers initiate a conversation, they take into account contextual features that determine the field, tenor and mode of the discourse at the onset of the interaction. However, the contextual configuration keeps changing as the conversation unfolds, and these changes are signalled via contextualisation cues that the co-participants need to recognise and process in real time. So, for an advanced-level student of English to have full pragmatic competence in the use of 'please', he/she should not only memorise all the possible patterns of usage, but should also be able to identify when and how frames have changed in a given interaction and how these changes might have an effect on subsequent turns. In the following sections, it is argued that DVD film clips are a good resource for ensuring EFL students become aware of these features.

4. The use of DVD clips for the analysis of context

The view of context as something dynamic and locally negotiated by participants through "[the] use [of] their bodies and behavior as a resource for framing and organizing their talk" (Goodwin, Duranti, 1992: 6) poses a problem for learning materials based on printed resources – such as textbooks – and/or audio recordings. In the case of the former, they are unable to capture all the nuances of verbal and non-verbal vocalisations and do not provide sufficient cues of the situational and interactional context. On the other hand, the context that the latter can provide is limited to vocal stimuli – both verbal and non-verbal. In either case, the lack of some contextual elements would make it very difficult for the student to find an analogy between what he/she has studied and real-life situations and it would be hard for him/her to draw inferences about how to frame real interactions except for the standard situation offered in the textbook and/or audio recording.

In ESL contexts, i.e. when learners of English live in the country of the target language, this could be a minor issue because everyday life would serve as the arena in which to practice whatever is learned in the classroom and real situations would provide the additional contextual features that traditional learning materials lack (Ochs, 1986; Walkinshaw, 2009: 212). However, in EFL contexts, where students live in their home countries and seldom have the chance to practise in real-life situations, having access to authentic or quasi-authentic multimodal material becomes a real asset (Tschirner, 2001: 306).

It is especially in this kind of learning environments that DVD films that are realistic and credible in their treatment of interactional, social and cultural contexts can offer students a good opportunity to experience – albeit as witnesses or eavesdroppers

– and learn how to interact in the target language and culture. This is even more so since recent technological advances have made it possible to have easy access to and control of digital visual resources – as opposed to cumbersome VHS videos – that allow for the minute analysis of interaction from a multimodal perspective, including gestures, facial expressions, body movements, and settings (Moreno Jaén, Pérez Basanta, 2009).

Additionally, the following advantages of the use of films for pedagogical purposes have been mentioned:

- the use of films has proved to be received by students with enthusiasm (King, 2002: 509; Shawback, Terhune, 2002: 94);
- films present colloquial English in real life contexts rather than artificial situations, and they expose students to a wide range of native speakers (King, 2002: 510);
- the realism of films provides a wealth of contextualised linguistic and paralinguistic terms and expressions, authentic cross-cultural information, classroom listening comprehension and fluency practice (King, 2002: 510);
- films offer endless opportunities to generate pedagogically sound activities for developing fluency (King, 2002: 511).

Of course, DVD films are not devoid of problems. The major issue that can be raised against films is the question of authenticity (Ackerley, Coccetta, 2007). Indeed, conversations in films may differ from those in natural and spontaneous language, mainly because film language is based on scripts which are "written to be spoken as if not written" (Gregory, Carroll, 1978: 42). This artificial nature has been highlighted by Taylor (2004), who found a considerable difference between the language of scripts and natural conversations in the Cobuild Bank of English and the San Diego corpus of spoken English (Taylor, 2004: 72), although the efforts made by actors and actresses to sound natural by "adapting the language given them in the script to the context in which they are supposed to find themselves" (Taylor, 2004: 80) somehow mitigate such a difference. Rodríguez Martín (in press) also reports certain differences between film language and a subset of conversations in the BNC corpus.

Against this shortcoming it could be argued that no approach is free from shortcomings. For example, the alternative of recording people role-playing conversations would still have the problem of being a performance, and hence, artificial. Besides that, we need to consider the observer's paradox (Labov, 1972), which has a bearing on people's behaviour. Finally, if we opted for recordings of real-life situations without the participants being aware of it, we would have to face ethical issues, not to mention that it would be extremely time consuming. DVD films, on the other hand, are appropriate for our purposes since they reproduce "communicative events, linguistically and pragmatically recognisable as socio-cultural situations" (Pérez Basanta, Rodríguez Martín, 2007: 149), which is what context is about.

5. The analysis of 'please' via films: an example

In order to illustrate the potential of DVD films for raising contextual awareness regarding the use of 'please', a short scene from the film *Love Actually* will be analysed from a multimodal perspective, leaving the possible pedagogical applications for the next section.

To begin with, we have argued that there are certain contextual features that set the initial frame of an interaction and that films usually provide. These are:

- the setting where the action takes place in terms of the location, the participants' positions, background noise, private or public area, etc.;
- the participants' background information, roles performed at the outset of the conversation, and their relationship in terms of rights and obligations due to power distance, status, etc.;
- the topic or objective of the transaction;
- the initial move that sets the starting point of the conversation.

The first point above establishes the mode of discourse, while points 2 and 4 are related to the tenor, and 3 has to do with the field. In the following extract taken from the film *Love Actually*, the above features can be summarised as follows:

- **Setting:** It is almost Christmas, and people are buying presents for the occasion. The interaction under study here takes place at the jewellery corner of a department store. It is a public place with people shopping all around. Harry, a customer, has just arrived in the store with his wife. She has gone to another section to buy something for her mother, leaving Harry alone. He approaches a showcase to have a look.
- **Background information:** Harry is a married middle-aged man with two young children. He is the boss in a company. His secretary, a sexy young woman, has just tried to seduce him and has asked him to buy something nice and special for her. He has just left the office to buy some Christmas presents with his wife. Finding himself alone in the store, he decides to buy a necklace for his secretary. **Roles:** Harry is a customer who wants to buy something as quick as possible so that his wife does not notice his purchase; the shop assistant (SA), also a middle-aged man, is eager to offer the best service by gift-wrapping the necklace in a gorgeous fashion, which takes time. **Rights and obligations**: Although both participants need to use polite language because they are not acquainted with each other, the SA, who is providing a service, is expected to show more respect and deference, and follow the customer's requests (Brown, Levinson, 1987).
- **Topic:** The conversation revolves around the necklace the customer intends to buy and the need or not to wrap it for a Christmas present.
- **Initial move:** The conversation is started by the shop assistant with the utterance 'Looking for anything in particular, sir?', which somehow forces Harry to decide whether to take action or just have a look. Harry decides to buy the necklace.

It is in this frame that the interaction is initiated, producing the seven turns (*Table 1*). Up to *line 07*, the transaction runs smoothly in line with the initial frame, both participants performing their roles as expected for the given context. Harry's facial expression when producing the turn 'Yes, all right' (*line 06*) confirms that everything is OK (see *Table 1*). It should be noticed that Harry has not produced the word 'please' at all, which goes against our (and possibly the student's) expectations.

LA_P23 (01:14:50-01:17:26)		
01	SA:	Looking for anything in particular, sir?
02	Harry:	Yes. That necklace there, how much is it?
03	SA:	It's £270.
04	Harry:	Erm, all right. Er, I'll have it.
05	SA:	Lovely. Would you like it… giftwrapped?
06	Harry:	Yes, all right.
07	SA:	Lovely. Let me just pop it in the box. There.

Table 1. Conversation in the film Love Actually *with a screen capture at 01:15:02 TCR (time code record)*

At this point, however, two different wants clash. While the SA wishes to please the customer with the most beautiful wrapping, Harry wants to end the transaction as fast as possible so that his wife does not catch him 'in the act'. Harry starts getting worried when he sees that the SA does not comply with his request to be quick. His face changes into a 'begging' expression (see *Table 2*) that accompanies the word-by-word repetition of his request to be quick. It is here that the politeness marker 'please' is produced.

LA_P23 (01:14:50-01:17:26)		
08	Harry:	Look, could we be quite quick?
09	SA:	Certainly, sir. Ready in the flashiest of flashes. There.
10	Harry:	That's great.
11	SA:	Not quite finished.
12	Harry:	I don't need a bag, I'll just put it in my pocket.
13	SA:	Oh, this isn't a bag, sir.
14	Harry:	Really?
15	SA:	This is so much more than a bag. Ooh!
16	Harry:	Could we be quite quick, *please*?
17	SA:	Prontissimo.
18	Harry:	What's that?
19	SA:	A cinnamon stick, sir.
20	Harry:	Actually, I really… I can't wait.

Table 2..Conversation in the film Love Actually *with a screen capture at 01:16:14 TCR*

The combination of the repeated request ('could you be quite quick?') with the addition of the word 'please', realised together with the 'begging' expression and tone of voice, mark Harry's change of frame from a typically standard transaction to one involving uneasiness and impatience. Although the SA seems to acknowledge Harry's haste, his behaviour seems to contradict his answer (*prontissimo*) by producing more ornaments for the gift. Again, this response to Harry's begging introduces a new frame of lack of cooperation that leads Harry to exasperation. His annoyance increases and reaches its *crescendo* when he bluntly tries to stop the SA (see *Table 3*).

LA_P23 (01:14:50-01:17:26)		
21	SA:	You won't regret it, sir.
22	Harry:	Wanna bet?
23	SA:	'Tis but the work of a moment. There we go. Almost finished.
24	Harry:	Are you gonna dip it in yogurt? Cover it with chocolate buttons?
25	SA:	No, sir, we're going to pop it in the Christmas box.
26	Harry:	But I don't want a Christmas box.
27	SA:	But you wanted it giftwrapped.
28	Harry:	I did but…
29	SA:	The final flourish.
30	Harry:	Can I pay?
31	SA:	All we need now…
32	Harry:	Oh, God.
33	SA:	… is a sprig of holly.
34	Harry:	NO, NO, NO, NO NO BLOODY HOLLY.
35	SA:	But sir…
36	Harry:	LEAVE IT, LEAVE IT, JUST LEAVE IT.
37	Karen:	Ooh! Loitering around the jewellery section?
38	Harry:	No. I was just looking around.

Table 3. Conversation in the film Love Actually *with a screen capture at 01:17:09 TCR*

In spite of SA's lack of cooperation as evidenced by his behaviour and his answers to Harry between *lines 21* and *35*, Harry still has room for a polite request in *line 30* using a Query Preparatory Conventionally Indirect form ('Can I pay?') although not upgraded by 'please'. In this case, the reason for not upgrading the utterance is different from that in *line 08*, since the frame has changed. Finally, politeness is completely discarded in *lines 32, 34* and *36*. In *32*, the vocative 'Oh, God' signals exasperation, while the blunt and loud series of negation markers with an expletive in *34* ('NO, NO, NO, NO. NO BLOODY HOLLY') and the direct requests using imperatives in *36* ('LEAVE IT, LEAVE IT, JUST LEAVE IT') indicate utter anger and despair, and the use of 'please' would be totally out of the question.

As the above description shows, several changes of frame take place in the course of the transaction. In this case, the changes are triggered by the SA's behaviour and Harry's reactions to it. As a result, Harry's realisations of requests also undergo modifications, which mark the onset of new frames. Clearly, this variety of realisations – changes in tenor

– cannot be explained in relation to a situation type, but are rather the result of Harry's recognition of the SA's locally displayed cues. Hence, for the learner of English to be native-like in the use or non-use of 'please', he/she needs to be able to (a) know the whole range of uses of 'please', (b) relate those uses to the appropriate frames, and (c) identify the contextualisation cues that mark the onset of those frames.

6. Pedagogical application

From a pedagogical perspective, this short scene can be used to bring the student's attention to the following features in relation to the (non)realisation of the politeness marker 'please':

1 **Situation type +/- 'please'** (House, 1989). In normal transactional circumstances, the absence of 'please' in requests does not necessarily imply impolite behaviour ('I'll have it; Yes, all right; Look, could we be quite quick?').
2 **Clause structure +/- 'please'** (House, 1989). When used, 'please' co-occurs with Query Preparatory Conventionally Indirect Speech Acts ('Could you...?').
3 **'Please' as urgency and insistence, to show impatience politely** (*Oxford Dictionary of English*). 'Please' can be used to upgrade a request in the form of a repeated utterance ('Could we be quite quick, please?') to show urgency (as in this case) or insistence.
4 **Imperatives without 'please', disregarding politeness (confrontational)** (Brown, Levinson, 1987; Watts, 2003; Terkourafi, 2005). Open confrontational interaction seems to be at odds with the use of 'please' ('NO, NO, NO, NO. NO BLOODY HOLLY; LEAVE IT, LEAVE IT, JUST LEAVE IT').
5 **Online processing of changes of frame via contextualisation cues** (Gumperz, 1992). The dynamic changes of frame might influence the use or non-use of 'please'. So, explicit training in these aspects should be helpful for students to learn how to recognise meaningful changes in the speakers' verbal and non-verbal behaviour in a conversation.

The aim would be to bring the students' attention to the importance of the contextualisation cues that are salient for the correct use and interpretation of the whole interaction and of individual turns of talk that shape the ongoing event. *Point 1* tackles the contextual features that are 'given' prior to and at the moment of starting the interaction. The presentation of the *situation* should include not only the setting at hand, but also all the information necessary to fully grasp all the variables of the interaction such as cultural schemata (rights and obligations, cultural norms), history of relationship, setting, and roles. *Point 2* refers to the possible grammatical structures that (typically) collocate with 'please'. In this case, only the Query Preparatory speech act was produced but there were other scenes in the film in which the Imperative + 'please' structure was found. *Point 3* focuses on a rather unexplored use of 'please' in the educational context, but equally important for a competent user of English. *Point 4*, although rather obvious, exemplifies a standard situation in which 'please' would be left out. Finally, *Point 5* represents the key element that gives cohesion and unity to the previous four points and helps understand the why and how of the transition from 'no please' to, again, 'no please' going through 'please' in a non-standard way. It focuses on the online (re)creation of context and the interplay between linguistic and non-linguistic behaviour via a multimodal analysis of conversational interaction.

In order to raise awareness of the above five points, the following possible exploitation of the material is suggested. This is intended merely as an orientation and not an exhaustive list of exercises, which are available on the ADELEX website supporting this volume (*http://www.ugr.es/local/inped/exploringnewpaths*).

- *Pre-viewing task.* Provide the script with blank spaces for students to fill in the word 'please' if needed. This can be done online using Hot Potatoes or similar programs. This exercise allows the student to make predictions about the appropriateness of using 'please' or not. Additionally, some questions could be asked regarding what the students consider to be appropriate uses of 'please' in terms of form and context.
- *Scene-viewing.* Watch the scene to check where 'please' has been actually used.
- *Post-viewing task.* Make the student reflect on the reasons why 'please' did (or did not) occur where expected, and draw inferences and principles of use (e.g., 'please' is not a requirement for customers to make requests in service encounters; 'please' can be emphatically marked to signal insistence, etc.). Questions should address contextualisation cues in all the aspects mentioned earlier.
- *Second viewing.* Watch the scene again (see Altman, 1989: 10; Bueno, 2009: 319, for the advantages of multiple viewing) and ask the student to find out what 'please' is used for in it:

  a. clause structure +/- 'please';
  b. situation type +/- 'please';
  c. rights and obligations +/- 'please';
  d. 'please' as urgency and insistence.

- *Third viewing.* Bring the students' attention to the verbal and non-verbal factors (locally displayed contextualisation cues) that determine the changes in frame in the service encounter interaction via guiding questions such as:

The conversation goes through three stages: (a) typical service encounter transaction in which the customer makes some requests to the shop assistant (Carter, McCarthy, 2006), (b) the customer's change of attitude to show uneasiness and impatience, and (c) the customer's final loss of self-control. (1) Identify the turn in which these transitions occur and how they are performed verbally and non-verbally. (2) Think of the reason(s) why the customer reacts the way he does.

Finally, no reference has been made to whether captions should be included in the scenes or not. My suggestion is that captions be omitted as much as possible for several reasons. Firstly, it would be impossible for the student to pay attention to all the nuances and details of the participants' behaviour and read the subtitles at the same time. Secondly, since pragmatic competence assumes a certain level of linguistic competence, the learner should be able to follow the interaction at the linguistic level so that he/she can focus on the paralinguistic elements. Finally, a transcription is already given to the student to work on (cloze exercises, etc.) and this can be used to check for difficult sections.

7. Conclusions

In this chapter, the potential of DVD film clips has been highlighted as a useful instrument to raise EFL learners' awareness of the contextual features involved in the correct production and understanding of the politeness marker 'please'. Using a scene from the film *Love Actually* as an example, I hope to have shown that this seemingly easy and unproblematic word has much more to it than expected if we attend – via multimodal analyses – to the dynamic changes in frame that take place in interaction. A possible pedagogical application has also been proposed.

Although the sample analysis of the DVD clip from *Love Actually* seems to suggest its potential as a learning tool, the next logical step should be to test the proposed activities among EFL learners and see whether their performance in the use of 'please' in different contexts (in all its senses) improves significantly after explicit instruction. This, of course, will be the following stage in the research, which should also include other markers of politeness.

Acknowledgements

I would like to express my gratitude to Dr. Graeme Porte for proof-reading an earlier version of this paper. I also wish to thank him and an anonymous reviewer for some insightful comments on it. All shortcomings and errors left remain my sole responsibility.

This paper is part of the ADELEX research project (Ref: HUM2007-61766/FILO), funded by the Spanish Ministry of Science and Innovation.

ADELEX CAT: A computer adaptive test for the lexical evaluation of university students

M. Teresa López-Mezquita Molina, University of Granada, Spain

1. Introduction

During the past thirty years we have witnessed a renewed interest in studies into the lexicon, which have brought to light a great number of questions related to the importance of lexical competence, considered by many to be at the core of communicative competence (Nation, 2001). Lexical competence is considered nowadays to be an essential step in the enhancement of L2 language proficiency but it is only very recently that a thorough knowledge of the lexicon has been recognised as an essential aspect of language ability. Vocabulary-related skills contribute significantly to all aspects of competence in a second language, to the extent that a speaker who has a wide vocabulary attains greater communicative ability than others with similar levels of skill in other linguistic spheres but with a smaller vocabulary. As some linguistic and pedagogic research has demonstrated (Laufer, 1992; Nation, 2001), communicative competence is in direct proportion to an individual's vocabulary size. Paul Meara (1996) has been one of the most persuasive researchers in convincing teachers of the need to enlarge their learners' vocabularies. He states: "The basic dimension of lexical competence is size. All other things being equal, learners with big vocabularies are more proficient in a wide range of language skills than others with smaller vocabularies" (Meara, 1996: 37).

However, until a few decades ago other aspects of communicative competence attracted more attention than vocabulary, which was relegated to a secondary role, and in fact, it was only in the 1980s that the study of the lexicon was given proper recognition in the context of L2 learning and acquisition. It was within this background of interest in lexical studies that the Department of English Philology at the University of Granada, undertook a study to evaluate the lexical competence of students in their final year of English Philology (Pérez Basanta et al., 2002). The results concluded that their level was not only insufficient for the academic requirements of the English Philology degree course, but also fell short of the professional demands which many of the future graduates would need to respond to as teachers of English. In view of these findings, Pérez Basanta co-ordinated a research group which developed into an officially funded research project, ADELEX ('Assessing and Developing Lexical Competence through the Internet'), whose main objective was to improve, enlarge and consolidate lexical competence among the students in the English Department.

The basic premise of the research team was to develop lexical aspects within the fields of lexicography, lexicology, semantics and discourse analysis by using new technologies that brought about full virtual learning (Pérez Basanta, 2004). Based on the assumption that the reliable assessment of lexical competence is a fundamental aspect in the process of developing L2 students' vocabularies, and given the attested lack of reliable, validated materials to measure vocabulary size (see, e.g., Read, 1997, 2000), one of the project's specific goals was the design of a series of computer-based vocabulary tests targeting the Spanish university context, which could be used for the accurate evaluation of students' receptive vocabulary in the initial stages of learning, and also to assess their lexical competence as part of the ongoing evaluation process.

This chapter thus describes the different stages in the design and construction of a computer adaptive vocabulary test for the assessment of lexical competence of English Philology students. The computer adaptive test (CAT) has contributed to increasing practicality, reliability and validity in a way that no other format has ever done before, as CATs include individualised and efficient implementation, instantaneous scoring, and continuous accessibility of assessment.

2. Assessing lexical competence

Lexical competence can be defined as the ability to recognise and use the words of a language in the same way as native speakers do. It thus includes the comprehension of the different relationships among word families and common collocations. As already noted, nowadays its important contribution to communicative competence is widely recognised in the field of Applied Linguistics.

Richards' (1976) description of the seven main aspects of word knowledge has been used as a general framework. Another taxonomy often cited is the one formulated by Nation (2001: 27), which expands Richards' components, specifying other features related to receptive and productive knowledge of the words in three aspects: form, meaning and use.

More recently, Jiménez Catalán (2002: 152) provides a double definition of the term: on the one hand, lexical competence is "the necessary knowledge to be able to use a word properly", and on the other hand, "the capacity to recognise, learn, retrieve and relate words both at an oral and written level". Drawing on Richards' taxonomy, Jiménez Catalán has compiled a number of additional aspects relating to what it means to know a word. Such knowledge would include its grammar, pronunciation, spelling, morphology and syntactic restrictions, its oral and written frequency in the language, the contexts in which it can be used, and the semantic and syntactic relations it holds with other words. Furthermore, the author mentions the ability to recognise the word in its oral and written form, the capacity to retrieve the word when it is needed, its conceptual and referential meaning, and finally its pragmatic meaning. In short, a complete evaluation of the knowledge of a word should verify that all these factors are known and to what depth.

Meara (1996) puts forward a more practical and operative approach which tries to simplify the question by reducing it to two dimensions of lexical knowledge: extension and organisation. To Meara, the assessment of lexical competence should establish first the breadth of vocabulary – that is to say, the number of words included in a student's vocabulary, and, second, the depth to which those words are known. In terms of breadth, Meara is strongly of the opinion that vocabulary size is a good indicator of the level of linguistic competence of an individual (Read, 1997; Nation, 2001; Laufer et al., 2004). He (1996) contends that the basic dimension of lexical competence is size and it is probably the only dimension of importance in small vocabularies. Similarly, Laufer (1998) agrees that size is more relevant than depth and an extensive vocabulary is crucial for pupils, since it directly affects their written compositions' quality and their speech fluency.

In any case, it seems that the evaluation of vocabulary should take into consideration, as a starting point, a series of fundamental aspects related to *what* vocabulary to assess and *how* to assess it – receptive/productive vocabulary, breadth and depth of vocabulary, selection of contents, item formats, etc. *Figure 1* lists all the aspects involved in these two areas, which will be dealt with in the following section.

3. Assessing lexical competence: contents and methods

3. 1. What to assess

The factors to be taken into account when considering what to assess could obviously be all those included in Nation's (2001) analytical table as well as those mentioned by Jiménez Catalán (2002), all of them referring to what is understood by *knowing a word*. The analysis of all these features receptively and productively will allow the teacher to know to what extent a word is known. Meara (1996), Laufer et al. (2004) and Henriksen (1999) also suggest a number of aspects worth considering within this field, such as breadth of vocabulary and lexicon organization, the notion of strength, or a set of three dimensions: partial to precise knowledge, depth of knowledge, and receptive to productive use ability.

Another central issue in the acquisition and also the assessment of vocabulary is the concept of word frequency. Some words appear more often than others in texts and therefore not every word demands the same attention. The words contained in frequency lists are of great interest to students and teachers because even a limited vocabulary of 2,000 words used correctly can allow the learner to understand and express a wide range of ideas. Such lists are a guide to the sort of vocabulary a student should learn in the first place in order to be able to read texts of average difficulty. They can also be used as a reliable guide for the design of vocabulary tests to check on the student's progress.

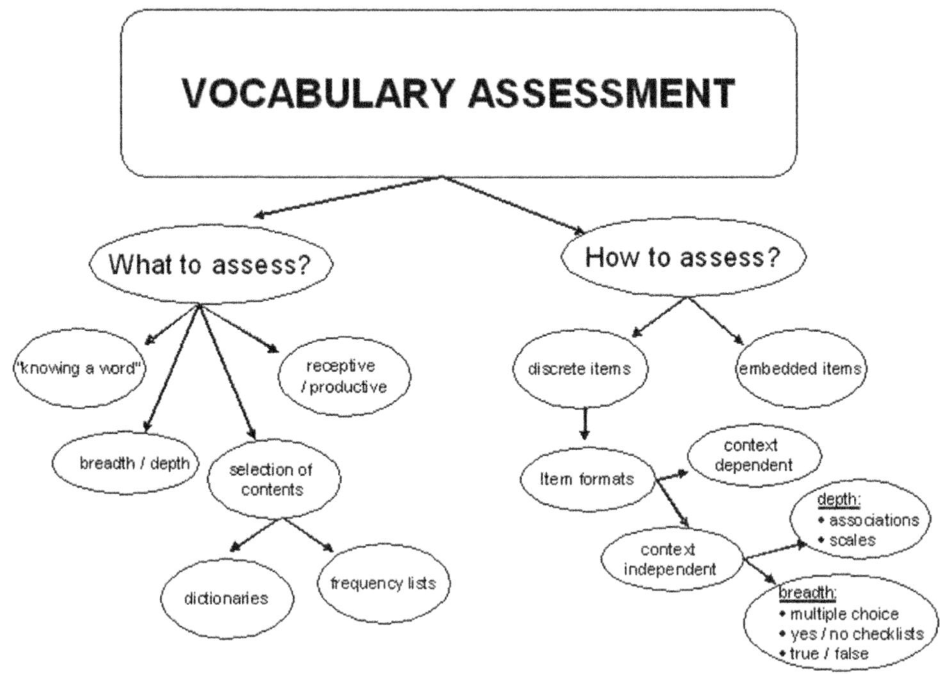

Figure 1: Key issues in vocabulary assessment

For a long time, the best-known word lists were manually compiled, such as the 2,000 word *General Service List* (West, 1953). Previous to this, Thorndike and Lorge (1944) built an eighteen-million word corpus combining several existing corpora, and some years later two one-million-word corpora were compiled: the Brown University Corpus (Kucera, Francis, 1967) with a focus on American English, and the Lancaster-Oslo/Bergen Corpus (LOB) (Hofland, Johanson, 1982) of British English.

However, in the last decades of the 20th century computational linguistics have opened up new horizons and widened the possibilities of compilation and analysis of vast amounts of data, which offer a much more accurate vision and enable reliable study of the real frequency with which words are used nowadays. Third-generation computerised corpora such as the Bank of English and the BNC, which include hundreds of millions words, have become the source of data for modern frequency lists.

One such list is that compiled by Adam Kilgarriff (1995), based upon data drawn from the BNC, which contains the 6,318 words that appear 800 or more times in the corpus, the words most frequently used, covering about 90% of the words to be found in normal texts (Sinclair, 2001; Nation, Waring, 1997). This frequency count and Clear's list (2003), from the Bank of English, completed with data from the Longman Corpus, have been used to compile a new frequency list especially designed for the ADELEX project (López-Mezquita, 2006a). This list will, henceforth, be referred to as the ADELEX list and will be described in greater detail in *Section 6.1.*

As an example of the burgeoning importance of word frequency, the Collins COBUILD dictionary offers the frequency of its entries according to information provided by the database of the Bank of English, (see *Table 1*). The frequency is represented by diamonds next to the entries in the dictionary. Five diamonds mark the most frequently used words, all included in band 1 (680 words).

From this chart we can see that a vocabulary of about 15,000 words would be necessary to understand 95% of an average text, which is the percentage it is assumed that a reader should be familiar with in order to achieve full text comprehension (i.e. an understanding of all the main points). If these figures are reliable, non-native speakers might be sufficiently equipped for university entrance with a vocabulary of only 5,000 words.

Sutarsyah et al. (1994, cited in Read, 2000) consider that a vocabulary of 4,000 to 5,000 words is sufficient for a student to understand a text in economics at university level. Nevertheless, other opinions are not so generous for languages other than English. Hazenberg and Hulstijn (1996) claim, for instance, that a non-native student wanting to enter a Dutch university would need to know about 10,000 words to understand first year subject material, whereas Groot (2000) considers that 7,000 words are needed to understand academic texts.

All these data have been taken into account in the process of design and construction of the ADELEX vocabulary tests in order to meet the requirements of English Philology undergraduates.

Band	Number of words	Cummulative total	Text coverage	
◆◆◆◆◆	680		75%	95%
◆◆◆◆◇	1040	1720		
◆◆◆◇◇	1580	3300		
◆◆◇◇◇	3200	6500	20%	
◆◇◇◇◇	8100	14600		

Table 1: Percentage of English text covered by the most frequently used words. Data from The Bank of English *(Collins COBUILD English Dictionary for Advanced Learners, 2001)*

3. 2. How to assess

Once the lexical construct has been determined and the contents to be tested have been selected, the next stage is to decide the most appropriate way to carry out this evaluation. In this respect, there are two main options in terms of vocabulary assessment: a) embedded items, i.e. integrated vocabulary within other skills such as reading or writing; b) discrete items, which evaluate the student's lexical knowledge independently (Read, 2000), which in turn can be subdivided into context-dependent or context-independent items. The use of context-independent items makes it possible to evaluate in detail, and separately, each of the lexical dimensions mentioned above (i.e. breadth and depth of knowledge). To this end, breadth of vocabulary is most commonly assessed by means of multiple choice, *yes/no* checklists and *true/false* items, whereas depth is often tested through associations and scales that provide information about different degrees of word knowledge.

In line with the renewed interest in vocabulary studies, the arrival of CALL has undoubtedly contributed to language evaluation. Certainly, the use of computers in language testing has opened up new paths for assessing lexical competence. Thus it is now widely recognised that computerised tests offer learners and teachers a number of advantages – with an array of new possibilities for test design and construction, item banking, test administration, scoring, immediate feedback and data analysis.

With hindsight it is clear that the first computer based tests were nothing more than a conversion of the pencil-and-paper tests to the new computerised format. Two generations of computerised tests have so far been developed: first-generation tests – *conventional* or *linear* tests, which present all test takers with the same items in the same sequence; and second-generation tests – *computer adaptive tests* (CATs), implemented by applying Item Response Theory (Lord, 1980), a measurement system based on probability theory, which takes account of both candidate and item characteristics; the programs used in CATs select the items from an item pool and present them according to the response pattern of the individual test taker. Thus, each test taker is provided with a unique tailor-made measurement for achieving valid and reliable vocabulary assessment insofar as fewer – but more valid and reliable – items are needed. In addition to this, automatic correction offers immediate feedback.

4. Vocabulary tests

Until recently there was widespread agreement concerning the limited availability of valid vocabulary tests that reliably measured both the breadth and depth of a speaker's lexical competence. Substantial consensus had been reached on the need for research in this field. Some scholars had noted the paucity of ideas leading to authentic innovation and a genuine need for modern accurate tests. According to Read (1997: 308):

> The predominant impressions to be gained from recent British books are, first, that the validity of vocabulary testing as such is rather dubious and, secondly, to the extent that vocabulary tests continue to be administered, there is a dearth of fresh ideas on how to design them, except perhaps for the stronger insistence that the lexical items to be tested should be presented in a whole text rather than a single sentence or in complete isolation.

Assertions such as this have undoubtedly played their part in influencing current research, to such an extent that it might be said that a change in trend has now taken place with a number of new vocabulary tests appearing. The goal of these tests is to give teachers access to tools that allow them to measure their students' receptive vocabulary reliably and thus analyse their students' needs and plan a syllabus suitable to consolidating their lexical competence.

According to Pérez Basanta (2005), vocabulary tests have traditionally fallen into two categories: those testing *breadth* of knowledge, or the number of words a learner recognises; and those assessing *depth* of knowledge, or different traits of word knowledge (Read, 2000; Schmitt et al., 2001). Within the first category, there are receptive and productive tests. Receptive tests include: *The Vocabulary Levels Tests* (Nation, 1983, 1990), *The Eurocentres Vocabulary Size Test* (EVST) (Meara, Jones, 1990), *The Revised Edition of The Vocabulary Levels Test* (Schmitt et al., 2001) and *ADELEX Levels Vocabulary Test* (ALVT) (López Mezquita, 2003, 2005). Of the very few productive tests, the best-known are: *The Productive Vocabulary Levels Test* (Laufer, Nation, 1999) and *Lex30* (Meara, Fitzpatrick, 2000). On the other hand, it is a widely held view that there is a dearth of *depth* tests, i.e. tests assessing all word dimensions (Read, 2000) with the possible exception of: *The Vocabulary Knowledge Scale* (VKS) (Paribakht, Wesche, 1993) and the *Depth of Vocabulary Knowledge Measure (DVK)* (Qian, Schedl, 2004).

Apart from traditional pen-and-paper tests, computer based tests (CBT) have recently come into play. They are classified into:

- web-based tests (WBT) such as Laufer and Nation's test (1999), available at *The Compleat Lexical Tutor, http://www.lextutor.ca/*, designed by Tom Cobb; *DIALANG, http://www.dialang.org/index.htm*, designed and financed by the European Council, and López-Mezquita's *ADELEX Levels Vocabulary Test on the Web* (2003, 2005);
- computer adaptive tests (CAT), highly technological computer tests, of which the most recent are: *Computer Adaptive Test of Size and Strength* (CATSS) (Laufer et al., 2004) and *Computer Adaptive ADELEX Vocabulary Test (CAAVT)* (López-Mezquita, 2005, 2006b).

5. Computer-assisted language testing

Within the field of educational technology, the introduction of the use of computers in the treatment and analysis of languages began with the use of machines and programs that had not been designed specifically for language learning. Nevertheless, the advantages offered by computers were immediately evident in the area of objective testing. According to Brown (1997), Olea and Hontangas (1999), and Olea and Ponsoda (2003), some of these advantages lie in the fact that computerised tests are marked and scored automatically, the testing conditions are more homogeneous and it is easier to preserve test security. Computers are much more accurate at marking, scoring and reporting scores of selected response tests than human beings. They can also give immediate feedback, process a huge amount of data quickly and register useful data such as the time every candidate takes to answer every item.

The practical benefits of using computer-based tests are considerable. From the test taker's point of view it allows him/her to work at his/her own pace, and from a pedagogical point of view, immediate feedback is likely to be more meaningful and to have more impact than delayed feedback (Alderson, 2000). The general name *computerized test* refers to all formats which can be subdivided basically into two categories:

- linear, or *first-generation* tests (Bunderson et al., 1989), where all the test takers are presented with the same items in the same sequence. The tests can be administered offline or online, thus becoming web-based tests;
- computer adaptive, or *second-generation* tests (Bunderson et al., 1989) in which a program selects the items from an item pool and presents them according to the response pattern of the individual test taker; the test content matches the skill level of the test taker and he or she gets a unique tailor-made test.

5. 1. Computer adaptive tests

Second-generation, computer adaptive tests (CAT) (Bunderson et al., 1989) consist basically of an item pool and a program which selects the items and offers them to students according to the response pattern of the individual test taker. When the CAT starts, the program chooses an item of medium-level difficulty from the item bank to estimate the test taker's ability. If the examinee responds correctly he or she will then be given a more difficult item. An incorrect answer will be followed by an easier question, and so on, with the computer algorithm adjusting the selection of the items interactively to the successful or failed responses of the test taker until the selected number of items is answered and/ or the standard error in the level of the estimation is reached. The basic notion of an adaptive test is to mimic automatically what a clever examiner would normally do. The flow chart (*Figure 2*) (Olea, Ponsoda, 2003: 49), shows the process of administration of a CAT summarizing the procedures described.

Computer adaptive tests are implemented by applying Item Response Theory (IRT) (Lord, 1980) so as to acquire the relevant statistical information for each item more reliably and accurately. IRT or "latent trait theory", a complex development of probability theory, is a measurement system which takes account of both candidate and item characteristics. It shows the probability of a learner's getting a particular item right, given his or her level of proficiency in a certain field and the difficulty and discrimination of the items he or she has to answer (Alderson et al., 1995).

According to Olea and Ponsoda (2003), a CAT is a test constructed for the purposes of psychological or educational evaluation; its items are presented and answered on a computer and its fundamental characteristic is that the test difficulty is adapted to the progressive level of competence shown by the test taker. In short, it consists of:

- an item pool with parameters calibrated according to an IRT model;
- a procedure that establishes the beginning and end of the test together with the criteria for progressively selecting the items which provide the highest information about the candidate's ability level;
- a statistical method for estimating capacity levels.

CATs add a number of advantages to linear computerised tests including the fact that a CAT is a unique test, tailored to the candidate's level of ability. Motivation is increased as frustration or boredom generated by items which are too difficult or too easy is eliminated, and time is saved because fewer items are needed to give more accurate assessment. As a result, students find CATs less overwhelming because the items are presented one at a time, thereby increasing reliability and security.

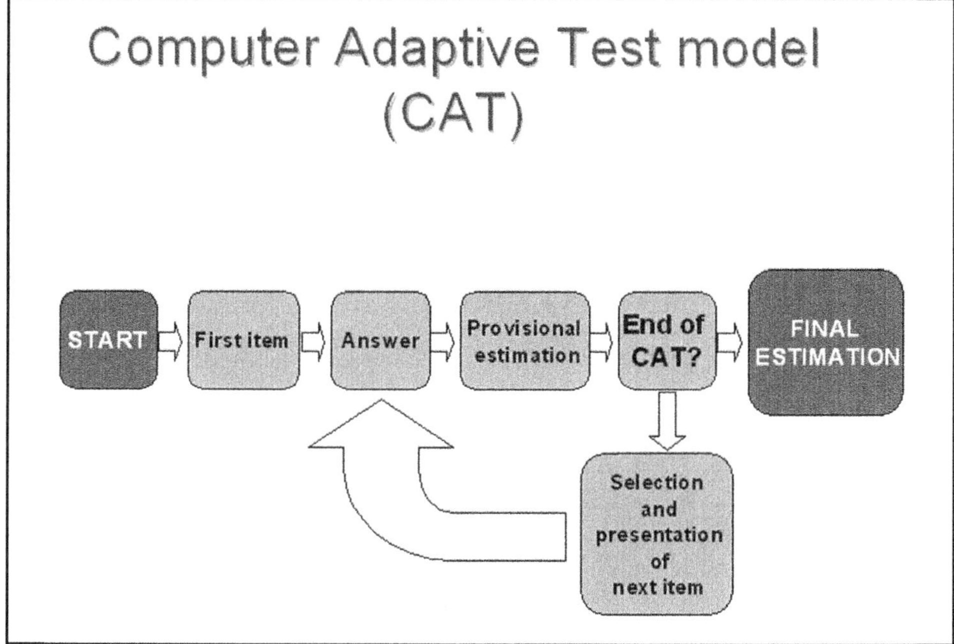

Figure 2: Process of application of a Computer Adaptive Test (Olea, Ponsoda, 2003: 49)

6. A vocabulary computer adaptive test for ADELEX

This chapter describes part of the work carried out by a research team coordinated by Pérez Basanta in the context of the ADELEX project designed to enhance L2 lexis. The project's full name – *ADELEX: Assessing and Developing Lexical Competence through New Technologies* – gives a strong clue as to its identity. The goal of this research is the implementation of a fully virtual online course to improve students' lexical competence, and within this research, to design and construct computer-based vocabulary tests targetting the Spanish University context so as to assess lexical competence for placement, progress and achievement evaluation purposes.

To this end a vocabulary test, described below, was designed and constructed; firstly, as a paper-and-pencil test, secondly, as a first-generation online test – 'conventional' or 'linear' test –, and finally, as a second-generation online test – 'computer adaptive' test, ADELEX CAT (López-Mezquita, 2009).

6. 1. Stage 1: the paper-and-pencil vocabulary test

The model followed for the test planning, design and construction was especially created ad hoc after thoughtful consideration of an extensive bibliography in the field of vocabulary assessment (Thorndike, Hagen, 1980; Madsen, 1983; Carroll, Hall, 1985; Heaton, 1989; Bachman, 1990; Pérez Basanta et al., 1992; Alderson et al., 1995; Frary, 1995; Bachman, Palmer, 1996; Murray, 2002; Abad et al., 2004). The main objective was to meet the fundamental test requirements: reliability and validity, the pillars on which any test must lay its foundations to measure accurately and consistently.

The first stage thus consisted of the creation of a vocabulary test, made up of 220 multiple-choice items. The students have to carry out simple recognition of the written word, i.e. the connection between form and meaning, to show their partial knowledge of the words, in relation to the following two questions formulated in Nation's taxonomy (2001: 27) on what it means to know a word. "Does the learner recognise the written form of the word?" and "Does the learner recall the appropriate meaning for this word form?" This knowledge can be considered a starting point and the first stage in the progressive learning of a word.

Discrete, context-independent items were most appropriate for this kind of test, since they allow the tester to reach a high level of intrinsic reliability and objectivity in the marking process. Also they require minimum reading and allow the student to answer a great number of items within a limited period of time, and thus cover the knowledge of a great number of words; in this way, according to Meara (1996), they provide valuable information about the student's vocabulary breadth. The idea was to check accurately how many words a learner recognises at a receptive level and hence get a picture of the general state of his/her vocabulary. On the other hand, multiple-choice items have excellent technical characteristics, as far as reliability and validity are concerned, and lend themselves to being computerised. On the whole, these advantages make this item format ideal for the project's purposes.

Using this format, 220 items were constructed, each composed of a stem, base or stimulus and five answer options, plus a last option, common to all the items in the test, 'none of these', which was designed to lessen the guess factor involved in multiple choice tests, which is inversely proportional to the number of answer options.

A crucial aspect of the test validity was the selection of the test contents. The first procedures had to do with ensuring appropriate selection of words and, to this end, a new frequency list was compiled to meet the lexical needs of the project's students and researchers. This word inventory was partly based upon Adam Kilgarriff's frequency list (1995), drawn from the British National Corpus, a 10,000-word frequency list from the Bank of English (Clear, 2003), and data from the *Longman Defining Vocabulary*, a 2,000-word list of highly frequent words in English according to the Longman Corpus, which the *Longman Dictionary of Contemporary English* uses for its definitions. This list, already mentioned in *Section 3.1.1.*, is referred to as the ADELEX list.

The ADELEX frequency list (López-Mezquita, 2006a) includes the 7,125 most frequent words in the English language according to reputable sources and has provided the contents for the vocabulary tests described in this chapter. As far as grammar categories are concerned, the ADELEX list includes 53.26% nouns, 19.48% verbs, 17.86% adjectives and 6.21% adverbs; the remaining percentage (3.17%) are function words.

Thus, all the words included in our test were selected from the 7,125-word ADELEX frequency list. The words for the construction of the items belong to the four lexical word classes (nouns, verbs, adjectives and adverbs) in a proportion that reflects the percentage of terms in the ADELEX list. Thus, 30 items are nouns, 13 items are verbs, 10 items are adjectives and 2 items are adverbs. In addition, certain grammar words which occur in paraphrases used in the test have been included in the item bases. Also the percentage of Latin and Germanic words kept a similar proportion as in real English; in fact, 50% are of Germanic origin and the same number of Latin origin.

The elements in every item belong to the same grammar category and all the distractors have a similar frequency to the target word. Thus their difficulty is more or less the same. The relationship between the base and the correct option is of synonymy, hyponymy or hyperonymy, and in some cases it is a paraphrase. The answer options have similar length and are ordered alphabetically. The distractors must seem reasonably attractive – otherwise they could easily be ruled out as absurd or incoherent, giving the student a better chance to give a correct answer by a process of elimination.

The test tries to determine a student's vocabulary level according to his/her percentage of correct answers. In other words, a score of 100% would imply that the student knows all the words included in the 7,000-word list and a score of 50% would mean that the student knows half that figure, i.e. 3,500 words, and so on. It was administered to 330 undergraduates of English Philology and to students of Translation and Interpretation Studies at two Spanish universities: Granada and Castellón. The results were analysed statistically by applying the Classical Theory of Tests (CTT) in order to obtain central measures – mean, mode, median, standard deviation, etc. – and then item analysis was performed to obtain the item facility value and the discrimination index. The facility value measures the level of difficulty of an item and the discrimination index measures the extent to which the results of an individual item correlate with the results from the whole test. Items with facility values higher than 0.80 were discarded as being too easy, and lower than

0.20 as being too difficult. As far as the discrimination index is concerned, we eliminated those items with an index below 0.25 and relied on those with higher values, which provide more information about the test and the test takers.

Test reliability was established by applying the Kuder-Richardson 20 index, which in this case, with all the items equally weighted and marked either right or wrong, was identical to Cronbach's Alpha. The desirable Alpha value for a vocabulary test is between 0.90 and 0.99 (Hughes, 1989) and the value obtained for the test was 0.9705, thus, indicating that the test was fully reliable.

6. 2. Stage 2: the first-generation computerised test

The next stage in the study was to turn the paper-and-pencil vocabulary test into a computer-based test to achieve a faster, more objective and reliable diagnosis of the candidates' vocabulary levels.

The initial and more natural application of computers to testing was simply to present and administer conventional paper-and-pencil tests by means of a computer. This process did not in fact change the test formats to any great extent but it did provide considerable advantages, such as the precise control of the presentation of the items on the screen, marking and automated saving of the answers, together with efficiency and speed at yielding results (Muñiz, Hambleton, 1999). In fact, the majority of computerised tests originated as versions of tests designed and constructed in a pencil-and-paper format (Fulcher, 2000), as did the ADELEX test.

From a formal point of view, the multiple choice item format used for the test lends itself perfectly to being computerised. Generally speaking, Muñiz and Hambleton (1999) consider that if the test implementation is properly done, from a technical point of view there do not seem to be any significant differences between the pencil-and-paper version and the computerised version. It is also logical to think that the test's psychometric properties must be similar if we consider that the test is essentially the same as the pencil-and-paper version, the only difference being the fact that the items appear on a screen instead of on paper, and the students must answer by means of the computer keyboard or the mouse (Muñiz, Hambleton, 1999).

The main factors affecting learners' performance and thus introducing a significant slant could be familiarity, the students' attitude towards computer technology, the types of tasks and time restrictions. In this case, these limitations were of no consequence since, on the one hand, it was a low-stakes situation (instrumental use, classroom tool) and on the other hand, the ADELEX students were very familiar with online learning.

Thus the paper-and-pencil test described in the previous section was computerised into a linear or 'first generation' test (Bunderson et al., 1989). All the test takers were presented with the same items in the same sequence; after the students had completed and submitted the answers to all the items, the test was automatically marked and the results were provided; immediate feedback on the correct and incorrect answers was given and the responses were stored on the computer for analysis.

The software used for this stage was *QuizStar, http://quizstar.4teachers.org/indexi.jsp*, a free web testing resource. The test was administered through *WebCT, http://www.webct. com/*, a digital platform used by the University of Granada for online courses. An offline version of the test was also created through the free authoring program *Hot Potatoes, http:// hotpot.uvic.ca/*.

6. 3. Final stage: ADELEX CAT

In order to increase validity, a questionnaire was designed to obtain feedback from the students, so that it might give information about length, timing, items, etc. Perhaps the most important piece of information obtained from this questionnaire was the test length: the students complained that there were too many items to answer on screen – however necessary for test reliability – causing some students to feel "overwhelmed" by the number of items. Considering this negative comment, the ADELEX team considered the possibility of turning the test into a computer adaptive test (CAT), and after weighing the pros and cons, it was decided that converting the linear test into a CAT version would be the best solution.

As mentioned above, CATs are tailor-made tests: every time the test is administered a different set of items is used, depending on the student's language ability level, so the learner gets a unique test. CATs add a number of very practical advantages, particularly that of saving time, as fewer items are needed to provide a more precise and reliable assessment under conditions of greater security.

As Chalhoub-Deville and Deville (1999) point out, a high level of expertise and sophistication in computer technology and psychometrics related to CAT is required. In this case, the software used to turn the ADELEX computerised linear test into a CAT was ADTEST (Ponsoda et al., 1994). The process of the conversion of the test was carried out in three stages:

- calibration of the item pool according to the IRT;
- comparison of the item parameters obtained by applying the CTT and the parameters obtained by applying IRT;
- implementation of CAT through ADTEST.

The item pool previously described for the paper-and-pencil test and analysed according to the CTT with SPSS was again calibrated, this time with ASCAL, following a three-parameter logistic model of IRT, which, in addition to the learner's linguistic ability, considers the parameters of difficulty, discrimination and the guessing factor. Once the results had established the model fit, those items whose values did not fit were rejected and eliminated from the bank.

The following step was to make a statistical comparison of the two tests; the first analysed by means of CTT and the other one by IRT procedures. But before correlating the two measures, all the values had to be converted to the same scale, since CTT values use a decimal scale in which 1 (100%) is the value of maximum facility, and IRT uses a scale in *logits*, units of interval measurement, in which value 0 equals 50%, and negative values indicate greater facility. After that, the (Pearson) correlation coefficient was calculated showing a 94.48% match. This was very high and gave an indication that the test was well constructed.

In the next stage, the CAT was implemented through ADTEST. The program consisted of four files: *adtest.exe, cga.bgi, items.str* and *param.str*, which respectively required to execute the program, provide statistical storage for the item pool, the parameters for item selection and the filing of the students' results. ADTEST implements the testing algorithm in such a way that the highest information item is selected (Ponsoda et al., 1994). When the student has given his/her answer and a maximum likelihood estimation of the new proficiency level has been calculated, the next highest information item is selected, and so on. Finally, the procedure stops when the standard error of proficiency estimation is below 0.32 or a pre-selected number of items – 30 items in this case – is reached. There is a maximum time of 30 seconds for each item, which means a maximum total time of 15 minutes for the whole test. When the test is finished the results (final proficiency level, standard error, time taken and number of items answered) are displayed on the computer screen.

7. ADELEX CAT on the web

ADELEX CAT has been used by students since the academic year 2004-2005. The many benefits of this assessment tool include accurate, reliable assessment of the students' vocabulary breadth carried out in about 15 minutes.

Initial teething problems included the fact that the University of Granada server would not allow program installations on the students' standalones; it was therefore necessary to use diskettes containing the program and all its components and take as many copies as there were students, so that each student could work individually at their computer. A general explanation was given before starting the test and after the students had finished, a file was created on the diskette to store all the information relating to the student's performance. All of the data were then saved and analysed. Improvements in subsequent years meant that the test was uploaded to the web and downloaded by the students taking the course (*http://sites.google.com/site/adelexcat/*), thus eliminating the need to use diskettes. The test can now be taken there by simply clicking on the URL and downloading the files. The need to make further improvements haseled the ADELEX team to work on the design and implementation of the project's own software.

At present a new online version of ADELEX CAT is undergoing piloting and validation (as illustrated in *Figure 3*) and, once this validation process is finished, it will be made available on the ADELEX website supporting this volume.

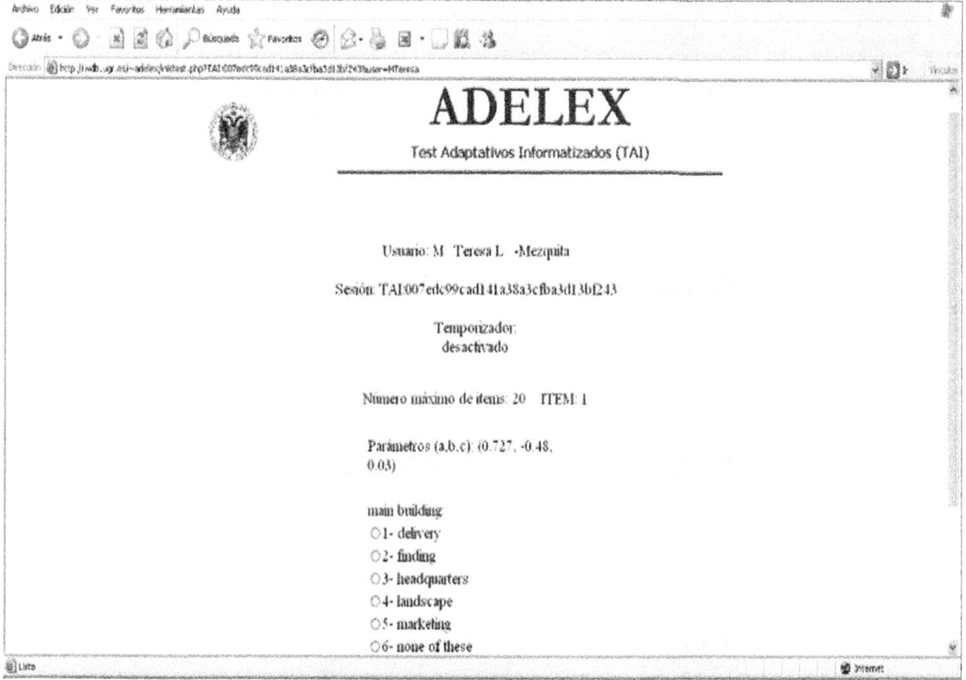

Figure 3: ADELEX CAT on the web (trial version)

8. Conclusions

This chapter has attempted to describe the process of design, development and implementation of a vocabulary computer adaptive test carried out within the ADELEX R&D project. The test, based on a 7,125-word frequency list especially compiled for this project (the ADELEX list), has undergone several phases of development and is currently available online at *http://sites.google.com/site/adelexcat*. This computerised evaluation tool is a 'tailor-made' test which objectively assesses the receptive lexical knowledge of university students. The advantages of this computer test in comparison with paper-and-pencil tests or linear computerised tests include a 15-minute maximum implementation time, which greatly reduces fatigue amongst test candidates, and the precision and reliability of the calculation of students' vocabulary thresholds. Together with other advantages mentioned in this chapter, they make this test format highly recommendable for vocabulary tests in which a range of items is required to obtain a valid and reliable estimate of learners' lexical capital.

Acknowledgements

Research leading to this publication has been funded by the Spanish Ministry of Innovation and Science under research project "ADELEX: Assessing and Developing Lexical Competence through New Technologies" (HUM2007-61766/FILO).

Reference section

(a) Published and unpublished articles and books

Abe, Mariko (2001). 'A corpus-based study of the use of conjunctions', in *PAC3 at JALT 2001: Conference proceedings*. Tokyo: JALT, pp. 541-7.

Ackerley, Katherine, Coccetta, Francesca (2007). 'Enriching language learning through a multimedia corpus'. *ReCALL* 19, 3: 351-70.

Ädel, Annelie (2006). *Metadiscourse in L1 and L2 English*. Amsterdam: John Benjamins.

Alameda, José R., Cuetos, Fernando (1995). *Diccionario de Frecuencias de las Unidades Lingüísticas del Castellano*. Oviedo: Universidad de Oviedo.

Alderson, J. Charles (2000). 'Technology in testing: The present and the future'. *System* 28: 593-603.

Alderson, J. Charles, et al. (1995). *Language Test Construction and Evaluation*. Cambridge: Cambridge University Press.

Allan, Rachel (2006). 'Data-driven learning and vocabulary: investigating the use of concordances with advanced learners of English'. *Centre for Language and Communication Studies, Occasional Paper* 66. Dublin: Trinity College Dublin.

Altenberg, Bengt, Tapper, Marie (1998). 'The use of adverbial connectors in advanced Swedish learners' written English', in Sylviane Granger (ed.), *Learner English on Computer*. London and New York: Addison Wesley Longman, pp. 80-93.

Altman, Robert (1989). *The Video Connection: Integrating video into language teaching*. Boston: Houghton Mifflin.

Anderson-Hsieh, Janet, Koehler, Kenneth (1988). 'The effect of foreign accent and speaking rate on native speaker comprehension'. *Language Learning* 38: 561-613.

Aston, Guy (1995). 'Corpora in language pedagogy: matching theory and practice', in Guy Cook and Barbara Seidlhofer (eds), *Principle and Practice in Applied Linguistics*. Oxford: Oxford University Press, pp. 257-70.

Aston, Guy (2001). 'Text categories and corpus users: A response to David Lee'. *Language Learning & Technology* 5, 3: 73-6.

Aston, Guy, et al. (eds) (2004). *Corpora and Language Learners*. Amsterdam: John Benjamins.

Bachman, Lyle F. (1990). *Fundamental Considerations in Language Testing*. Oxford: Oxford University Press.

Bachman, Lyle F., Palmer, Adrian S. (1996). *Language Testing in Practice*. Oxford: Oxford University Press.

Baddeley, Alan (1992). 'Working memory'. *Science* 255: 556-59.

Baddock, Barry (1996). *Using Films in the English Classroom*. Hertfordshire: Phoenix Ltd.

Bahns, Jens (1993). 'Lexical collocations: A contrastive view'. *ELT Journal* 47, 1: 56-63.

Bahns, Jens, Eldaw, Moira (1993). 'Should we teach EFL students collocations?'. *System* 21, 1: 101-14.

Baker, Judith (1998). 'Metaphor'. *English Teaching Professional* 7: 13-4.

Baldry, Anthony, Coccetta, Francesca (2010 in press). *Web-based Concordancing and Annotation: Self-access project work and syllabus construction through structured web explorations*. London: Equinox Publishing.

Baldry, Anthony, et al. (2010 in press). '*MWS* and *MWB*: multimodal website concordancing and annotation tools', in Anthony Baldry and Elena Montagna (eds), *Interdisciplinary Approaches to Multimodality: Theory and practice. Readings in intersemiosis and multimedia*. Palladino: Campobasso.

Baldry, Anthony, O'Halloran, Kay L. (2010 in press). 'Research into the annotation of a multimodal corpus of university websites: An illustration of multimodal corpus linguistics', in Tony Harris and María Moreno Jaén (eds), *Corpus Linguistics in Language Teaching*. Bern: Peter Lang.

Baldry, Anthony, Thibault, Paul J. (2006a). *Multimodal Transcription and Text Analysis: A multimodal toolkit and coursebook with associated on-line course*. London: Equinox Publishing.

Baldry, Anthony, Thibault, Paul J. (2006b). 'Multimodal corpus linguistics', in Geoff Thompson and Susan Hunston (eds), *System and Corpus: Exploring connections*. London: Equinox Publishing, pp. 164-83.

Baldry, Anthony, Thibault, Paul J. (2007). 'Multimodal transcription and text analysis', in Ruqaiya Hasan et al. (eds), *Continuing Discourse on Language. A functional perspective*. Volume I. London: Equinox Publishing, pp. 174-6.

Baldry, Anthony, Thibault, Paul J. (2008). 'Applications of multimodal concordances'. *HERMES* 41: 11-41.

Bally, Charles (1951 [1909]). *Traité de Stylistique Française*. 2 vols. 3rd edition. Paris: Librairie C. Klincksieck.

Barcroft, Joe (2002). 'Semantic and structural elaboration in L2 lexical acquisition'. *Language Learning* 52: 323-63.

Barfield, Andy (2006). *An Exploration of Second Language Collocation Knowledge and Development*. Unpublished PhD Thesis. University of Wales, Swansea, UK.

Barlow, Michael, Kemmer, Suzanne (eds) (2000). *Usage-Based Models of Language*. Stanford: Centre for the Study of Language and Information Publications.

Baroni, Marco, Bernardini, Silvia (eds) (2006). *Wacky! Working papers on the web as corpus*. Bologna: Gedit.

Baroni, Marco, et al. (2004). 'Introducing the La Repubblica corpus: A large, annotated, TEI(XML)-compliant corpus of newspaper Italian', in *Proceedings of the Fourth Language Resources and Evaluation Conference*, pp. 1771-4.

Bavelas, Janet, et al. (2000). 'Listeners as co-narrators'. *Journal of Personality and Social Psychology* 79, 6: 941-52.

Béacco, Jean-Claude (1995). 'À propos de la structuration des communautés discursives: beaux-arts et appreciatif', in Jean-Claude Béacco and Sophie Moirand (eds), *Les Enjeux des Discours Spécialisés*. Paris: Presses de la Sorbonne Nouvelle, pp. 135-53.

Béjoint, Henri (2000). *Modern Lexicography: An introduction*. Oxford: Oxford University Press.

Belz, Julie A., Vyatkina, Nina (2005a). 'Learner corpus analysis and the development of L2 pragmatic competence in networked intercultural language study: the case of German modal particles'. *Canadian Modern Language Review* 62, 1: 17-48.

Belz, Julie A., Vyatkina, Nina (2005b). 'Computer-mediated learner corpus research and the data-driven teaching of L2 pragmatic competence: the case of German modal particles'. *CALPER Working Papers* 4, April.

Belz, Julie A., Vyatkina, Nina (2008). 'The pedagogical mediation of a developmental learner corpus for classroom-based language instruction'. *Language Learning & Technology* 12, 3: 35-52.

Benson, Morton (1990). 'Collocations and general-purpose dictionaries'. *International Journal of Lexicography* 3, 1: 23-34.

Bernardini, Silvia (2002). 'Exploring new directions for discovery learning', in Bernhard Kettemann and Georg Marko (eds), *Teaching and Learning by Doing Corpus Analysis*. Amsterdam: Rodopi, pp. 165-82.

Bernardini, Silvia (2004). 'Corpora in the classroom: An overview and some reflections on future developments', in John Sinclair (ed.), *How to Use Corpora in Language Teaching*. Amsterdam: John Benjamins, pp. 15-36.

Biber, Douglas (1988). *Variation across Speech and Writing*. Cambridge: Cambridge University Press.

Biber, Douglas, et al. (1999). *Longman Grammar of Spoken and Written English*. Harlow: Longman.

Bikeliene, Lina (2008). 'Resultive connectors in advanced Lithuanian learners' English writing'. *KALBOTYRA* 59, 3: 30-7.

Blum-Kulka, Shoshana, et al. (eds) (1989). *Cross-Cultural Pragmatics: Requests and apologies*. Norwood, N.J.: Ablex Publishing.

Boers, Frank (2000). 'Metaphor awareness and vocabulary retention'. *Applied Linguistics* 21: 553-71.

Boers, Frank, et al. (2004). 'Etymological elaboration as a strategy for learning figurative idioms', in Paul Bogaards and Batia Laufer (eds), *Vocabulary in a Second Language: Selection, acquisition and testing*. Amsterdam: John Benjamins, pp. 53-78.

Boers, Frank, et al. (2006). 'Formulaic sequences and perceived oral proficiency: putting a lexical approach to the test'. *Language Teaching Research* 10: 245-61.

Boers, Frank, Lindstromberg, Seth (2005). 'Finding ways to make phrase-learning feasible: the mnemonic effect of alliteration'. *System* 33, 225-38.

Boers, Frank, Lindstromberg, Seth (2009). *Optimizing a Lexical Approach to Instructed Second Language Acquisition*. Basingstoke: Palgrave Macmillan.

Bogaards, Paul (1999). 'Access structures of learners' dictionaries', in Thomas Herbst and Kerstin Popp (eds), *The Perfect Learners' Dictionary (?)*. Tübingen: Max Niemeyer Verlag, pp. 113-30.

Bolinger, Dwight (1972). *Degree Words*. The Hague: Mouton.

Bolinger, Dwight (1976). 'Review article of Adam Makkai (1976) *Idiom Structure in English*'. *Language* 52, 1: 238-41.

Bolinger, Dwight (1985). 'Defining the indefinable', in Robert Ilson (ed.), *Dictionaries, Lexicography and Language Learning*. Oxford: Pergamon Press, pp. 69-73.

Bolton, Kingsley, et al. (2002). 'A corpus-based study of conjunctions in student writing: research from the International Corpus of English in Hong Kong (ICE-HK)'. *International Journal of Corpus Linguistics* 7, 2: 165-82.

Bosque, Ignacio (1999). 'El sintagma adjetival: modificadores y complementos del adjetivo: adjetivo y participio', in Ignacio Bosque and Violeta Demonte (eds), *Gramática Descriptiva de la Lengua Espanola*. Madrid: Espasa Calpe, pp. 217-310.

Boulton, Alex (2008). 'DDL: reaching the parts other teaching can't reach?', in Ana Frankenberg-Garcia (ed.), *Proceedings of the 8th Teaching and Language Corpora Conference*. Lisbon: Associação de Estudos e de Investigação Científica do ISLA-Lisboa, pp. 38-44.

Boulton, Alex (2009a). 'Testing the limits of data-driven learning: Language proficiency and training'. *ReCALL* 21, 11: 37-51.

Boulton, Alex (2009b). 'Language awareness and medium-term benefits of corpus consultation'. *Proceedings of EuroCALL 2009: New trends in CALL – working together*. Valencia: Universidad Politécnica de Valencia.

Boulton, Alex (2009c). 'Data-driven learning: Reasonable fears and rational reassurance'. *Indian Journal of Applied Linguistics* 35, 1: 81-106.

Boulton, Alex (2010). 'Data-driven learning: Taking the computer out of the equation'. *Language Learning* 60, 3: 534-72.

Boulton, Alex (2010 in press). 'Data-driven learning: On paper, in practice', in Tony Harris and María Moreno Jaén (eds), *Corpus Linguistics in Language Teaching*. Bern: Peter Lang.

Boulton, Alex (in press). 'Data-driven learning: The perpetual enigma', in Stanislaw Roszkowski and Barbara Lewandowska-Tomaszczyk (eds), *PALC 2009*. Frankfurt: Peter Lang.

Boulton, Alex (Forthcoming). 'Corpora for all? Learning styles and data-driven learning'. *Proceedings of the 5ᵗʰ Corpus Linguistics Conference.*

Bowker, David, Lodge, Patricia (1997). *Accelerate: Starter.* Oxford: Heinemann ELT.

Brand, Christiane, Kämmerer, Susanne (2006). 'The Louvain International Database of Spoken English Interlanguage (LINDSEI): Compiling the German component', in Sabine Braun et al. (eds), *Corpus Technology and Language Pedagogy: New resources, new tools, new methods.* Frankfurt am Main: Peter Lang, pp. 127-40.

Braun, Sabine (2007). 'Integrating corpus work into secondary education: from data-driven learning to needs-driven corpora'. *ReCALL* 19, 3: 307-28.

Brown, Dan (2003a). *The Da Vinci Code.* London: Corgi Edition.

Brown, Dan (2003b). *El Código Da Vinci* [trans. Juan J. Estrella]. Barcelona: Ediciones Urano.

Brown, Dorothy F. (1974). 'Advanced vocabulary teaching: the problem'. *RELC Journal* 5, 2: 1-11.

Brown, James D. (1997). 'Computers in language testing: Present research and some future directions'. *Language Learning & Technology* 1, 1: 44-59.

Brown, Penelope, Levinson, Stephen C. (1987). *Politeness: Some universals of language use.* Cambridge: Cambridge University Press.

Brunner, Martin, Süb, Heinz-Martin (2005). 'Analysing the reliability of multidimensional measures: an example from intelligence research'. *Educational and Psychological Measurement* 65, 2: 227-40.

Bueno, Kathleen A. (2009). 'Got film? Is it a readily accessible window to the target language and culture for your students?'. *Foreign Language Annals* 42, 2: 318-39.

Bunderson, C. Victor, et al. (1989). 'The four generations of computerized testing', in Robert L. Linn (ed.), *Educational Measurement.* London: Macmillan, pp. 367-407.

Bunker, Ellen L. (1988). *Towards Comprehensive Guidelines for the Preparation of Material in English for EFL Adults with Limited Education.* Unpublished MA Thesis, Brigham Young University, USA.

Burger, Harald (1998). *Phraseologie: Eine Einfuhrung am Beispiel des Deutschen.* Berlin: Erich Schmidt Publishing.

Butler, Christopher S. (2005). 'Formulaic language: an overview with particular reference to the cross-linguistic perspective', in Christopher S. Butler et al. (eds), *The Dynamics of Language Use.* Amsterdam: John Benjamins, pp. 221-42.

Bybee, Joan (2006). 'From usage to grammar: the mind's response to repetition'. *Language* 82, 4: 711-33.

Bybee, Joan (2008). 'Usage-based grammar and second language acquisition', in Peter Robinson and Nick C. Ellis (eds), *Handbook of Cognitive Linguistics and Second Language Acquisition.* New York: Routledge, pp. 216-36.

Bybee, Joan, Eddington, David (2006). 'A usage-based approach to Spanish verbs of becoming'. *Language* 82, 2: 323-410.

Bybee, Joan, Hopper, Paul (eds) (2001). *Frequency and the Emergence of Linguistic Structure.* Amsterdam: John Benjamins.

Byrne, Donn (1988). *Teaching Writing Skills.* London: Longman.

Canale, Michael (1983). 'From communicative competence to communicative language pedagogy', in Jack Richards and Richard Schmidt (eds), *Language and Communication.* New York: Longman, pp. 2-27.

Carroll, Brendan J., Hall, Patrick J. (1985). *Make your Own Language Tests. A practical guide to writing language performance tests.* Oxford: Pergamon Press.

Carroll, Donald (2004). 'Restarts in novice turn beginnings: disfluencies or interactional achievements?', in Rod Gardner and Johannes Wagner (eds), *Second Language Conversations.* London: Continuum, pp. 201-20.

Carter-Thomas, Shirley (2007). 'The *iffiness* of medical research articles: a comparison of English *if* and French *si*', in Kjersti Flottum (ed.), *Language and Discipline Perspectives on Academic Discourse.* Cambridge: Cambridge Scholars Publishing, pp. 150-75.

Carter-Thomas, Shirley, Rowley-Jolivet, Elizabeth (2001). 'Syntactic differences in oral and written scientific discourse: the role of information structure'. *ASp* 31-33: 19-38.

Carter, Ronald (1987). 'Vocabulary and second/foreign language teaching'. *Language Teaching* 20, 1: 3-16.

Carter, Ronald (1998). 'Orders of reality: CANCODE, communication, and culture'; and 'A reply to Guy Cook'. *ELT Journal* 52, 1: 43-56; 64.

Carter, Ronald, McCarthy, Michael (1995). 'Grammar and the spoken language'. *Applied Linguistics* 16, 2: 141-58.

Carter, Ronald, McCarthy, Michael (2006). *Cambridge Grammar of English: A comprehensive guide: Spoken and written English grammar and usage.* Cambridge: Cambridge University Press.

Castillo Carballo, María Auxiliadora (1998). 'El término 'colocación' en la lingüística actual'. *Lingüística Española Actual* 20, 1: 41-54.

Castillo Carballo, María Auxiliadora (2001). 'Colocaciones léxicas y variación lingüística: implicaciones didácticas'. *Lingüística Española Actual* 23, 1: 133-43.

Celce-Murcia, Marianne, Larsen-Freeman, Dianne (1999). *The Grammar Book: An ESL/EFL teacher's course.* Boston: Heinle & Heinle Publishers.

Cermak, Laird S., Fergus, Craik I. (1979). *Levels of Processing in Human Memory.* Hillsdale: Lawrence Erlbaum.

Chafe, Wallace (1980a). 'Some reasons for hesitating', in Hans W. Dechert and Manfred Raupach (eds), *Temporal Variables in Speech: Studies in honour of Frieda Goldman-Eisler.* Paris: Mouton Publishers, pp. 169-80.

Chafe, Wallace (ed.) (1980b). *The Pear Stories: Cognitive, cultural, and linguistic aspects of narrative production.* Norwood, NJ: Ablex.

Chafe, Wallace (1992). 'Intonation units and prominences in English natural discourse', in *Proceedings of the IRCS Workshop on Prosody in Natural Speech.* Philadelphia: University of Pennsylvania.

Chafe, Wallace (1994). *Discourse, Consciousness, and Time: The flow and displacement of conscious experience in speaking and writing.* Chicago: University of Chicago Press.

Chalhoub-Deville, Micheline, Deville, Craig (1999). 'Computer adaptive testing in second language contexts'. *Annual Review of Applied Linguistics* 19: 273-99.

Chambers, Angela (2005). 'Integrating corpus consultation in language studies'. *Language Learning & Technology* 9, 2: 111-25.

Chambers, Angela (2007). 'Popularising corpus consultation by language learners and teachers', in Encarnación Hidalgo et al. (eds), *Corpora in the Foreign Language Classroom*. Amsterdam: Rodopi, pp. 3-16.

Chambers, Angela, Wynne, Martin (2008). 'Sharing corpus resources in language learning', in Felicia Zhang and Beth Barber (eds), *Handbook of Research on Computer-Enhanced Language Acquisition and Learning*. Hershey, PA: IGI Global, pp. 438-51.

Chan, Tun-Pei, Liou, Hsien-Chin (2005). 'Effects of web-based concordancing instruction on EFL students' learning of verb-noun collocations'. *Computer Assisted Language Learning* 18, 3: 231-51.

Charles, Maggie (2007) 'Reconciling top-down and bottom-up approaches to graduate writing: using a corpus to teach rhetorical functions'. *Journal of English for Academic Purposes* 6, 4: 289-302.

Charteris-Black, Jonathan (2000). 'Metaphor and vocabulary teaching in ESP economics'. *English for Specific Purposes* 19: 149-65.

Cheng, Winnie, et al. (2003). 'The language learner as language researcher: putting corpus linguistics on the timetable'. *System* 31, 2: 173-86.

Ciesielska-Ciupek, Maria (2001). 'Teaching with the internet and corpus materials: preparation of the ELT materials using the internet and corpus resources', in Barbara Lewandowska-Tomaszczyk (ed.), *PALC 2001: Practical applications in language corpora*. Frankfurt: Peter Lang, pp. 521-31.

Clear, Jim (2003). *10,000 Most Frequent Lemmas from 211m.* (personal communication).

Clements, J. Clancy (1988). 'The semantics and pragmatics of the Spanish (copula + adjective) construction'. *Linguistics* 26: 779-822.

Cobb, Tom (1997a). *From Concord to Lexicon: Development and test of a corpus-based lexical tutor.* Montreal: Concordia University.

Cobb, Tom (1997b). 'Is there any measurable learning from hands-on concordancing?'. *System* 25, 3: 301-15.

Cobb, Tom (1999). 'Breadth and depth of lexical acquisition with hands-on concordancing'. *Computer Assisted Language Learning* 12, 4: 345-60.

Cobb, Tom, et al. (2001). 'Can the rate of lexical acquisition from reading be increased? An experiment in reading French with a suite of on-line resources'. Translation of 'Peut-on augmenter le rythme d'acquisition lexicale par la lecture? Une expérience de lecture en français appuyée sur une série de ressources en ligne', in Patricia M. Raymond and Claudette Cornaire (eds), *Regards sur la Didactique des Langues Secondes*. Montreal: Editions Logique, pp. 133-53.

Cobb, Tom, Horst, Marlise (2001). 'Growing academic vocabulary with a collaborative on-line data-base', in Bruce Morrison et al. (eds), *ELT Perspectives on IT and Multimedia: Selected papers from the ITMELT conference 2001*. Hong Kong: Hong Kong Polytechnic University, pp. 189-225.

Cohen, Gillian, et al. (1986). *Memory: A cognitive approach*. Milton Keynes: Open University Press.

Condamines, Anne (2000). '*Chez* dans un corpus de sciences naturelles: un marqueur de méronymie?'. *Cahiers de Lexicologie* 77: 165-87.

Condamines, Anne (2002). 'Corpus analysis and conceptual relation patterns'. *Terminology* 8, 1: 141-62.

Connor, Ulla (1984). 'A study of cohesion and coherence in English as a second language students' writing'. *Papers in Linguistics* 17, 301-16.

Conrad, Susan, Biber, Douglas (eds) (2001). *Variation in English: Multi-dimensional studies*. London: Longman.

Cop, Margaret (1988). 'The function of collocations in dictionaries', in Tamas Magay and Judit Zigány (eds), *BUDALEX Proceedings: Papers from the EURALEX Third International Congress*. Budapest: Akademiai Kiado, pp. 35-46.

Corley, Martin, et al. (2007). 'It's the way that you, er, say it: hesitations in speech affect language comprehension'. *Cognition* 105, 3: 658-68.

Corpas Pastor, Gloria (1996). *Manual de Fraseología Española*. Madrid: Gredos.

Cowie, Anthony P. (1981). 'The treatment of collocations and idioms in learners' dictionaries'. *Applied Linguistics* 2, 3: 223-35.

Cowie, Anthony P. (1998). 'Introduction', in Anthony P. Cowie (ed.), *Phraseology: Theory, analysis, and applications*. Oxford: Clarendon Press, pp. 1-20.

Coxhead, Averil (2000). 'A new academic word list'. *TESOL Quarterly* 34, 2: 213-38.

Cresswell, Andy (2007). 'Getting to "know" connectors? Evaluating data-driven learning in a writing skills course', in Encarnación Hidalgo et al. (eds), *Corpora in the Foreign Language Classroom*. Amsterdam: Rodopi, pp. 267-87.

Crew, William (1990). 'The illogic of logical connectives'. *ELT Journal* 44: 316-25.

Crystal, David (2001). *Language and the Internet*. Cambridge: Cambridge University Press.

Culicover, Peter (1999). *Syntactic Nuts: Hard cases in syntax*. Oxford: Oxford University Press.

Curado Fuentes, Alejandro (2002). 'Exploitation and assessment of a business English corpus through language learning tasks'. *ICAME Journal* 26: 5-32.

Curado Fuentes, Alejandro (2003). 'The use of corpora and IT in a comparative evaluation approach for oral business English'. *ReCALL* 15, 2: 189-201.

Curado Fuentes, Alejandro (2007). 'A corpus-based assessment of reading comprehension in English', in Encarnación Hidalgo et al. (eds), *Corpora in the Foreign Language Classroom*. Amsterdam: Rodopi, pp. 309-26.

De Cock, Sylvie (1998). 'Corpora of learner speech and writing and ELT', in Aurelia Usoniene (ed.), *Proceedings of the International Conference on Germanic and Baltic Linguistic Studies and Translation*. Vilnius: Homo Liber, pp. 56-66.

De Cock, Sylvie (2004). 'Preferred sequences of words in NS and NNS speech'. *Belgian Journal of English Language and Literatures* 2, 225-46.

de Haan, Pieter (1999). 'English writing by Dutch-speaking students', in Hilde Hasselgård and Signe Oksefjell (eds), *Out of Corpora*. Amsterdam: Rodopi, pp. 203-12.

De Smeet, Hendrik, Verstraete, Jean-Christophe (2006). 'Coming to terms with subjectivity'. *Cognitive Linguistics* 17, 3: 365-92.

De Souza, Clarisse (2005). *The Semiotic Engineering of Human-Computer Interaction*. Camb. Mass and London: MIT Press.

Dechert, Hans W. (1980). 'Pauses and intonation as indicators of verbal planning in second-language speech productions', in Hans W. Dechert and Manfred Raupach (eds), *Temporal Variables in Speech: Studies in honour of Frieda Goldman-Eisler*. Paris: Mouton Publishers, pp. 269-85.

Dechert, Hans W. (1983). 'How a story is done in a second language', in Claus Faerch and Gabriele Kasper (eds), *Strategies in Interlanguage Communication*. New York: Longman, pp. 175-95.

Deconinck, Julie, et al. (2009). 'Music to their ears? Assessing learners' sensitivity to the form of multi-word units', in Tom Koole et al. (eds), *Artikelen van de Zesde Anéla Conferentie*. Delft: Eburon, pp. 63-72.

Deese, James (1980). 'Pauses, prosody, and the demands of production in language', in Hans W. Dechert and Manfred Raupach (eds), *Temporal Variables in Speech: Studies in honour of Frieda Goldman-Eisler*. Paris: Mouton, pp. 69-84.

Dewaele, Jean-Marc (2002). 'Individual differences in L2 fluency: the effect of neurobiological correlates', in Vivian Cook (ed.), *Portraits of the L2 User*. Clevedon: Multilingual Matters, pp. 219-50.

Dixon, Robert M.W. (1991). *A New Approach to English Grammar: On semantic principles*. Oxford: Clarendon Press.

Dodd, Bill (1997). 'Exploiting a corpus of written German for advanced language learning', in Anne Wichmann et al. (eds), *Teaching and Language Corpora*. London: Longman, pp. 131-45.

Dodd, Steven (1989). 'Lexicomputing and the dictionary of the future'. In Gregory James (ed.), *Lexicographers and their Works*. Exeter: University of Exeter, pp. 83-93.

Dörnyei, Zoltán (2009). *The Psychology of Second Language Acquisition*. Oxford: Oxford University Press.

Duranti, Alessandro (1992). 'Language in context and language as context: the Samoan respect vocabulary', in Alessandro Duranti and Charles Goodwin (eds), *Rethinking Context: Language as an interactive phenomenon*. Cambridge: Cambridge University Press, pp. 77-99.

Ejzenberg, Roseli (2000). 'The juggling act of oral fluency: a psycho-sociolinguistic metaphor', in Heidi Riggenbach (ed.), *Perspectives on Fluency*. Ann Arbor: University of Michigan Press, pp. 287-313.

Ellis, Nick C. (1996). 'Sequencing in SLA: phonological memory, chunking, and points of order'. *Studies in Second Language Acquisition* 18, 91-126.

Ellis, Nick C. (2002a). 'Frequency effects in language acquisition: a review with implications for theories of implicit and explicit language acquisition'. *Studies in Second Language Acquisition* 24, 143-88.

Ellis, Nick C. (2002b). 'Reflections on frequency effects in language acquisition: a response to commentaries'. *Studies in Second Language Acquisition* 24, 297-339.

Ellis, Nick C. (2005). 'At the interface: dynamic interactions of explicit and implicit language knowledge'. *Studies in Second Language Acquisition* 27, 305-52.

Ellis, Nick C. (2008). 'Phraseology: the periphery and the heart of the language', in Fanny Meunier and Sylviane Granger (eds), *Phraseology in Foreign Language Learning and Teaching*. Amsterdam: John Benjamins, pp. 1-13.

Ellis, Nick C., Beaton, Alan (1993). 'Psycholinguistic determinants of foreign language vocabulary learning'. *Language Learning* 43, 4: 559-617.

Ellis, Nick C., et al. (2008). 'Formulaic language in native and second language speakers: psycholinguistics, corpus linguistics, and TESOL'. *TESOL Quarterly* 42, 3: 375-96.

Erman, Britt, Warren, Beatrice (2000). 'The idiom principle and the open choice principle'. *Text* 20, 87-120.

Estling Vannestål, Maria, Lindquist, Hans (2007). 'Learning English grammar with a corpus: experimenting with concordancing in a university grammar course'. *ReCALL* 19, 3: 329-50.

Eubank, Lynn, et al. (1997). "Tom eats slowly cooked eggs': Thematic verb-raising in L2 knowledge'. *Language Acquisition* 6: 171-99.

Eubank, Lynn, Grace, Sabine (1998). 'V-to-I and inflection in non-native grammars', in Maria-Luise Beck (ed.), *Morphology and its Interfaces in L2 Knowledge*. Amsterdam: John Benjamins, pp. 69-88.

Evensen, Lars (1990). 'Pointers to superstructure in student writing'. In Ulla Connor and Ann Johns (eds), *Coherence in Writing*. Alexandria VA: TESOL, pp. 46-77.

Eyckmans, June (2007). 'Taking SLA research to interpreter-training: does knowledge of phrases foster fluency?', in Frank Boers et al. (eds), *Multilingualism and Applied Comparative Linguistics: Pedagogical perspectives*. Newcastle: Cambridge Scholars Publishing, pp. 89-104.

Eyckmans, June (2009). 'Towards an assessment of learners' receptive and productive syntagmatic knowledge', in Andy Barfield and Henrik Gyllstad (eds), *Researching Collocations in Another Language. Multiple interpretations*. Basingstoke: Palgrave Macmillan, pp. 139-52.

Eyckmans, June, et al. (2007). 'Identifying chunks: Who can see the wood for the trees?'. *Language Forum* 33, 85-100.

Faerch, Claus, Kasper, Gabriele (1984). 'Pragmatic knowledge: Rules and procedures'. *Applied Linguistics* 5: 214-25.

Fan, May (2009). 'An exploratory study of collocational use by ESL students – A task based approach'. *System* 37: 110-23.

Fei, Deng (2006). 'The effect of the use of adverbial conjunctions in Chinese EFL learners' English writing quality'. *CELEA Journal* 29, 1: 105-11.

Feldt, Leonard S. (2005). 'Estimating the reliability of dichotomous or trichotomous scores'. *Educational and Psychological Measurement* 65, 1: 28-41.

Fellbaum, Christiane (2007). 'Introduction', in Christiane Fellbaum (ed.), *Idioms and Collocations: Corpus-based linguistic and lexicographic studies*. London and New York: Continuum, pp. 1-19.

Field, Yvette, Yip, Lee M. O. (1992). 'A comparison of internal conjunctive cohesion in the English essay writing of Cantonese speakers and native speakers of English'. *RELC Journal* 23: 15-28.

Fiksdal, Susan (2000). 'Fluency as a function of time and rapport', in Heidi Riggenbach (ed.), *Perspectives on Fluency*. Ann Arbor: University of Michigan Press, pp. 128-40.

Fillmore, Charles (1979). 'On fluency', in Charles Fillmore et al. (eds), *Individual Differences in Language Ability and Language Behavior*. New York: Academic Press, pp. 85-101.

Fillmore, Charles (2000). 'On fluency', in Heidi Riggenbach (ed.), *Perspectives on Fluency*. Ann Arbor: University of Michigan Press, pp. 43-60.

Fillmore, Charles, et al. (1988). 'Regularity and idiomaticity in grammatical constructions: the case of *let alone*'. *Language* 64, 3: 501-38.

Firth, John R. (1957). 'Modes of meaning', in John R. Firth, *Papers in Linguistics: 1934-1951*. Oxford: Oxford University Press, pp. 190-215.

Fleischer, Wolfgang (1997). *Phraseologie der Deutschen Gegenwartssprache*. Tübingen: Niemeyer.

Fløttum, Kjersti, et al. (2006). *Academic Voices: Across languages and disciplines*. Amsterdam: John Benjamins.

Folse, Keith S. (2006). 'The effect of type of written exercise on L2 vocabulary retention'. *TESOL Quarterly* 40, 2: 27-93.

Fontenelle, Thierry (1994). 'What on earth are collocations?'. *English Today* 40, 10, 4: 42-8.

Foster, Pauline (2001). 'Rules and routines: a consideration of their role in task-based language production of native and non-native speakers', in Martin Bygate et al. (eds), *Researching Pedagogic Tasks: Second language learning, teaching, and testing*. London: Longman, pp. 75-93.

Freed, Barbara (1995). 'What makes us think that students who study abroad become fluent?', in Barbara Freed (ed.), *Second Language Acquisition in a Study Abroad Context*. Amsterdam: John Benjamins, pp. 123-48.

Fulcher, Glenn (1996). 'Does thick description lead to smart tests? A data-based approach to rating scale construction'. *Language Testing* 13, 2: 208-38.

Fulcher, Glenn (2000). 'Computers in language testing', in Paul Brett and Gary Motteram (eds), *A Special Interest in Computers: Learning and teaching with information and communication technologies.* Whitstable, Kent: IATEFL, pp. 93-106.

Gadet, Françoise (2003). '"Français populaire" : un "classificateur déclassant"?'. *Marges Linguistiques* 6: 103-15.

Gairns, Ruth, Redman, Stuart (1986). *Working with Words.* Cambridge: Cambridge University Press.

Gan, Siowck-Lee, et al. (1996). 'Modeling teaching with a computer-based concordancer in a TESL preservice teacher education program'. *Journal of Computing in Teacher Education* 12, 4: 28-32.

Garza, Thomas J. (1991). 'Evaluating the use of captioned video materials in advanced foreign language learning'. *Foreign Language Annals* 24, 3: 239-57.

Gasser, Michael (1990). 'Connectionism and universals of second language acquisition'. *Studies in Second Language Acquisition* 12: 179-99.

Gilquin, Gaëtanelle, et al. (2007). 'Learner corpora: the missing link in EAP pedagogy'. *Journal of English for Academic Purposes* 6, 4: 319-35.

Gilquin, Gaëtanelle, Gries, Stefan Th. (2009). 'Corpora and experimental methods: a state-of-the-art review'. *Corpus Linguistics and Linguistic Theory* 5, 1: 1-26.

Gitsaki, Christina (1996). *The Development of ESL Collocational Knowledge.* Unpublished PhD Thesis. Centre for Language Teaching and Research, The University of Queensland, Brisbane, Australia.

Goldberg, Adele E. (1995). *Constructions: A construction grammar approach to argument structure.* Chicago: University of Chicago Press.

Goldberg, Adele E. (2006). *Constructions at Work: The nature of generalization in language.* Oxford: Oxford University Press.

Goldberg, Adele E., Jackendoff, Ray (2004). 'The English resultative as a family of constructions'. *Language* 80: 532-68.

Goldman-Eisler, Frieda (1968). *Psycholinguistics: Experiments in spontaneous speech.* New York: Academic Press.

Goodale, Malcolm (1995). *COBUILD Concordance Samplers 2: Phrasal verbs.* London: HarperCollins.

Goodwin, Charles, Duranti, Alessandro (1992). 'Rethinking context: an introduction', in Alessandro Duranti and Charles Goodwin (eds), *Rethinking Context: Language as an interactive phenomenon.* Cambridge: Cambridge University Press, pp. 1-42.

Goodwin, Charles, Goodwin, Marjorie H. (1992). 'Assessments and the construction of context', in Alessandro Duranti and Charles Goodwin (eds), *Rethinking Context: Language as an interactive phenomenon.* Cambridge: Cambridge University Press, pp. 147-89.

Granger, Sylviane (1993). 'The International Corpus of Learner English', in Jan Aarts et al. (eds), *English Language Corpora: Design, analysis and exploitation.* Amsterdam: Rodopi, pp. 57-69.

Granger, Sylviane (ed.) (1998). *Learner English on Computer.* London: Longman.

Granger, Sylviane, Meunier, Fanny (2008). 'Phraseology in language learning and teaching: where to from here?', in Fanny Meunier and Sylviane Granger (eds), *Phraseology in Foreign Language Learning and Teaching.* Amsterdam: John Benjamins, pp. 247-52.

Granger, Sylviane, Paquot, Magali (2008). 'Disentangling the phraseological web', in Sylviane Granger and Fanny Meunier (eds), *Phraseology. An interdisciplinary perspective.* Amsterdam: John Benjamins, pp. 27-49.

Granger, Sylviane, Tyson, Stephanie (1996). 'Connector usage in the English essay writing of native and non-native EFL speakers of English'. *World Englishes* 15, 1: 17-27.

Gregory, Michael, Carroll, Susanne (1978). *Language and Situation: Language varieties and their social contexts*. London, Henley and Boston: Routledge & Kegan Paul.

Gries, Stefan Th. (2010 in press). 'Methodological skills in corpus linguistics: A polemic and some pointers towards quantitative methods', in Tony Harris and María Moreno Jaén (eds), *Corpus Linguistics in Language Teaching*. Bern: Peter Lang.

Groot, Peter J. M. (2000). 'Computer assisted second language vocabulary acquisition'. *Language Learning & Technology* 4, 1: 60-81.

Gross, Gaston (1996). *Les Expressions Figées en Français: Noms composés et autres locutions*. Paris: Ophrys.

Guillot, Marie-Noëlle (1999). *Fluency and its Teaching*. Clevedon: Multilingual Matters Ltd.

Gumperz, John J. (1982). *Discourse Strategies*. Cambridge: Cambridge University Press.

Gumperz, John J. (1992). 'Contextualization and understanding', in Alessandro Duranti and Charles Goodwin (eds), *Rethinking Context: Language as an interactive phenomenon*. Cambridge: Cambridge University Press, pp. 229-52.

Gyllstad, Henrik (2007). *Testing English Collocations: Developing receptive tests for use with advanced Swedish learners*. PhD Thesis. Lund: Lund University.

Hadley, Gregory (2002). 'Sensing the winds of change: an introduction to data-driven learning'. *RELC Journal* 33, 2: 99-124.

Haines, David (1996). 'Survival of the fittest'. *The Bookseller* (Feb.), 26-34.

Halliday, Michael (1961). 'Categories of the theory of grammar'. *Word* 17, 3: 241-92.

Halliday, Michael (1978). *Language as a Social Semiotic*. London: Arnold.

Halliday, Michael, Hasan, Ruqaiya (1976). *Cohesion in English*. London: Longman.

Halliday, Michael, Hasan, Ruqaiya (1989 [1985]). *Language, Context and Text: A social semiotic perspective*. Australia: Deakin University Press.

Halliday, Michael, Matthiessen, Christian (2004). *An Introduction to Functional Grammar* (3rd ed.). London: Arnold.

Handl, Susanne (2008). 'Essential collocations for learners of English: the role of collocational direction and weight', in Fanny Meunier and Sylviane Granger (eds), *Phraseology in Foreign Language Learning and Teaching*. Amsterdam: John Benjamins, pp. 43-66.

Harder, Peter (2007). 'Grammar, flow and procedural knowledge', in Mike Hannay and Gerard J. Steen (eds), *Structural-Functional Studies in English Grammar*. Amsterdam: John Benjamins, pp. 309-35.

Hartley, Bernard, Viney, Peter (1978). *Streamline English: Departures*. Oxford: Oxford University Press.

Hartmann, Reinhard (2001). *Teaching and Researching Lexicography*. Harlow: Pearson Education Limited.

Hasselgreen, Angela (2005). *Testing the Spoken English of Young Norwegians: A study of test validity and the role of "smallwords" in contributing to pupils' fluency*. New York: Cambridge University Press.

Hausmann, Franz (1979). 'Un dictionnaire des collocations est-il possible?'. *Travaux de Linguistique et de Littérature* 17: 187-95.

Hazenberg, Suzanne, Hulstijn, Jan H. (1996). 'Defining a minimal receptive second-language vocabulary for non-native university students: An empirical investigation'. *Applied Linguistics* 17, 2: 145-61.

Heaton, John B. (1989). *Writing English Language Tests*. New York: Longman Group Limited.

Henriksen, Birgit (1999). 'Three dimensions of vocabulary development'. *Studies in Second Language Acquisition* 21: 303-17.

Higgins, John, Johns, Tim (1984). *Computers in Language Learning.* London: Collins.

Higueras, Marta (2004). *La Enseñanza-Aprendizaje de las Colocaciones en el Desarrollo de la Competencia Léxica en el Español como Lengua Extranjera.* Unpublished PhD Thesis. Universidad Complutense de Madrid, Spain.

Higueras, Marta (2007). *Estudio de las Colocaciones Léxicas y su Enseñanza en Español como Lengua Extranjera.* Málaga: ASELE.

Hill, Jimmie (2000). 'Revising priorities: from grammatical failure to collocational success' in Michael Lewis (ed.), *Teaching Collocation: Further developments in the Lexical Approach.* London: Language Teaching Publications, pp. 47-69.

Hill, Jimmie, et al. (2000). 'Classroom strategies, activities, and exercises' in Michael Lewis (ed.), *Teaching Collocation: Further developments in the Lexical Approach.* London: Language Teaching Publications, pp. 88-126.

Hoey, Michael (2005). *Lexical Priming: A new theory of words and language.* London and New York: Routledge.

Hofland, Knut, Johansson, Stig (1982). *Word Frequencies in British and American English.* Bergen: Norwegian Computing Centre for the Humanities.

Horst, Marlise, et al. (2001). 'Expanding academic vocabulary with an interactive on-line database'. *Language Learning & Technology* 9, 2: 90-110.

Hosenfeld, Carol (1976). 'Learning about learning: discovering our students' strategies'. *Foreign Language Annals* 9, 2: 117-29.

House, Juliane (1989). 'Politeness in English and German: the functions of *please* and *bitte*', in Shoshana Blum-Kulka et al. (eds), *Cross-Cultural Pragmatics: Requests and apologies.* Norwood, N.J.: Ablex Publishing, pp. 96-119.

House, Juliane, Kasper, Gabriele (1981). 'Politeness markers in English and German', in Florian Coulmas (ed.), *Conversational Routine.* The Hague: Mouton de Gruyter, pp. 157-85.

Howarth, Peter (1996). *Phraseology in English Academic Writing: Some implications for language learning and dictionary making.* Tübingen: Max Niemeyer Verlag.

Howarth, Peter (1998). 'Phraseology and second language proficiency'. *Applied Linguistics* 19, 22-44.

Hsue-Hueh Shih, Rebecca (2000). 'Compiling Taiwanese Learner Corpus of English'. *Computational Linguistics and Chinese Language Processing* 5, 2: 87-100.

Huang, Hung-Tzu, Liou, Hsien-Chin (2007). 'Vocabulary learning in an automated graded reading program'. *Language Learning & Technology* 11, 3: 64-82.

Huddleston, Rodney, Pullum, Geoffrey K. (2002). *The Cambridge Grammar of the English Language.* Cambridge: Cambridge University Press.

Hughes, Arthur (1989). *Testing for Language Teachers.* Cambridge: Cambridge University Press.

Hughes, Rebecca (1996). *English in Speech and Writing.* New York: Routledge.

Hughes, Rebecca (2002). *Teaching and Researching Speaking.* Essex: Pearson Education.

Hulstijn, Jan, Laufer, Batia (2001). 'Some empirical evidence for the involvement load hypothesis in vocabulary acquisition'. *Language Learning* 51, 3: 539-58.

Hundt, Marianne, et al. (eds) (2007). *Corpus Linguistics and the Web.* Amsterdam: Rodopi.

Hunston, Susan (2002). *Corpora in Applied Linguistics.* Cambridge: Cambridge University Press.

Hussein, Fayez (1990). 'Collocations, the missing link in vocabulary acquisition amongst EFL learners'. *Papers and Studies in Contrastive Linguistics* 26, 26: 123-36.

Hyland, Ken (1996). 'Writing without conviction? Hedging in scientific research articles'. *Applied Linguistics* 17, 4: 433-54.

Hyland, Ken (1998). *Hedging in Scientific Research Articles.* Amsterdam: John Benjamins.

Instituto Cervantes (1994). *Report on Linguistic Resources for Spanish (I): Written and spoken corpora available or in progress in Spain.* Alcalá de Henares: Instituto Cervantes.

Instituto Cervantes (1996). *Informe sobre Recursos Lingüísticos para el Español (II): Corpus escritos y orales disponibles y en desarrollo en España.* Alcalá de Henares: Instituto Cervantes.

Írsula Peña, Jesús (1994). 'Entre el verbo y el sustantivo, ¿quién rige a quién? El verbo en las colocaciones sustantivo-verbales' in Alexander Endruschat et al. (eds), *Verbo e Estructuras Frásicas. Actas do IV Colóquio Internacional de Linguística Hispânica de Leipzig.* Oporto: University of Oporto, pp. 277-86.

Ivir, Vladimir (1988). 'Collocations in dictionaries monolingual and bilingual', in Tom Burton and Jill Burton (eds), *Lexicographical and Linguistic Studies in Honour of George W. Turner.* Cambridge: D. J. Brewer, pp. 43-50.

Jackendoff, Ray (2008). '*Construction after construction* and its theoretical challenges'. *Language* 84, 1: 8-28.

Jalilifar, Alireza (2008). 'Discourse markers in composition writings: the case of Iranian learners of English as a foreign language'. *English Language Teaching* 1, 2: 114-22.

Jenkins, Joseph R., Dixon, Robert (1984). 'Vocabulary learning'. *Contemporary Educational Psychology* 8: 237-60.

Jiménez Catalán, Rosa M. (2002). 'El concepto de competencia léxica en los estudios de aprendizaje y enseñanza de segundas lenguas'. *ATLANTIS* 24, 1: 149-62.

Jiménez Catalán, Rosa M., Mancebo, Rocío (2008). 'Vocabulary input in EFL textbooks'. *RESLA* 21: 147-65.

Joe, Angela (1998). 'What effects do text-based tasks promoting generation have on incidental vocabulary acquisition?'. *Applied Linguistics* 19, 3: 357-77.

Johansson, Stig (2009). 'Some thoughts on corpora and second-language acquisition', in Karin Aijmer (ed.), *Corpora and Language Teaching.* Amsterdam: John Benjamins, pp. 33-44.

Johansson, Stig, Oksefjell, Signe (eds) (1998). *Corpora and Cross-Linguistic Research: Theory, method and case studies.* Amsterdam: Rodopi.

Johns, Tim (1986). 'Micro-concord: A language learner's research tool'. *System* 14, 2: 151-62.

Johns, Tim (1988). 'Whence and whither classroom concordancing?', in Theo Bongaerts et al. (eds), *Computer Applications in Language Learning.* Dordrecht: Foris, pp. 9-27.

Johns, Tim (1990). 'From printout to handout: Grammar and vocabulary teaching in the context of data-driven learning'. *CALL Austria* 10: 14-34. [Reprinted in Tim Johns and Philip King (eds), *Classroom Concordancing. English Language Research Journal* 4: 27-45].

Johns, Tim (2002). 'Data-driven learning: The perpetual challenge', in Bernhard Kettemann and Georg Marko (eds), *Teaching and Learning by Doing Corpus Analysis.* Amsterdam: Rodopi, pp. 107-17.

Johns, Tim, et al. (2008). 'Integrating corpus-based CALL programs and teaching English through children's literature'. *CALL* 21, 5: 483-506.

Joiner, Elizabeth G. (1990). 'Choosing and using videotexts'. *Foreign Language Annals* 23, 1: 53-64.

Kasper, Gabriele (2004). 'Speech acts in (inter)action: Repeated questions'. *Intercultural Pragmatics* 1, 1: 125-33.

Kasper, Gabriele (2006). 'When once is not enough: Politeness of multiple requests in oral proficiency interviews'. *Multilingua* 25: 323-50.

Kaur, Jagdish, Hegelheimer, Volker (2005). 'ESL students' use of concordance in the transfer of academic word knowledge: an exploratory study'. *CALL* 18, 4: 287-310.

Keating, Gregory D. (2008). 'Task effectiveness and word learning in a second language: the involvement load hypothesis on trial'. *Language Teaching Research* 12: 365-86.

Kennedy, Claire, Miceli, Tiziana (2001). 'An evaluation of intermediate students' approaches to corpus investigation'. *Language Learning & Technology* 5, 3: 77-90.

Kim, Youjin J. (2008). 'The role of task-induced involvement and learner proficiency in L2 vocabulary acquisition'. *Language Learning* 58, 2: 285-325.

King, Jane (2002). 'Using DVD feature films in the EFL classroom'. *Computer Assisted Language Learning* 15, 5: 509-23.

Klein-Braley, Christine, Raatz, Ulrich (1984). 'A survey of research on the c-test'. *Language Testing* 1, 2: 134-46.

Koike, Kazumi (2001). *Colocaciones Léxicas en el Español Actual: Estudio formal y léxico-semántico*. Madrid: University of Alcalá and University of Takushoku.

Koosha, Mansour, Jafarpour, Ali Akbar (2006). 'Data-driven learning and teaching collocation of prepositions: the case of Iranian EFL adult learners'. *Asian EFL Journal Quarterly* 8, 4: 192-209.

Koponen, Matti, Riggenbach, Heidi (2000). 'Overview: varying perspectives on fluency', in Heidi Riggenbach (ed.), *Perspectives on Fluency*. Ann Arbor: University of Michigan Press, pp. 5-24.

Kovacci, Ofelia (1999). 'El adverbio', in Ignacio Bosque and Violeta Demonte (eds), *Gramática Descriptiva de la Lengua Española*. Madrid: Espasa Calpe, pp. 705-86.

Kozloff, Sarah (2001). *Overhearing Film Dialogue*. Berkeley: University of California Press.

Krauss, Robert M., Weinheimer, Sidney (1966). 'Concurrent feedback, confirmation, and the encoding of referents in verbal communication'. *Journal of Personality and Social Psychology* 35: 523-29.

Kraut, Robert E., et al. (1982). 'Listener responsiveness and the coordination of conversation'. *Journal of Personality and Social Psychology* 43: 718-31.

Kucera, Henry, Francis, W. Nelson (1967). *A Computational Analysis of Present Day American English*. Providence, RI: Brown University Press.

Labov, William (1972). *Sociolinguistic Patterns*. Philadelphia: University of Pennsylvania Press.

Langacker, Ronald W. (1987). *Foundations of Cognitive Grammar, Vol. I: Theoretical prerequisites*. Stanford: Stanford University Press.

Larsen-Freeman, Diane, Cameron, Lynne (2008). *Complex Systems and Applied Linguistics*. Oxford: Oxford University Press.

Laufer, Batia (1992). 'Reading in a foreign language: How does L2 lexical knowledge interact with the reader's general academic ability?'. *Journal of Research in Reading* 15, 2: 95-103.

Laufer, Batia (1998). 'The development of passive and active vocabulary in a second language: Same or different?'. *Applied Linguistics* 19, 2: 255-71.

Laufer, Batia (2005a). 'Focus on form in second language vocabulary acquisition', in Susan Foster-Cohen (ed.), *EUROSLA Yearbook 5*. Amsterdam: John Benjamins, pp. 223-50.

Laufer, Batia (2005b). 'Ten best ideas for teaching vocabulary'. *The Language Teacher* 29, 10: 3-8.

Laufer, Batia, et al. (2004). 'Size and strength: Do we need both to measure vocabulary knowledge?'. *Language Testing* 21, 2: 202-26.

Laufer, Batia, Girsai, Nany (2008). 'Form-focused instruction in second language vocabulary learning: a case for contrastive analysis and translation'. *Applied Linguistics* 29, 694-716.

Laufer, Batia, Hulstijn, Jan (2001). 'Incidental vocabulary acquisition in a second language: the construct of task-induced involvement'. *Applied Linguistics* 22, 1: 1-26.

Laufer, Batia, Nation, Paul (1999). 'A vocabulary size test of controlled productive ability'. *Language Testing* 16, 1: 33-51.

Lawley, James (2000, June). 'Muchos libros de inglés dan más problemas que soluciones'. *El País*, p. 6.

Lee, Chuen-Yi, Liou, Hsien-Chin (2003). 'A study of using web concordancing for English vocabulary learning in a Taiwanese high school context'. *English Teaching and Learning* 27, 3: 35-56.

Lee, David Y. (2007). 'Corpora and discourse analysis: New ways of doing old things', in Vijay K. Bhatia et al. (eds), *Advances in Discourse Studies*. London and New York: Routledge, pp. 86-99.

Lee, David Y., Swales, John (2006). 'A corpus-based EAP course for NNS doctoral students: moving from available specialized corpora to self-compiled corpora'. *English for Specific Purposes* 25, 1: 56 75.

Lee, Miranda Y.-P. (2003). 'Structure and cohesion of English narratives by Nordic and Chinese students', in Anne Dahl et al. (eds), *Proceedings of the 19th Scandinavian Conference of Linguistics*, vol. 31, 2: 290-302.

Leech, Geoffrey, et al. (2001). *Word Frequencies in Written and Spoken English: Based on the British National Corpus*. London: Longman.

Leed, Richard L., Nakhimovsky, Alexander D. (1979). 'Lexical functions and language learning'. *Slavic and East European Journal* 23, 1: 104-13.

Lehtonen, Jaakko (1978). 'On the problems of measuring fluency', in Matti Leiwo and Anne Rasanen (eds), *AFinLA Yearbook 1978*. Jyväskylä: AFinLA, pp. 53-68.

Lehtonen, Jaakko, et al. (1977). *Spoken English: The perception and production of English on a Finnish-English contrastive basis*. Jyväskylä: Gummerus.

Lennon, Paul (1990). 'Investigating fluency in EFL: A quantitative approach'. *Language Learning* 40: 387-417.

Lennon, Paul (2000). 'The lexical element in spoken second language fluency', in Heidi Riggenbach (ed.), *Perspectives on Fluency*. Ann Arbor: University of Michigan Press, pp. 25-42.

Lewis, Michael (1993). *The Lexical Approach: The state of ELT and a way forward*. Hove: Language Teaching Publications.

Lewis, Michael (1997). *Implementing the Lexical Approach: Putting theory into practice*. Hove: Language Teaching Publications.

Lewis, Michael (ed.) (2000a). *Teaching Collocation. Further developments in the Lexical Approach*. Hove: Language Teaching Publications.

Lewis, Michael (2000b). 'Introduction', in Michael Lewis (ed.), *Teaching Collocation. Further developments in the Lexical Approach*. Hove: Language Teaching Publications, pp. 8-9.

Lewis, Michael (2000c). 'Language in the Lexical Approach', in Michael Lewis (ed.), *Teaching Collocation. Further developments in the Lexical Approach*. Hove: Language Teaching Publications, pp. 126-54.

Lewis, Morgan (2000). 'There is nothing as practical as a good theory' in Michael Lewis (ed.), *Teaching Collocation: Further developments in the Lexical Approach*. London: Language Teaching Publications, pp. 10-27.

Lin, Ming-Chia (2008). 'Building a lexical syllabus on Moodle with web concordancers for EFL productive academic vocabulary'. *Proceedings of WorldCALL 2008*. Fukuoka: Fukuoka University.

Lindquist, Hans, Levin, Magnus (2009). 'The grammatical properties of recurrent phrases with body-part nouns: the N_1 *to* N_1 pattern', in Ute Römer and Rainer Schultze (eds), *Exploring the Lexis-Grammar Interface*. Amsterdam: John Benjamins, pp. 171-88.

Lindstromberg, Seth, Boers, Frank (2008). *Teaching Chunks of Language*. Rum: Helbling Languages.

Liou, Hsien-Chin, et al. (2006). 'Corpora processing and computational scaffolding for an innovative web-based English learning environment: the CANDLE project'. *CALICO Journal* 24, 1: 77-95.

López-Mezquita, M. Teresa (2003). 'La construcción de un instrumento de medida para la evaluación de la competencia léxica de los traductores de inglés al español'. *Apuntes* 11, 4: 17-20.

López-Mezquita, M. Teresa (2006a). 'El vocabulario y la lingüística de corpus: Elaboración de una lista de frecuencias para el programa ADELEX', in Carmen Pérez Basanta (ed.), *Fundamentos Teóricos y Prácticos de ADELEX: Una investigación sobre la evaluación y el desarrollo de la competencia léxica a través de las nuevas tecnologías*. Granada: Comares, pp. 105-27.

López-Mezquita, M. Teresa (2006b). 'El vocabulario y la evaluación', in Carmen Pérez Basanta (ed.), *Fundamentos Teóricos y Prácticos de ADELEX: Una investigación sobre la evaluación y el desarrollo de la competencia léxica a través de las nuevas tecnologías*. Granada: Comares, pp. 129-53.

López-Mezquita, M. Teresa (2007). *La Evaluación de la Competencia Léxica: Tests de vocabulario. Su fiabilidad y validez. Tesis doctoral. Primer premio de los Premios Nacionales de Investigación Educativa y Tesis Doctorales 2005*. Madrid: Ministerio de Educación y Ciencia.

López-Mezquita, M. Teresa (2009). 'A computer-adaptive vocabulary test'. *Indian Journal of Applied Linguistics* 35, 1: 121-38.

Lord, Frederic M. (1980). *Applications of Item Response Theory to Practical Testing Problems*. Hillsdale, NJ: Lawrence Erlbaum.

Lorenz, Gunter (1999). *Adjective Intensification: Learners versus native speakers: A corpus study of argumentative writing*. Amsterdam: Rodopi.

Louw, Bill (1993). 'Irony in the text or insincerity in the writer? The diagnostic potential of semantic prosodies', in Mona Baker et al. (eds), *Text and Technology*. Amsterdam: John Benjamins, pp. 157-76.

Lozano, Cristóbal (2008). 'Variability and optionality in second language grammars: a quantitative approach', in Ángeles Linde López et al. (eds), *Studies in Honour of Neil McLaren: A man for all seasons*. Granada: Editorial Universidad de Granada, pp. 59-75.

MacKay, Donald G. (1982). 'The problems of flexibility, fluency, and speed-accuracy tradeoff in skilled behavior'. *Psychological Review* 89: 483-506.

Madsen, Harold S. (1983). *Techniques in Testing*. Oxford: Oxford University Press.

Masuhara, Hitomi (1998). 'What do teachers really want from coursebooks?', in Brian Tomlinson (ed.), *Materials Development in Language Teaching*. Cambridge: Cambridge University Press, pp. 239-60.

Matsuyama, Tetsuya (2004). 'The N *after* N construction: a constructional idiom'. *English Linguistics* 21: 55-84.

Mauranen, Anna (2004a). 'Speech corpora in the classroom', in Guy Aston et al. (eds), *Corpora and Language Learners*. Amsterdam: John Benjamins, pp. 195-211.

Mauranen, Anna (2004b). 'Spoken corpus for an ordinary learner', in John McH. Sinclair (ed.), *How to Use Corpora in Language Teaching*. Amsterdam: John Benjamins, pp. 89-105.

McAlpine, Janice, Myles, Johanne (2003). 'Capturing phraseology in an online dictionary for advanced users of English as a second language: a response to user needs'. *System* 31: 71-84.

McCarthy, Michael (1990). *Vocabulary*. Oxford: Oxford University Press.

McCarthy, Michael (1993). *Discourse Analysis for Language Teachers*. Cambridge: Cambridge University Press.

McCarthy, Michael (2005). 'Fluency and confluence: what fluent speakers do'. *The Language Teacher* 29, 6: 26-8.

McCarthy, Michael (2008a). 'Spoken fluency revisited'. Paper presented at the *34th JALT International Conference on Language Teaching*, Tokyo, Japan.

McCarthy, Michael (2008b). 'Accessing and interpreting corpus information in the teacher education context'. *Language Teaching* 41, 4: 563-74.

McCarthy, Michael, Carter, Ronald (1995). 'What is spoken grammar and how should we teach it?'. *ELT Journal* 49, 3: 207-18.

McCarthy, Michael, O'Dell, Felicity (1999). *English Vocabulary in Use: Elementary*. Cambridge: Cambridge University Press.

McCarthy, Michael, O'Dell, Felicity (2005). *English Collocations in Use*. Cambridge: Cambridge University Press.

McEnery, Tony, Wilson, Andrew (1996). *Corpus Linguistics*. Edinburgh: Edinburgh University Press.

McEnery, Tony, Wilson, Andrew (1997). 'Teaching and language corpora'. *ReCALL* 9, 1: 5-14.

McKay, Sandra (1980). 'Teaching the syntactic, semantic and pragmatic dimensions of verbs'. *TESOL Quarterly* 14, 1: 17-26.

McKeown, Margaret G., Curtis, Mary E. (1987). *The Nature of Vocabulary Acquisition*. Hillsdale, New Jersey: Lawrence Erlbaum Associates.

McVey-Gill, Mary, et al. (2002). *Cinema for Spanish Conversation*. Newburyport, MA: Focus Publishing.

Meara, Paul M. (1995). 'The importance of early emphasis on L2 vocabulary'. *The Language Teacher* 19, 2: 8-11.

Meara, Paul M. (1996). 'The dimensions of lexical competence', in Gillian Brown et al. (eds), *Performance and Competence in Second Language Acquisition*. Cambridge: Cambridge University Press, pp. 35-53.

Meara, Paul M. (2002). 'The rediscovery of vocabulary'. *Second Language Research* 18, 4: 393-407.

Meara, Paul M., Fitzpatrick, Tess (2000). 'Lex30: An improved method of assessing productive vocabulary in an L2'. *System* 28: 19-30.

Meara, Paul M., Jones, Glyn (1990). *Eurocentres Vocabulary Size Test 10KA*. Zurich: Eurocentres.

Mejri, Salah (1997). *Le Figement Lexical: Descriptions linguistiques et structuration sémantique*. Tunis: Publications de la Faculté des Lettres de la Manouba.

Meunier, Fanny, Granger, Sylviane (eds) (2008). *Phraseology in Foreign Language Learning and Teaching*. Amsterdam: John Benjamins.

Millar, Neil (submitted for review). 'The processing of malformed formulaic language'. *Applied Linguistics*.

Miller, George A. (1956). 'The magical number seven, plus or minus two: some limits on our capacity for processing information'. *Psychological Review* 63: 81-97.

Milton, John, Tsang, Elza S. C. (1993). 'A corpus-based study of logical connectors in EFL students' writing: directions for future research'. In Richard Pemberton and Elza Tsang (eds), *Studies in Lexis*. Hong Kong: The Hong Kong University of Science and Technology, pp. 215-46.

Mittmann, Brigitta (1999). 'The treatment of collocations in OALD5, LDOCE3, COBUILD2 and CIDE', in Thomas Herbst and Kerstin Popp (eds), *The Perfect Learners' Dictionary (?)*. Tübingen: Max Niemeyer Verlag, pp. 101-11.

Montoro del Arco, Esteban Tomás (2006). *Teoría Fraseológica de las Locuciones Particulares: Las locuciones prepositivas, conjuntivas y marcadoras en español*. Frankfurt am Main: Peter Lang.

Moon, Rosamund (2008). 'Dictionaries and collocation', in Sylviane Granger and Fanny Meunier (eds), *Phraseology: An interdisciplinary perspective*. Amsterdam: John Benjamins, pp. 313-36.

Moreno Jaén, María (2007). 'A corpus-driven design of a test for assessing the ESL collocational competence of university students'. *International Journal of English Studies* 7, 2: 127-47.

Moreno Jaén, María (2008). 'Teaching collocations through DDL: Design, implementation and preliminary results of a corpus-based learning experience', in *Proceedings of the 8th Teaching and Language Corpora Conference*. Lisbon: Associaçao de Estudos e de Investigaçao Científica do ISLA, pp. 231-8.

Moreno Jaén, María (2009). *Recopilación, Desarrollo Pedagógico y Evaluación de un Banco de Colocaciones Frecuentes de la Lengua Inglesa a través de la Lingüística de Corpus y Computacional*. Unpublished PhD Thesis. University of Granada, Spain.

Moreno Jaén, María (2010). 'Teaching collocations: A corpus-based approach', in Begoña Bellés-Fortuño et al. (eds), *Exploring Corpus-Based Research in English Language Teaching*. Castellón de la Plana: Publicacions de la Universitat Jaume I, pp. 13-22.

Moreno Jaén, María, Pérez Basanta, Carmen (2009). 'Developing conversational competence through language awareness and multimodality: the use of DVDs'. *ReCALL* 21, 3: 283-301.

Moreno Jaén, María, Pérez Basanta, Carmen (2010). 'An update of ADELEX: Developing the lexical competence of Spanish university students through ICT in the ESHE'. *Computer Assisted Language Learning* 23, 1: 59-85.

Mukherjee, Joybrato (2009). 'The grammar of conversation in advanced spoken learner English', in Karin Aijmer (ed.), *Corpora and Language Teaching*. Amsterdam: John Benjamins, pp. 203-30.

Muñiz, José, Hambleton, Ronald K. (1999). 'Evaluación psicométrica de los tests informatizados', In Julio Olea et al. (eds), *Tests Informatizados. Fundamentos y aplicaciones*. Madrid: Ediciones Pirámide S.A., pp. 23-59.

Munro, Murray, Derwing, Tracey (2001). 'Modeling perceptions of the accentedness and comprehensibility of L2 speech: the role of speaking rate'. *Studies in Second Language Acquisition* 23, 4: 451-68.

Murray, Joel (2002). 'Creating placement tests'. *ESL Magazine* 5, 6: 22-4.

Narita, Masumi, et al. (2004). 'Connector usage in the English essay writing of Japanese EFL learners', in *Proceedings of the IV International Conference on Language Resources and Evaluation: In memory of Antonio Zampolli*, pp. 1171-4.

Nation, I. S. Paul (1983). 'Testing and teaching vocabulary'. *Guidelines* 5: 12-25.

Nation, I. S. Paul (1986). *Word Lists: Words, affixes, stems*. Wellington: Victoria University of Wellington. English Language Institute.

Nation, I. S. Paul (1990). *Teaching and Learning Vocabulary*. New York: Newbury House.

Nation, I. S. Paul (2000). 'Learning vocabulary in lexical sets: Dangers and guidelines'. *TESOL Journal* 9, 2: 6-10.

Nation, I. S. Paul (2001). *Learning Vocabulary in Another Language*. Cambridge: Cambridge University Press.

Nation, I. S. Paul (2007). 'The four strands'. *Innovation in Language Learning and Teaching* 1, 1: 2-13.

Nation, I. S. Paul, Waring, Robert (1997). 'Vocabulary size, text coverage and word lists', in Norbert Schmitt and Michael McCarthy (eds), *Vocabulary: Description, acquisition and pedagogy*. Cambridge: Cambridge University Press, pp. 6-19.

Nattinger, James R., DeCarrico, Jeannette S. (1992). *Lexical Phrases and Language Teaching*. Oxford: Oxford University Press.

Nesi, Hilary (1996). 'Review article: for future reference? Current English learners' dictionaries in electronic form'. *System* 24, 4: 537-46.

Nesi, Hilary (1999). 'A user's guide to electronic dictionaries for language learners'. *International Journal of Lexicography* 12, 1: 55-66.

Nesselhauf, Nadja (2003). 'The use of collocations by advanced learners of English and some implications for teaching'. *Applied Linguistics* 24, 2: 223-42.

Nesselhauf, Nadja (2005). *Collocations in a Learner Corpus*. Amsterdam: John Benjamins.

Nesselhauf, Nadja, Tschichold, Cornelia (2002). 'Collocations in CALL: An investigation of vocabulary-building software for EFL'. *Computer Assisted Language Learning* 15, 3: 251-79.

Newman, Aryeh (1988). 'The contrastive analysis of Hebrew and English dress and cooking collocations: some linguistic and pedagogic parameter'. *Applied Linguistics* 9, 3: 293-305.

O'Keeffe, Anne, et al. (2007). *From Corpus to Classroom: Language use and language teaching*. Cambridge: Cambridge University Press.

O'Sullivan, Íde, Chambers, Angela (2006). 'Learners' writing skills in French: corpus consultation and learner evaluation'. *Journal of Second Language Writing* 15: 49-68.

Ochs, Elinor (1986). 'Introduction', in Bambi B. Schieffelin and Elinor Ochs (eds), *Language Socialization Across Cultures*. New York: Cambridge University Press, pp. 1-13.

Olea, Julio, Hontangas, Pedro (1999). 'Tests informatizados de primera generación', in Julio Olea et al. (eds), *Tests Informatizados. Fundamentos y aplicaciones*. Madrid: Ediciones Pirámide S.A., pp. 111-25.

Olea, Julio, Ponsoda, Vicente (2003). *Tests Adaptativos Informatizados*. Madrid: Aula Abierta. Universidad Nacional de Educación a Distancia.

Oppentocht, Lineke, Schutz, Rik (2003). 'Developments in electronic dictionary design', in Piet van Sterkenburg (ed.), *A Practical Guide to Lexicography*. Amsterdam: John Benjamins, pp. 215-27.

Osborne, John (2008). 'Adverb placement in post-intermediate learner English: a contrastive study of learner corpora', in Gaëtanelle Gilquin et al. (eds), *Linking up Contrastive and Learner Corpus Research*. Amsterdam: Rodopi, pp. 127-46.

Oxenden, Clive, et al. (2004). *New English File: Elementary*. Oxford: Oxford University Press.

Ozturk, Ismet (2007). 'The textual organization of research article introductions in Applied Linguistics: Variability within a single discipline'. *English for Specific Purposes* 26, 1: 25-38.

Paivio, Alan (1986). *Mental Representations: A dual-coding approach*. Oxford: Oxford University Press.

Palmer, Harold (ed.) (1933). *Second Interim Report on English Collocations*. Tokyo: Institute for Research in English Teaching.

Paradis, Michel (1994). 'Neurolinguistic aspects of implicit and explicit memory: implications for bilingualism and SLA', in Nick C. Ellis (ed.), *Implicit and Explicit Learning of Languages*. London and San Diego: Academic Press, pp. 393-419.

Paribakht, Tahereh S., Wesche, Marjorie B. (1993). 'Reading comprehension and second language development in a comprehension-based ESL program'. *TESL Canada Journal* 11: 9-27.

Park, Kyung-Ja, Lee, On-Soon (2005). 'Idiosyncratic features of English expressions used by NNSs of English: with reference to online chatting data'. *Journal of Pan-Pacific Association of Applied Linguistics* 2005, 9, 2: 181-207.

Pavesi, Maria (2008). 'Spoken language in film dubbing: target language norms, interference and translational routines'. In Delia Chiaro et al. (eds), *Spoken Text and Image: Updating research in screen translation*. Amsterdam: John Benjamins, pp. 79-89.

Pawley, Andrew, Syder, Frances (1983). 'Two puzzles for linguistic theory: nativelike selection and nativelike fluency', in Jack C. Richards and Richard W. Schmidt (eds), *Language and Communication*. London: Longman, pp. 191-226.

Pawley, Andrew, Syder, Francis (2000). 'The one-clause-at-a-time hypothesis', in Heidi Riggenbach (ed.), *Perspectives on Fluency*. Ann Arbor: University of Michigan Press, pp. 163-99.

Penadés Martínez, Inmaculada (2004). 'La enseñanza de la fraseología en el aula de ELE'. *Carabela* 56: 51-68.

Pérez Basanta, Carmen (2004). 'Pedagogic aspects of the design and content of an online course for the development of lexical competence: ADELEX'. *ReCALL* 16, 1: 29-49.

Pérez Basanta, Carmen (2005). 'Assessing the receptive vocabulary of Spanish students of English philology: an empirical investigation', in José L. Martínez-Dueñas Espejo et al. (eds), *Towards an Understanding of the English Language: Past, present and future: Studies in honour of Fernando Serrano*. Granada: Servicio de Publicaciones de la Universidad de Granada, pp. 545-64.

Pérez Basanta, Carmen (Forthcoming). 'A second-generation CALL vocabulary-learning programme (ADELEX): In search of a psychopedagogic model', in Rubén Chacón-Beltrán et al. (eds), *Teaching, Learning and Using L2 Vocabulary*. London: Multilingual Matters.

Pérez Basanta, Carmen, et al. (1992). 'Fundamentaciones teóricas del testing', in José A. Martínez López (ed.), *Actas de las VIII Jornadas Pedagógicas para la Enseñanza del Inglés*. Granada: GRETA, pp. 141-62.

Pérez Basanta, Carmen, et al. (2002). 'Assessing and developing lexical competence through the Internet', in Antonio Méndez et al. (eds), *International Conference on Information and Communication Technologies in Education* (Vol. 1). Badajoz: Serie de la Sociedad de la Información, pp. 1545-8.

Pérez Basanta, Carmen, Rodríguez Martín, M. Elena (2006a). 'A corpus-driven approach to teaching conversation: using the British National Corpus', in Cristina Mourón Figueroa and Teresa I. Moralejo Gárate (eds), *Studies in Contrastive Linguistics: Proceedings of the 4th International Contrastive Linguistics Conference*. Santiago de Compostela: Servicio de Publicaciones de la Universidad de Santiago de Compostela, pp. 779-85.

Pérez Basanta, Carmen, Rodríguez Martín, M. Elena (2006b). 'The application of data-driven learning to a small-scale corpus of conversational texts form the BNC – British National Corpus'. *The International Journal of Learning* 12, 8: 183-92.

Pérez Basanta, Carmen, Rodríguez Martín, M. Elena (2007). 'The application of data-driven learning to a small-scale corpus: using film transcripts for teaching conversational skills', in Encarnación Hidalgo et al. (eds), *Corpora in the Foreign Language Classroom*. Amsterdam: Rodopi, pp. 141-58.

Pérez-Fernández, Ángela (2003). *Las Colocaciones Léxicas de los Adverbios Intensificadores Ingleses: Propuesta de un diccionario*. PhD Thesis on CD-ROM. Jaén: Servicio de Publicaciones de la Universidad de Jaén.

Pérez-Paredes, Pascual (2010 in press). 'Appropriation and integration issues in corpus methods and mainstream language education', in Tony Harris and María Moreno Jaén (eds), *Corpus Linguistics in Language Teaching*. Bern: Peter Lang.

Pérez-Paredes, Pascual, et al. (Forthcoming). 'The use of adverbial hedges in EAP students' oral performance: a cross-language analysis', in Vijai Bhatia et al. (eds), *Researching Specialized Languages*.

Philip, Gill (2007). 'Decomposition and delexicalisation in learners' collocational (mis)behaviour'. Paper presented at the *4th Corpus Linguistics Conference*, Birmingham, 27-30 July, 2007.

Ponsoda, Vicente, et al. (1994). 'ADTEST: A computer adaptive test based on the maximum information principle'. *Educational and Psychological Measurement* 54, 3: 680-6.

Postma, Gertjan (1995). 'Zero-semantics: the syntactic encoding of quantificational meaning', in Marcel den Dikken and Kees Hengeveld (eds), *Linguistics in the Netherlands, 1995*. Amsterdam: John Benjamins, pp. 175-90.

Pridham, Francesca (2001). *The Language of Conversation*. London and New York: Routledge.

Proust, Marcel (1954 [1913]). *Du Côté de chez Swann*. Paris: Gallimard.

Qian, David D., Schedl, Mary (2004). 'Evaluation of an in-depth vocabulary knowledge measure for assessing reading performance'. *Language Testing* 21, 1: 28-52.

Quirk, Randolph, et al. (1985). *A Comprehensive Grammar of the English Language*. Harlow: Longman.

Rasinger, Sebastian M. (2008), *Quantitative Research in Linguistics*. London: Continuum.

Rayson, Paul (2003). *Matrix: A statistical method and software tool for linguistic analysis through corpus comparison*. Unpublished PhD Thesis. Lancaster University, UK.

Read, John (1997). 'Vocabulary and testing', in Norbert Schmitt and Michael McCarthy (eds), *Vocabulary: Description, acquisition and pedagogy*. Cambridge: Cambridge University Press, pp. 303-20.

Read, John (2000). *Assessing Vocabulary*. Cambridge: Cambridge University Press.

Renouf, Antoinette, et al. (2007). 'WebCorp: An integrated system for web text search', in Marianne Hundt et al. (eds), *Corpus Linguistics and the Web*. Amsterdam: Rodopi, pp. 47-67.

Reyes, M. Josefa (1999). 'Descripción de la incorporación del léxico nuevo por los alumnos de primero de BUP'. *REALE* 12: 85-92.

Richards, Jack C. (1976). 'The role of vocabulary teaching'. *TESOL Quarterly* 10, 1: 77-89.

Riggenbach, Heidi (1991). 'Towards an understanding of fluency: a microanalysis of nonnative speaker conversation'. *Discourse Processes* 14: 423-41.

Rixon, Shelagh (2000). 'Where do the words in EYL textbooks come from?', in Shelagh Rixon (ed.), *Young Learners of English: Some research perspectives*. London: Longman, pp. 55-71.

Rizo-Rodríguez, Alfonso (2004). 'Current lexicographical tools in EFL: monolingual resources for the advanced learner'. *Language Teaching* 37, 1: 29-46.

Rizo-Rodríguez, Alfonso (2005). 'Advanced monolingual learners' dictionaries of English in book form: a preliminary state-of-the-art survey', in José Luis Martínez-Dueñas et al. (eds), *Towards an Understanding of the English Language: Past, present and future: Studies in honour of Fernando Serrano*. Granada: Editorial Universidad de Granada, pp. 565-80.

Rizo-Rodríguez, Alfonso (2008). 'Review of five English learners' dictionaries on CD-ROM'. *Language Learning & Technology* 12, 1: 23-42.

Rizo-Rodríguez, Alfonso (2009). 'Syntactic and semantic specifications in online English learners' dictionaries'. *Indian Journal of Applied Linguistics* 35, 1: 25-43.

Rodríguez Martín, M. Elena (2006). 'La enseñanza del léxico a través del cine en un entorno virtual', in Carmen Pérez Basanta (ed.), *Fundamentos Teóricos y Prácticos de ADELEX: Una investigación sobre la evaluación y el desarrollo de la competencia léxica a través de las nuevas tecnologías*. Granada: Comares, pp. 229-48.

Rodríguez Martín, M. Elena (2010 in press). 'Comparing parts of speech and semantic fields in the BNC and a micro-corpus of movies: Is film language the "real thing"?', in Tony Harris and María Moreno Jaén (eds), *Corpus Linguistics in Language Teaching*. Bern: Peter Lang.

Rodríguez Martín, M. Elena (in press). 'Comparing conversational processes in the BNC and a micro-corpus of movies: Is film language the "real thing"?'. *Language Forum* 36, 1.

Rodríguez Martín, M. Elena, Moreno Jaén, María (2009). 'Teaching conversation through films: A comparison of conversational features and collocations in the BNC and a micro-corpus of movies'. *The International Journal of Learning* 16, 7: 445-58.

Römer, Ute (2009). 'Corpus research and practice: what help do teachers need and what can we offer?', in Karin Aijmer (ed.), *Corpora and Language Teaching*. Amsterdam: John Benjamins, pp. 83-98.

Rowling, Joanne K. (2005). *Harry Potter and the Half-Blood Prince*. London: Bloomsbury.

Rowling, Joanne K. (2006). *Harry Potter y el Misterio del Príncipe* [trans. Gemma Rovira Ortega]. Barcelona: Salamandra.

Rühlemann, Christoph (2006). 'Coming to terms with conversational grammar: 'dislocation' and 'disfluency''. *International Journal of Corpus Linguistics* 11, 4: 385-409.

Rühlemann, Christoph (2007). *Conversation in Context. A corpus-driven approach*. London: Continuum.

Rühlemann, Christoph (2008). 'A register approach to teaching conversation: farewell to standard English'. *Applied Linguistics* 29, 4: 672-93.

Ruiz Gurillo, Leonor (2001). *Las Locuciones en Español Actual*. Madrid: Arco Libros.

Sacks, Harvey, et al. (1974). 'A simplest systematics for the organization of turn-taking in conversation'. *Language* 54, 4: 696-735.

Sajavaara, Kari (1987). 'Second language speech production: factors affecting fluency', in Hans W. Dechert and Manfred Raupach (eds), *Psycholinguistic Models of Production*. Norwood, N.J.: Ablex Publishing Company, pp. 45-65.

Samraj, Betty (2002). 'Introductions in research articles: Variations across disciplines'. *English for Specific Purposes* 21, 1: 1-17.

Sánchez López, Cristina (1999). 'Los cuantificadores: clases de cuantificadores y estructuras cuantificativas', in Ignacio Bosque and Violeta Demonte (eds), *Gramática Descriptiva de la Lengua Española*. Madrid: Espasa Calpe, pp. 1025-128.

Sánchez-Hernández, Purificación, Pérez-Paredes, Pascual (2005). 'Examining English for Academic Purposes students' vocabulary output: Corpus-aided analysis and learner corpora'. *RESLA* 2005: 201-12.

Schegloff, Emanuel (1987). 'Recycled turn beginnings: a precise repair mechanism in conversation's turn-taking organisation', in Graham Button and John R. E. Lee (eds), *Talk and Social Organisation*. Clevedon, England: Multilingual Matters, pp. 70-85.

Schegloff, Emanuel (1996). 'Turn organization: one intersection of grammar and interaction', in Elinor Ochs et al. (eds), *Interaction and Grammar*. Cambridge: Cambridge University Press, pp. 52-133.

Scheibman, Joanne (2002). *Point of View and Grammar*. Amsterdam: John Benjamins.

Schmidt, Richard (1990). 'The role of consciousness in second language learning'. *Applied Linguistics* 11, 2: 129-58.

Schmidt, Richard (1992). 'Psychological mechanisms underlying second language fluency'. *Studies in Second Language Acquisition* 14: 357-85.

Schmidt, Richard (2001). 'Attention', in Peter Robinson (ed.), *Cognition and Second Language Acquisition*. New York: Cambridge University Press, pp. 3-32.

Schmitt, Norbert (1998). 'Measuring collocational knowledge: key issues and an experimental assessment procedure'. *ITL Review of Applied Linguistics* 119-120, 27-47.

Schmitt, Norbert (2000). *Vocabulary in Language Teaching*. Cambridge: Cambridge University Press.

Schmitt, Norbert (ed.) (2004). *Formulaic Sequences: Acquisition, processing and use*. Amsterdam: John Benjamins.

Schmitt, Norbert, Carter, Ronald (2004). 'Formulaic sequences in action: an introduction', in Norbert Schmitt (ed.), *Formulaic Sequences: Acquisition, processing and use*. Amsterdam: John Benjamins, pp. 1-22.

Schmitt, Norbert, et al. (2001). 'Developing and exploring the behaviour of two new versions of the Vocabulary Levels Test'. *Language Testing* 18, 1: 55-88.

Schweickert, Robert, Boruff, Brian (1986). 'Short-term memory capacity: Magic number or magic spell?'. *Journal of Experimental Psychology: Learning memory and cognition* 12: 419-25.

Shawback, Michael J., Terhune, Noel M. (2002). 'Online interactive courseware: using movies to promote cultural understanding in a CALL environment'. *ReCALL* 14, 1: 85-95.

Shin, Dongkwang, Nation, I. S. Paul (2008). 'Beyond single words: The most frequent collocations in spoken English'. *ELT Journal* 62, 4: 339-48.

Siepmann, Dirk (2005). 'Collocation, colligation, and encoding dictionaries. Part I: lexicological aspects'. *International Journal of Lexicography* 18, 4: 409-43.

Siepmann, Dirk (2006). 'Collocation, colligation, and encoding dictionaries. Part II: lexicographical aspects'. *International Journal of Lexicography* 19, 1: 1-39.

Siepmann, Dirk (2008). 'Phraseology in learners' dictionaries: What, where and how?', in Fanny Meunier and Sylviane Granger (eds), *Phraseology in Foreign Language Learning and Teaching*. Amsterdam: John Benjamins, pp. 185-202.

Sinclair, John (1987). 'Collocation: A progress report', in Ross Steele and Terry Threadgold (eds), *Language Topics: Essays in honour of Michael Halliday*, vol. 2. Amsterdam: John Benjamins, pp. 319-31.

Sinclair, John (1991). *Corpus, Concordance, Collocation*. Oxford: Oxford University Press.

Sinclair, John (2008). 'The phrase, the whole phrase and nothing but the phrase', in Sylviane Granger and Fanny Meunier (eds), *Phraseology: An interdisciplinary perspective*. Amsterdam: John Benjamins, pp. 407-10.

Siyanova, Anna, Schmitt, Norbert (2007). 'Native and nonnative use of multiword versus one-word verbs'. *International Review of Applied Linguistics in Language Teaching* 45, 2: 119-39.

Skehan, Peter (1998). *A Cognitive Approach to Language Learning*. Oxford: Oxford University Press.

Smith, Simon, et al. (2008). 'A corpus query tool for SLA: Learning Mandarin with the help of SketchEngine', in Barbara Lewandowska-Tomaszczyk (ed.), *Corpus Linguistics, Computer Tools, and Applications: State of the art*. Frankfurt: Peter Lang, p. 673-86.

Sperber, Dan, Wilson, Deirdre (1995). *Relevance*. Oxford: Blackwell.

Stengers, Helene (2007). 'Is English exceptionally idiomatic? Testing the waters for a lexical approach to Spanish', in Frank Boers et al. (eds), *Multilingualism and Applied Comparative Linguistics: Pedagogical perspectives*. Newcastle: Cambridge Scholars Publishing, pp. 107-25.

Stengers, Helene (2009). *The Idiom Principle Put to the Test: An exercise in applied comparative linguistics*. Unpublished PhD Thesis. Free University of Brussels, Belgium.

Stevens, Vance (1990). 'Concordance-based vocabulary exercises: A viable alternative to gap-fillers?'. *Classroom Concordancing: English Language Research Journal* 4: 47-61.

Stewart, Melissa A., Pertusa, Inmaculada (2004). 'Gains to language learners from viewing target language close-captioned films'. *Foreign Language Annals* 37: 438-47.

Stoller, Fredericka (1990). 'Films and videotapes in the content-based ESL/EFL classroom'. *English Teaching Forum* 28, 4: 10-4.

Strayer, David L., Kramer, Arthur F. (1990). 'An analysis of memory-based theories of automaticity'. *Journal of Experimental Psychology: Learning memory and cognition* 16: 291-304.

Sun, Yu-Chih, Wang, Li-Yuch (2003). 'Concordancers in the EFL classroom: cognitive approaches and collocation difficulty'. *Computer Assisted Language Learning* 16, 1: 83-94.

Swales, John (1990). *Genre Analysis: English in academic and research settings*. Cambridge: Cambridge University Press.

Swales, John (2004). *Research Genres: Exploration and applications*. Cambridge: Cambridge University Press.

Tang Eunice, Ng, Christina (1995). 'A study on the use of conjunctions in ESL student's writing'. *Perspectives Working Papers* 7, 1: 38-45.

Tao, Hongyin (2003). 'Turn initiators in spoken English: a corpus-based approach to interaction and grammar'. *Language and Computers* 46: 187-207.

Taylor, Christopher (2000). 'The subtitling of film: reaching another community', in Eija Ventola (ed.), *Discourse and Community: Doing functional linguistics*. Tübingen: Narr, pp. 309-27.

Taylor, Christopher (2004). 'The language of film: corpora and statistics in the search for authenticity. *Notting Hill* (1998) – a case study'. *Miscelánea: A Journal of English and American Studies* 30: 71-85.

Terkourafi, Marina (2005). 'Beyond the micro-level in politeness research'. *Journal of Politeness Research* 1: 264-80.

Thibault, Paul J. (2000). 'The multimodal transcription of a television advertisement: theory and practice', in Anthony Baldry (ed.), *Multimodality and Multimediality in the Distance Learning Age*. Campo Basso: Palladino, pp. 311-85.

Thomas, Jenny (1983). 'Cross-cultural pragmatic failure'. *Applied Linguistics* 4, 2: 91-112.

Thomas, Jenny (1995). *Meaning in Interaction: An introduction to pragmatics*. London: Longman.

Thornbury, Scott (2002). *How to Teach Vocabulary*. Essex, England: Longman.

Thornbury, Scott (2004). *Natural Grammar: The keywords of English and how they work*. Oxford: Oxford University Press.

Thorndike, Robert L., Hagen, Elisabeth (1980). *Tests y Técnicas de Medición en Psicología y Educación*. Mexico: Editorial Trillas.

Tian, Shiauping (2005a). 'Data-driven learning: do learning tasks and proficiency make a difference?'. *Proceedings of the 9th Conference of the Pan-Pacific Association of Applied Linguistics*. Tokyo: Waseda University Media Mix Corp, pp. 360-71.

Tian, Shiauping (2005b). 'The impact of learning tasks and learner proficiency on the effectiveness of data-driven learning'. *Journal of Pan-Pacific Association of Applied Linguistics* 9, 2: 263-75.

Timmis, Ivor (2005). 'Towards a framework for teaching spoken grammar'. *ELT Journal* 59, 2: 117-25.

Tomasello, Michael (2003). *Constructing a Language: A usage-based theory of language acquisition*. Cambridge, MA: Harvard University Press.

Tomlinson, Brian (1991). 'Survey: vocabulary practice books'. *ELT Journal* 45, 2: 169-73.

Tomlinson, Brian (2008). *English Language Learning Materials*. London: Continuum.

Tono, Yukio (2000). 'On the effects of different types of electronic dictionary interfaces on L2 learners' reference behaviour in productive/receptive tasks', in Ulrich Heid et al. (eds), *Proceedings of the Ninth Euralex International Congress, EURALEX 2000*. Stuttgart: Universität Stuttgart, pp. 855-61.

Towell, Richard, et al. (1996). 'The development of fluency in advanced learners of French'. *Applied Linguistics* 7, 1: 84-119.

Tribble, Chris, Jones, Glyn (1990). *Concordances in the Classroom: A resource book for teachers.* London: Longman.

Tschirner, Erwin (2001). 'Language acquisition in the classroom: the role of digital video'. *Computer Assisted Language Learning* 14, 3-4: 305-19.

Voller, Peter, Widdows, Steven (1993). 'Feature film as text: a framework for classroom use'. *ELT Journal* 47, 4: 342-49.

Walker, Crayton (2008). 'Factors which influence the process of collocation', in Frank Boers and Seth Lindstromberg (eds), *Cognitive Linguistic Approaches to Teaching Vocabulary and Phraseology.* Berlin and New York: Mouton de Gruyter, pp. 291-308.

Walkinshaw, Ian (2009). *Learning Politeness: Disagreement in a second language.* Oxford, Bern and Berlin: Peter Lang.

Watts, Richard J. (2003). *Politeness.* Cambridge: Cambridge University Press.

Webb, Stuart (2005). 'Receptive and productive vocabulary learning: the effects of reading and writing on word knowledge'. *Studies in Second Language Acquisition* 27, 1: 33-52.

Wei-Yun Chen, Cheryl (2006). 'The use of conjunctive adverbials in the academic papers of advanced Taiwanese EFL learners'. *International Journal of Corpus Linguistics* 11, 1: 113-30.

Weir, Cyril J. (1990). *Communicative Language Testing.* Hemptstead: Prentice Hall.

Weng, Li-Jen (2004). 'Impact of the number of response categories and anchor labels on coefficient alpha and test-retest reliability'. *Educational and Psychological Measurement* 64, 6: 956-72.

Wennerstrom, Ann (2000). 'The role of intonation in second language fluency', in Heidi Riggenbach (ed.), *Perspectives on Fluency.* Ann Arbor: University of Michigan Press, pp. 102-27.

Whistle, Jeremy (1999). 'Concordancing with students using an *off-the-web* corpus'. *ReCALL* 11, 2: 74-80.

Wible, David (2008). 'Multiword expressions and the digital turn', in Fanny Meunier and Sylviane Granger (eds), *Phraseology in Foreign Language Learning and Teaching.* Amsterdam: John Benjamins, pp. 163-81.

Widdowson, Henry G. (1996). 'Comment: Authenticity and autonomy in ELT'. *ELT Journal* 50: 67-8.

Widdowson, Henry G. (2000). 'On the limitations of linguistics applied'. *Applied Linguistics* 21, 1: 3-25.

Willis, Dave (1990). *The Lexical Syllabus: A new approach to language teaching.* London: Collins English Language Teaching.

Wingate, Marcel (1987). 'Fluency and disfluency: illusion and identification'. *Journal of Fluency Disorders* 12, 2: 79-101.

Winkler, Birgit (2001). 'English learners' dictionaries on CD-ROM as reference and language learning tools'. *ReCALL* 12, 2: 191-205.

Woolard, George (2000). 'Collocation: encouraging learner independence', in Michael Lewis (ed.), *Teaching Collocation: Further developments in the Lexical Approach.* Hove: Language Teaching Publications, pp. 28-46.

Woolard, George (2005). *Key Words for Fluency. Learning and practising the most useful words of English.* London: Thomson.

Wray, Alison (2002). *Formulaic Language and the Lexicon.* Cambridge: Cambridge University Press.

Wray, Alison (2008). *Formulaic Language: Pushing the boundaries*. Oxford: Oxford University Press.

Yeh, Yuli, et al. (2007). 'Online synonym materials and concordancing for EFL college writing'. *Computer Assisted Language Learning* 20, 2: 131-52.

Yoon, Hyunsook (2008). 'More than a linguistic reference: the influence of corpus technology on L2 academic writing'. *Language Learning & Technology* 12, 2: 31-49.

Yoon, Hyunsook, Hirvela, Alan (2004). 'ESL student attitudes towards corpus use in L2 writing'. *Journal of Second Language Writing* 13, 257-83.

Yorio, Carlos A. (1980). 'Conventionalized language forms and the development of communicative competence'. *TESOL Quarterly* 14, 4: 433-42.

Yorio, Carlos A. (1989). 'Idiomaticity as an indicator of second language proficiency', in Kenneth Hyltenstam and Loraine K. Obler (eds), *Bilingualism across the Lifespan*. Cambridge: Cambridge University Press, pp. 55-72.

Zhang, Meisuo Z. (2000). 'Cohesive features in the expository writing of undergraduates in two Chinese universities'. *RELC Journal* 31, 1: 61-95.

Zhang, Xiaolin (1993). *English Collocations and their Effect on the Writing of Native and Non-Native College Freshmen*. Unpublished PhD Thesis. Indiana University of Pennsylvania, USA.

Zhang, Xuemei (2007). 'A corpus-based study on Chinese WFL learners' use of adverbial conjuncts'. *CELEA Journal* 30, 2: 34-40.

(b) Online references (corpora, software and publications accessible online)

Note: a date followed by a dash indicate a corpus that is being constantly updated

Abad, Francisco J., et al. (2004). 'Ayuda a la creación de exámenes'. Available at: <http://www.uam.es/docencia/ace> [accessed 9 August 2010].

Boubel, Aurélie, Pansard, Fabrice (2003). 'Les investisseurs institutionnels et l'épargne retraite'. *Économie Internationale* 96: 43-62. Available at: <www.cairn.info/load_pdf.php?ID_ARTICLE=ECOI_096_0043> [accessed 28 November 2009].

Canning-Wilson, Christine (2000). 'Practical aspects of using video in the foreign language classroom'. *The Internet TESL Journal* 6, 11. Available at: <http://iteslj.org/Articles/Canning-Video.html> [accessed 15 February 2009].

Chambers, Angela, Le Baron, Florence (eds) (2007). *Le Corpus Chambers-Le Baron D'Articles de Recherche en Français/The Chambers-Le Baron Corpus of Research Articles in French*. Oxford: Oxford Text Archive. Available at: <http://ota.ahds.ac.uk/headers/2527.xml> [accessed 28 November 2009].

Chambers, Angela, Rostand, Séverine (eds) (2005). *Le Corpus Chambers-Rostand de Français Journalistique/The Chambers-Rostand Corpus of Journalistic French*. Oxford: Oxford Text Archive. Available at: <http://ota.ahds.ac.uk /headers/2491.xml> [accessed 28 November 2009].

Davies, Mark (2002-). *Corpus del Español (100 million words, 1200s-1900s)*. Available at: <http://www.corpusdelespanol.org> [accessed 3 December 2009].

fluent (2008). *Merriam-Webster Online Dictionary*. Retrieved November 17, 2008, from <http://www.merriam-webster.com/dictionary/fluent>.

Frary, Robert B. (1995). 'More multiple-choice item writing do's and don'ts'. Available at: <http://www.ericdigests.org/1997-1/more.html> [accessed 9 August 2010].

Giunchiglia, Fausto, et al. (2009). *Foundations for the Representation of Diversity, Evolution, Opinion and Bias*. Technical Report DISI-09-063, Ingegneria e Scienza dell'Informazione, University of Trento. Available at <http://eprints.biblio.unitn.it/archive/00001758> [accessed 10 August 2010].

Haïk, Isabelle (2008). 'Symmetric structures'. Available at: <http://www.crisco.unicaen.fr/IMG/pdf/Symmetric_structures-TLR.pdf> [accessed 8 December 2009].

Keene, Malcolm D. (2006). 'Viewing video and DVD in the EFL classroom'. *Research Bulletin of the Faculty of Anthropology of Bunkyo Gakuin University* 8, 1: 217-34. Available at: <http://www.lib.u-bunkyo.ac.jp/kiyo/2006 /kyukiyo/KENKYU217-234.pdf> [accessed 15 June 2009].

Kilgarriff, Adam (1995). *BNC Database and Word Frequency Lists*. Available at: <http://www.kilgarriff.co.uk/bnc-readme.html> [accessed 9 August 2010].

Kilgarriff, Adam (2004). *The Sketch Engine*. London: Lexical Computing Ltd. Available at: <http://www.sketchengine.co.uk/> [accessed 10 August 2010].

Lindstromberg, Seth, Boers, Frank (2005). 'Means of mass memorization of multi-word expressions (part one): The power of sound patterns'. *Humanising Language Teaching* 7, 1: 1-14. Availabe at: <http://www.hltmag.co.uk/jan05/ mart03.rtf> [accessed 8 August 2010].

Longman Corpus Network. Information available at: <http://www. pearsonlongman.com/dictionaries/corpus/index.html> [accessed 9 August 2010].

Philip, Gill (2008). 'Adverb use in EFL student writing: from learner dictionary to text production', in *Proceedings of EURALEX XIII International Lexicography Congress*. Available at: <http://amsacta.cib.unibo.it/2436/1/ EURALEX2008.pdf> [accessed 5 October 2009].

Poss, Michaela (2007). 'Structural versus constructional semantics: the case of Dutch NPN'. *Leiden Working Papers in Linguistics* 4, 1: 21-39. Available at: <http://www.let.leidenuniv.nl/pdf/lucl/lwpl/4.1/poss.pdf> [accessed 5 October 2009].

Rayson, Paul (2009). *Wmatrix: A web-based corpus processing environment*. Computing Department, Lancaster University. Available at: <http://ucrel.lancs.ac.uk/ wmatrix/> [accessed 1 December 2009].

SACODEYL Corpora. Available at: <http://www.um.es/sacodeyl/> [accessed 21 November 2009].

Scott, Michael (2004). *WordSmith Tools version 4*. Oxford: Oxford University Press.

Taylor, Christopher (1999). 'The translation of film dialogue', in Susan Bassnett et al. (eds), *Textus* 12, 2. Genova: Tilgher. Available at: <http://claweb.cla. unipd.it/citatal/documenti/trieste/textus.rtf> [accessed 9 February 2009].

Taylor, Christopher (2006). '*I knew he'd say that!* A consideration of the predictability of language use in film'. *Mutra 2006 – Audiovisual Translation Scenarios: Conference proceedings*. Available at: <http://www.euroconferences. info/proceedings/2006_Proceedings/2006_Taylor_Christopher.pdf> [accessed 4 October 2009].

The Bank of English / Wordbanks Online. Information and trial version available at: <http://www.collinslanguage.com/wordbanks/default.aspx> [accessed 10 August 2010].

Walker, Carolyn (1999). *Penguin Readers Teacher's Guide to Using Film and TV*. London: Longman. Available at: <http://www.longman.pl/files/ Penguin%20Readers%20PDF/using_films_and_tv_guide.pdf> [accessed 15 November 2009].

(c) Other references including reference books, textbooks and coursebooks

Addison, Charlotte, Field, Pamela (2006). *Challenge*. Cyprus: Burlington Books.

Álvarez, M. Victoria, Watson, Anthony (1965). *¡Oigan Señores!* London: British Broadcasting Corporation.

Ball, William J. (1986). *Dictionary of Link Words in English Discourse*. London: Macmillan.

Benson, Morton, et al. (1997 [1986]). *The BBI Dictionary of English Word Combinations*. Second edition. Amsterdam: John Benjamins.

Benson, Morton, et al. (2010 [1986]). *The BBI Dictionary of English Word Combinations*. Third edition. Amsterdam: John Benjamins.

Corréard, Marie-Hélène (1997). *The Oxford-Hachette French Dictionary*. Second edition [first edition edited by Marie-Hélène Corréard and Valerie Grundy]. Oxford: Oxford University Press.

Crowther, Jonathan, et al. (eds) (2002). *Oxford Collocations Dictionary for Students of English*. Oxford: Oxford University Press.

Crystal, David (1987). *The Cambridge Encyclopedia of Language*. Cambridge: Cambridge University Press.

Crystal, David (1995). *The Cambridge Encyclopedia of the English Language*. Cambridge: Cambridge University Press.

Dutton, Brian, García de Paredes, Ángel (1967). *Starting Spanish*. London: British Broadcasting Corporation.

Escribano, José G. (1978). *Dígame*. London: British Broadcasting Corporation.

Gammidge, Mick, Ben, Wetz (2002). *Oxford Exchange 2*. Oxford: Oxford University Press.

González, Mike, Placencia, M. Elena (1995). *Sueños: World Spanish*. London: British Broadcasting Corporation.

Kjellmer, Goran (1994). *A Dictionary of English Collocations: Based on the Brown Corpus*. 3 volumes. Oxford: Clarendon Press.

Mansion, Jean E. (ed.) (1940 [1934]). *Harrap's Standard French and English Dictionary. Part 1 French-English*. London: Harrap. [Reprinted with corrections 1948].

Prieto Gállego, Rosa M., Martínez Álvarez, Ana M. (1997). *Making Moves 2: First move*. Zaragoza: Edelvives Baula.

Richards, Jack, Schmidt, Richard (2002). *Longman Dictionary of Language Teaching and Applied Linguistics*. Malaysia: Pearson Education Limited.

Sánchez, Aquilino, et al. (1995). *Cumbre: Curso de español para extranjeros*. Madrid: SGEL.

Sinclair, John (ed.) (2001). *Collins COBUILD English Dictionary for Advanced Learners*. Third edition. HarperCollins Publishers.

Soanes, Catherine, Stevenson, Angus (eds) (2003 [1998]). *Oxford English Dictionary* (2nd Ed). Oxford: Oxford University Press.

Sperber, Milo, Fernández-Gasalla, Manuel (1971). *Zarabanda*. London: British Broadcasting Corporation.

Trask, Robert L. (1993). *A Dictionary of Grammatical Terms in Linguistics*. London and New York: Routledge.

Utley, Derek (1987). *España Viva*. London: British Broadcasting Corporation.

Wehmeier, Sally (ed.) (1994). *Oxford Wordpower Dictionary*. Oxford: Oxford University Press.

West, Michael P. (1953). *A General Service List of English Words*. Harlow: Longman.

Wetz, Ben, et al. (2005). *English Alive!* Oxford: Oxford University Press.

Appendix: ADELEX and EEL Websites

The Editors and Series Editors

With its practical advice on how to cope with and develop lexical contents, to explain what the latest innovations are regarding electronic dictionaries and EFL textbooks, or what corpora to use and how to explore and exploit them in the classroom, this volume cried out for links to supporting websites. There are in fact two: the ADELEX website (*http://www.ugr.es/local/inped/exploringnewpaths*) and the EEL website (*http://mcaweb.unipv.it:8080/mcaweb/publications.html*) both of which, in their respective ways, help to promote the integration between cutting-edge research and grass-roots classroom practice, the hallmark of this volume and this series. Though partially overlapping, the sites fulfil different functions corresponding, at least in part, to the different ends of the research and teaching spectrum.

The ADELEX website

Awarded the European Label for Pedagogic Innovation by the European Commission and the Spanish Ministry of Education, ADELEX is funded by the Spanish Ministry of Science and Innovation within the National Research Programme (*http://www.ugr.es/local/inped*). Keywords in the ADELEX project are lexical competence, web-based learning, computer-based testing and Spanish university students. In its present incarnation, and as evidenced by the website, the project has evolved into a dynamic online program that approaches vocabulary learning and assessment from many different perspectives. It researches into: (a) the nature of lexis (i.e. lexicology, semantics, pedagogical lexicography, phraseology, etc.); (b) state-of-the-art digital methodology that promotes linguistic interaction and autonomous and cooperative learning; (c) second-generation computer-based testing of lexical competence (not only lexical but also phraseological knowledge).

The website does what a book cannot do. It provides examples of digital materials ready to be used in online learning environments. The three modules included on the website present innovative ways to bring current research into the ELT classroom. From data-driven tasks focused on collocations, to new multimodal approaches to exploit film clips for the teaching of conversation, the materials provided in the online supplement appear as a genuine opportunity to explore new paths in language pedagogy.

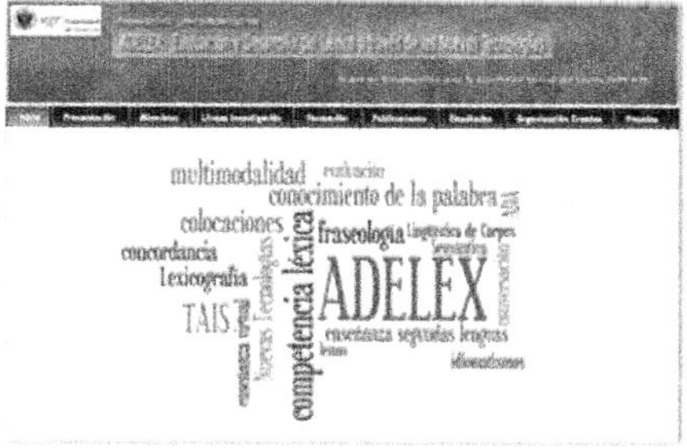

The EEL 1 website

Like all the volumes in the series, the first volume in the *Equinox English Linguistics and ELT* series (EEL for short) has a website which tracks all the chapters in the volume providing the reader with support and extensions as they read through each chapter. The site can be accessed as illustrated below by going to *http://mcaweb.unipv.it*. Clicking on the left-hand icon takes you to the *WEBSITE SUPPORT FOR THE EEL SERIES* icon shown in the centre, while a second click takes you to the EEL 1 site on the right.

A click on the *GO TO THE EEL WEBSITE FOR THIS VOLUME* icon (omitted) will take you to the EEL 1 home page. Each of the individual chapters can be accessed by the numerical menu bar in the top part of the page.

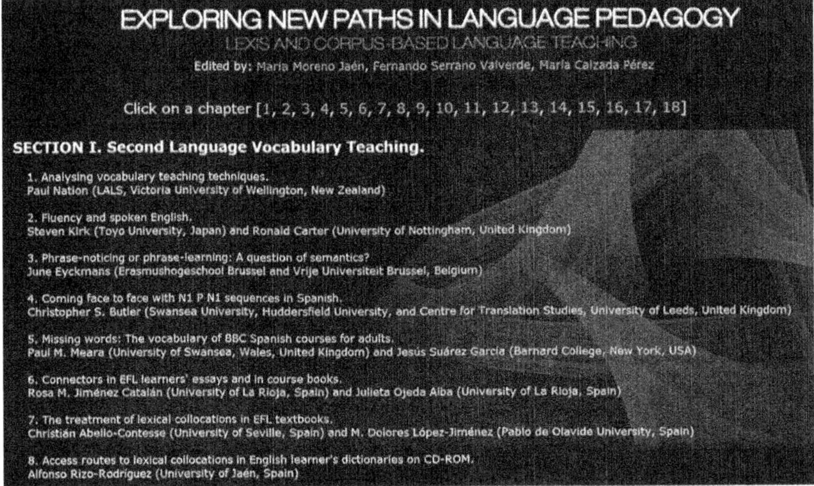

The individual chapters mention websites and website resources. The laborious task of checking them out is eased by the fact that the sites mentioned in each chapter, and many more associated sites, are listed with active links in the EEL website which thus provides hundreds of time-saving quicklinks. The website is constantly updated as new sites and resources become available and, for this reason, there may be some changes in the way that the website is presented vis-à-vis what is shown above. Indeed, it is impossible to give a complete description of either the ADELEX or EEL 1 websites as they are destined to grow, thanks to the ongoing contributions made by the editors, authors, readers and, of course, teachers and students.

Index

A

Activities **10-20**, 104

ADELEX 213-4, 229, 279-81, 315

Adjectives 72-4, 100-1, 103, 118-9, 121,
220-1, 224-6
adjectival collocates 116-8, 121, 231
predicate adjective constructions 215-7,
219

Adverbs 119, 149-51, **157-72**, 219-20, 281
adverbial collocates 117, 121
adverbial hedges 159-60
adverbial use 54, **58-67**, 71-5
amplifier adverbs **160-71**, 220

Annotation 173, 185-6, 189, 199

Antonymy 98
antonyms 182
opposites 17

Assessment 13, 15, 40, 47-9, 112, 136, 143,
160, 169, 170-1, 180, 229, 234, 243, **272-7**,
283-5

Australia 187

C

Canada 134, 187

CARS model 147-8, 153

Clinton, Hilary 194-5, 200-10

Clusters 27, 136, 175-6, 179

COBUILD 43, 112, 114-5, 117-9, 121, 124,
144, 168, 238, 264, 275

Cognitive linguistics 40, 45, 49

Coherence 47-8, 188

Collocations 42-3, 47-9, 95, **97-103**, 105-9,
111-24, 136-7, 139, 218, **229-43**, 253
grammatical collocations 106
lexical collocations 98, 108-9, 113

Communication:
communicative approaches 77, 96, 107,
142
communicative intentions 28, 31
communicative language teaching 39
communicative situations 29

Computing:
Computer Assisted Language Learning
(CALL) 134-5, 276
computer-mediated communication 234
Computer Vision and Multimedia
Laboratory (CVML) 173, 177, 189

Concordances 137, 139, **145-55**, 179, 196

Connectors 85-93, 136, 139, 145

Context 11, 15, 30-1, 40, 44, 83, 131, 147-50,
152, 214, 224, **245-52**, 260-4, 269, 276, 280

Conversation 27-38, 96, 146, 165-7, 170-1,
214, 219-20, **245-55**, 259, 261-9

Co-occurrence 41-2, 98, 113, 120, 230, 243

Corpora:
Bank of English (BoE) 43, 69, 207, 191,
196, 231, 252-3, 264, 274-5, 281
British National Corpus (BNC) 42-3, 52,
135, 147, 245, 264, 274, 281
Brown University Corpus 274
Corpus del Español 52
Lancaster-Oslo/Bergen Corpus 274
LINDSEI 159, 171-2

Corpus linguistics 37, 40-1, 47, 128-9, 141,
157-9, 173, 186, 189, 191, 230, 250

Critical Discourse Analysis (CDA) 194

D

Data-Driven Learning (DDL) 129-31, **134-44**,
146, 231-3, 242-3

Discourse 31, 40, 43-4, 85, 92, 128, 146-7,
151, 192-4, 215, 225, **245-50**, 261-5

markers 31, 36-7, 249, 253

particles 160, 162-5, 169-70

discourse-functional approaches 215-6, 224, 226-7, 238, 260

Downtowners 160-3, 165, 168-70, 220

DVD (see also *Films*) 151, 159-60, 163-5, 270

Dysfluency 26-8, 30-1, 36

E

Electronic dictionaries 120

English for Academic Purposes 158-9, 169-70

English for Specific Purposes 173-4, 191

Evaluation 10-11, 13, 18-20, 130, 136, 139, 168-9, 214, 225, 271-3, 275-8, 280, 285

F

Films (see also *DVD*) 159, 245, **251-6**, 259, 264-5, 268, 270

Fluency 9, 20, **25-38**, 41, 48, 96, 107, 109, 229, 264, 273

Formality 31, 97

Formulaic language 29, 36, 38, 249, 252, 261

Formulaic sequences 29, 36-8, 41

Frequency 31, 36-7, 39

G

General Service List (GSL) 274

Grammar:
conversational grammar **245-51**, 254-5

grammatical competence 30, 39

grammatical constructions/patterns 37, 39, 51, 111, 122, 268

grammaticalisation 219

lexicalised grammar 39, 97

Grammaticalised lexis 39, 40, 97

Genre/text type 92-3, 111, 136, 138, 148, 151-2, 155, 168, 172-4, 176-8, 183-5, 188-9, 191-5, 254

hypergenres 174, 176-7

micro-genres 174, 176-7

mini-genres **173-9**, 181-3, 189

subgenres 173, 183-4

H

Homonymy 42

Hyponymy 98, 281

I

Ideology 194-5, 205-8

Idioms 41, 43, 45, 49, 98, 106, 111, 121, 230-2, 239

idiomatic expressions 49, 121

idiomaticity 43, 48, 97, 100-1, 109

idiomatic phrases 43

ILIAS 229, 233

Imaging 14, 16, 18-9

Imperatives 261, 267-8

Institutionalized expressions 98

Interlanguage 39, 45, 47, 48, 86, 91-2

Interpersonal communication 159, 205, 247, 259, 262

Interviews 130, 136, 159, 165-7, 170-2

Involvement Load Hypothesis 10-2, 14-24

Item Response Theory 276, 278

K

KWIC concordances 137, 142, 173, 181

L

Languages/nationalities:
Chinese 133-4

Dutch 52, 158, 275

French 96, 132-4, **145-55**, 158, 187

German 132-4, 158, 260

Irish 182

Italian 146, 158

Japanese 32-3, 35, 52, 86, 168, 260

Korean 168

Polish 133

Spanish 26, 40, 43, **51-75**, 76-83, 85-7, 91-3, 95, 96, 99, 104, 106, 108, 157-9, 168-70, 213, **215-27**, 233, 261

Swedish 86, 158

Language skills 104, 159, 271

    academic writing 62, 65-8, 74, 145-6, 151, 153

    L1 to L2 transfer 49-50, 92, 97, 102

    listening 9, 15, 30, 33, 264

    reading 9-11, 15, 44, 97, 150, 136-7, 276

    speaking 15, 25, 28, 157, 163, 169, 245, 250, 252, 255

    writing 15, 20, 91-3, 97, 130, 245-51, 276

Learnability 47

Levels of Processing Theory 11, 45

Lexical:

    lexical approaches 39, 42-4, 97-8

    lexical competence 158, 229, 243, 271-3

    lexical items 27, 98, 108, 113, 173

    lexical patterns 111, 173

    lexical phrases 40-4, 46

    lexical priming 111

    lexical sets 17

Lexicalization 226

Lexicogrammatical patterns 51, 173

Lexicon 39-41, 98-102, 204, 220, 271-3

LexTutor 135, 198

Living Knowledge Project (LK) 173, 179, 185-90

M

Meaning:

    conceptual meaning 272

    descriptive meaning 61, 75

    compositional meaning 113, 116

    experiential meaning 205

    figurative meaning 45, 103

    referential meaning 272

    pragmatic meaning 37, 52, 272

Memory 11, 15-6, 18-29, 32, 37, 41, 44-5, 49

Moodle 229

Motivation 11, 15, 45-6, 49, 143, 214, 279

Multimodality 186, 251

    multimodal corpus linguistics 128, 173, 176

    multimodal genre analysis 173, 185, 188

    multimodal text 174, 214, 251, 259

N

Neural networks 29

Newspapers:

    The Daily Telegraph 178-81

    The Independent 52, 178

    The New York Times 52

New Zealand 187

Nouns 53, 81, 101, 118-22, 231

    lexicalised nouns 52, 69

    nominal collocates 118, 231

    nominal use/occurrence 59-60, 62-4, 71, 74, 217

    nominalization 72, 160, 167

    NPN construction/structure 51-3, 69, 73-4

    proper nouns 205-7

O

Obama, Barack 187, 192, 194, 195, 200-10

Orality 159, 251-2

    oral discourse/language 60-3, 65-8, 74, 85, 245

    oral proficiency 26, 30, 44, 168

    oratory techniques 195

P

Pauses 26-7, 29, 32, 34-6, 226, 246, 249

Phraseology 27, 41, 43, 45, 49, 111, 128

Politeness 247, 260-1, 266-8, 270

Polysemy 43, 114

Polysystems theory 193

Prepositions 51-4, 63-4, **68-75**, 103, 145

Pronunciation 27, 260, 272

Prosody 32, 37, 151-2, 246

Psycholinguistics 28, 30, 32, 36, 41

Q

Query strategies 261, 267-8

R

Register 73-74, 92, 102, 111, 160, 166-72, 192, 245, 247, 250, 255, 278

Relevance Theory 31

Retrieval 11, 13-5, 18-9, 18, 45

S

Second Language Acquisition (SLA) 25, 39, 41, 42, 44, 97, 98

Skills:
    bottom-up processing skills 40
    conversational skills 38, 259
    corpus skills 232
    dictionary-using skills 112
    ICT skills 139, 142
    noticing skills 138, 143
    translating skills 192

Software:
    concordancing software 147, 231
    lexicographical software 113, 120, 122, 124

Software tools:
    ADTEST 283

AntConc 194, 195, 197-200

CLAWS 199

JLookup 231

Lexical Frequency Profiler 198

Multimodal Web Search (MWS) 128, 173-4, 178-81, 185-6, 188-90

Range 197-9, 207, 210

SketchEngine 135

VocabProfile 197-199, 201, 210

WebCorp 135, 188

Wmatrix 197, 199, 205, 208, 210, 252-3

WordSmith 87, 135, 148, 192, 194-7, 199-201, 205, 210, 252-3

South Africa 187

Speech (see also *Oral discourse*) **25-38**, 41, 165-71, 245-247, 249-52, 273
    parts of speech 53-4, 103, 253
    speech acts 254, 259, 268

Speeches:
    political speeches 194-6, 200, 204-7
    film transcripts/language 227, 245, **251-6**, 264

Statistical measures:
    chi-square 88
    Mutual Information (MI) 36-7, 46
    t-score 231
    t-test 236, 240

Synonymy 98, 281
    Synonyms 17, 58, 182

Syntagmatic relationship 17, 48

T

Tasks 10-4, 269
    closed tasks 136
    communicative tasks 109, 157
    productive tasks 116, 118
    speaking tasks 159-60, 163, 169-70
    writing tasks 85-7, 91-3

Technique feature analysis 14, 17, 19-20

Tests:

  computer adaptative test (CAT) **272-85**

  computer-based test (CBT) 277, 278, 282

  Depth of Vocabulary Knowledge Measure 277

  gap-fill test 48, 234, 241

  Lex30 277

  linear test 280, 283

  reading comprehension test 48

  The Eurocentres Vocabulary Size Test 227

  Vocabulary Knowledge Scale 277

  Vocabulary Levels Test 136, 277

  web-based test (WBT) 277, 278

Text:

  argumentative text 92, 145

  expository text 92

Text types (see *Genre*)

Text-based approach 145

Textbooks (TB) 37, **77-84**, 87, 95, 103, 109, 226, 254-5, 259-60, 263

Tone 34, 267

Translation 15, 23, 28, 48, 51, 57, 62, 65, 68, 77, 99, 130, 134, 136, 216-7, 219, 226, 234

  corpus-based translation studies 193

  translation studies 134, 191, 194, 281

Typology 104, 105, 107

U

USA 133-4, 159, 205

V

Verbs:

  copular verbs **216-20**, 226-7

  delexicalized verbs 101, 103

  phrasal verbs 49, 98, 106, 121

  stative verbs 227

  verbs of movement 59, 67

  verbal collocates 59, 61, 63, 65, 118, 121, 231

VHS videos 259, 264

Vocabulary:

  vocabulary learning load 82

  vocabulary lists 42, 78-83, 136, 196, 198-9, 205, 226, 231, 252-3, 273-4, 281

  vocabulary size 27, 41, 47, 271-3

W

Websites 174, 181, 185, 188

  ADELEX website (see *ADELEX*)

  EEL website 315-6

Words:

  Chunks 29, 37, 43, 46, 48, 229

  Multiwords (lexical item) **40-9**, 78, 98, 108, 214, 230, 232

  Polywords 98

  Smallwords 31-2, 35, 37

CPSIA information can be obtained
at www.ICGtesting.com
Printed in the USA
BVOW09s2240070517
483390BV00005B/16/P